Eating Bitterness

Contemporary Chinese Studies

This series, a joint initiative of UBC Press and the UBC Institute of Asian Research, Centre for Chinese Research, seeks to make available the best scholarly work on contemporary China. Volumes cover a wide range of subjects related to China, Taiwan, and the overseas Chinese world.

Glen Peterson, *The Power of Words: Literacy and Revolution in South China, 1949-95*

Wing Chung Ng, *The Chinese in Vancouver 1945-80: The Pursuit of Identity and Power*

Yijiang Ding, *Chinese Democracy after Tiananmen*

Diana Lary and Stephen MacKinnon, eds., *Scars of War: The Impact of Warfare on Modern China*

Eliza W.Y. Lee, ed., *Gender and Change in Hong Kong: Globalization, Postcolonialism, and Chinese Patriarchy*

Christopher A. Reed, *Gutenberg in Shanghai: Chinese Print Capitalism, 1876-1937*

James A. Flath, *The Cult of Happiness: Nianhua, Art, and History in Rural North China*

Erika E.S. Evasdottir, *Obedient Autonomy: Chinese Intellectuals and the Achievement of Orderly Life*

Hsiao-ting Lin, *Tibet and Nationalist China's Frontier: Intrigues and Ethnopolitics, 1928-49*

Xiaoping Cong, *Teachers' Schools and the Making of the Modern Chinese Nation-State, 1897-1937*

Diana Lary, ed., *The Chinese State at the Borders*

Norman Smith, *Resisting Manchukuo: Chinese Women Writers and the Japanese Occupation*

Hasan H. Karrar, *The New Silk Road Diplomacy: China's Central Asian Foreign Policy since the Cold War*

Richard King, ed., *Art in Turmoil: The Chinese Cultural Revolution, 1966-76*

Blaine R. Chiasson, *Administering the Colonizer: Manchuria's Russians under Chinese Rule, 1918-29*

Eating Bitterness

New Perspectives on China's
Great Leap Forward and Famine

EDITED BY KIMBERLEY ENS MANNING
AND FELIX WEMHEUER

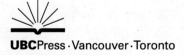

UBCPress · Vancouver · Toronto

20 19 18 17 16 15 14 13 12 11   5 4 3 2 1

Printed in Canada on FSC-certified ancient-forest-free paper (100% post-consumer recycled) that is processed chlorine- and acid-free.

Library and Archives Canada Cataloguing in Publication

Eating bitterness : new perspectives on China's great leap forward and famine / edited by Kimberley Ens Manning and Felix Wemheuer.

(Contemporary Chinese studies, 1206-9523)
Includes bibliographical references and index.
ISBN 978-0-7748-1726-4

1. China – History – 1949-1976. 2. Famines – China – History – 20th century. 3. China – Politics and government – 1949-1976. 4. China – Economic policy – 1949-1976. 5. China – Social conditions – 1949-1976. 6. China – Economic conditions – 1949-1976. I. Manning, Kimberley Ens II. Wemheuer, Felix III. Series: Contemporary Chinese studies

DS777.56.E28 2011   951.05   C2010-905264-1

UBC Press gratefully acknowledges the financial support for our publishing program of the Government of Canada (through the Canada Book Fund) and the British Columbia Arts Council.

Additional funding from the Chiang Ching-kuo Foundation and Concordia University is greatly appreciated.

UBC Press
The University of British Columbia
2029 West Mall
Vancouver, BC V6T 1Z2
www.ubcpress.ca

Contents

Preface

Eating Bitterness grows out of a workshop held under the same title at the Institute for East Asian Studies (Sinology) at the University of Vienna in November 2006. At the workshop, Chinese and Western scholars gathered together to discuss their findings about the Great Leap Forward and famine and to raise new questions about state-society interaction during this decisive period in People's Republic of China (PRC) history. We hope that this volume contributes to what is emerging as a rich field of study in both China and the West.

There are a number of individuals and institutions that aided in the publication of Eating Bitterness. We are indebted to Professor Susanne Weigelin-Schwiedrzik for hosting the original workshop and encouraging us to develop this project to its present state. Professor Timothy Cheek also served as an important early advocate as we sought to move the volume forward. By providing translation funding at an early stage of the project, Concordia University enabled us to include the chapters written by the four Chinese scholars. We also wish to thank the Chiang Ching Kuo Foundation and Concordia University for providing the necessary subvention funding for the publication of Eating Bitterness as well as the University of Vienna for providing support for some of the copyediting. Finally, Felix Wemheuer thanks the Austrian Science Foundation (FWF) for his Erwin Schrödinger Fellowship Abroad. Much of the work on this book was completed while he was in residence at Harvard University during the 2008-9 academic year.

A volume with as many authors as this could not have come to pass without the support of a wider community of colleagues. We are particularly indebted to three anonymous reviewers for providing detailed and extremely valuable comments at the review stage of the publication process. We also wish to thank those who read and provided comments on the introductory chapter: Jeremy Brown, Heath B. Chamberlain, Yixin Chen, Richard King, Ralph A. Thaxton, Susanne Weigelin-Schwiedrzik, and

Susan Whiting. We hope that the final version of the introduction and book does some modicum of justice to their extensive knowledge and insights.

Finally, we wish to thank those with whom we worked most closely on this project over the past three years: the volume's contributors; our editors, translators, and assistants; and our families. We feel extremely fortunate to have had the opportunity to work with such a talented group of scholars. Indeed, although the contributors have been trained in a wide variety of disciplines and are at varying stages of their careers, we believe they offer some of the finest examples of cutting-edge scholarship being produced on the Maoist era today. We are also grateful to the numerous people who contributed their editing and translation skills to the realization of this project. Our editors at UBC Press, Emily Andrew and Randy Schmidt, skilfully and professionally guided us through the publication process. Laraine Coates, our production editor, guided us through the editing process with admirable organization and efficiency. We were also aided by the timely assistance of several translators: Jiagu Richter, Sascha Mundstein, and Robert Mackie. We especially appreciate the contributions of Robert Mackie, who oversaw the final translation of all of the Chinese chapters included in *Eating Bitterness*, and Wolfgang Zeidl, who carefully combed the manuscript to ensure the accuracy of the *pinyin*. We also wish to thank Sarah Comrie for her wonderful editing and organizational skills as we prepared the manuscript for submission.

On a final note, we wish to thank our families for their support as we developed this project. Felix Wemheuer would like to thank his wife, Li Xiaoqing. Kimberley Manning is especially grateful to Jason Ens and Patricia Manning, who made sure she had the time and means to write and edit during a period of family expansion, and her children Elijah and Thea, who have been a source of tremendous joy and sustenance.

Acronyms

ACWF	All China Women's Federation
CCP	Chinese Communist Party
CUHKA	Chinese University of Hong Kong Archive of Contemporary Chinese History
GCAWF	Gaoshan County Archives Women's Federation
HAPC	Higher Agricultural Producer Cooperatives
HPA	Hebei Provincial Archives
HDA	Hexi District Archives
HCAWF	Huoye County Archives Women's Federation
LAPC	Lower Agricultural Producer Cooperatives
MCPCA	Macheng County Party Committee Archives
NBCK	Neibu cankao [Internal reference]
PLA	People's Liberation Army
PRC	People's Republic of China
WCAWF	Wenhe County Archives-Women's Federation Documents

Eating Bitterness

Introduction

Kimberley Ens Manning and Felix Wemheuer

When the Chinese Communist Party (CCP) assumed power in 1949, Mao Zedong declared that "not even one person shall die of hunger (*buxu esi yi ge ren*)." Hunger, however, was endemic; during the winter of 1949-50, for example, approximately 7 million refugees were fleeing famine conditions. Moreover, it was clear that, despite orders to prevent famine deaths, provincial Party authorities were not complying with instructions to publicize the anti-famine mandate in Hebei Province, a region particularly hard struck. Dong Biwu, future head of the Central Relief Committee, instructed the Hebei authorities that they would only be able to fulfill Mao's mandate were each cadre at each level of government willing to investigate the situation: openness was best.[1] And yet, despite Mao's vow and the administration's attempts to build an open government system that could both prevent and respond to natural disaster, China would find itself beset by the most devastating famine in modern history within ten short years. Indeed, between 1959 and 1961 some 15 million to 43 million peasants starved to death.[2]

Until the 1980s and the Chinese government's release of population statistics, few outside of China understood the seriousness of the deprivation that swept the country at the end of the CCP's first decade in power. While several major English-language works were subsequently published on the topic, however, neither the famine nor the Great Leap Forward Campaign (which contributed to the onset of the famine) has attracted the same sustained level of scrutiny in either China or the West as has, for example, the Cultural Revolution. In many ways, this is not surprising. The CCP authorities are reluctant to draw attention to an event for which they bear much responsibility. It was thus not until the 1980s, when Western scholars began to examine population records themselves, that many began to understand the depth of the famine. But while censorship explains part of the silence, it does not tell the whole story. The particular violence inflicted on the urban-based intellectuals during the Cultural Revolution rendered a skewed vision of the events that preceded it, including the Great Leap Forward and the Great Leap Forward Famine. Indeed, while the Cultural Revolution preoccupied a whole generation of Chinese intellectuals, China-watchers, and China scholars, the relationship between the Great Leap Forward and famine has largely been overlooked, treated as a precursor to the Cultural Revolution or explained away as a Maoist aberration.[3]

With the approach of the fiftieth anniversary of the famine, however, it would seem that a sea change is under way. In 2008 alone, two new major studies on the topic were published: Yang Jisheng's *Tombstone* (*Mubei*) and Ralph Thaxton's *Catastrophe and Contention in Rural China*.[4] Insofar as both of these works draw upon a wealth of previously unavailable sources, they offer important new insights into the famine, many of which reflect the perspectives of peasants who struggled to survive this calamity. But these works do more than this. Indeed, they not only lay bare the immediate devastation wrought by the famine, but they also begin to reconstruct alternative histories of China's experiment with state socialism. In Yang's and Thaxton's retellings, the Great Leap Forward and famine are symptomatic of a deeply flawed system of state terror. Their works thus stand as significant political interventions at a key moment when the CCP leadership is striving to maintain its legitimacy.

Like Yang and Thaxton, *Eating Bitterness* draws on a wealth of new sources to ask new questions about the Great Leap Forward and famine – questions that focus, in particular, on the many non-central Party elite actors who contributed to, ameliorated, suffered from, and resisted the events that played out in the years between 1957 and 1962. In the following chapters, contributors make use of a variety of sources, including oral histories, ethnographic research, and archival research, as well as more traditionally available sources, such as print media, biographies, and socialist realist literature. Insofar as the contributors are engaged in a variety of larger research projects – projects that reflect different disciplinary preoccupations and curiosities – they build outward from past works (including those of Yang and Thaxton) while simultaneously pointing to new lines of inquiry. It is in this way that questions regarding historiography, peasant resistance, state power, and gender politics (to name just a few subjects of interest) are rendered in a new light in the chapters presented here. Moreover, by presenting work from two research communities in one collection, work that has for the most part been undertaken in mutual isolation, we hope to spur further academic cross-fertilization. Ultimately, we hope that *Eating*

Bitterness will contribute to emerging debates about the production of the historiography of the PRC, including the often complicated challenge of interpreting China's socialist past through its globalizing present.

The Great Leap Forward and famine are usefully understood in both historical and comparative contexts. Therefore, we begin this introduction by offering a brief discussion of China's historical struggle with famine, the emergence of famine under state socialism, and comparative explanations of famine more generally. We then highlight the key events surrounding the start of the Great Leap Forward and famine before going on to explore why elite explanations of these phenomena have dominated scholarly discussion in the West. After that, we introduce some of the new scholarship on the grassroots that is emerging in China and the West, and then we discuss the major themes of *Eating Bitterness:* ideology and discourse, grassroots turmoil and party responses, and the politics of peasant resistance. Finally, we conclude with some brief thoughts on the politics of memory.

China: State Socialism in a "Land of Famine"

China has often been described as a land of famine.[5] According to Lillian Li, "no other civilization has had such a continuous tradition of thinking about famine, and no other nation's modern history has been so influenced by hunger and famine."[6] And, indeed, the worldview of imperial China made the ruler responsible for providing relief aid in the event of famine. Rulers who ignored this responsibility risked losing the "Mandate of Heaven," or the right to govern.[7]

Famine did, in fact, periodically devastate large regions of China from the late nineteenth century through until the founding of the People's Republic. Scholars estimate that between 9 million and 20 million people died in the North China Famine of 1876-79.[8] Historians similarly estimate the excess mortality at 10 million for famines that took place between 1896 and 1900.[9] After the fall of the Qing dynasty in 1911, many famines continued to occur. Among the most serious are those that saw the deaths of 500,000 people during the 1920-21 drought[10] and the deaths of 10 million during the North China Drought (between 1928 and 1930).[11] During the Sino-Japanese War in 1942-43, 2 million to 3 million people died of famine in Republican-controlled areas of Henan Province.[12]

When the CCP assumed power in 1949, China was one of the poorest countries in the world. The Chinese GDP per head in 1950 was only one-fourth of that of the United Kingdom in 1820, and it was less than the Irish GDP on the eve of the Great Famine of 1847-50.[13] On the eve of collectivization in the Soviet Union in 1928, per capita grain output stood at nearly 500 kilograms, while China produced only 285 kilograms per capita in 1952.[14] The new revolutionary government in Beijing gained a large part of its legitimacy thanks to its promise to end poverty and famine in China. These were not easy goals, considering that China was devastated by the many years of Japanese occupation and by the civil war between the Communists and the Guomindang. Indeed, for much of the 1950s, China stood on the brink of catastrophe. In order to overcome poverty, the CCP promoted industrialization; launched large irrigation projects; and organized education, hygiene, and health campaigns in the villages and cities. Millions of peasants were mobilized to reclaim new land. In 1953, the central leadership, under the urging of Mao Zedong, concluded that only collective agriculture could solve China's problems. Despite a series of crises with collectivization, however, the CCP managed to prevent widespread famine until the Great Leap Forward Famine began in 1959.[15]

China's Great Leap Forward Famine resulted in a higher death toll than any previous famine. And yet this was not the first famine to occur under state socialism.[16] When Mao declared in 1949 that China should "lean to one side" and learn from the Soviet Union, three major famines had already taken place in the Union of Soviet Socialist Republics. Specifically, between 10 million and 15 million people died in civil war-related famines in Russia and Ukraine between 1918 and 1921;[17] some 6 million to 8 million people died of famine in the aftermath of the collectivization of agriculture in 1931-33;[18] and between 1 million and 2 million people perished in the famine of 1947.[19]

Although overall famine mortality in the Soviet Union and China was significantly higher than the mortality rates of the twentieth-century famines in Africa and India combined, major theories of famines have not given much consideration to famine under state socialism.[20] When Amartya Sen's major work, *Poverty and Famine,* was first published in 1981, for example, little was known about the real extent of the Great Leap Forward Famine.[21] His entitlement approach, which suggests that famine could occur without a serious decrease in production, is primarily based on his analysis of the Bengal Famine of 1943. Sen argues that people starved not for lack of food but, rather, because they lost their entitlement to food.[22] Later Sen and Dreze pointed out that the lack of democracy and free press in China was a major reason for the Great Leap Forward Famine, while India managed to escape major famine after gaining its independence in 1947 thanks to the development of democratic institutions.[23] However, while Dreze and Sen acknowledge that, by forcing a government to take action, a free press can prevent major famines, it is less successful in preventing endemic malnutrition in everyday life. Comparing India's and China's death rates and applying that difference to the Indian population of 781 million in 1986, they estimate the excess normal mortality in India caused by malnutrition and related diseases at 3.9 million people per year.[24] While democracies are more likely to prevent famine than are dictatorships, some scholars argue that certain dictatorships did establish effective systems of food security. Others criticize the argument linking democracy and famine prevention because political systems such as the Suharto dictatorship in Indonesia and the Soviet Union during the Khrushchev and Brezhnev eras successfully prevented famine despite the lack of free press and other democratic institutions.[25] Stephen Wheatcroft even argues that the Soviet Union and China finally managed to break out of the historical cycles of famine after the Communist parties learned their lessons from the earlier major catastrophes.[26] While it is true that no major deadly famine occurred in the Soviet Union after 1947 or in China after 1962, it must be said that poor nutrition and hunger were widespread in rural China until the mid-1980s.[27]

Many questions remain regarding the origins of the Great Leap Forward Famine and its consequences for the people who experienced it. Before discussing some of this volume's contributions to comparative understandings of famine, we offer a brief overview and analysis of the pre-existing scholarship on the Great Leap Forward and famine.

From the Cusp of Communism to Descent into Famine

The Great Leap Forward began slowly in the late fall of 1957 before picking up speed in the spring and summer of 1958. After Mao Zedong famously announced in November 1957 that China would overtake Great Britain in steel production within fifteen years,[28] the Party began to encourage the development of large infrastructure projects such as the building of new dams and irrigation works. Over the winter of 1957-58, hundreds of thousands of peasants were mobilized by rural authorities to work for weeks or even months on job sites far from their homes. In March 1958, the Central Committee decided to establish big collectives (*dashe*) and push rural industrialization.[29] An even bigger push towards radicalization began in the summer of that year.

In August 1958, at a conference held at the summer resort of Beidaihe, the Central Committee decided to organize peasants into a new administrative unit: the People's Commune (*renmin gongshe*). Within a few short weeks, the People's Commune was being celebrated as the most important bridge to a communist society. A massive new administrative unit that encompassed up to fifty thousand people, the People's Commune was expected to abolish the sharp disparities between countryside and city, peasants and workers, and intellectual labour and manual labour. Ultimately, the People's Commune was to serve as the basic unit of communist society when the state finally withered away. Indeed, in August 1958, the Chinese government declared that the realization of communism was close at hand.[30] For the first time in the history of state socialism, a ruling communist party placed the transition to communism on its immediate agenda.

The Great Leap Forward fused classic Marxism with Maoist experimentation. On the one hand, it sought to realize Karl Marx's vision of the abolition of the differences between manual work and intellectual work, city and countryside;[31] on the other hand, it embraced a Maoist utopianism in which the individual could overcome great odds through willpower alone.[32] Furthermore, the newly founded theoretical organ of the CCP, *Red Flag* (*Hongqi zazhi*), sought to develop a Chinese program for the transformation to communism. Its editor, Chen Boda, dreamed of a new all-round communist man (*quanmian fazhan de gongchanzhuyi xinren*) who was simultaneously a soldier, peasant, worker, and intellectual.[33] To this end, the *Red Flag* made numerous references to the young Marx, who considered the abolition of the division of labour as a key element of communist society.

Prior to the Beidaihe Conference, the Great Leap Forward was primarily conducted as a program for rapid economic development. With the establishment of the commune system, the Great Leap Forward became the most radical social revolution that Chinese villagers had ever experienced. Model communes in provinces such as Henan and Hebei abolished almost every form of private property.[34] The borders of "natural villages" were dismantled. Tens of thousands of peasants and many villages were now administered by one commune. In some places, local CCP organizations sought to abolish family structures – a goal aided by the fact that, in some areas, husbands and wives were assigned to work in different brigades, that the elderly were sent to the old people's homes, and that children were placed in the newly established daycares and kindergartens (see Manning and Wang Yanni, this volume).

Of all of the new institutions established during the Great Leap Forward, the CCP leadership considered the establishment of public dining halls (*gonggong shitang*) as the key factor in the transformation of rural habits and the means of creating a collective spirit among the peasants.[35] Similar to the expansion of collective daycares and nursing homes, the establishment of public dining halls was also celebrated in the public press as a means of liberating the female workforce. Cooking at home was prohibited.

As a result, the communes took over the management of the food supply and its distribution. As envisioned by the CCP leadership, the public dining halls were to become the primary locus for social activities, including meetings and weddings. Mao Zedong equated the ultimate goals of the Great Leap Forward and the establishment of the communes with the dining halls, arguing that "communism means eating for free."[36] On model communes, the communist principle of distribution according to need (*an xu fenpei*) was introduced (see Xin Yi in Chapter 5 of this volume), theoretically rendering hunger a problem of the past.

The militarization of the rural workforce proved a key element of this development strategy. As Chen Jian argues, the People's Liberation Army attacked Guomindang forces on Jinmen Island as a means of rousing enthusiasm for the Great Leap Forward.[37] Under the slogan "militarize the organization, move as if in battle, and collectivize everyday life" (*zuzhi junshihua, xingdong zhandouhua, shenghuo jitihua*), communes and brigades were organized according to military ranks, and Party secretaries were made "commanders" (*shuji dang tongshuai*). *Red Flag* proclaimed that the peasants were naturally attuned to militarization.[38] Indeed, the same military methods that resulted in the CCP's victory over Japanese imperialism and the Guomindang were adopted to fight a war against nature in order to minimize the threat of droughts and floods. Moreover, the Central Committee decided that every Chinese peasant between the ages of sixteen and sixty years should become a soldier of the People's Militia (*minbing*).[39] The days of inefficient and "unscientific" organization of rural production were seemingly over.

The dream of an accelerated transformation to communism, however, quickly turned into a nightmare of unforeseen proportions. As early as the winter of 1958-59, reports of local famines were beginning to emerge. Both Mao and the rest of the CCP leadership recognized that the People's Communes were leading to mismanagement and thus sought to moderate the Great Leap policies during the first half of 1959. During the two important conferences held in Zhengzhou in February and April of 1959, the CCP leadership tried to calm the "winds of communism" (*gongchanfeng*).[40] At these meetings, the Party leadership clarified that the present goal of the Great Leap Forward was the construction of socialism rather than the transformation to communism. The Central Committee decided to reintroduce plots for private use (*ziliudi*) and to allocate distribution according to work performance (*an lao fenpei*). Emphasis on the mandatory nature of the dining halls was revised: peasants could eat in the public dining halls on a voluntary basis.[41] At this time, the Central Committee condemned practices of "absolute egalitarianism" (*juedui pingjunzhuyi*), while, in his letters to Party cadres, Mao criticized ineffective production methods and false reports.[42] The Central Committee authorized smaller brigades to become the central units of production in the commune. As a result of these new policies, the Great Leap continued, but the CCP leadership tried to correct the most serious mistakes and to rectify (*zhengdun*) the movement.

The period of readjustment lasted only a few short months. Indeed, in July 1959 any hopes of moderating the impact of the Great Leap Forward were dashed at the now infamous Lushan Conference. In a personal letter to Mao, Minister of Defence Peng Dehuai criticized the steel campaigns and voiced his concerns about the severity of the crisis facing the nation. Mao condemned Peng's criticisms as "right-wing opportunism" (*youqing jihuizhuyi*) and opened up a power struggle.[43] As a result of the Lushan Conference, Peng was dismissed from office. During the next few months, the CCP leadership launched a "clean-up" campaign within the Party against thousands of so-called "right-wing opportunists." As a consequence, the Great Leap Forward became infused with radicalism for the remainder of 1959. Planning targets, especially for steel production, again sky-rocketed.[44] According to official statistics, over 70 percent of peasants were forced to eat communally, despite the fact that the public dining halls offered less and less food.[45] In January 1960, the Central Committee even decided to expand the People's Communes to the cities. The Party leadership, once again, made the transformation to communism a top priority.

In the meantime, famine deepened and spread across rural China. Reports of mass starvation in the Xinyang region of Henan Province reached the central government in Beijing in October 1960.[46] While the so-called "Xinyang Incident" (*Xinyang shijian*) seems to have played a central role in changing the minds of the leadership regarding the Great Leap Forward,[47] the near depletion of grain reserves in Shanghai, Beijing, and Tianjin may have been an equal source of concern, as Jeremy Brown makes evident in his chapter. In the late autumn of 1960, the central leadership introduced new policies to stop the famine. Against the backdrop of this growing crisis, Mao could no longer ignore the severe problems that the Great Leap Forward had generated.

Despite the fact that it was never officially declared over, the Great Leap Forward quietly came to an end when the central government made the decision to redefine commune management according to the so-called Sixty Articles (or the "Work Regulations on Rural Communes") in 1961.[48] As a consequence of the new regulations, private plots were reintroduced, and production teams were once again based on family and village structures. In addition, the Party abolished the public dining-hall system and prohibited production teams from organizing steel production. Grain was imported from the West in order to feed the population, and the tax burden of the peasants was lowered. In January 1962, at the Seven Thousand Cadres Conference, Liu Shaoqi and Mao Zedong sought to analyze the origin of the "leftist mistakes" of the Great Leap.[49] In the aftermath of the Seven Thousand Cadres Conference, however, the CCP leadership focused on the future, and all discussion of the origins of the disaster ceased. As far as the leadership was concerned, the nightmare of the Great Leap Forward Famine was over.

The Great Leap Forward and Famine: Perspectives on the Party Centre and Emerging Questions about the Grassroots

The historical narrative that we have just laid out, one very much focused on Mao and his colleagues, is no doubt familiar to most scholars of modern history in China and the West. And, indeed, most research on the Great Leap Forward has focused on the Party centre. The original focus on elite decision making during the Great Leap Forward and famine makes sense, however, for four very good reasons. First, up until the late 1980s and early 1990s, scholars were limited in their ability to gain access to primary source material other than media reports and documents authorized for publication by the CCP. Moreover, the vast bulk of this primary material was itself written by and focused on political elites. In other words, scholars did not look to non-elite sources because there was little available at the time scholarship on this topic began.

Second, there were pressing questions to answer about the Party centre. And, indeed, despite the limitations of earlier source material, a whole generation of China scholars became very astute at deciphering inner-Party manoeuvrings to explain pivotal events in the evolution of the PRC – including the events surrounding the Great Leap Forward. To this end, debates both inside and outside China have focused on why the Party leadership launched the Great Leap Forward, why it sided with Mao Zedong after Peng Dehuai gave voice to the widespread criticism among the provincial leadership, and why it continued with the Great Leap Forward once its disastrous consequences became apparent.[50]

Elite-centred scholarship has also produced important hypotheses about the major contributing factors to the onset of famine. In two of the earliest studies carried out by Western scholars, for example, economists Walker and Kueh re-evaluate Chinese statistics to explore the relationship between the Great Leap Forward and famine. In his work, Walker argues that agricultural production was highly unstable in the 1950s and that the government sought to balance the huge disparities between the grain surplus and non-surplus regions. Before 1958, Walker suggests, the CCP successfully prevented famine, but the grain procurement policies nonetheless generated dissatisfaction at the grassroots. This carefully balanced system between the provinces, however, collapsed when over-enthusiasm and the "winds of exaggeration" blew during the Great Leap. According to Walker, high procurement rates ultimately contributed to famine.[51] Kueh, on the other hand, lays greater emphasis on bad weather than does Walker for the serious declines in production in 1959 and 1960. However, he believes that, without the government's decision to reduce the grain-sown area and to institute high procurement rates, peasants would have been able to survive the natural disaster.[52] By way of contrast, Yang as well as Wen and Chang argue that the policy of eating in public dining halls was a major contributing factor of the famine.[53]

The third reason for the original focus on elite decision making during the Great Leap Forward and famine also has to do with disciplinary training. When the Great Leap Forward and famine occurred fifty years ago, Western historians and political scientists were still being trained to focus on elite policy making and structures of governance. At the same time, and just as important, many scholars had no way of knowing what was actually transpiring on the ground. While the radical political movements of the late 1960s and 1970s transformed many academic assumptions and led to new lines of scholarship, it has taken some time for new grassroots understandings of the Great Leap Forward and famine to emerge.[54] Ultimately, it was not an academic but a journalist who "broke the story" of the famine by focusing on the grassroots. In 1996, Jasper Becker received international attention for the publication of *Hungry Ghosts: China's Secret Famine*. In this work Becker documents the famine where it hit hardest – places such as Xinyang in Henan Province and Fengyang County in Anhui Province. For the first time, stories of mass starvation, cannibalism, and terror reached a broader audience in the West.

The final reason that grassroots perspectives on the Great Leap Forward and famine have taken time to emerge has to do with the fact that the Great Leap Forward itself was not implemented in a unified way. As it happened, the first Western studies undertaken at the village level in the late 1970s and early 1980s were located in the provinces of Guangdong and Jiangxi, areas removed from the epicentre of the famine (see Chen's chapter in this volume for a discussion of Jiangxi). In contrast to the massive number of deaths experienced in Henan, Anhui, and Sichuan, many people residing in South China fared much better. As a result, the authors mention shortages but no widespread mass starvation and, consequently, devote only a few pages to the famine.[55]

It was not until the publication of *Chinese Village, Socialist State* that an academic work tackled the Great Leap Forward and famine at the village level in any detail.[56] Both this path-breaking study and Eric Mueggler's widely acclaimed *The Age of Wild Ghosts* illustrate some common dynamics of the period of the advanced collectives and the Great Leap Forward – specifically, the challenge of meeting high procurement rates, the toll of the mass mobilizations on local populations, and the loss of women's power. But even within these similarities there are marked differences. Whereas Friedman, Pickowicz, and Selden, the authors of *Chinese Village, Socialist State*, focus on the development of the "model" Wugong People's Commune in the famous Raoyang County (Hebei Province), Mueggler's study documents the struggles of the Lòlop'ò people in the area of Zhizuo, Yunnan. Vast regional, political, and cultural differences separate the field sites: for example, while Friedman, Pickowicz, and Selden argue that the famine ended the "honeymoon" between the peasants and the CCP, many of the Lòlop'ò viewed the increasing encroachment of the new state (especially on the practice of rites) as ominous from the earliest days of the regime. The loss of female power was in some ways more acute in Zhizuo as well, especially once powerful women elders were deprived of their spiritual and practical roles in maintaining family granaries.[57]

Writing on the early 1950s, Brown and Pickowicz suggest that how one experienced this period "depended on geography, social standing, timing, and chance."[58] We would argue that the same insight should be applied to the Great Leap Forward and the intense period of deprivation that began during this movement. The tremendous diversity in implementation and outcome means that learning about the grassroots during this period is a great challenge. Moreover, because scholars are starting somewhat late to focus on the social dimensions of the Great Leap and the famine, we have a great deal of catching up to do. Many open questions, both old and new, remain before us. For example, we still know little about the utopian dimensions of the Great Leap Forward and how they relate to the emergence of famine. Indeed, Schoenhals' study of utopianism in 1958 is an intellectual history that does not consider ideological developments within the broader society.[59] The pivotal year of 1960 remains a large gap in both Western and Chinese scholarship as well. Moreover, there is still much to understand about the long-term consequences of the Great Leap Forward and famine, including the period of readjustment (1961-63). To date, MacFarquhar and Zweig have considered the relationship between the Great Leap Forward and the Cultural Revolution (1966-69), and Yang has considered the impact of the Great Leap Forward on the start of the economic reforms (1978).[60] However, MacFarquhar's work on the Great Leap

Forward and the famine comes from the perspective of historical background – indeed, it is an analysis of the origins of the Cultural Revolution, which MacFarquhar traces back to the mid-1950s.[61] It is only recently, with the publication of Mueggler's and Thaxton's work, that we are beginning to build on Yang's earlier insights to comprehend the lasting impact that the famine had on rural communes and its role in catalyzing the agricultural reforms of the late 1970s and early 1980s. Finally, we also need to revisit questions regarding the cause of famine itself. In this vein, one of the most important puzzles with which we need to come to terms is why famine deaths were so variable across provinces, regions, and even villages. When it comes to rewriting the history of the PRC and solving the puzzle of mass starvation in the modern era, both the Great Leap Forward and the famine require more sustained attention, particularly to the grassroots.

Linking New Perspectives from China and the West

At least three major research projects, by Wemheuer,[62] Thaxton,[63] and Manning,[64] respectively, focus on the Great Leap Forward and use ethnographic, oral history, and archival tools to better understand village life during this time. These three scholars conducted oral history interviews in different counties in Henan Province in order to better understand how ordinary people contributed to, experienced, and resisted the Great Leap Forward and famine. In another extensive project on the Great Leap Forward, Chen Yixin uses similar methodological tools to understand the role of provincial-level leadership as well as grassroots factors in the provinces of Anhui and Jiangxi.[65] Brown, Chen, King,[66] Manning, Thaxton, Weigelin-Schwiedrzik,[67] and Wemheuer all ask questions about how the Great Leap Forward has been remembered in official histories and literary texts, about the institutional and ideological foundations of villager and activist participation in this movement, about gender politics, about urban-rural relations, about the origins of the famine, and about the long-term impact of the famine with regard to acts of resistance and violence during the Cultural Revolution and Reform eras. Of particular interest to several of these scholars are the deeply differentiated experiences of the Great Leap Forward and of the famine, and they ask questions that, in many ways, re-examine the role of local leaders. Why did some local leaders turn a blind eye to behaviour that undermined the collective before, during, and after the famine? Why did other local leaders choose to openly contest certain policies and/or petition for relief? And why did others, perhaps the majority, continue to implement policies (including turning over remaining grain reserves) that imposed such sustained suffering?

At the same time, in the PRC, some extraordinary scholars have also been carrying out research on the Great Leap Forward and famine. With the publication of several books in Chinese, this small group of scholars has ignited a new set of debates about the Great Leap Forward on the mainland.[68] One of the most outstanding of these works is the two-volume *Mubei* (Tombstone).[69] Yang, a former journalist with the New China News Agency, was personally affected by the events that occurred between 1958 and 1961: his father starved to death during the famine. In the first volume of this work, Yang documents horrifying details about the famine and the political terror waged against the peasants in the most affected provinces, including Henan, Sichuan, and Anhui. The second volume offers harsh criticism of the "emperor" Mao Zedong.[70]

Many of the Mainland scholars covered their own research costs to travel to villages and conduct oral history interviews as well as to explore new sources in local archives. They have also been actively training a new generation of scholars. Gao Wangling (from People's University in Beijing) and Gao Hua (from Nanjing University), for example, have encouraged many of their students to carry out research on the Great Leap. This scholarship offers the promise of providing divergent explanations of the Great Leap Forward and famine from those of the CCP, an issue Weigelin-Schwiedrzik addresses in her chapter. The questions being considered by these scholars include: How did the People's Communes operate? Who made decisions about resource allocation? How was power distributed at the local level? What forms did rural resistance take during the Great Leap Forward? Why did the vast majority of peasants *not* rise up in violent rebellion when so many were dying around them? Why was the Party able to maintain its power structure at the local level during such an unprecedented social and political crisis?

Eating Bitterness brings these two, largely independent, research communities together. As we believe this volume makes clear, European-, North American-, and Chinese-based research communities have much to learn from close exchange and collaboration. Indeed, we are pleased to present some very challenging findings from the PRC to an English-speaking public and to link these findings to the growing body of research in the West.

Regimes of Truth: Discourses of Emancipation and Fear in the Great Leap Forward

Eating Bitterness begins with an examination of several important studies published by scholars working in mainland China. Whereas intellectuals in China have made the Cultural Revolution a sustained topic of research and rumination for over twenty years, the Great Leap Forward is only beginning to receive the attention of Chinese scholars and public critics. Indeed, for much of the 1980s the "scar literature," or literature of the wounded, focused on losses that intellectuals suffered during the Cultural Revolution – an intellectual effort that was initially sanctioned by the CCP as it, too, tried to distance itself from its Maoist past. The Great Leap Forward and famine, however, were topics of an altogether different nature. It was China's peasants, not intellectuals, who suffered the most during this period, whether from forced labour assignments or from the hunger that gripped most of rural China from 1959 into 1962 and even 1963. Because the CCP has considered peasants a natural revolutionary ally in the establishment of the People's Republic, the Party leadership has been less tolerant of public discussion of what essentially produced the greatest crisis of its now near-sixty-year rule; instead, it sought to define the historical record in its 1981 "Resolution on Some Questions Concerning the History of the Party since the Founding of the People's Republic of China." According to the Resolution, the Great Leap Forward was the result of a leftist (Maoist) leadership in which economic laws were ignored. The Resolution also cites the withdrawal of the Soviet Union and a series of natural disasters during this key period as contributing to the famine.

As Susanne Weigelin-Schwiedrzik argues in her chapter, much of the scholarship on the Great Leap Forward and famine that has emerged in China does not directly contest the 1981 Resolution. Nonetheless, as more detailed information about the famine has become available in China, emerging scholarship (including several of the chapters in this volume) is beginning to directly challenge the idea of the Party's "natural" alliance with Chinese peasants. In "Re-Imagining the Chinese Peasant," Weigelin-Schwiedrzik offers an important analysis of several recent texts published by Chinese intellectuals, including the writing of Mao's former secretary, Li Rui, and the research of social scientists Zhang Letian and Gao Wangling. The scholarship of Zhang and Gao decentralizes history and diversifies the historical record, she argues, because of the local nature of their sources: county archives and, in the case of Gao, oral interviews with peasants as well. Moreover, the idea of "peasant power," whether active or reactive, is central to this scholarship – an idea that implicitly acknowledges that the interests of peasants have been, and in some cases continue to be, directly at odds with those of the Party-state. The theme of peasant power has been an important source of debate in English scholarship on Maoist China as well, a topic to which we shall return shortly.

Ironically, and as Weigelin-Schwiedrzik discusses, it was fiction writers, not social scientists, who, in some of the earliest treatments of the famine, began to explore the theme of peasant resistance in the root-seeking literature of the post-Mao era. In their fictionalized historiographies, writers such as Yu Hua and Mo Yan have offered some of the most evocative accounts of the famine and of how peasants struggled to survive it. As Richard King reminds us, some intellectuals may have contributed to the construction of a "curtain of ignorance" by publishing glowing accounts of the Great Leap Forward during its height in 1958 and 1959. In his chapter, King discusses intellectual efforts both to collect and to record "new folk songs" (*xin minge*) as well as to develop fiction to inspire the labouring masses during the Great Leap Forward. By the time of the Great Leap, the Anti-Rightist Campaign had effectively silenced the CCP's critics, so all that was left were efforts that matched the Party's agenda of the moment. King documents the role these intellectuals played in mobilizing individuals to commit to the campaign and also points to their silence when it came to recording the devastation that followed.

King also focuses on a central, albeit often overlooked, aspect of the Great Leap Forward: the mass mobilization of women. With the development and expansion of universal child care, nursing homes, and public dining halls on the new communes, the CCP leadership sought to liberate the labour of rural women from the home, thus enabling them to devote themselves fully to the tasks of socialist construction. Fictionalized characters such as Li Shuangshuang, as well as local labour models, were exalted throughout the land for their ability to outdo men in competitions and to work in twenty-four-hour shifts. But what did this look like on the ground? Kimberley Ens Manning's chapter examines how the expansion of social welfare facilities interacted with powerful discourses of sexual equality in rural Henan and Jiangsu during the Great Leap Forward. Her work suggests that some women, with little regard for health and safety, not only willingly embraced the mobilization but also pushed themselves and others to achieve the heroic tasks assigned to them. In so doing, they ended up subverting long-standing CCP policies regarding the protection of women's physiological and reproductive health. Radicalism during the Great Leap Forward was ignited, in part, by powerful state discourses about sexual equality – albeit discourses that contained serious contradictions as they manifest in local Party institutions.

Radicalism, however, was also motivated by fear. While scholars have long assumed that rural cadres exaggerated production and relied on coercive mobilization methods during the height of the Great Leap Forward in order to avoid censure from the Party, little is known about how the Anti-Rightist Campaign transpired in rural areas. Felix Wemheuer argues that the Socialist Education Campaign, the rural extension of the Anti-Rightist Campaign, actually shaped how individuals could speak and think about hunger over the course of the fall of 1957. In his chapter, Wemheuer analyzes the Socialist Education Campaign as a discourse that established a truth regime regarding the relationship between food and hunger. Indeed, Wemheuer shows how the Party effectively established a narrative that told of peasants "faking" hunger in order to obtain food aid from the state. Simply put, peasants who complained of hunger were accused of hiding grain reserves. Thus, eighteen months before severe hunger began to afflict parts of rural China, it became impossible to openly discuss food shortages. Wemheuer argues that hunger turned into famine, in part, because to name deprivation was to be labelled a "rightist."

Coping with Loss: The Politics of Appropriation, Substitution, and Deprivation

For many peasants the earliest months of the Great Leap Forward were a time of confusion and hope, promise and fear. As Xin Yi documents in his chapter, the initial wildly enthusiastic reception of peasants and rural cadres to the nationwide effort to transform the countryside quickly gave way under the weight of broken promises and mounting chaos. In his study of the free-supply system (*gongjizhi*), Xin Yi shows that the practice actually varied widely from region to region and failed to provide people with many of their basic needs. Instead of ensuring the livelihood of peasants, the free-supply system was marked by instability, disunity, and low pay. Ultimately, Xin Yi argues that the severe dysfunction of the free-supply system increased the power of rural cadres and undermined the social order.

Wang Yanni provides additional compelling evidence as to the sheer arbitrariness and chaotic nature of the earliest months of the Great Leap Forward. Whereas Xin Yi focuses on the shortcomings of the free-supply system, Wang focuses on communization more generally – that is, the efforts to collectivize labour and property. Drawing on reports from county archives as well as oral interviews in Macheng County, Hubei Province, Wang documents the overwhelming impact that house demolition, grave destruction, and the militarization of daily life had on the peasants of her home county. As a consequence of her findings, Wang rejects the idea that communization was in any way driven by the utopian ideals of peasants; rather, she sees rapid communization as a kind of "industrialization" and "militarization" of the people.

The loss and deprivation experienced by many peasants, and described so vividly by Wang, contributed to and exacerbated a mounting nationwide problem: famine. Both Gao Hua and Chen Yixin examine how various levels of leadership confronted the famine after it began to emerge in 1959.

Gao Hua focuses in particular on the Party's advocacy of campaigns to "augment" and "substitute" the dwindling food supply. His research reveals a great deal about the CCP's attempts to create a new scientific discourse focused on food substitutes to compensate for what was, in fact, inadequate nutritional sources. His research also reveals a great deal about the Party's initial unwillingness to face the growing crisis as well as how, once it finally did so, it prioritized the health of cadres (especially urban cadres) over the health of "the masses."

One of the most remarkable aspects of the Great Leap Forward is that, while few were untouched by the severe shortages that plagued China in the late 1950s and early 1960s, not everyone suffered equally. In his insightful chapter, Chen Yixin compares the provinces of Jiangxi and Anhui during the Great Leap Forward and famine. Whereas, between 1958 and 1961, excessive deaths accounted for 18.37 percent of Anhui's population, they accounted for only 1.06 percent of Jiangxi's population for the same period – a shocking disparity given that these are neighbouring provinces. Chen attributes the wide gap in the two provinces to several important factors, including agricultural conditions, the in-kind agricultural tax, and the political attitudes of the provincial leadership. Chen's work highlights the need for future studies to focus on how local conditions contributed to or minimized famine devastation.

Urban Promises, Peasant Power, and the Party's Struggle for Legitimacy in a Post-1949 China

Of all the disparities that increased during the Great Leap Forward and famine, one of the greatest was the urban-rural divide. Over the course of the late 1950s, the CCP placed increasing restrictions on the ability of peasants to migrate within the nation – especially from villages to cities. Urban and rural society was divided by the household registration system (*hukouzhi*), which forced peasants to stay in their villages. Whereas urbanites were supported by a state-organized food distribution system, villagers had to depend upon themselves for their survival.[71] At the same time, peasants were becoming increasingly aware that state grain requisitions were being used to feed urbanites. As Wemheuer discusses in his chapter, the Socialist Education Campaign was waged, in part, to counter peasant protests regarding differences between city and country. However, while millions of peasants managed to acquire temporary employment in urban factories and workshops during the early stages of the Great Leap Forward, few achieved the same rights and benefits as did workers in the state-owned system. The gaping disparity between urban and rural dwellers during the famine, a disparity enforced by municipal and central leaders, would contribute to the decline of the CCP's legitimacy in the eyes of the many peasants forced to feed urban workers, even when their own survival was at stake. Between 1962 and 1963, some 20 million people were sent back to the countryside in order to decrease the burden of the state and the urban society. Back in the countryside, they disappeared from the payroll of the state and had to rely on work points in the People's Communes and, later, on the production output of private plots (after they were re-introduced in 1961).

Jeremy Brown's careful study of state-society relations in Tianjin during the Great Leap and famine suggests that those in the cities may have known a lot more about the rural famine than was previously believed. According to Brown, the human toll of the famine was very visible in Tianjin during the winters of 1959 and 1960. Indeed, Tianjin residents witnessed starving farmers on the city streets, while some hosted rural relatives who sought refuge in their homes. Even more significantly, Brown shows that, during the Great Leap Forward, city leaders actively ignored the famine plaguing the rural counties surrounding Tianjin – counties for which they were responsible. Brown's study offers compelling evidence of the Party leadership's determination (municipal and central) to maintain the livelihood of urban workers at the expense of that of peasants.

The porous boundaries between city and village also meant that peasants in many locales were increasingly aware of the urban-rural disparity. This glaring inequality, Ralph Thaxton argues, severely undermined the legitimacy of the CCP and led to peasants resisting and undermining state appropriation of grain. In his chapter, Thaxton discusses the practice of *chiqing*, or eating unripened standing crops, as a popular form both of survival and of resistance during the famine. By the early 1960s, the practice had become so widespread that it threatened the state's ability to extract the grain it needed to feed workers in the cities. The CCP thus implemented the household responsibility system to protect its ability to continue to expropriate grain from the countryside. In contrast to the widely held belief that the Party devised the household responsibility system to save the peasants from famine (what Thaxton calls the "administrative intervention paradigm"), he argues that the delegation of responsibility for the fulfillment of the grain quotas to peasant families was a way for the state to gain greater control of the harvest and, thus, to exert more power over the peasantry.

Like Thaxton, Gao Wangling also focuses on peasant interactions with the Party-state. Drawing upon ten years of research in Mancheng County, Gao analyzes peasant resistance to collective economic structures and how this resistance evolved over the course of the famine. He shows how

Chinese peasants not only carried out what he calls counter-action (*fanx-ingwei*) but also how this counter-action deconstructed and transformed state regulations. According to Gao, counter-action includes behaviour such as stealing grain, going slowly (*mo yanggong*), and "concealing production and distributing privately" (*manchan sifen*). Gao emphasizes that the peasants were forced to carry out counter-action in order to survive. The accumulated consequences of nationwide practices of counter-action, Gao argues, harmed the grain policies of the state and caused a serious crisis within collective agriculture.

Concluding Thoughts

As a number of the chapters in *Eating Bitterness* make clear, surviving the famine depended in no small part on one's ability to negotiate with the Party-state. In this respect, they shed new light on debates within Western scholarship regarding the role of peasant power and resistance in the Mao era. In this final section, we would like to briefly comment on this issue as well as to return to our earlier discussion about modern state famine. We conclude with a few brief remarks about the politics of memory.

Some twenty years ago Vivienne Shue argued that rural communities were effectively able to deflect the Maoist state through subversive practices.[72] The state's reach, she contends, was limited by the fact that CCP policies had increased the insularity of rural communities (or what she refers to as "cellularity"). Daniel Kelliher's *Peasant Power in China* goes one step further, arguing that peasants were not only autonomous from the Party-state but also provided the impetus behind the decollectivization of agriculture.[73] According to Kelliher, local experimentation led to the state implementation of the household responsibility system in the reform era. Interestingly, Thaxton, Shue, and Kelliher all acknowledge the influence of James C. Scott. Scott's notion of "everyday forms of resistance,"[74] or the slow and often silent struggle over crops, rent, labour, and taxes through pilfering, poaching, and foot dragging, plays a central role in their understanding of how peasants related to the socialist state. Gao's concept of "counter-action" is also similar to Scott's concept of "everyday forms of resistance."[75] Peasants not only undertook collective action, submitted petitions, and participated in minor forms of pilfering of communal goods but also fled famine areas on foot. Despite the increasing restrictions of the *hukou* system, peasants were much more mobile during the famine than has previously been acknowledged. Thus, while it was true that peasants could not easily flee certain regions (such as Xinyang) because of administrative and military fiat, others continued to enter cities (Brown) and neighbouring provinces (Chen) in order to ensure their survival. The fact that a number of these chapters find compelling evidence of peasant resistance and ways of escape during what, arguably, was the most repressive period for China's peasants lends greater weight to the argument that peasants have never been passive victims when confronted with twentieth-century modernization projects.

But surviving the famine did not just depend on one's ingenuity, courage, and resourcefulness: it also depended on the kind of state encountered. To this end, what stands out with respect to the Great Leap Forward is not so much the unified imposition of authoritarian high modernism, as is suggested in Scott's more recent work,[76] but, rather, a dynamic and highly fragmented process in which local leadership often played a role in determining life or death.[77] Chen Yixin's work, for example, deftly illustrates the crucial role that provincial leadership played in Jiangxi in preventing greater famine deaths. Similarly, leaders at lower levels of the state either exacerbated the famine by aggressively pursuing state procurement policies or alleviated it by turning a blind eye to peasant counter-action. China's lack of democratic institutions during this period cannot tell us why some local leaders *did* try to protect their communities.

These findings thus bring us back to some older questions about local leadership during this key period.[78] In the volume as a whole, we see that leaders in cities, counties, and villages played complex roles at the margins of the state. Their subjectivity as actors, state, or society was not always readily apprehended and, indeed, often changed depending upon the issue at hand. In his recent book, Thaxton suggests that local officials in Da Fo Village, Henan Province, had been shaped by their previous experience of being marginalized as poor peasants in the "old society" and by their involvement in war. They imposed the Great Leap Forward on their neighbours with a particular self-righteousness. Like Thaxton's work and that of Friedman, Pickowicz, and Selden, Manning's work on women's activism emphasizes the importance of local leadership ties; however, in this case, the gendered dimensions of mass mobilization wove an intricate web of relations between leaders and their kin and between leaders and led. Local women leaders were not hardened war veterans, although some acted as though they were.

Comparative studies of famine, we would suggest, would be well served by including a much sharper focus on local actors. Comparative political scientists, including some China scholars, have increasingly called for the need to disaggregate both state and society, "to recognize the blurred and moving boundaries between states and societies and to view states and societies as mutually transforming."[79] To apply such a perspective to the Great Leap Forward and famine is not to dispute the highly militarized, regimented, and often brutal way in which people were mobilized during the Great Leap, as is so evident in Wang Yanni's chapter. Nor is it to embrace the CCP's official explanation of the famine: that lower-level leaders were responsible for much of the excess and violence while the central government was responsible for setting the incorrect strategy of the Great Leap Forward. But it is to suggest that we might be well served to apply a longer and more textured view of the institutionalization of the grassroots Party structure. The fact that, as early as the winter of 1950, Hebei Party authorities were not promoting the policy to prevent famine deaths suggests that something within the political system rendered it unpalatable to report the local crisis – a tendency that would only be magnified in successive campaigns (especially the 1957 Socialist Education Campaign). While much more study is still needed, *Eating Bitterness* suggests that a variety of complexly interacting factors, including ideological commitment, fear of reprisal, local conditions, and personal allegiances, shaped how local leaders contributed to and sought to ameliorate the famine in their local communities.

Many of the local perspectives on the Great Leap Forward and famine presented in *Eating Bitterness* were informed by the use of interview data. Given that many of the individuals who lived through this period as teenagers or adults are rapidly aging, a certain kind of urgency accompanies this task. How do we understand or, as Joan Scott urges, *explain* the memories shared?[80] Recent scholarship on the "politics of memory" in China suggests that collective memory is complex, uneven terrain and that it is never wholly innocent.[81] The task of explaining what happened and why it happened is rendered even more difficult given the trauma that so many endured as a consequence of the Great Leap Forward mobilizations and famine. Indeed, the famine itself presents a dilemma with which holocaust historians have struggled for years: how to name the unnameable.[82] And yet the perils of ceding collective memory to the Party-state may outweigh the perils involved in reconstructing new visions of the past. In the absence of a physical memorial or a truth and reconciliation commission, we hope that this volume provides one means of marking the fiftieth anniversary of the famine and its continuing impact on the development of the People's Republic.

Notes

1 Zhuan Xiezu, *Dong Biwu zhuan* [The Biography of Dong Biwu] (Beijing: Zhongyang wenxian chubanshe, 2006), see 685-92.
2 Estimating the total number of famine deaths remains a controversial issue. Based on Chinese population statistics published in the early 1980s, scholars have derived different figures. Peng Xizhe calculates 23 million deaths in fourteen provinces (see Peng

Xizhe, "Demographic Consequences of the Great Leap Forward in China's Provinces," *Population and Development Review* 13, 4 [1987]: 649). Ansley Coale comes to the conclusion that 16.5 million people died, while Basil Ashton counts 30 million deaths and 30 million missing births (see Ansley Coale, "Population Trends, Population Policy, and Population Studies in China," *Population and Development Review* 7, 1 [1981]: 85-97; and Basil Ashton and Kenneth Hill, "Famine in China, 1958-1961," *Population and Development Review* 10, 4 [1984]: 613-45). Jasper Becker estimates 43 million to 46 million casualties on the basis of an internal investigation of the Chinese government (see Jasper Becker, *Hungry Ghosts: Mao's Secret Famine* [London: John Murray, 1996]). See also Penny Kane, *Famine in China, 1959-61: Demographic and Social Implications* (New York: St. Martin's Press, 1988); and Carl Riskin, "Seven Questions about the Chinese Famine of 1959-61," *China Economic Review* 9, 2 (1998): 111-24.

3   David Bachman's work on the institutional origins of the Great Leap Forward is an important early exception in this regard. See David Bachman, *Bureaucracy, Economy, and Leadership in China: The Institutional Origins of the Great Leap Forward* (New York: Cambridge University Press, 1991).

4   Two other important works by mainland authors were recently published as well: Dong Fu (a pen name), *Maimiaoqing, caihua huang* [Wheat Sprouts Green, Rape Flowers Yellow] (Hong Kong: Tianyuan shuwu, 2008); and Qiao Peihua, *Xinyang shijian* [The Xinyang Disaster] (Hong Kong: Kaifang chubanshe, 2009). See also the recently edited collection of mainland scholarship by Song Yongyi and Ding Shu, *Dayuejin – Dajihuang: Lishi he bijiao shiye xia de shishi he sibian* [Great Leap Forward – Great Leap Famine: The Truth and Analysis under Historical and Comparative Perspectives] (Hong Kong: Tianyuan shuwu, 2009).

5   Walter Hampton Mallory, *China: Land of Famine* (New York: American Geographical Society, 1926).

6   Lillian Li, *Fighting Famine in North China* (Stanford: Stanford University Press, 2007), 2.

7   Jennifer Eileen Downs, "Famine Policy and Discourses on Famine in Ming China, 1368-1644" (PhD diss., University of Minnesota, 1995), 42. See also Pierre-Ethienne Will and R. Bin Wong, *Nourish the People: The State Civilian Granary System in China, 1650-1850* (Ann Arbor: Center for Chinese Studies, University of Michigan, 1991).

8   Li, *Fighting Famine in North China*, 284; Mike Davis, *Late Victorian Holocausts: El Niño Famines and the Making of the Third World* (London: Verso, 2001), 7.

9   Davis, *Late Victorian Holocausts*, 7.

10 Li, *Fighting Famine in North China*, 284.

11 Ibid., 304.

12 Li, *Fighting Famine in North China*, 284.

13 Cormac O'Grada, *Famine: A Short History*, (Princeton University Press, 2008), 244.

14 Y.Y. Kueh, *Agricultural Instability in China, 1931-1991: Weather, Technology, and Institutions* (Oxford: Clarendon Press, 1995), 17.

15 Kenneth R. Walker, *Food Grain Procurement and Consumption in China* (Cambridge: Cambridge University Press, 1984).

16 Regarding comparative research, see Thomas Bernstein, "Stalinism, Famine, and Chinese Peasants," *Theory and Society* 13 (1984): 339-77; Felix Wemheuer, "Regime Changes of Memories: Creating Official History of the Ukrainian and Chinese Famine under State Socialism and after the Cold War," *Kritika: Explorations in Russian and Eurasian History* 10, 1 (2009): 31-59; and Matthias Middell and Felix Wemheuer, eds., *Hunger and Scarcity under Socialist Rule* (Leipzig: University of Leipzig Press, forthcoming 2010).

17 R.W. Davis and Stephen Wheatcroft, *The Years of Hunger: Soviet Agriculture, 1931-1933* (New York: Palgrave Macmillan, 2004), 403.

18 See Wemheuer, "Regime Changes of Memories," 31.

19 Elena Zubkova, *Russia after War: Hopes, Illusions, and Disappointments, 1945-1957* (London: M.E. Sharpe, 1998), 47.

20 Devereux's book on theories of famine is mainly based on the African and Indian cases. See Stephen Devereux, *Theories of Famine* (New York: Harvester/Wheatsheaf, 1993). For an important and recent exception, see Dennis Tao Yang, "China's Agricultural Crisis and Famine of 1959-1961: A Survey and Comparison to Soviet Famines," *Comparative Economic Studies* 50 (2008): 1-29.

21 For a critique of Sen's treatment of the famines under socialism, see Peter Nolan, "The Causation and Prevention of Famines: A Critique of A.K. Sen," *Journal of Peasant Studies* 21, 1 (1993): 4-5. Sen's reply, "The Causation and Prevention of Famines: A Reply," was published in the same issue (29-40).

22 See Amartya Sen, *Poverty and Famine: An Essay on Entitlement and Deprivation* (Oxford: Clarendon Press, 1997).

23 Jean Dreze and Amartya Sen, *Hunger and Public Action* (New York: Oxford University Press, 1989), 214.

24 Ibid.

25 For a discussion of these debates, see Michael Ellman, "The 1947 Soviet Famine and the Entitlement Approach to Famine," *Cambridge Journal of Economics* 24, 5 (2000): 620.

26 Stephen Wheatcroft, "Soviet and Chinese Famines in Historical Perspective," in *Hunger and Scarcity under Socialist Rule*, ed. Matthias Middell and Felix Wemheuer (Leipzig: University of Leipzig Press, forthcoming 2010).

27 See, for example, Jean Chun Oi, *State and Peasant in Contemporary China: The Political Economy of Village Government* (Berkeley: University of California Press, 1989); Fu Shenglun, *Gaobie ji'e* [Farewell to Hunger] (Beijing: Renmin chubanshe, 1999); and Wheatcroft, "Soviet and Chinese Famines." The Tibetan government in exile argues that major famines occurred in Tibet between 1961 and 1964 and between 1968 and 1973, during which time a total of 342,970 Tibetans starved to death. See *Tibet: Proving Truth from the Facts* (1996), http://www.tibet.net/.

28 Zhang Wenhe and Li Yan, *Kouhao yu Zhongguo* [Slogans and China] (Beijing: Zhonggong dangshi chubanshe, 1998), 381.

29 "Zhonggong zhongyang guanyu ba xiaoxing de nongye hezuoshe shidang de hebing wei dashe de yijian" [View of the Central Committee on the Merger of the Small Collectives into Big Collectives] and "Zhonggong zhongyang guanyu fazhan difang gongye wenti de yijian" [View of the Central Committee Regarding the Development of Local Industry], in *Jianguo yilai zhongyao wenxian* [Selected Important Documents since the Founding of the People's Republic of China], ed. Zhonggong zhongyang wenxian yanjiushi (Beijing: Zhonggong zhongyang wenxian chubanshe, 1995), 11:223-30.

30 "Zhonggong zhongyang guanyu zai nongcun jianli renmin gongshe wenti de jueyi" [Resolution of the Central Committee of the CCP Regarding Problems with the Establishment of the People's Communes in the Countryside], in *Jianguo yilai zhongyao wenxian*, 11:450.

31 Maurice Meisner, "Marx, Mao, and Deng on the Division of Labour in History," in *Marxism and the Chinese Experience*, ed. Arif Dirlik and Maurice Meisner (London: M.E. Sharpe, 1989), 96.

32 Michael Schoenhals, *Saltationist Socialism: Mao Zedong and the Great Leap Forward* (Stockholm: University of Stockholm Department of Oriental Languages, 1987), 28.

33 Chen Boda, "Quanxin de shehui, quanxin de ren" [All New Society, All New Men], *Hongqi* [Red Flag] 4 (1958): 7-8.

34 Li Youjiu, "Henan Xinyang laixin" [A Letter from Xinyang, Henan], *Hongqi* [Red Flag] 7 (1958): 23.

35 *Renmin ribao* [People's Daily], 24 October 1958.

36 Luo Pinghan, *Daguofan: Gonggong shitang shimo* [Eating out of the Big Pot: The History of the Public Dining Halls] (Nanning: Guangxi renmin chubanshe, 2001), 55.

37 Jian Chen, *Mao's China and the Cold War* (Chapel Hill, NC: University of North Carolina Press, 2001). For further discussion of the Jinmen conflict during this period, see two

recent works: Michael Szonyi, *Cold War Island* (Cambridge: Cambridge University Press, 2008); and Lorenz Luthi, *The Sino-Soviet Split: Cold War in the Communist World* (Princeton, NJ: Princeton University Press, 2008).

38   Fu Xiutao, "Quanmin jie bing" [People in Arms], *Hongqi* [Red Flag] (1958): 22.

39   "Zhonggong zhongyang guanyu minbing wenti de jueding" [The Decision of the Central Committee Regarding the Problem of the People's Militia], in *Jianguo yilai zhongyao wenxian*, 11:469; Elizabeth Perry, *Patrolling the Revolution: Worker Militias, Citizenship, and the Modern Chinese State* (Lanham: Rowman and Littlefield, 2006), 184-96.

40   Zhonggong zhongyang wenxian yanjiushi, ed., "Mao Zedong tongzhi de jianghua" [The Speech of Comrade Mao Zedong], in *Jianguo yilai zhongyao wenxian*, 124-34.

41   Luo, *Daguofan*, 118.

42   Mao Zedong, "Dang nei tongxin," *Neibu cankao* [Internal Reference], 12:283-86.

43   See Kenneth Lieberthal, "The Great Leap Forward and the Split in the Yan'an Leadership, 1958-1965," in *Politics of China, 1949-1989*, ed. Roderick MacFarquhar (Cambridge: Cambridge University Press, 1993), 87-147.

44   Sun Jian, *Zhonghua renmin gongheguo jingjishi* [An Economic History of the People's Republic of China] (Beijing: Zhongguo renmin daxue chubanshe, 1992), 267.

45   Luo, *Daguofan*, 176.

46   Regarding the Xinyang Incident, see Zhang Shufan, "Xinyang shijian: Yige chentong de lishi jiaoxun" [The Xinyang Incident: Bitter Lessons from History], *Bainian chao* [The Current Century] 12 (1998): 39-44; She Dehong, "Guanyu 'Xinyang shijian' de yishu" [Memories of the "Xinyang" Incident], *Bainian chao* [The Current Century] 12 (1998): 325-54; Becker, *Hungry Ghosts*, 113-20; Li Rui, "Xinyang shijian" [The Xinyang Incident], *Yanhuang Chunqiu* [China Chronicle] 4 (2002): 19-22; and Qiao Peihua, *Xinyang shijian* [The Xinyang Disaster] (Hong Kong: Kaifang chubanshe, 2009).

47   Qiao, *Xinyang shijian*.

48   "Nongye renmin gongshe gongzuo tiaoli xuizheng'an" [Labour Regulations in People's Communes (revised draft)], in *Jianguo yilai zhongyao wenxian*, 14:385-411.

49   For details, see Felix Wemheuer, "Dealing with the Great Leap Famine in China: The Question of Responsibilty," *China Quarterly*, 201 (2010): 176-94.

50   Bachman, *Bureaucracy, Economy, and Leadership*; Alfred Chan, *Mao's Crusade: Politics and Policy Implementation in China's Great Leap Forward* (Oxford: Oxford University Press, 2001); Thomas B. Bernstein, "Mao Zedong and the Famine of 1959-1960: A Study in Willfulness," *China Quarterly* 186 (2006): 421-45; Bo Yibo, *Ruogan zhongda juece yu shijian de huigu (xiudingben)* [Reflections on Certain Major Decisions and Events], vol. 2 (Beijing: Renmin chubanshe, 1997); Li Rui, *Lushan huiyi shilu, zengdingben* [Memorandum on the Lushan Conference] (Zhengzhou: Henan renmin chubanshe, 1995); Li Rui, *Dayuejin qinliji* [Personal Account of the Great Leap Forward], vols. 1-2 (Haikou: Nanfang chubanshe, 1999); Roderick MacFarquhar, *The Origins of the Cultural Revolution*, 3 vols. (New York: Columbia University Press, 1974); Frederick Teiwes and Warren Sun, *China's Road to Disaster: Mao, Central Politicians, and Provincial Leaders in the Unfolding of the Great Leap Forward, 1955-1959* (London: Sharpe, 1999).

51   Walker, *Food Grain Procurement*, 155.

52   Kueh, *Agricultural Instability in China*, 260.

53   Dali L. Yang, *Calamity and Reform in China: State, Rural Society, and Institutional Change since the Great Leap Famine* (Stanford: Stanford University Press, 1996); Guanzhong James Wen and Gene Chang, "Communal Dining and the Chinese Famine of 1958-1961," *Economic and Cultural Change* 46 (1997): 2-34.

54   Currently, a whole new generation of scholarship on the Maoist era is beginning to emerge. For an early review of this scholarship, see Elizabeth J. Perry, "Trends in the Study of Chinese Politics: State-Society Relations," *China Quarterly* 139 (1994): 704-13. For a more recent discussion of these issues as well as examples of the latest work on

the 1950s, see Jeremy Brown and Paul G. Pickowicz, *Dilemmas of Victory: The Early Years of the People's Republic of China* (Cambridge, MA: Harvard University Press, 2008).

55   See, for example, Anita Chan, Richard Madsen, and Jonathan Unger, *Chen Village under Mao and Deng: The Recent History of a Peasant Community in Mao's China* (Berkeley: University of California Press, 1992); Jack Potter and Sulamith Potter, *China's Peasants: The Anthropology of a Revolution* (Cambridge: Cambridge University Press, 1990); and Mobo C.F. Gao, *Gao Village: Rural Life in Modern China* (London: Hurst and Company, 1999).

56   Edward Friedman, Paul Pickowicz, and Mark Selden, *Chinese Village, Socialist State* (New Haven: Yale University Press, 1991).

57   Erik Mueggler, *The Age of the Wild Ghosts: Memory, Violence, and Place in Southwest China* (Berkeley: University of California Press, 2001).

58   Jeremy Brown and Paul Pickowicz, "The Early Years of the People's Republic of China: An Introduction," in Brown and Pickowicz, *Dilemmas of Victory*, 1-18.

59   Schoenhals, Michael, *Doing Things with Words in Chinese Politics* (Berkeley: University of California Press, 1992).

60   MacFarquhar, *Origins of the Cultural Revolution*; David Zweig, *Agrarian Radicalism in China, 1968-1981* (Cambridge, MA: Harvard University Press, 1989); Yang, *Calamity and Reform.*

61   One early exception is Simon Leys, *The Chairman's New Clothes: Mao and the Cultural Revolution* (New York: St. Martin's Press, 1977). Leys introduces the challenging idea that the Cultural Revolution was, in effect, "new clothes" that Mao used to cover up the large catastrophe of the Great Leap Forward.

62   Felix Wemheuer, *Steinnudeln: Ländliche Erinnerungen und staatliche Vergangenheitsbewältigung der "Großen Sprung" – Hungersnot in der chinesischen Provinz Henan* [Stone Noodles: Rural and Official Memory of the Great Leap Famine in the Chinese Province of Henan] (Frankfurt: Peter Lang, 2007).

63   Ralph A. Thaxton, *Catastrophe and Contention in Rural China: Mao's Great Leap Forward Famine and the Origins of Righteous Resistance in Da Fo Village* (New York: Cambridge University Press, 2008).

64   Kimberley Ens Manning, "Making a Great Leap Forward? The Politics of Women's Liberation in Maoist China," *Gender and History* 18, 3 (2006): 574-93; Kimberley Ens Manning, "Communes, Canteens, and Crèches: The Gendered Politics of Remembering the Great Leap Forward," in *Re-Envisioning the Chinese Revolution*, ed. Ching Kwan Lee and Guobin Yang, 93-118 (Stanford: Woodrow Wilson and Stanford University Press, 2007). Manning's work also draws upon research conducted in the province of Jiangsu.

65   See, for example, Yixin Chen, "Cold War Competition and Food Production in China, 1957-1962," *Agricultural History* 83, 1 (2009): 51-78.

66   Richard King, *Heroes of China's Great Leap Forward: Two Stories* (Honolulu: University Press of Hawaii, 2010).

67   Susanne Weigelin-Schweidrzik, "Trauma and Memory: The Case of the Great Famine in the People's Republic of China (1959-1961)," *Historiography East and West* 1, 1 (2003): 39-67.

68   Gao Wangling, *Renmin gongshe shiqi Zhongguo nongmin fanxingwei diaocha* [Investigations of Counter-Action: The Chinese Peasants in the Era of the People's Commune] (Beijing: Zhonggong dangshi chubanshe, 2006); Jia Yanmin, *Dayuejin shiqi xiangcun zhengzhi de dianxing: Henan Chayashan weixing renmin gongshe yanjiu* [A Typical Example of Rural Politics during the Great Leap Forward: A Study of Henan's Chayashan Satellite Commune] (Beijing: Zhishi chanquan chubanshe, 2006). For example, see also Cao Shuji, *Dajihuang* [The Great Famine] (Hong Kong: Shidai guoji chuban you xian gongsi, 2005). This book re-estimates population statistics during the famine based on the county gazetteers. Yu Xiguang's *Dayuejin: Ku rizi* [Great Leap: A Bitter Life], vol. 1 (Xianggang:

Chaoliu chuban gongsi, 2005), on the other hand, is a collection of archival documents and letters written during the famine.

69 Yang Jisheng, *Mubei: Zhongguo liushi niandai dajihuang jishi* [Tombstone: A Report on the Great Famine in the 1960s in China] (Hong Kong: Tiandi tushu, 2008).

70 More recently, Qiao Peihua, a faculty member at the Henan Party school, has published an in-depth account of the starvation that afflicted many of the residents of the Xinyang region of Henan. See Qiao, *Xinyang shijian*.

71 Regarding the separation between rural and urban society, see Sulamith Potter and Jack Potter, "The Position of Peasants in Modern China's Social Order," *Modern China* 9, 4 (1983): 465-99; Tiejun Cheng and Mark Selden, "The Construction of Spatial Hierarchies: China's Hukou and Danwei Systems," in *New Perspectives on State Socialism in China*, ed. Timothy Cheek and Tony Saich, 23-50 (New York: M.E. Sharpe, 1997); and Kam Wing Chan, "The Chinese Hukou System at 50," *Eurasian Geography and Economics* 50, 2 (2009): 197-221.

72 Vivienne Shue, *The Reach of the State: Sketches of the Chinese Body Politic* (Stanford: Stanford University Press, 1988).

73 See Daniel Kelliher, *Peasant Power in China: The Era of Rural Reform, 1979-1989* (New Haven, CT: Yale University Press, 1993); and Kate Xiao Zhou, *How the Farmers Changed China: Power of the People* (Boulder, CO: Westview Press, 1996).

74 See James C. Scott, "Everyday Forms of Resistance," in *Everyday Forms of Peasant Resistance*, ed. Forrest D. Colburn, 3-33 (New York: M.E. Sharpe, 1989).

75 Although Gao suggests that counter-action had characteristics that were particular to the socialist collective system and that had major consequences for the fate of collective agriculture – features that ultimately should distinguish them from Scott's "everyday forms of resistance." See Gao Wangling in Chapter 11 of this volume.

76 James C. Scott, *Seeing Like a State: How Certain Schemes to Improve the Human Condition Have Failed* (New Haven, CT: Yale University Press, 1998).

77 For a recent critique of the concept of "authoritarian high modernism" as it was applied in Tanzania's villagization, see Leander Schneider, "High on Modernity? Explaining the Failings of Tanzanian Villagization," *African Studies* 66, 1 (2007): 9-38. See Joel S. Migdal, *State in Society: Studying How States and Societies Transform and Constitute One Another* (New York: Cambridge University Press, 2001), for his process-oriented understanding of the modern state.

78 See, for example, Michael Oksenberg, "Local Leaders in Rural China, 1962-65: Individual Attributes, Bureaucratic Positions, and Political Recruitment," in *Chinese Communist Politics in Action*, ed. A. Doak Barnett, 155-215 (Seattle: University of Washington Press, 1969); Thomas P. Bernstein, "Cadre and Peasant Behavior under Conditions of Insecurity and Deprivation: The Grain Supply Crisis of the Spring of 1955," in *Chinese Communist Politics in Action*, ed. A. Doak Barnett, 365-99 (Seattle: University of Washington Press, 1969). Jean Oi's seminal study on the division of the harvest emphasizes the importance of local leaders in this process. Oi documents compelling evidence of the role that team leaders played in evading state grain procurement. See Jean Chun Oi, *State and Peasant in Contemporary China* (Berkeley: University of California Press, 1989).

79 Joel Migdal, Atul Kohli, and Vivienne Shue, "Introduction: Developing a State-in-Society Perspective," in *State Power and Social Forces*, ed. Joel Migdal, Atul Kohli, and Vivienne Shue, 293-326 (Cambridge: Cambridge University Press, 1994); Peter Hays Gries and Stanley Rosen, "Introduction: Popular Protest and State Legitimation in 21st-Century China," in *State and Society in 21st-Century China*, ed. Peter Hays Gries and Stanley Rosen, 1-23 (New York: RoutledgeCurzon, 2004).

80 Joan Scott, "Experience," in *Feminists Theorize the Political*, ed. Judith Butler and Joan Scott, 22-40 (New York: Routledge, 1992).

81 Ching Kwan Lee and Guobin Yang, eds., *Re-Envisioning the Chinese Revolution: The Politics and Poetics of Collective Memories in Reform China* (Washington, DC: Woodrow Wilson Center Press, 2007). Many scholars have thoughtfully engaged similar questions about the politics of memory in China. See, for example, Erik Mueggler, *The Age of the Wild Ghosts;* Gail Hershatter, "The Gender of Memory: Rural Chinese Women and the 1950s," *Signs* 28, 1 (2002): 43-70; and Ralph Thaxton, *Catastrophe and Contention.*

82 See, for example, Dominick LaCapra, *Representing the Holocaust: History, Theory, Trauma* (Ithaca: Cornell University Press, 1994).

1   Re-Imagining the Chinese Peasant: The Historiography on the Great Leap Forward

Susanne Weigelin-Schwiedrzik

Up until quite recently, the Great Leap Forward was both a myth and a taboo in Chinese historiography. The myth is related to the question of successfully combining the "general truth of Marxist-Leninism to the concrete practice of the Chinese revolution"; the taboo is related to the Great Famine as being the most abominable effect of the Great Leap on Chinese society and economy.[1] Myth and taboo are closely connected: as long as the myth about the Great Leap dominated the historiography of the post-1949 era, the taboo about the famine had to be upheld. However, as soon as the myth about Mao's ability to successfully sinicize Marxism was open to deconstruction,[2] the taboo about the famine was no longer enforced. And, vice versa, the more the Chinese public learned about the Great Famine, the less it was prepared to believe in the myth that the Chinese Communist Party had found a successful path to socialism. Recent discussions about the Great Leap Forward and its relationship to the Great Famine are part and parcel of re-imagining the relationship between the CCP and the Chinese peasantry. As a result, what was imagined as a natural alliance is now regarded as a strained relationship full of conflict and mistrust. This conflict exists today and will shape China's future for many years to come.

The Historiography of the Great Leap before 1976

Party history textbooks of the Maoist era usually refrain from going into detailed descriptions of the post-1949 era, and they especially avoid referring to the Great Leap Forward.[3] However, textbooks that came out during the early 1970s, after universities had been reopened and students had to attend CCP history classes, discuss the Great Leap at some length.[4] They argue that, in the initial years after the communist takeover, China suffered under the pressure of having to imitate the Soviet Union and, therefore, ended up in the same kind of crisis as was encountered in Eastern Europe in the early 1950s. Mao Zedong analyzed the situation and came to the conclusion that socialism in China had to be different from socialism in Russia and Eastern Europe. He strongly criticized Stalin's approach to the political economy of socialism and came up with the idea that, in developing its own economy, China mainly had to rely on its enormously large workforce. In discussing the experience of organizing cooperatives in the Chinese countryside, he convinced himself that Chinese peasants supported the idea of collectivization and, thus, that the reorganization of the countryside would work out much better in China than it had in the Soviet Union. This is why Cultural Revolution textbooks on Party history argue that the Great Leap was the first success that the Party, under Mao's leadership, could claim with regard to distancing itself from the Russian experience and in finding its own path towards socialism – a path that would be fundamentally different from what the Communist Party of the Soviet Union summarized as its own experience in the "Short Course of the History of the Communist Party of the Soviet Union,"[5] which was instituted under Stalin's leadership.[6]

It is interesting to note that the pattern on which post-1949 Party history was modelled resembles the pattern for pre-1949 Party history. In its initial phase, the CCP was highly dependent on Comintern advisers and followed their ideas about the future of the Chinese revolution closely. After the defeat of the First United Front, however, the Party, step by step and through several rounds of struggle between the correct revolutionary line and wrong "leftist" or "rightist" lines, learned its lesson. It realized that only by defining a strategy for the Chinese revolution that was based on Marxist-Leninism as well as on an in-depth understanding of the particularities of Chinese society could it lead the revolution to victory.[7] The ability to combine Marxist-Leninism with the particularity of China was the basis for victory, and the particularity of China consisted of the fact that the peasants were the main force of the revolution. Consequently, the CCP showed its ability to adapt to the situation in China by gradually retreating to the countryside and developing its strength through organizing the peasants. When the CCP took over China in 1949, it shifted its attention from the countryside to the cities; however, with the Great Leap Forward, it invented a strategy for socialism in China that was based on peasant support, agriculture, and the countryside. So it shifted its focus back to the rural areas. In both cases, the learning process took six to seven years and was accompanied by line struggles inside the Party. However, the parallels between the two stories ends when it comes to discussing the problem of defeat. Whereas, in the case of pre-1949 CCP history, the defeat of the First United Front and the loss of many lives in 1927 were openly declared to be the beginning of the learning process, in post-1949 CCP history the Party could not risk admitting another such defeat. The learning process, which involved adapting to China's particular situation, is therefore described as one that resulted not from fundamental failure but, rather, from Chairman Mao's ability to analyze the situation and to convince his comrades of his ideas.[8]

Rare examples of a more detailed account of what happened during the Great Leap Forward are to be found in internal teaching materials distributed to worker, peasant, and army students during the later years of the Cultural Revolution. In these textbooks, the Great Leap Forward is described within the aforementioned framework and is closely related to the eighth inner-Party line struggle against Peng Dehuai. The Great Famine is euphemized as "temporary economic difficulties"[9] that were brought about by "the treacherous clique under Khrushchev tearing existing contracts to pieces and forcing their specialists to return to the Soviet Union as well as several years of natural disasters."[10] The anti-Chinese and anti-communist attacks by Russian revisionists were matched by those from other imperialist and revisionist countries and were accepted by revisionists in China such as Liu Shaoqi. During the "Meeting of 7,000 Cadres" in January 1962, Liu Shaoqi criticized Mao for having attacked Peng Dehuai too strongly and for not having acknowledged that Peng Dehuai's arguments against the Great Leap were correct. This showed, according to the CCP textbook, that Liu Shaoqi was a member of Peng Dehuai's clique and was strongly opposed to Mao's ideas about socialism in China. This, it said, is when Liu showed his true face for the first time.

The Great Famine and its death toll are not mentioned. Nor does the text admit that Liu Shaoqi had expressed the Party's apologies during the Meeting of 7,000 Cadres in light of the terrible losses brought about by the Great Leap. Instead, the narrative of success and victory relates the Great Leap to the Cultural Revolution and praises both as signs of Mao's ability to fight revisionism.

The Historiography on the Great Leap since the End of the Maoist Era

With the death of Mao Zedong and the end of the Cultural Revolution, the argument about the need to fight revisionism lost its persuasiveness, and the model that replaced the old narrative put the 1950s in a positive light while juxtaposing them to the ten years of chaos that occurred between 1966 and 1976.[11] The Great Leap is seen as an early example of Mao Zedong's development of "ultra-leftist" ideas about socialism in China, which would turn out to be highly erroneous. The 1981 "Resolution on Some Questions Concerning the History of the Party since the Founding of the People's Republic of China" states:

> The 2nd Plenary Session of the 8th Party Congress passed the resolution on the general line and other points of fundamental importance. The correct side about this resolution is its reflecting the wish and strong demand of the masses to change the state of underdevelopment of our economy. Its mistake consisted in underestimating the role of economic laws. However, because of the lack of experience in building socialism and a lack of knowledge regarding the laws of economic development as well as the overall economic situation in our country, but even more so because Comrade Mao Zedong as well as many comrades from the central to the local levels became self-satisfied and arrogant as a result of our victory, we started to become impatient in expecting success and to overestimate the role of subjective willingness and subjective endeavour.[12]

The Great Famine is still not depicted as such: "During the years 1959 to 1961 the economy of our country came across severe problems, and the state as well as the people had to suffer great damages because of mistakes that had been committed during the Great Leap Forward and the Campaign against Rightists, as well as because of natural calamities having taken place. On top of that, the economy was badly affected by the Soviet Union perfidiously tearing contracts into pieces."[13] The volume, which was specially prepared for members of the army, gives explanations of the most important arguments presented in the 1981 Resolution. Explanation 94 discusses the "three difficult years" as a problem related to the Soviet Union. It refers to the Soviets as having signed a friendship treaty with China in order to help socialism to develop but then, as a consequence of ideological conflicts that arose since the mid-1950s, suddenly retreating and leaving China with many unfinished projects and a great debt to repay.[14]

The explanations given by the Central Documentary Bureau on Party History (*Zhonggong zhongyang wenxian yanjiushi*) treat the topic in a similar fashion to the 1981 Resolution, with the slight but important difference that it gives the Great Leap Forward and the Anti-Rightist Campaign the greatest share of blame for the catastrophe, while natural disasters and the retreat of the Soviet Union are seen as problems that exacerbated the situation.[15] The Great Leap Forward is clearly no longer regarded as a sign of the CCP's ability to find a successful road to socialism; rather, it is regarded as a major mistake that caused harm to the people. The myth of the Great Leap was no longer upheld, and, subsequently, more and more details about the Great Famine were revealed to the public.

Ten years after the 1981 Resolution had been passed, Hu Sheng's 1991 volume *Seventy Years of the Chinese Communist Party* stated quite bluntly:

> Comparing the year 1960 with the year 1957, the average amount of consumed grain among the urban and rural population sank by 19.4 percent, with grain consumption among the rural population dropping by 23.7 percent. Consumption of vegetable oil sank by 23 percent, the per capita consumption of meat by 70 percent. Because some areas were not sufficiently supplied with food, edema was a disease that frequently occurred. The death rate rose notably. According to official statistics the population of the whole country decreased by 10 million in 1960 compared to the year before. In special areas such as the Xinyang district in Henan, there was a death rate of more than one hundred per thousand in nine counties, more than double the usual rate. Even though we had hoped for the masses of the people to live through better days as soon as possible, the consequences were that these facts made people grieve. These are the most serious consequences and a lesson to learn from the mistakes made during the course of the Great Leap Forward and the organization of People's Communes.[16]

Six years later, the discussion of the Great Leap Forward and the Great Famine had reached a point at which the death toll could no longer be kept secret. It was under these conditions that Li Chengrui, then the director of the Statistical Bureau of the PRC, published an article in the official PRC journal of Party historiography, *Research on CCP History* (*Zhonggong dangshi yanjiu*), discussing the research that had been conducted inside and outside the PRC regarding the number of casualties caused by the Great Leap Famine. Obviously, his article is not concerned with giving an explanation of why the famine could have taken place; rather, his purpose is to define the correct method of counting casualties. Thus, he tries to convince the reader that 17 million people died as a consequence of the Great Leap Famine and that calculations indicating higher numbers were incorrect.[17] After the myth of the Great Leap was replaced by criticism of the Great Leap, the taboo about the Great Famine was replaced by a "scientific method" of dealing with the death toll and by acknowledging the fact that millions of people had died as a consequence of the Great Leap. By that time, quite a few monographs on the Great Leap and the Great Famine had been published outside China. Some of them were translated into Chinese,[18] and questions about the Great Famine could no longer be suppressed. However, it took Chinese-language academic research on the Great Leap and the Great Famine quite some time to discuss these issues in public.

Explaining the Famine

Three approaches to explaining the relationship between the Great Leap and the Great Famine – the political, the structuralist, and the socio-logical – have emerged so far. Li Rui, as a major player at the central leadership level during the Great Leap, represents the political approach. He looks at the reasons for the Great Leap and views the Great Famine as the sign of a political defeat caused by Mao's false assessment of the situation. His focus is on elite politics.[19] Zhang Letian, who represents unofficial historiography, takes a structuralist approach. He tries to explain the relationship between the Great Leap and the Great Famine by referring to the Big Commune System (*dagongshe zhidu*) as the major reason for the nutrition crisis in the Chinese countryside.[20] Gao Wangling, a historian from outside the system of Party historiography, represents the socio-logical approach to the question. His focus is on state-society relations, and he stresses the fact that state and peasant society were diametrically opposed in the pursuit of their respective interests. The Great Famine was a consequence of the state's inability to safeguard the interest of the peas-antry, and it was a turning point in the relationship between the state and rural society.[21]

Li Rui draws on his personal memories in writing his two-volume book on the Great Leap, but he stresses several times that his interpretation of the situation is in accord with the 1981 Resolution.[22] His book spells out in great detail what the Resolution only hints at. In his conclusion, however, he is much more outspoken than is the Resolution in his critique of the myth that Mao Zedong's path to socialism was more adequate for China and better than the path taken in Stalin's Soviet Union. "We did not invent a new model," he explains, and he argues that the idea that socialism needed heavy industrialization was as accepted in China as it had been in the Soviet Union.[23] The so-called "Chinese path towards socialism" is, in his view, simply a matter of combining the Soviet model of developing a socialist economy with the wartime experience of mass mobilization.[24] He vividly describes Mao's doubts about adhering to Marxism and his pride in developing new theories about socialism in underdeveloped countries, and he summarizes the discourse of the time as follows: "What the Great Leap meant when demanding 'to get rid of superstition' was, speaking frankly, that one felt Marxism would no longer have any vitality."[25] Mao played a crucial role in this and, therefore, is to be held responsible for the disaster that was the Great Leap Famine. He developed a utopian approach to solving the problem of China's lagging behind in economic development, and he based it on the idea that the "masses" would be willing and able to engage in overcoming China's poverty: "When the majority of the masses is in a low state of cultural refinement, these mass movements can easily become blind and have devastating consequences ... The chaos that came by during the 'Great Leap' and the 'Great Cultural Revolution' as a consequence of mobilizing the masses constitutes a painful lesson that will stay with our nation for a long time to come."[26]

Quite interestingly, Li Rui traces Mao's tendency to develop utopian ideas back to Kang Youwei and the "Book of Great Harmony," which, according to Li Rui, must have had a deep influence on Mao.[27] However, that Mao could find support for his ideas is due to the fact that China was an underdeveloped country in which, despite the scarcity of resources, both the masses and the leaders hoped to achieve equality in the shortest possible period of time. This is where the tendency to "underestimate the role of economic laws" originates. Mao related directly to the masses and their wish to overcome poverty, and he did not listen to other leading members of the CCP, who finally gave in to him: "It is sad to say, but the Party did not do anything about Mao Zedong's incorrect ideas and actions, which is why he developed these things to the extreme."[28] Li Rui's analysis of the Great Leap indicates that the CCP was unable to make use of its victory by developing China's economy and having the Chinese people live under decent conditions. It is a story of the tragedy of good intentions, and his point of departure is the fact that, since 1978, the CCP leadership has been pursuing more successful policies. He warns against the possibility of "chaos" re-emerging in China if people do not analyze the reasons for past defeat, and he is critical of the fact that "capitalism has already been restored."[29]

Zhang Letian also wants to draw his readers' attention to the potential of utopianism to mobilize the peasant masses in China:

> When the People's Communes were first founded, the government painted a wonderful image of a new socialist village for the peasants. Two-storied houses, electricity and a telephone, good living conditions, an egalitarian and harmonious society, a happy and nice life. However, after one year, the commune had not led the peasants to what they had anticipated as a "paradise of happiness." To the contrary, the commune had led peasants to a life of widespread hunger and starvation. With the village economy stagnating, the ideal started to dissolve. The logic of rural

economy and social evolution defeated inventions based on subjectivism and nice words of mobilization. They forced the government into compromise. Consequently, the system of big communes had to transform into a system of small communes.[30]

Neither bad weather nor conflicts with the Soviet Union had caused the troubles.[31] Production sank even though most production factors were developing quite well: "The centralized commune system strained the natural village, it destroyed the traditional way of life of the peasants, and the peasants only complied because of political pressure."[32] Under these circumstances, the peasants became passive, and the cadres at the local level replaced adequate management with waste and insanity. Because the peasants were under heavy political pressure, they had no way to organize their own survival and to resist the local cadres. Thus, the idea of solving the problem by retreating to a smaller collective was not the result of pressure from below but, rather, of pressure from the top. The peasants accepted this, however, because it meant "more freedom," which they used to reshape the commune to an extent that fundamentally changed its structure. Subsequently, it no longer conformed to the ideas of the CCP leadership and, in fact, generated an incessant fight between peasants and Party over what was the right form of collectivization.[33]

For Zhang Letian, collectivization per se was not a problem; rather, it was a viable solution to the plight of peasants and agricultural production in China. However, when Mao ordered the organization of communes, he overtaxed the peasants and organized the communes in a manner that had an unhealthy effect both on peasant life and on agricultural production. After the commune adjusted to the reality of the Chinese countryside, things went much better for the peasants. The commune, however, never realized its positive potential. Consequently, the peasants were unable to enjoy the positive aspects of collectivization and instead had to pay a high price for something that had no discernible advantage.

Obviously, Zhang Letian regards the Great Famine as the result of a system failure. As stated in the 1981 Resolution, the Party erred because it underestimated the time necessary to overcome traditional structures in the Chinese countryside. Its desire to organize peasants beyond the constraints of rural traditions coincided with the peasants' hope for a better future. This is how the idea of the Great Leap was accepted by the Party, the local cadres, and the peasants, and this is how it generated the Great Famine, leaving the people without any way of escaping its deadly effects. In Zhang's narrative, the Great Leap is an erroneous idea that generated an erroneous system. The peasants did not have the power to change the system, and the local cadres did not understand that it had to be changed. This is why relief could only come from the very top. Only when the CCP leadership, which came up with the idea, realized that it was a mistake could the peasantry be relieved from the famine. Zhang Letian seems to imply that, had the Party left the organization of agricultural production to rural society, the peasants would have invented a form of collectivization that could have been beneficial to everyone.

Gao Wangling's explanation is similar to Zhang Letian's.[34] However, Gao does not look at the problem mainly from the state and Party's point of view but, rather, talks to people at the grassroots level and uses their testimonies to develop his arguments. According to him, peasants developed a special form of "counter-action" (*fanxingwei*) when reacting to the policies of the state and the CCP.[35] This counter-action (also discussed in Chapter 11 of this volume) was necessary to preserve their lifestyle and their ability to survive the risks and hardships of life in the countryside. For Gao Wangling, the Great Leap is a classic example of how the actions of the CCP and the state generated counter-action from the peasants and the cadres in the countryside. Rather than focusing on how corrupt and unsophisticated cadres at the grassroots level increased the hardships of rural society, he quotes from interviews conducted with all echelons of rural society to show that the peasants had invented a myriad number of survival strategies. The state demanded more and more agricultural support for its project of industrialization, but the peasants were unable and/or unwilling to accede to these demands. So the state started cheating the peasants, and the peasants started cheating the state. By painting a rosy picture of the egalitarian society that would be brought about through collectivization, the state duped the peasantry into allowing more state control over their production and lifestyle. For its part, the peasantry reported incorrect production figures and hid grain from the state. The state distrusted the peasants, and the peasants distrusted the state.[36]

Decentralizing the Historical Account

Li Rui's account of the Great Leap Forward is well known and widely accepted. Although Li is often regarded in the West as presenting fresh if not dissenting views, a close analysis of his text shows that he usually stays within the limits set by the 1981 Resolution.[37] The most important contribution of his book consists in supplying the reader with a lot of interesting details. Party historiography is, by definition, not much more than a very rough interpretation of what happened in the past. And, up until the 1980s, additional information filtered into the hermetic system of Party historiography only when provided by top-level people whose job it was to decide what was to be known.[38] Li Rui is one of these people. He is interested in presenting his view on inner-Party struggle and gives details of those issues that are of interest to inner-Party discussions on the history of the CCP. This is why he focuses on critiquing the myth of Mao's path to socialism, and this is why he is not interested in breaking the taboo of silence surrounding the Great Famine. His is a mainstream perspective, in which the legitimacy of CCP rule is always at stake. And this is why the problem of the Great Famine is so difficult to address. Li Rui was accused of participating in Peng Dehuai's clique and of supporting Peng's criticism of the Great Leap. He knows from experience that addressing the disaster of the Great Famine is the highest possible risk a leading Party member can take. He also knows that the number of casualties during the Great Famine was given in the initial draft of the 1981 Resolution but that it was eventually omitted. Given that many of the leading CCP members of the 1980s had supported Mao's criticism of Peng Dehuai, Li Rui would have isolated himself from them by insisting on the correctness of his criticism of the Great Leap. By not openly referring to the Great Famine, he shows an understanding of the predicament from which the Party leadership cannot escape and therefore tries to forget.

However, in 2002, Li Rui openly addressed the problem of the Great Famine for the first time. In an article written as a foreword to a publication on the Xinyang Incident in Henan, which was only to reach a wider public in 2008,[39] he describes in some detail the humanitarian catastrophe caused by starvation in the Chinese countryside. Again, he argues that the reason for what happened stemmed from inner-Party conflict at different levels of the system. He stresses that the central government was made aware of the problem and sent investigative teams to Xinyang. Their report alerted the central leadership to the problem of widespread starvation, but it held that, due to its radicalism, the provincial committee of Henan had generated the problem. In quoting from this report, Li Rui alludes to unhealthy tendencies at all levels of the CCP and seems to side with the conclusion of one of the cadres who, in 1985, was punished in the aftermath of the incident: "For the Xinyang Incident, the provincial Party committee has to take over responsibility, the district committee has to take over responsibility, the county committee has to take over responsibility, and also the Central Committee has to take over responsibility. Only to punish the grassroots level is not fair."[40]

In contrast to Li Rui, Zhang Letian and Gao Wangling contextualize the Great Famine and avoid explanations related to political decisions taken at the top of the CCP hierarchy. They explicitly develop a bottom-up perspective and rely on grassroots-level information to develop their ideas.

While Zhang Letian relies primarily on county-level archives for his work, Gao Wangling combines these with oral history. He makes use of his relationship with the village to which he was despatched as a "sent-down youth" (*shangshanxiaxiang zhishi qingnian*) and revisits his former friends and colleagues. These people turn out to be willing and able to explain many of the things about which they did not speak in the 1970s. The peasants he interviews remember the past in light of their experience in the present, a time in which they have gained an enormous amount of autonomy from the state and from Party rule and are using this autonomy in order to bargain the terms of their relationship with the state.[41] They openly admit that they could not reveal their thoughts in former times, and, in comparing their relationship to the state in those times to the situation in China under Japanese occupation, they are extremely daring.[42]

There are several groups of young researchers who are using oral history in order to circumvent strict Party control over the archives and in order to retrieve the memories of survivors. Very often this kind of historical research is not conducted by those institutions that should be responsible for writing the history of the CCP and the PRC. Academic historians still seem to shy away from allowing their students to contact people in the villages in order to find out about major events and their effects on life in the countryside during the Maoist era. They still insist that oral history is not as reliable as the kind of historiography based on written sources.[43] But the kind of social history that Gao Wangling and others write is more and more appreciated, and oral history interviews are no longer conducted only with leading Party members and intellectuals.[44]

Based on local sources – be they local archives or local people – we learn that the situation in the countryside differed from location to location. Very often the local administration was of major importance in shaping the livelihood of the people. This is an important addition to the perspective of CCP historiography, which always views China from a centrist viewpoint and claims that central policies shaped the reality in every corner of the country. The decentralization of history and the diversification of the historical account are logical consequences of writing history from a grassroots perspective. Rather than focusing on a political analysis of top-level decisions, they bring an anthropological perspective to the analysis of rural China in the 1950s and clearly indicate that the "reach of the state" was much more limited than the Party would like to admit.[45] Gao tells us that there were places where local cadres helped the peasants to survive the famine through collectively organized cheating and stealing.[46] In other places, local cadres made life for the peasants even harder than it already was, which is why peasants had to find individual solutions to the threat of famine. Leaving parts of the crops in the fields and coming back to pick them up during the night was one of these solutions; going to the fields and stealing immature corn was another. Local cadres were neither corrupt in all cases nor obedient to the centre under all conditions. Similarly, peasants were neither simply the object of Party policies nor always free to determine their own fate. In the words of Gao:

> So far most of the research on Chinese peasants has been focused on the "top level," that is to say on the process of deciding on and implementing state policies. However, the object of these policies, the peasants (i.e., the social side), rested outside the researchers' perspectives. I realized after a period of examinations and research that peasants are in effect not what many people believed they were. They were not the passive recipients of a certain system but had their own hopes, ideas, and demands. They always had their "counter-actions" and measures by which they changed, corrected, or made the policies and systems of upper levels impossible. This reciprocity between the government and the peasants runs through the whole process and still exists today.[47]

The Strained Relationship between Peasants and Party

Although there are important differences between the three approaches to the Great Leap and famine, there are also astonishing similarities. One of the latter is the fact that, in all three cases, the authors no longer describe the relationship between the CCP and the peasants as that of natural allies. For Li Rui, the problem lies in the idea that industrialization was essential to the maximum exploitation of agriculture. This is what he calls the Soviet model, and this is what made life so difficult for the Chinese peasantry. This model splits society into two realms, one of which enjoys the pleasure of living in the cities, while the other suffers under the disadvantage of living in the countryside. The inner logic of this model was not discussed in public until a few years ago. To the contrary, what was propagated was the romantic idea that the Chinese peasants needed the CCP just as much as the CCP needed the peasants. During the Cultural Revolution, the peasants were seen not only seen as allies of the communist revolution but also as the most revolutionary part of the population. Young people from the cities were sent to the countryside to undergo a second (i.e., more revolutionary) education. Cadres had to experience the hardship of life in the rural areas in order to freshen up their revolutionary spirits. The more the peasants were forced into living in severe poverty, the more they were propagandized as the most revolutionary force in Chinese society. This paradox – that the Chinese peasantry helped the CCP to victory but was robbed of the fruits of that victory – was kept secret for a long time. Li Rui was one of the first to openly discuss and analyze this issue. By critiquing the Chinese path to socialism as a combination of the Soviet model and mass mobilization, he surpassed the limits set by the 1981 Resolution, which critiqued the Party for its mistakes but still held that it was the only legitimate representative of the interests of all classes in Chinese society. It was not until the Party and the state leadership passed Document No. 1 of 2004 that it was acknowledged that the "dualism" of Chinese society had to be overcome and that industrialization had reached a point at which it no longer required support from agriculture.[48] To the contrary, agriculture was now to be supported by the industrial sector. Still, the CCP does not admit to having harmed the interests of the peasants, only that its strategy was at least temporarily detrimental to them.

Zhang Letian looks at the problem of the Great Leap and famine from the perspective of its social organization and political implications. The Big Commune System was the system through which the Party and the state tried to impose what Li Rui calls the Soviet model onto Chinese society. Using the peasants' hope of reducing individual risks to get them organized into communes, the state and the Party then used the commune system to force peasants into complying with the needs of industrialization and urban privileges. The peasants, however, soon realized that they had to defend themselves against the state and its policy of privileging the cities and the industrial sector. Zhang Letian shows how the strained relationship between the Party and the state on the one side and the peasantry on the other generated an ideological system and an administrative system that complemented one another in depowering the Chinese peasantry. However, the peasants still had enough power to force the state into changing the Big Commune System into a form of collectivization that was more in line with their interests. Zhang Letian's argument clearly goes beyond the limits of the 1981 Resolution, implying that the interests of the state and the peasants are not only not identical but also contradictory.

Gao Wangling regards the state as strong enough to enforce its regime on the peasants. He does not seem to agree with Zhang Letian that the peasants had the power to reshape the commune system; instead, he views them as mostly reactive and as blind to the overall situation. In trying to understand peasant survival strategies, he focuses on their reactions to a state that imposes upon them disadvantageous terms of trade. These reactions are difficult to discern as "counter-actions" that cannot fundamentally change the commune system or state-society relations but that can help the peasants to survive and enhance their living conditions. Gao Wangling does not spell this argument out but, rather, leaves his readers with the impression that peasants, due to their sheer numbers, had the power to continuously subvert the socialist state and thus drive the Soviet model to a reductio ad absurdum. They did not consciously struggle to change the system but, rather, finally forced it to change simply by pursuing their own survival. The Soviet model Li Rui criticizes was incompatible with the form of agriculture to which Chinese peasants were accustomed and that they preserved even under the conditions the newly established communist state attempted to impose upon them. Again, this shows the fundamental conflict between the state and rural society.

Lifting the Taboo by Writing Literature: Wang Zhiliang's *The Starving Village*

The taboo of silence surrounding the Great Famine, although, since the 1981 Resolution, no longer imposed on society by Party directives, still lingers in post-1949 Chinese historiography.[49] As was seen above, although the myth of the Great Leap has lost its persuasiveness, the taboo around the Great Famine still lingers as historians continue to shy away from this topic. Thus, the first person to actually give an account of what happened in the Chinese countryside during the Great Famine is Wang Zhiliang, who addressed this topic in his 1994 novel *The Starving Village*.[50] Wang Zhiliang offers a documentary fiction about his experiences in different regions of China as a sent-down "rightist." He writes about starving peasants, whom he depicts as victims of local cadres, bad weather, and helplessness. He writes that their sufferings not only involved a lack of nutrition but also, and especially, a situation that drove them to violate their basic moral beliefs (this being their only chance of survival). For Wang Zhiliang, the disaster of the Great Leap is not only that it led to the Great Famine, in which many millions died of starvation, but also that it robbed people of their innate humanism. People who survived the Great Famine would never be the same.

Wang does not offer any explanation for why things happened the way they did. He does not deal with CCP politics; rather, he tells us the story of local suffering. Two things stand out: (1) the absolute helplessness of the local peasants, who, according to Wang Zhiliang's narrative, are devoid of any means of freeing themselves from the situation that threatens their lives; and (2) the victimization of the peasants by local cadres, who misuse their power to add to the hardships these people have to endure. People spend all day searching desperately for something to eat and drink. They go to the forest to pick herbs as a replacement for vegetables and grain. They run off to the nearby railway track hoping that passengers will throw out leftovers and garbage. Despite all these efforts, food is so scarce that they have to decide whether to abandon the grandmother or the baby in order to enhance the chances of survival for other members of the family. Eventually, they get so tired and weak that they can only lie down and wait for the next rain. Once it comes, people run out of their houses, take off their clothes, and enjoy a rare opportunity to wash their bodies. As time goes by, they are reduced to seeking survival on an individual basis. No collective can help them, no family can support them. They are individuals in the most radical sense of the word, alone against everybody else.

The local cadres Wang Zhiliang depicts in his story make things even worse for the peasants. They use their power to establish a network of friends and family with privileged access to food, information, and women. The centre of this network is the public dining hall, which ensures that the peasants have to depend on food supplied by the local administration. Those who supported the local cadre system benefited from this form of food supply; those who were not allowed, were unable, or were unwilling to support it had to live on the leftovers. Further, they were exposed to enforced labour, which was often insane and unnecessary, and kept ignorant of anything going on outside the village. Women were usually excluded from the network of those enjoying privileges, and the enforced labour they had to suffer included involuntary sexual services in exchange for food.

Wang Zhiliang's perspective on the Great Leap and the Great Famine is based on the intellectual's moral obligation towards the peasantry. Wang feels ashamed over what he experienced in the countryside, and he feels sorry for the peasants who had to suffer not only from the famine but also from the fact that their lot was not pitied and their deaths not mourned. His perspective on the Great Famine resembles that of Hu Sheng.[51]

In Search of a New Image for the Chinese Peasantry: The Root-Seeking Literature on the Great Leap

The gradual rewriting of the image of the Chinese peasant that we encounter in books on post-1949 Chinese history transgresses the limits of the traditional moral obligation of intellectuals towards the peasants. However, what we find in Zhang Letian and Gao Wangling appeared much earlier in the field of literature and has a forerunner in the root-seeking literature (*xungen wenxue*) of the 1990s. It is especially in the literature of new historicism, most prominently in prose written by Ge Fei, Mo Yan, Su Tong, and Yu Hua, that we find many of the aforementioned thoughts.[52] In contrast to the situation before 1976, when discussions in the realm of historiography were often more daring and avant-garde than were those in the field of literature, at the end of the Cultural Revolution, the focus of the debate on issues related to understanding China's twentieth century shifted from the field of historiography to the field of literature. This is true of the literature of the wounded (*shanghen wenxue*), which was the first form of writing that tried to come to terms with the Cultural Revolution, and it is also true of the root-seeking literature, which, by revisiting the Chinese countryside, also deals with the Great Leap Forward and, especially, the Great Famine. While the field of academic historiography is still searching for a new model to enable it to rewrite twentieth-century Chinese history, writers of the root-seeking literature have already tried out multiple ways of remodelling China's contemporary history.[53]

Yu Hua's novella *To Live* is a family saga that runs through most of the twentieth century.[54] Fu Gui, the narrator of the story, is his family's only survivor. Having lost all his wealth through gambling, he is a poor peasant in post-1949 China and is reduced to seeking survival amidst poverty, war, turmoil, and mass mobilizations. During the Great Leap, he loses his only son. Although the villagers are already starving, his son is called to the hospital along with his classmates and asked to donate blood for the principal of their school, who is losing blood while giving birth to a child. Fu Gui's son Youqing dies as the doctor takes more and more blood from him in order to rescue the headmistress, who is the wife of the county head.[55] Only when Fu Gui is called to the scene does he realize that the county head is his former friend Chunsheng, with whom he had spent many difficult days in pre-1949 China. In Chapter 7, the friends meet for the first time after many years and do not dare to openly speak of the fact that Fu Gui's son lost his life while Chunsheng's wife was rescued. Fu Gui buries his son before telling his wife what happened. However, although she herself nearly starved to death, she soon realizes that her son is dead and that the county head is somehow involved in this. When Chunsheng comes to bring them money as a compensation for the loss of their son, she does not allow him to enter the house.[56]

The relationship between the narrator and his friend is symbolic of the relationship between the peasants and the Party. The natural friendship that had evolved during the pre-1949 wars and turmoil is destroyed during the Great Leap, never to be repaired. Youqing dies while donating blood to the headmistress of his school. His life is clearly regarded as less precious than that of the teacher and wife of the county head. The local elite lives off of the peasants. In contrast to the well-known movie based on Yu Hua's novel, the story does not end with a positive perspective on the future. The friend turned Party head commits suicide. The narrator loses his daughter and wife as well as his son-in-law and his grandson. Only by telling his story can he, the only survivor of his family, leave something for future generations. Although he was always willing to adapt, to comply, and to obey, circumstances did not allow him to do what he thought was most important: to preserve the continuity of his lineage. Yu Hua's perspective resembles Zhang Letian's insofar as Yu sees the relationship between peasant and Party as irreparable and the politics of the CCP as irreconcilable with the interests of the peasants, despite their willingness to cooperate with the Party.[57]

In contrast to Yu Hua, who was born and raised in a small city, Mo Yan is the offspring of a family that was categorized as belonging to the village's richer echelons. In his more recent novels, he depicts the peasantry as the root of Chinese culture and society and, therefore, as more enduring than any political power that might be trying to establish its rule over China.[58] In many of his early short stories, however, his perspective is close to what we find in Wang Zhiliang's and Yu Hua's stories.[59] We read about hunger in the countryside, which occurs at any given time, not only during the Great Leap Forward. We read about peasants suffering from local power holders, be they nationalists, communists, or Japanese. One of his stories depicts a mother working in a granary and swallowing grain in order to hide it from the guards. Once at home, she vomits up the grain and cooks it as a meal for her children.[60] In another story, he tells of a little boy who tries to reach the next town in an attempt to buy medicine for his mother. The fact that Chinese peasants were robbed of their freedom of mobility by the household registration system is represented by the little boy's being handcuffed to a tree in the burning sun, with nobody either willing or able to help him. Quite clearly, the peasants are the victims of nature, political systems, and economic scarcity.[61]

In *Big Breasts and Wide Hips,*[62] Mo Yan's peasants are victims and perpetrators, subjects and objects of oppression, blind and curious, stupid, silly, and awkward, yet cunning, clever, and crafty. However, they are "peasants without the Party" (Lucien Bianco),[63] peasants who do not know about the grand mass movements, who tumble from one event to the other without having the words to describe them, peasants who organize their survival within larger circumstances that are utterly unknown to them. At no point does the reader encounter the Party as an institution in the Chinese countryside. In some cases, we learn that there are Party members among the villagers, but they are introduced as individuals and members of clans and families rather than as people affiliated with the CCP. If the peasants admire them or follow their advice, it is out of trust for the individual and not out of support for a political program. Shangguan Lu is the centre of the story, which starts with the Boxer Rebellion in the year 1900 and comes to a close a few years before the end of the twentieth century. As the mother of eight daughters and one son, Shangguan Lu organizes their survival without male support. She represents sustainability in the countryside and is juxtaposed to men who are either too weak or too violent to guarantee survival. Her daughters marry the representatives of all the different political forces in China. They depart from the traditions of the countryside by seeking allies among local bandits, the Guomindang, the CCP, and US advisers. But they all die a premature death. Jintong, born during the Sino-Japanese War of 1937-45 as the son of a Swedish missionary, is the only one of the family to survive. He is so weak that he cannot depart from rural traditions, and it is this weakness, represented by his unusual dependence on his mother's milk, that enables him to survive all the abominable events that hit the village. Through this weakness he is able to sustain the hybridism of the situation into which he was born – a situation in which femininity stands for continuity and masculinity for change.

Through Jintong we learn about the Great Leap in Mo Yan's favourite location, which is both real and imaginative – Gaomi County in Shandong Province.[64] As a young adolescent, Jintong is sent to a state farm, where he meets women who run the place according to what the Party tells them. They engage in insane breeding experiments and organize life in the countryside according to a rationality whose logic is indiscernible to Jintong. His first explicit encounter with a member of the CCP occurs within this setting. Commander Long, a woman who lost one arm, wants to copulate with him. Jintong refuses and only fulfills her wish after finding her dead as a consequence of suicide. Subsequently, he is accused of having killed her; however, as a flood covers the state farm with mud, no evidence of his alleged murder can be traced, and he is sent home unpunished. For the time being, the incident slips into oblivion.

Mo Yan extracts the scene of the Great Leap from the village, positioning it within an artificial setting that underlines the peasants' distance from the Great Leap and their inability to understand its rationale. In contrast to what we read in Party historiography about the Great Leap, Mo Yan's peasants show no enthusiasm for it. The people involved in the Great Leap are either forced to do so or are alien to the situation in the countryside. Jintong meets one of his sisters in the state farm, but he is unable to identify her. She has changed her name and identity since he last saw her and only reveals her affiliation with the Shangguan family in her last will. She dies as a consequence of eating too much after a long period of hunger, a form of death depicted in many narratives on starvation in China. However, in *Big Breasts and Wide Hips* hunger is a constant threat, and peasants know how to handle it. Only people who lost contact with the countryside and the accumulated wisdom of survival to be found in the villages would die such an unnecessary death.

In Mo Yan's story, Jintong is the perpetrator, and Commander Long, member of the CCP, is the victim. What does this imply about our understanding of the Great Leap? Several readings seem possible. First of all, we have to take into account the fact that the scene represents the peasants' perspective on the situation. As such, it shows the inability of the Party to enforce its policies in the countryside and to punish peasants who supposedly do harm to it and its members. The local population is more concerned about Jintong than about punishing a crime committed against a Party member from outside the village. Also, we might read the scene as a discussion of the peasants' ability to forget. The crime scene is covered by mud, so there is no need to bother about what actually happened. However, what seems to have fallen into oblivion reappears during the Cultural Revolution, and Jintong is sentenced to work in a labour camp for having killed Commander Long.[65] Finally, we cannot overlook the fact that the scene constitutes one of the very few direct encounters between Jintong and the CCP and that the Great Leap is depicted in more detail than are other historical incidents. Perhaps Mo Yan turns common knowledge about the Great Leap upside down in order to make his readers realize how the CCP has so far handled the question of responsibility and guilt for the casualties caused by its policies. If so, the scene can be read as an allusion to the Party's hiding its responsibility for the Great Leap and the Great Famine behind the screen of natural disasters. As a consequence, the responsibility for the disaster remains unclear, which is why the peasants are unable to take action against the source of their hardships. In this respect, Mo Yan comes to conclusions that are quite similar to those of Yu Hua. Everybody seems to know who is responsible for what; however, while those who are responsible remain unpunished, those who have to live through the disaster lose their lives.

No matter how disastrous the situation, mother Shangguan Lu knows how to survive. Not only does she have a wide range of survival strategies, but she is also able to adapt to, and to display autonomy within, the different political systems and settings under which she has to live. Her pragmatism knows no ideological or religious constraints, which is why she is able to adapt to rapid changes of regime and conventions yet, when necessary, still defy rules and regulations. No regime can make her submit, yet she is ready to comply with any regime that is imposed on her. It is this combination of adaptability and autonomy that forms the basis of her sustainability. Through Shangguan Lu, Mo Yan explains to us that the traditional way of life in the Chinese countryside, which the CCP wanted to get rid of during the Great Leap Forward, is more sustainable than any system that might try to change it.

Conclusion: Re-Imagining the Chinese Peasants Means Rewriting Twentieth-Century Chinese History

While most foreign observers of the recent miracle of economic development in China focus on the situation in China's cities and megacities when trying to understand what future this country is heading for, some Chinese intellectuals focus on the countryside and the peasantry. They seem to be more astonished by China's recent past than by its present, and they anticipate the future by referring to China's long history. In light of a rapidly changing present, they turn to the Maoist era and realize that they need to understand the revolution under communist leadership in terms that are fundamentally different from those they had learned in their Party history lessons. And they come to the conclusion that, despite all the blood that was shed during the course of the twentieth century, the changes that took place were less fundamental than they had been led to believe. The experience of the Great Leap plays a crucial role in reconceptualizing the possibility of change in China's twentieth century. It shows that the CCP, which was able to unite most of China under its rule and bring civil war to an end, was unable to penetrate the Chinese countryside with its ideas and institutions. It met with peasant counter-actions, which eventually forced it to adjust its policies to the reality of the countryside. Instead of the Party changing the peasants, the peasants changed the Party. As Jiang Yihua, a veteran economic historian from Fudan University (known for his fresh views on Chinese history) explains, the main problem of China's moving towards modernity is the peasant problem. By this he means that, as long as the peasants are the majority of Chinese society, they have the power to determine to what degree it can be changed. Any political power that tries to force the peasantry into a direction it does not support will be met with implicit or explicit, direct or indirect, forms of resistance. This is what Jiang refers to as the "survival capacity" and the "powerful regenerative capacity" of the Chinese peasants.[66] Whether we look at the historiography on the Great Leap or the fiction on the Great Leap, what is clear is this: there is no future for China that the peasants cannot accept as their future.

Notes

1 For a discussion of the relationship between taboo and trauma in the case of the Great Famine, see Susanne Weigelin-Schwiedrzik, "Trauma and Memory: The Case of the Great Famine in the People's Republic of China (1959-1961)," *Historiography East and West* 1, 1 (2003): 39-67.

2 In the course of discussing the Cultural Revolution, some voices in the PRC have recently been inclined towards going back to a more positive interpretation of the Great Leap Forward. They argue that the deconstruction of the Great Leap should not go so far as to totally negate it; instead, one should acknowledge that the Great Leap made

important contributions to social equity. Negating the Great Leap is, for them, equivalent to negating the problem of social disparities in today's China.

3 I am only referring to recent historiographical discussions in the PRC. For the state of the art in the field of Chinese studies, see Felix Wemheuer, *China's "Großer Sprung nach vorne" (1958-1961): Von der kommunistischen Offensive in die Hungersnot: Intellektuelle erinnern sich* [China's "Great Leap Forward" (1958-1961): From the Communist Offensive to Famine: Intellectuals Remember] (Münster: Lit-Verlag, 2004), 9-19.

4 See "Nankai daxue Zhonggong dangshi jiangyi bianxiezu: Zhongguo gongchandang lishi jiangyi" [Lecture on the History of the Chinese Communist Party] (Tianjin, 1976) and "Zhongguo gongchandang liangtiao luxian douzhengshi jiangyi bianxiezu: Zhongguo gongchandang liangtiao luxian douzhengshi jiangyi" [Lecture on the History of the Two Line Struggle of the Chinese Communist Party] (1974).

5 Commission of the Central Committee of the C.P.S.U.(B.), ed., *History of the Communist Party of the Soviet Union (Bolsheviks) Short Course* (Moscow: Foreign Languages Publishing House, 1939).

6 For a summary of the Maoist view on this question, see Zhang Letian, *Gaobie lixiang: Renmin gongshe zhidu yanjiu* [Farewell to Idealism: A Study of the People's Commune System] (Shanghai: Dongfang chuban zhongxin, 1998), 4.

7 This official view of the Chinese Revolution was first put down in "Guanyu ruogan lishi wenti de jueyi mingci jieshi" [Word Explanations for the Resolution on Some Questions Concerning the History since the Founding of the People's Republic of China], *Renmin ribao* [People's Daily], 1 July 1981, 1-7.

8 See note 3.

9 "Zhongguo gongchandang shici luxian douzheng jiangyi (chugao)" [Lecture on the Ten Inner Party Line Struggles of the Chinese Communist Party (first draft)], n.d., 209.

10 Ibid.

11 For the official version of this narrative, see Renmin chubanshe, ed., "Guanyu jianguo yilai dang de ruogan lishi wenti de jueyi" [Resolution on Some Questions Regarding the History of the Party since the Founding of the People's Republic of China], in *Guanyu jianguo yilai dang de ruogan lishi wenti de jueyi zhushiben* (Beijing: Renmin chubanshe, 1985), 3-72.

12 Ibid., 23.

13 Ibid., 24.

14 "Guanyu jianguo yilai dang de ruogan lishi wenti de jueyi mingci jieshi"; *Guanyu jianguo yilai dang de ruogan lishi wenti de jueyi zhushiben*, 136.

15 *Guanyu jianguo yilai dang de ruogan lishi wenti de jueyi zhushiben*, 374.

16 Hu Sheng, ed., *Zhongguo gongchandang de qishi nian* [Seventy Years of the Chinese Communist Party] (Beijing: Zhonggong dangshi chubanshe, 1991), 369. I would like to thank Paul Cohen and Stuart Schram for drawing my attention to Hu Sheng's unprecedented and still unusual openness about the famine.

17 Li Chengrui, "'Dayuejin' yinqi de renkou biandong" [Changes in Demography as Induced by the "Great Leap Forward"], *Zhonggong dangshi yanjiu* [Research on CCP History] 2 (1997): 1-13.

18 For an example, see Penny Kane, *Famine in China, 1959-61: Demographic and Social Implications* (New York: St. Martin's Press, 1988). This is translated into Chinese as Pengni Kai'en (i.e., Penny Kane), *Zhongguo de dajihuang*.

19 Li Rui, *Dayuejin qinliji* [Personal Account of the Great Leap Forward] (Haikou: Nanfang chubanshe, 1999), 2 vols.

20 Zhang, *Gaobie lixiang*.

21 Gao Wangling, *Renmin gongshe shiqi Zhongguo nongmin "fanxingwei" diaocha* [An Investigation of Peasant "Resistance" during the Time of the People's Communes] (Beijing: Zhonggong dangshi chubanshe, 2006).

22 Renmin chubanshe, ed., "Guanyu jianguo yilai dang de ruogan lishi wenti de jueyi."
23 Li Rui, *Dayuejin qinliji*, 515.
24 Ibid., 517.
25 Ibid., 519.
26 Ibid., 525.
27 Ibid., 530.
28 Ibid., 539.
29 Ibid.
30 Zhang, *Gaobie lixiang*, 74.
31 Ibid., 77.
32 Ibid., 78.
33 Ibid., 85.
34 Gao, *Renmin gongshe shiqi Zhongguo nongmin "fanxingwei,"* 19.
35 For the author's explanation of this term, see ibid., 3.
36 Ibid., 192-93.
37 "Zhongguo gongchandang shici luxian douzheng jiangyi (chugao)," n.d., 209.
38 For a more detailed English-language discussion of Party historiography, see Susanne Weigelin-Schwiedrzik, "Party Historiography in the People's Republic of China," *Australian Journal of Chinese Affairs* 17 (1987): 77-94.
39 Qiao Peihua, *Xinyang shijian* [The Xinyang Disaster] (Hong Kong: Kaifang chubanshe, 2009). Li Rui originally published the piece as "'Xinyang shijian' ji qi jiaoxun" [Lessons of the Xinyang Incident] in *Yanhuang chunqiu* [China Chronicle] 4 (2002): 19-22.
40 Li Rui. "Xinyang shijian' ji qi jiaoxun," 21.
41 See Susanne Weigelin-Schwiedrzik, "The Distance between State and Rural Society in the PRC," *Journal of Environmental Management* 87, 2 (2008): 216-25.
42 Gao, *Renmin gongshe shiqi Zhongguo nongmin "fanxingwei,"* 9.
43 For a discussion of oral history in the PRC, see Wang Junyi and Ding Dong, eds., *Koushu lishi* [Oral History], vol. 1 (Beijing: Zhongguo shehui kexue chubanshe, 2003).
44 Increasingly, students in the history and sociology departments at Renmin Daxue, Fudan Daxue, and Qinghua University write their MA theses on the basis of oral history sources. See Liu Xin, "Remember to Forget: Critique of a Critical Case Study," *Historiography East and West* 2, 1 (2004): 45-85.
45 Vivienne Shue, *The Reach of the State* (Stanford: Stanford University Press, 1988).
46 Gao, *Renmin gongshe shiqi Zhongguo nongmin "fanxingwei,"* 11.
47 Ibid., 192.
48 Document No. 1 of 2004 states: "the difficulty of boosting farmers' incomes ... is also a concentrated reflection of deep-rooted contradictions having built up over a long time inside the dual system of city and countryside." See *Zhonggong zhongyang guowuyuan guanyu cujin nongmin zengjia shouru ruogan zhengce de yijian* [Chinese Communist Party Central Committee and State Council Resolution on Some Political Suggestions for Boosting Peasant Incomes], available at www.people.com.cn.
49 Recently, Yang Jisheng, an author living in Beijing, published his book on the Great Famine – a book he had researched for more than twenty years in Hong Kong. See Yang Jisheng, *Mubei: Zhongguo liushi niandai de dajihuang jishi* [Tombstone: An Account of China's Great Famine of the 1960s] (Hong Kong: Tiandi tushu, 2008).
50 [Wang] Zhi Liang, "Ji'e de shancun," *Renditions* 68 (2007): 112-42. For a partially translated English version, see Andrew Endrey, "Zhiliang: Hungry Mountain Village – Excerpts," *Renditions* 68 (2007): 112-42.
51 Hu, *Zhongguo gongchandang de qishi nian*.
52 For discussions of the root-seeking literature, see, for example, Yi-tsi Feuerwerker, *Ideology, Power, Text: Self-Representation and the Peasant "Other" in Modern Chinese Literature* (Stanford: Stanford University Press, 1998); Howard Choy, *Remapping the Past: Fictions*

of History in Deng's China, 1979-1997 (Boston: Brill, 2008); Michael S. Duke, "Past, Present, and Future in Mo Yan's Fiction of the 1980s," in *From May Fourth to June Fourth: Fiction and Film in 20th-Century China*, ed. David Der-wei Wang and Ellen Widmer, 43-70 (Cambridge, MA: Harvard University Press, 1993); and Andrea Riemenschnitter, "Nationale Mythen und Konfigurationen kulturellen Wandels in der chinesischen Literatur des 20." Jahrhunderts [National Myths and Configurations of Cultural Change in the Chinese Literature of the 20th Century] (Unveröffentlichte Habilitationsschrift [Habilitation thesis], University of Heidelberg, 2001), 140-50.

53 For a discussion of the relationship between literature and historiography, see Choy, *Remapping the Past;* Ching-kiu Stephen Chan, "Split China or the Historical/Imaginary: Toward a Theory of the Displacement of Subjectivity in Modern China," in *Politics, Ideology, and Literary Discourse in Modern China*, ed. Kang Liu and Tang Xiaobing, 70-101 (Durham: Duke University Press, 1993).

54 Yu Hua, "Huozhe" [To Live], in *Yu Hua zuopinji* [Collected Works of Yu Hua] (Shanghai: Shanghai wenyi chubanshe, 2004 [1993]).

55 Ibid., chap. 6.

56 Ibid., chap. 7.

57 Zhang, *Gaobie lixiang.*

58 See, for example, Mo Yan, *Fengru feitun* [Big Breasts and Wide Hips] (Beijing: Dangdai shijie chubanshe, 2004). For an English translation, see Mo Yan and Howard Goldblatt, trans., *Big Breasts and Wide Hips* (New York: Arcade Publishing, 2004).

59 See, for example, Mo Yan, "Chishi san pian" [Three Pieces about Eating], in *Qingxing de shuomengzhe* [A Clear-Headed Dreamer] (Jinan: Shandong wenyi chubanshe, 2002); and Mo Yan, "Liangshi" [Grain], in *Zuiguo: Duanpian xiaoshuoji* [Guilty: Collection of Short Stories] (Jinan: Shandong wenyi chubanshe, 2002), 267-80. For a choice of early short stories translated into English, see Mo Yan and Janice Wickeri, trans., *Explosions and Other Stories* (Hong Kong: Renditions Paperback, 1991). For a discussion of Mo Yan's literature on hunger and starvation, see Angelika Schönegger-Men, "Beherrscht von Hunger und Leid: Übersetzung und gesellschaftspolitischer Kommentar zu vier autobiographischen Geschichten und zwei kurzen Erzählungen von Mo Yan" [Under the Pressure of Hunger and Suffering: A Translation and a Socio-Political Commentary on Four Autobiographical Accounts and Two Short Stories by Mo Yan] (Diploma thesis, University of Vienna, 2004).

60 Mo, "Liangshi."

61 Mo Yan, "Muzhikao" [Thumbscrew], in *Muzhikao: Duanpian xiaoshuoji* [Thumbscrew: Collection of Short Stories] (Jinan: Shandong wenyi chubanshe, 2002), 189-215.

62 Mo, *Fengru feitun.*

63 Lucien Bianco, *Peasants without the Party* (New York: M.E. Sharpe, 2001).

64 Mo, *Fengru feitun*, chap. 25.

65 Ibid., chap. 26.

66 Jiang Yihua, "Zongxu" [General Introduction], in *Geming yu xiangcun, guojia, sheng, xian yu liangshi tonggou tongxiao zhidu, 1953-1957* [The Revolution and the Countryside: The Central State, the Province, the County, and the System of Controlled Grain Allocation, 1953-1957], ed. Tian Xiquan (Shanghai: Shanghai shehui kexue chubanshe, 2006), 2-3.

2 Romancing the Leap:
Euphoria in the Moment before Disaster
Richard King

Revolution, as Mao Zedong famously observed, is not a matter of inviting people to dinner or other such gentilities: it is, as he wrote in his "Report on an investigation of the peasant movement in [his native province of] Hunan," in a paragraph that was later included in the "little Red Book" and sung by Cultural Revolution youth as a quotation song, "an act of violence by which one class overthrows another."[1] Despite, or perhaps in part because of, their violent quality, great revolutionary movements inspire romantic enthusiasm in their adherents. This is especially so with the young, be they participants, beneficiaries, or merely observers longing for a change that will improve their world, their nation, or the group with which they identify. Thus, the twenty-year-old William Wordsworth, a Cambridge undergraduate on a summer walking tour of France in 1790, was seduced by the changes brought about by the French Revolution of the previous year, endowing it with the qualities of hope and youth:

> Bliss was it in that dawn to be alive,
> But to be young was very heaven! – Oh! Times,
> In which the meagre, stale, forbidding ways
> Of custom, law, and statute, took at once
> The attraction of a country in romance![2]

In the France of Wordsworth's observation and imagining, all would find the means for fulfillment "Not in Utopia, subterranean fields, / Or some secreted island, Heaven knows where! / But in the very world, which is the world / Of all of us, – the place where in the end / We find our happiness, or not at all!"[3] Wordsworth's French romanticism had an aphrodisiac, as well as a politically uplifting, effect: the young poet fathered a child in the course of his European vacation.[4]

The Chinese revolution through which Mao Zedong led the Chinese people for forty years was, as he had predicted in 1927, no dinner party;

but it, like the French and Russian revolutions before it, demonstrated a capacity to arouse passion. At various crucial stages in its turbulent development – notably in the revolutionary base areas of Yan'an and in the opening phases of both the Great Leap Forward and the Cultural Revolution – the Chinese Communist Party contrived to channel this passion into the production of uplifting propaganda recast in traditional popular artistic forms that would present to a mass audience what Susanne Weigelin-Schwiedrzik characterizes in the previous chapter as a "narrative of success and victory." In Yan'an, the form chosen as the vessel for Party instruction was a local drama called *Yangge* (Rice-Sprout Song), transformed from bawdy entertainment into educational tool; in the case of the Great Leap, the movement for the mass campaign to mobilize the populace began with an orchestrated attempt to compose and collect "new folk songs" (*xin minge*) written for the campaign and celebrating a new dawn of unlimited possibility. Like wheat and steel, respectively the totemic products for agriculture and industry in the Great Leap, these poems were to be produced in unprecedented quantities. Indeed, following the call to collect folk songs in early 1958, "several million pieces were collected" in Shanghai alone, of which two thousand were published.[5] Zhou Yang, who oversaw the arts from the Ministry of Propaganda, wrote in May 1958 of a harvest of verse that was already "a thousand basketsful and ten thousand basketsful."[6]

The poems were followed by works in other forms in the visual, literary, and performing arts, which, while they may have been produced more slowly and in smaller quantities, similarly extolled the innovations and achievements of the Great Leap in a fervour of revolutionary and sentimental romanticism. This chapter focuses on three texts from the early stages of the Great Leap: the definitive collection of "new folk songs," *Red Flag Ballads*, and two stories by leading practitioners of village fiction in the Mao era – Hao Ran and Li Zhun. A reading of these texts demonstrates the ways in which literature was intended to inspire enthusiasm for the initiatives and innovations of the time as well as compliance with the demands placed on the Chinese peasantry to meet the goals set for them by the Party and Chairman Mao. The two young fiction writers, whose works were written later than the poems, may be accused of complicity in concealing the darker side of the Great Leap, which was evident when their stories were published (although the full horror of the subsequent famines could not have been anticipated). The disastrous consequences of the Great Leap, while known to those who suffered them and the subject of hearsay and rumour, remained unspoken at home and abroad, denied by the official media and overseas friends of the Chinese government.

Songs of Revolutionary Romanticism

The campaign to produce new folk songs, like the Great Leap of which it was a part, came as the Anti-Rightist Campaign was under way. The leadership of the CCP was still smarting from the criticism that it had invited, but still not fully expected, in the Hundred Flowers Campaign of 1956, and it was in the process of purging large numbers of real or imagined dissenters, particularly among the intellectuals.[7] The Anti-Rightist Campaign began in 1957, with attacks on members of the urban intelligentsia – scientists, educators, creative writers, and others – who had criticized the CCP's management of their endeavours. It was broadened to include condemnation of "rural rightists" who were opposed to the speed with which the collectivization of land, livestock, and property was being implemented. This came at a time when the world's two major communist parties, the Soviet and the Chinese, were moving from cautious fraternity to outright hostility following Khrushchev's criticism of Stalin. Party chairman Mao Zedong's mistrust of intellectuals meant that other groups within Chinese society – the peasantry and the industrial proletariat – had to make additional contributions in the pursuit of the grandiose and unattainable goals Mao set for China's military and industrial development in international isolation: a Chinese-made atom bomb and a higher output of steel than the United Kingdom chief among them. Folk songs, based on indigenous rural forms that owed nothing to intellectual or Soviet traditions, were chosen to reflect and inspire the determination and boundless optimism needed to vault China into the ranks of powerful industrialized nations. The utopian fantasy of state policy, and the similar spirit called for in the new poetry, also necessitated a new creative methodology that went beyond the socialist realism imported from the Soviet Union. This was to be "the combination of revolutionary realism and revolutionary romanticism" proposed by Mao and said to be embodied in his poetry.[8] The Mao poem most praised for combining romanticism and realism is his "Reply to Li Shuyi" (*Da Li Shuyi*), written in 1957 in memory of Mao's second wife, Yang Kaihui (the first being from an arranged marriage that Mao rejected), and Li's husband (and Mao's colleague) Liu Zhixun, both of whom perished in the battles with the Nationalist government in the early 1930s.[9] In the poem, the two of them are imagined transported to heaven. The second stanza reads: "The lonely moon goddess spreads her ample sleeves / To dance for these loyal souls in infinite space. / Earth suddenly reports the tiger subdued, / Tears of joy pour forth falling as mighty rain."[10] In the essay celebrating the new poetry quoted above, Zhou Yang explains the new formulation, saying that, without romanticism, realism would degenerate into naturalism, which he describes as a "distortion and vulgarization of realism," and that without realism romanticism would be mere "revolutionary noise-making, or intellectual-style self-indulgent fantasy."[11]

A mere three hundred of the millions of "new folk songs" were collected in a 1959 anthology prepared by Zhou Yang and the People's Republic's senior poet Guo Moruo.[12] The number matches the three hundred items in the most popular collection of Tang poetry and is similar to the number of verses in the classical *Book of Odes* (*Shijing*) traditionally ascribed to Confucius. Zhou and Guo's collection was intended to be similarly definitive.

Most of the new folk songs have a rural setting, and it is these poems that are considered here. The themes of the poems are the same as those that appear in other Great Leap propaganda, both print and visual, and they include the victory of humanity in its war with nature, the superiority of socialist humanity to heroes of the past, the celebration of the achievements of the Great Leap, the emergence of women as an equal force in production, and equality and shared purpose as a basis for romantic love.

The Struggle with Nature

In her book *Mao's War against Nature*, Judith Shapiro quotes a celebrated poetic fragment from Mao's youth to illustrate not only his obsession with struggle but also his adversarial view of nature: "To struggle against Heaven is endless joy, / To struggle against the earth is endless joy, / To struggle against people is endless joy."[13] Shapiro notes that:

> The ideology of Marxism-Leninism-Mao Zedong Thought, with the conviction that nature was conquerable through military mobilization, attack and victory, shaped the human-nature relationship, as did a traditional culture that provided conditions under which such models and leaders could take hold.[14]

The Great Leap was to exhaust both raw materials and human bodies in massive irrigation and construction projects, many of them poorly designed and (especially in the case of dams constructed of beaten earth) destined to collapse. In *Red Flag Ballads*, the mood is one of revolutionary-romantic indomitability in the war against nature. The best known of all of the poems, "Here I Come," celebrates digging through mountains to ensure a supply of water. The narrator declares, "I order the Three Mountains and the Five Peaks: / Make way there, / Here I come!"[15] (Zhou Yang's gloss to this poem reads, "this 'I' is of course not the [individual] 'small I,' but the

A notorious faked photograph of children supposedly standing on a rice crop so dense it will bear their weight (they are actually standing on an artfully concealed bench). This photo was released in 1958 by New China News Agency and reprinted in the English-language *China Pictorial*. This image also appears in Becker, *Hungry Ghosts*.

'great I,' a general title for the collective peasantry; and only for that reason does it possess such great and irresistible force."[16]) Another poem, also enthusiastically quoted by Zhou Yang, introduces the dangerous assumption that sleep is hardly necessary for those working towards great goals. Peasants boast that they work much longer days than the sun and issue this challenge: "Sun, sun, I ask you, / Do you dare to compete with us?"[17] In a poem celebrating the construction of irrigation projects and terraced fields on mountainsides, comparison is made to heroes of the past. The poet questions rhetorically: "How can [the legendary master craftsman] Lu Ban compare with us?"[18] For the balladeers of 1958, nothing was impossible; their poetic imaginings were to be turned disastrously into philosophical leaps and economic projections by Henan Province's newly appointed first Party secretary, Wu Zhipu, and were in turn quite possibly, if implausibly, accepted as fact by Mao.[19]

The Achievements of the Leap

Two of the most famous (or infamous) innovations of the Great Leap in the countryside were (1) the "backyard furnaces" made by peasants to supply iron to factories in the cities and (2) the public dining halls designed to free up labour (principally female) for massive construction projects. The iron smelters and canteens were valorized only briefly in the literature of the Great Leap, for example in the stories by Hao Ran and Li Zhun considered below. Shortly afterwards, both were abandoned, and, when Chinese authors were allowed to address the Great Leap more than twenty years after the event, they were portrayed as wasteful adventures in a misguided rush to communism.[20]

Red Flag Ballads includes no poems in praise of the village iron smelters (or backyard furnaces), a quixotic initiative that squandered vast resources of raw material (ore, coal, timber, and requisitioned metal products) and human energy to produce unusable iron. Poems of this kind were written; however, their absence in the official anthology may well be because the smelters had been dismantled and the initiative abandoned before the selection of poems for the original collection was made.[21] I have been able to locate only one such, and that only in an English translation. The report in which it appears claims that it is one of 120 Great Leap poems penned by a peasant girl from Shanxi. The poem offers a powerful, even sensual, image of the smelting process:

> The rising sun bathes the hill in light,
> Precious stone, black ore glistening.
> Carried on men's strong backs,
> Swinging baskets, shoulder poles,
> Sweating, but hearts full of joy.
> For molten iron bubbles in furnaces
> Pouring out in bright, shining waves.[22]

In contrast to the grandiloquent verses about major construction projects quoted above is the charming poem "A Basket," which focuses on the virtues of the People's Communes and the short-lived public dining halls, citing a past of begging and subsistence and contrasting it with a present in which the dining hall supplies superior food:

> Granny took this basket
> To beg for food with Dad in tow.
> Mother took this basket
> For herbs to see the famine through.

Aunty took this basket
With cornmeal buns out to the fields.
And now I'll take this basket
To our canteen [i.e., dining hall] to fetch white rolls.
The People's Communes' merits know no bounds
The Party's kindness is greater than Heaven's.[23]

The poem captures a sense of well-being, recalled by some as characteristic of the early months of the Great Leap. Later events were to erase this rosy view from popular memory.

Women Taking Charge

The Great Leap Forward was not the first time that the Chinese state, through its media, had given publicity to women's breaking into areas that had been exclusively male. Tina Mai Chen's research on *nüjie di'yi* (first women) model workers in the 1950s demonstrates that, by associating women with technology and machinery, viewed by the state as essential for socialist construction, "the potential existed for the future to have a female and feminist face."[24] In rural China, the image of female emancipation was the tractor driver, "one of the most widely circulating icons of modernity in the P[eople's] R[epublic of] C[hina]," a role promoted in China by showings of the Soviet film *Tractor Driver* and celebrated in reports, photographs, posters, and the one-*yuan* note first issued in 1958.[25] Portrayal in the pages of *Xin Zhongguo funü* (New Women of China) is, of course, no guarantee of general social practice; however, like other socialist works of art and reportage, these images were as much a vision of the future as a portrait of the moment. In the Great Leap, women entered the rural workforce in unprecedented numbers, in part because of the urgent need for labourers in the massive irrigation, terracing, and other construction projects of 1958 and 1959, and the concurrent need to maintain agricultural production in the newly formed People's Communes.

No female tractor drivers appear in the poems selected for *Red Flag Ballads*, but there are poems depicting young men and women (frequently referred to in the love-song personae of *ge* "elder brother" and *mei* "younger sister") matching each other in feats of labour. For example, the man digging up soil and the woman carrying it away: "Hauling a thousand loads and not feeling tired ... She is a heroine (*yingxiong*) and he a stout fellow (*haohan*) / Digging until the stars go down to make way for the sun."[26] Where both are carrying loads, she vows to keep up: "Even if you fly up to the clouds, / I will go all out to keep up with you."[27] Here, as in the stories that celebrate the achievements of women at the iron smelters and the communal kitchens, there is no suggestion that anything less should be demanded of female labour than of male labour, an ideal which, as Kimberley Ens Manning shows in Chapter 3 of this volume, was on occasion harshly enforced by officials responsible for mobilizing village women.

Romance in a Common Cause

A few of the works in *Red Flag Ballads* combine revolutionary romanticism with a more conventional romance, a combination that can be observed more clearly in the fiction of the period considered below. In one poem, a new bride being escorted by her husband on the traditional visit home to her mother's house promises to return soon to avoid delay to production and study.[28] In this and other poems, it seems to be implicitly understood that productive labour and learning (*xue wenhua*) make women more attractive. Love in shared labour is charmingly described in "At the Well-Head" (*Jingtai shang*):

> Hearts as one, the boy and girl
> With equal force propel the wheel.
> She keeps pace as firm he pushes,
> Silver water swishing gushes.
> A thousand *li* they walk each day,
> But never from the well they stray.
> Water springs from deep below,
> But deeper still does their love flow.[29]

The *Red Flag Ballads*, as the first works in the newly announced spirit of the combination of revolutionary realism and revolutionary romanticism, set the tone for the fiction that was to follow. The imperative of fast production meant that the works of the period tended to be short- or mid-length stories rather than novels. The two works considered below, by two of the leading writers of rural fiction in the Mao era – Hao Ran and Li Zhun – are fairly long short stories.[30]

The Fires of Love

Hao Ran's story "Dawn Clouds Red as Flame" is dated 11 January 1959. It was published in a local journal in May of that year and, the following year, was included in the young author's third volume of short stories.[31] Perhaps because of the ephemeral nature of its subject matter – love among the rural iron furnaces – it was not included in subsequent collections of the author's work. It is the only Great Leap fiction on this subject that I have found, though it was not the only work written at that time against the background of iron smelting.[32]

Hao Ran was as close to being a "peasant author" as one could then find in the People's Republic and was, thus, like the unnamed authors collected in *Red Flag Ballads*, free of the taint of association with the "rightists" then being purged from literary organizations.[33] Now best known for his two epic novels of class and line struggle in the countryside, *Bright Sunny Skies* (*Yanyangtian*) and *The Golden Road* (*Jinguang dadao*), and his celebrity as the nation's leading author in the Cultural Revolution, Hao Ran began his literary career in the mid-1950s as a writer of socialist pastorals. Then, in 1962, he turned to the subject of class struggle with *Bright Sunny Skies*. His early stories consist of vignettes of village life, character sketches, and simple love stories. In an early review, the veteran writer Ye Shengtao praised the young writer's portrayals of young peasant women.[34] The romantic tales feature young peasant activists whose path to life is grounded in shared enthusiasm for innovation and productive labour as, for example, in the story "Delivering Vegetable Seeds," in which a young man travels long distances to provide superior seeds for a young woman's experimental plot. Mothers meddling in their children's marital affairs appear to add some tension and humour, but any conservative thinking is put in its place by more enlightened peers and sage Party officials, and the overall impression is one of rural harmony.[35] This harmonious image of the countryside was criticized in an otherwise favourable review by the leftist critic and later Gang of Four member Yao Wenyuan, who felt that, among Hao Ran's stories, "too few [were] concerned with *class relationships and class struggle in the countryside*" (emphasis Yao's).[36]

There is now no way of finding out if Hao Ran chose to write about the iron-smelting campaign himself or if the topic was recommended to him by mentors or Party superiors.[37] Whichever is the case, he crafted a story more dramatic, with more romantic intrigue and with sharper generational conflicts, than is typical of his writing in that period. The story begins by presenting two young people whose personal histories and characters mark them as ideal: Ding Dachuan, the son of a revolutionary martyr and the image of his father, who has performed an act of heroism in fighting floods (the most typical exploit in the war against nature), and Jin Huazhen, who has prevented former landlords (inspired by urban rightists) from seizing grain from the local granary. Further, Jin Huazhen is an exemplary "first woman," the first in her village (Red Date Village, the model for advanced social practice in a number of Hao Ran's stories) to succeed in producing iron, and she is the leader of an all-female iron-smelting group. The narrator quotes an aphorism to the effect that heroes fall in love with other heroes.[38] The two meet as delegates at a conference and become further acquainted when he gives her a ride home on his bicycle after she misses the bus. When Ding Dachuan is selected to head his own village's attempt to build iron smelters, he goes back to Red Date Village; then Jin Huazhen goes to his village to teach advanced techniques for smelter-building, and the two fall in love. The impediment to the course of true love is Ding Dachuan's aunt (and adoptive mother), who wants to marry the young man to her own niece, the vivacious Qin Yuzhu, and refuses to accept his choice. Jin Huazhen befriends Qin Yuzhu at another conference and is distraught when she finds out about Qin Yuzhu's aunt's choice of a husband for her and when her new friend (in a plot device reminiscent of more classic romantic fiction) asks her advice as to the young man's suitability and her own next step.[39] The aunt's scheme is revealed, and the two heroes set a date for their marriage.

A more serious challenge occurs when Jin Huazhen, now an explosives expert, is heroically but horribly injured in a blasting accident (the accident is a male colleague's fault, and Huazhen throws herself on the explosives to prevent injury to others). Aunt Ding conceals the news from Dachuan and summons Qin Yuzhu to her house on the wedding day, planning to substitute her niece for the injured Huazhen. The young man predictably refuses and, at Qin Yuzhu's prompting, rushes through the night to see Jin Huazhen in hospital and declare his continued love. The final scene comes at dawn, with a celebration of youth in bliss and hope for the future reminiscent of the Wordsworth poem quoted at the start of this chapter:

> They looked up at the same time to see the red clouds of dawn filling the sky, so red they looked as if they were on fire!
> Ah, what a lovely morning, what radiant youth![40]

The story is full of images of fire: relations between the girls at the conference and the atmosphere at the smelters are both "ardent" (*huore*), and passion and fury are described in the same metaphorical terms. A fiery scene of furnaces proliferating on the North China Plain, then a glorious image of the triumph of the Great Leap, now reads more as dystopia than utopia:

> The whole area in front of Mount Pan was aflame, a dramatic scene unequalled in history. No matter what village you went to, there were iron-smelting furnaces everywhere, and people battling everywhere for iron and steel. The roads were filled with throngs of carts, smoke and dust

rolled and billowed, as the jet-black iron flowed ceaselessly towards the city. The furnaces increased in number, needing ever more raw materials.[41]

As contrived as the romance may be, this is still one of Hao Ran's boldest, and most troubling, stories; Hao was venturing into a world about which he clearly knew little (the descriptions of the construction and form of the smelters are vague at best), with all the blind enthusiasm of the day.[42] The rural rightists had been condemned for their adherence to the Party's former policy of "opposing rash advance" (*fan maojin*). It seems, from Hao Ran's story, that rash advance was now the order of the day: furnaces are built overnight, and advanced skills (e.g., with explosives) are acquired almost as quickly. The story itself is a product of Great Leap impetuosity: youthful passion and revolutionary romanticism meeting in the flames of the smelters, with a heroine nobly maimed in a glorious cause that had been abandoned before the book that contained the story was published.

The Alchemy of Noodles

The eponymous heroine of "A Brief Biography of Li Shuangshuang" takes advantage of the opportunities provided by the Great Leap Forward – the need for increased labour, the right to put up big-character posters, the campaign for literacy, and the public dining halls – to achieve the impossible for a village housewife: escape from domestic drudgery, the right to be known by her own name, the respect and love of her formerly abusive husband, and celebrity status. Li Shuangshuang, in the many works that bear her name, was the cultural success story of the Great Leap. The author believed that the story had been reprinted over four hundred times in various editions, read by 300 million people, and praised by the state premier. In addition, it was made into a comic strip and comic books, was produced in numerous local operatic forms, and was made into a popular film.[43] Throughout the many plot variations, the core of the story remained the same: the relationship between the forthright young peasant woman Li Shuangshuang and her much less progressive husband Sun Xiwang.

The version dated earliest, March 1959, can be briefly summarized as follows. As the story opens, a poster in verse form signed by Li Shuangshuang has been pasted up in her village's main street, proposing a village public dining hall so that women could be freed from cooking and participate in the Great Leap Forward. The poster's writer, whose name is unfamiliar to most villagers, is identified as the wife of Sun Xiwang, who customarily refers to her as "the one at my home," "Little Chrysanthemum's Mother," or "the one who cooks for me,"[44] thus denying that she has any identity of her own. However, the downtrodden (and frequently beaten) young wife has been emboldened by attending literacy classes that allow her to leave notes for her husband in a combination of images and characters. She volunteers for, and works on, an irrigation project. Even though she is out at work, Xiwang refuses to help with household chores, leading first to a quarrel when he fails to prepare lunch and then to her public dining hall proposal. The proposal is adopted, and Xiwang, who had worked in a restaurant before 1949, becomes its first cook. However, Xiwang allows himself to be tricked into using publicly owned ingredients in preparing a meal for the former landowner on whose premises the dining hall is located, and the kitchen is messy and unhygienic. Shuangshuang takes over, cleans the place up (discovering in the process a water pump the owner had buried at the time of collectivization rather than share with his neighbours), and runs the dining hall to everyone's satisfaction. Her achievements are publicized on the local radio, and she wins the admiration and love of her husband after ten years of marriage. In a revised version of the story, which appeared in March of the next year (1960) in the major literary journal *People's Literature* (*Renmin wenxue*), Li Shuangshuang also devises a recipe for "Great Leap" noodles, which are made, in part, with flour from sweet potatoes when wheat flour is in short supply; she also joins the CCP, and she is chosen to attend a national conference of model workers. In subsequent versions of the Li Shuangshuang story, the plot is as malleable as the heroine's noodles: the film was made in 1962, after the demise of the public dining halls, and the focus of the plot shifted to the allocation of work points (especially to women) in the new commune system, with a subplot added by Li Zhun (who also wrote the screenplay), in which a young couple choose each other as marriage partners despite the girl's parents' desire to marry her to someone with more status than a peasant (even as Shuangshuang and Xiwang are falling in love after marriage).

"A Brief Biography of Li Shuangshuang" is a more sophisticated and polished piece of writing than is "Dawn Clouds Red as Flame," which was written by an author slightly older, better educated, and more widely read than Hao Ran. By 1959, Li Zhun was already a celebrated author who had gained attention when his 1953 land-reform story "Not That Road" was shown to Mao Zedong, who ordered it printed in newspapers across the nation.[45]

The story repeatedly promotes the Great Leap and its policies: the central character constantly repeats her determination to "leap forward" and is instructed by the local Party secretary of the need to "put politics in command" (*zhengzhi guashuai*) by being obedient to the CCP. While the

initiative for setting up the canteen is presented as coming from Li Shuangshuang herself, the Party authorities in the story are only too happy to
promote the idea. Li Zhun's achievement is to enliven the political message
(one which, at the time of his first writing of the story, he would have had
little reason to doubt) with his trademark humour, both in the squabbling
between husband and wife and in the attempts of the newly literate to
master political as well as practical language. The humour can be seen in
this exchange between husband and wife, which takes place after Shuangshuang explains the merits of the public dining hall with regard to freeing
up labour for construction:

> Xiwang nodded and thought, "She's got a point." He thought a little while
> longer and remarked carelessly: "Little Whistle [their son]'s mother, I
> heard someone say today that Ma Kesi said we ought to operate canteens
> [i.e., public dining halls], have you read that book?" Shuangshuang said:
> "No. But I heard it was Lie Ning!" Xiwang said: "No, I'm sure it was that
> Ma guy."[46]

The transformation of Li Shuangshuang from anonymous village wife
to public dining hall manager, at the accelerated pace of the Great Leap
Forward, is matched by a transformation in her relationship with Xiwang.
Near the end of the story (in the March 1959 version), Xiwang admits to
this transformation, in the process addressing her by name:

> [Xiwang] realized that his wife he had married ten years before had sud-
> denly become greater than himself, and he could not stop himself from
> saying:
> "This labour business really does change people! ... I said you've
> changed, Shuangshuang, you've become cleverer, more sensible, and your
> ideology is superior to mine. When I think of the little brat you were when
> you came to my house, it seems to me that you've become a different
> person!"
> Shuangshuang, moved, spoke emotionally: "Well, you've changed too!
> I feel that I love you more than before!" She giggled: "Xiwang, look at the
> two of us, we're courting!"
> Xiwang said seriously: "In matters of love, young people fall in love and
> then marry, we married first and then fell in love!"[47]

Thus, in this second story by a male author about female empowerment,
the sentimental romantic and revolutionary romantic are again united:
the pioneering woman who proves herself a man's equal (or superior) in

Image 80 from the *Lianhuan huabao* (Comic-Book Journal) version of "Li Shuangshuang," 6 June 1960, text by Bai Zi and illustrations by Hua Sanchuan. The caption reads: "After the insulated cart was opened up, everyone cried out in delight. Someone said: 'What kind of noodles are these, they're even better than those made with white flour.' Another said: 'Auntie Shuangshuang, the canteen has fired off a sputnik! We're going to put up a big-character poster in praise of you!'"

initiative, labour, and ideology becomes more attractive in the process. Li Shuangshuang and her friends, like the women of the *Red Flag Ballads,* are capable of prodigious feats of labour, including entire nights of extra work, and of social and technical innovation. In the 1960 version of the story, Shuangshuang, with Xiwang, designs a stove that will produce flapjacks faster and, with her female colleagues, an insulated cart that will keep food hot when it is delivered to the fields. In addition, she invents her "Great Leap noodles," which are made partly of sweet potatoes when wheat is in short supply and are judged to be superior to noodles made only of white flour. The nationwide shortage of grain in 1958 and 1959 was caused by unprecedentedly high state requisitioning, which was based on accounting that took seriously Wu Zhipu's "philosophy of the Great Leap" and obliged local officials to predict and report harvests that were unattainable. Consequently, there was a need for the kind of science, or alchemy, that would magically transform the unpalatable into the delicious (as Shuangshuang's recipe did) and the uneatable into the nourishing. None of this historical background is mentioned in the story, of course, but much is made of the public dining hall and its manager's capacity to exceed all expectations and send the peasants into the future well fed.

Curtains of Ignorance

In 1965, the author and documentary filmmaker Felix Greene published a book entitled *A Curtain of Ignorance*, written to counter reports about China that had appeared in the American press, in particular claims that there had been famine in the years between 1959 and 1962. Based on the evidence of his own travels in China, and his conversations with foreign residents, including diplomats, UN officials, and the China-based British surgeon Joshua Horn, Greene maintained: "The indisputable fact is that the famines that in one area or another constantly ravaged the farm lands of China, and the fear of starvation, which for so long had haunted the lives of China's peasants, are today things of the past."[48] It would now appear not only that Greene's own view was obstructed by a curtain of ignorance but also that there were, in fact, multiple curtains of ignorance and deception concerning the situation in the Chinese countryside in those years, some of them lifted by the contributors to the present volume, and some of which may never be lifted. Greene and his American readers were not alone in their ignorance of the fact that famines had indeed taken place; the extent of the disaster was a secret even in China, where the famines were never reported in the state media, never photographed, and never filmed.[49] Mao appears to have chosen to remain behind a curtain of his own, accepting the mendacious accounts and contrived displays of rich harvests prepared for him by officials keen either to advance their careers by these deceptions or to avoid punishment for failing to produce the expected. Mao rejected the case against the Great Leap presented by Peng Dehuai at the Lushan Plenum in 1959, and, as Jeremy Brown shows in Chapter 9 of this volume, only moved to mitigate the effects of the famine when the inhabitants of the city faced a crisis in food supplies.[50] Others in positions of leadership who knew of the famines were too loyal, or too cowed, to speak. Even those who were suffering hunger may well have believed that the worst of the famine conditions were limited to their own localities, ignorant of the larger disaster that was unfolding.

And what of the writers who wrote in praise of the Great Leap Forward, and the others of China's intellectuals who had survived the Anti-Rightist Campaign and should have been in a position to observe and describe what was happening? Was their view also obscured by a curtain of ignorance? Or were they simply hacks producing propaganda-to-order for a massive deception of their readers? The "village author" Ma Feng and his wife Duan Xingmian, interviewed in 2002, claimed that, in 1958, the

Party had not exhausted its credibility (or perhaps their credulity) and that they were disposed to accept the reports of phenomenal increases in agricultural production they read and heard. They believed, Duan Xingmian admitted, because they wanted to believe. As for Hao Ran, an incident recounted in his oral autobiography reveals an improbably naïve acceptance of fraudulent newspaper reports and pictures, finally disabused in the summer of 1958. The author, then on the staff of a journal reporting on the success of the Chinese revolution to Russian-language readers, visited his friend Xiao Yongshun (later the inspiration for the character Xiao Changchun, hero of the novel *Bright Sunny Skies*) and stated his intention to go to a commune and write about the farming techniques there, which had reportedly produced a rice crop so dense that children could stand on top of the plants:

> Without waiting for me to finish, Xiao Yongshun had to laugh; don't go there, he said, it's fake, if you write your story you'll be conspiring in the deception. We shouldn't do that kind of thing.
>
> I said, it was clearly a photograph, not a painting, children were standing on the rice-plants, and there were others standing to the side, it can't be faked.
>
> Xiao Yongshun said, there was a bench in among the plants, the children were standing on the bench, so that from the front it looked as if they were standing on the plants, to show that the grain had grown miraculously and could take people's weight. It's a pack of lies!
>
> I listened incredulously; can it really be so? The photo was published in a Party journal!
>
> Xiao Yongshun sighed and said, this year [1958] those above and those below are lying and boasting, it's bound to end in disaster.[51]

By the time Hao Ran and Li Zhun wrote their first drafts of "Dawn Clouds Red as Flame" and "A Brief Biography of Li Shuangshuang" in early 1959, they would have been aware of the "lying and boasting" that characterized public life in the heady days of the Great Leap. However, both, as loyal servants of the state and beneficiaries of its nurturing of young writers, went ahead and produced works glorifying two of the short-lived social experiments of the day. They may have believed, in the spirit of combining revolutionary realism and revolutionary romanticism demanded of authors, that the problems they witnessed were small potholes on the road to utopia and that it was the larger picture upon which they should focus. They would also have known, from their observation of the treatment of the "rightists," which they had escaped, the fate that lay in store for them should they write stories that painted a less than optimistic picture of the Great Leap.

The compliance of the Chinese intelligentsia in the Great Leap, and its failure to register any protest at either the absurd projections for harvests or the demands placed on the peasantry to produce iron and build canals and dams while growing unprecedented quantities of grain, can be explained in large part by the Anti-Rightist Campaign, which removed those most likely to speak out and left those who were afraid for their own safety. However, their behaviour still compares poorly with the courage, or fool-hardiness, of the intellectuals in Hungary only a couple of years before. A demand by the Hungarian leadership for a 27 percent increase in agricultural production (a minute amount by the standards of the Great Leap) was derided in a June 1956 meeting of the Hungarian Writers' Union, where it was ridiculed by a certain György Szüdi as "simply idiotic." This show of defiance was to result in the dissolution of the Writers' Union.[52]

What seems to me more surprising than the failure of writers in the 1960s to show the disastrous results of the Great Leap is the fact that, even in the period of considerable liberalization between 1978 and 1981, writers and other intellectuals returning from years of ostracism and imprisonment (dating from early in the Cultural Revolution or even as far back as the Anti-Rightist Campaign two decades earlier) should have written so little about the mistakes of the Great Leap and the famines that followed, choosing, instead, to concentrate overwhelmingly on the sufferings of their own peer group – urban intellectuals and state and Party officials in the Cultural Revolution. There are distinguished exceptions, the most obvious of them being Zhang Yigong's *The Story of the Criminal Li Tongzhong*, a short novel published in 1980, towards the end of the brief post-Mao liberalization, which does depict the famines in Henan (Zhang's native province as well as Li Zhun's), laying the blame on ambitious officials (the toxic "hot-shot official" in Zhang's work is seemingly modelled on Henan's Great Leap first Party secretary Wu Zhipu) who were prepared to requisition food grain to meet quotas even if it meant that the peasants who grew it were left with nothing.[53] By and large, however, this tragic phase in the history of modern China was set aside by Chinese authors until, as Susanne Weigelin-Schwiedrzik notes above, writers like Mo Yan and Yu Hua incorporated it into fictional narratives recounting the fates of individuals and families in modern China from the mid-century civil war to the time they were writing. Part of this is clearly due to a disinclination in successive generations of leadership – a disinclination clearly conveyed to artists – to recall a shameful part of the CCP's record. However, a further factor that must be taken into account is the relative indifference of many of the survivors of the Cultural Revolution towards the sufferings of the peasantry and a marked preference for airing their own grievances.

I have not yet heard of calls for the construction of a Museum of the Great Leap Forward, along the lines of the Museum of the Cultural Revolution proposed by the author Ba Jin. The pillars are in place for a virtual museum, at least: they include the fiction and poetry cited above, the *China Famine* website, Yu Xiguang's book *Great Leap: Bitter Days*,[54] Jasper Becker's ground-breaking English-language study *Hungry Ghosts*,[55] an archive of Great Leap memoirs being developed at the University Services Centre for Chinese Studies at the Chinese University of Hong Kong, and the outstanding recent research of colleagues represented in *Eating Bitterness*. Any such museum should record not only the final tragedy but also the initial euphoria and the mythology of "a country in romance" that sent the Chinese people, the peasantry most of all, rushing headlong down a road that would lead most to exhaustion and deprivation, and many millions to starvation.[56]

Notes

1 Mao Zedong, "Investigation of the Peasant Movement in Hunan," in *Selected Works of Mao Tse-tung Vol. 1* (Beijing: Foreign Languages Press, 1967), 23-62.

2 William Wordsworth, "French Revolution as It Appeared to Enthusiasts at Its Commencement," 1805, http://www.poetryfoundation.org/.

3 Ibid.

4 I am grateful to David Pollard for this final piece of information.

5 The figure is quoted in Lars Ragvald, "The Emergence of 'Worker-Writers' in Shanghai," in *Shanghai: Revolution and Development in an Asian Metropolis*, ed. Christopher Howe (Cambridge: Cambridge University Press, 1981), 318. An early collection of 179 of these poems, edited by the Propaganda Division of the Shanghai Municipal Communist Party Committee, was published in October 1958 as *Shanghai minge xuan* [Selected Folk Songs of Shanghai] (Shanghai: Shanghai wenyi chubanshe, 1958).

6 Zhou Yang, "Xin minge kaituole shige de xin daolu" [New Folk Songs Have Opened a New Road for Poetry], *Hongqi* [Red Flag] 1 (1958): 33.

7 See Richard King, "The Hundred Flowers," in *The Columbia Companion to Modern East Asian Literature*, ed. Joshua Mostow, 476-80 (New York: Columbia University Press, 2003).

8 See Ban Wang, "Revolutionary Realism and Revolutionary Romanticism: The Song of Youth," in *The Columbia Companion to Modern East Asian Literature*, ed. Joshua Mostow, 471-75 (New York: Columbia University Press, 2003).

9 Yang Kaihui was executed in 1930 after the communist Red Army withdrew from Changsha; Liu Zhixun died in battle in 1933.

10 Mao Zedong, "Reply to Li Shu-yi," 33. For a heavily annotated version of the Chinese text, see *Mao zhuxi shi-ci jangjie* [Explanations of Chairman Mao's Poetry] (Shenyang: Liaoning Daxue zhongwenxi xiandai wenxue jiao-yan shi, 1973), 201-8.

11 Zhou, "Xin minge kaituole shige xin daolu," 35.

12 Guo Moruo and Zhou Yang, eds., *Hongqi geyao* [Red Flag Ballads] (Beijing: Renmin wenxue chubanshe, 1979 [1959]). References are to the 1979 edition.

13 Judith Shapiro, *Mao's War against Nature: Politics and the Environment in Revolutionary China* (Cambridge: Cambridge University Press, 2001), 9. Shapiro's source for this

quotation is a "Chinese scholar from Yunnan Province." These lines are also quoted in *Mao Zedong tongzhi de qingshaonian shidai* [The Childhood and Youth of Comrade Mao Zedong] (Beijing: Renmin chubanshe, 1951), 33. I am grateful to Michael Schoenhals for helping me locate this reference.

14 Shapiro, *Mao's War against Nature*, 12-13.

15 This is not so much a single poem as a compilation. As the poet He Qifang later revealed, the first two couplets originated in different parts of Shaanxi Province (the second couplet being from Ankang, the place named in the anthology), with the final two lines being added by an editorial board. See He Qifang, *Wenxue yishu de chuntian* [Spring in Literature and Art] (Beijing: Zuojia chubanshe, 1964), 58; Guo and Zhou, *Hongqi geyao*, 159.

16 Zhou, ""Xin minge kaituole shige de xin daolu," 34.

17 Ibid., 35.

18 Guo and Zhou, *Hongqi geyao*, 64.

19 In 1958, Wu Zhipu claimed that, as a result of a philosophical leap forward on the part of the peasants of Henan, rice paddies in that province yielded seventy times as much as they had in the past. See Wu Zhipu, "Yuejin de zhexue yu zhexue de yuejin" [The Philosophy of the Great Leap and a Great Leap in Philosophy], *Zhexue yanjiu* [Philosophical Research] 6 (1958): 15. Wu Zhipu's ideas recall those of the Stalin-era Soviet agronomist Trofim Lysenko, who claimed that yields could be quadrupled through the pseudo-science of "vernalization." For more on Wu Zhipu's public pronouncements, and his meeting with Mao in March 1958, see Michael Schoenhals, *Saltationist Socialism: Mao Zedong and the Great Leap Forward* (Stockholm: University of Stockholm Department of Oriental Languages, 1987), 49-51.

20 The canteens and iron smelting appear briefly in historical novels written in the 1990s by Yu Hua. Both innovations appear in *Huozhe*, first published in 1993, and the canteens alone appear in *Xu Sanguan mai xue ji* [An Account of Xu Sanguan Selling His Blood] (Shanghai: Shanghai wenyi chubanshe, 2004 [1995]). Zhang Yimou's 1994 film version of *Huozhe* presents both at greater length. See Yu Hua, "Huozhe" [To Live], in *Yu Hua zuopinji* [Collected Works of Yu Hua] (Shanghai: Shanghai wenyi chubanshe, 2004 [1993]), 83-91, translated by Michael Berry as *To Live* (New York: Anchor Books, 2000), 100-10; Yu, *Xu sanguan mai xue ji*, 109-11, translated by Andrew F. Jones as *Chronicle of a Blood Merchant* (New York: Pantheon Books, 2003).

21 The authors of one recent survey confirm that there were new folk songs in praise of the iron smelters, or "little furnaces" (*xiaogaolu*). See Wang Jialiang and Jin Han, *Zhongguo xian-dangdaiwenxue* [Modern and Contemporary Chinese Literature] (Hangzhou: Zhejiang daxue chubanshe, 2001), 394.

22 The young poet's name is given as Li Chin-chih, and her age is given as sixteen. See Wang Feng, "Poets Old and Young," in *Chinese Women in the Great Leap Forward* (Beijing: Foreign Language Press, 1960), 45. The names of the poets are not given in the *Red Flag Ballads*.

23 Guo and Zhou, *Hongqi geyao*, 74.

24 Tina Mai Chen, "Female Icons, Feminist Iconography? Social Rhetoric and Women's Agency in 1950s China," *Gender and History* 15, 2 (2003): 289-90.

25 Ibid., 268. The woman on the banknote was Liang Jun, China's first female tractor driver. See also the report "Woman Tractor Driver Breaks New Ground," *China Daily*, March 23, 2004, http://www.chinadaily.com.cn/.

26 Guo and Zhou, *Hongqi geyao*, 124.

27 Ibid., 123.

28 Ibid., 137-38.

29 Ibid., 168.

30 For a translation of Hao Ran's "Zhaoxia hong si huo" by Haydn Shook and Richard King as "Dawn Clouds Red as Flame," see *Renditions* 68 (2007): 18-49. A partial translation

of the March 1960 *Renmin wenxue* text of "Li Shuangshuang xiaozhuan" by Johanna Hood and Robert Mackie, as "A Brief Biography of Li Shuangshuang," appears in the same issue, pp. 52-76. *Renditions* 68 is a special issue dedicated to "Village Literature and the Great Leap Forward." A full translation of "Li Shuangshuang xiaozhuan" appears in Richard King, ed., *Heroes of China's Great Leap Forward* (Honolulu: University of Hawaii Press, 2010), 15-61.

31 Hao Ran, "Zhaoxia hong si huo," first published in the journal *Wenyi hongqi* [Red Flag in the Arts] in May 1959 and reprinted in *Xin chun qu* [Songs of a New Dawn] (Beijing: Zhongguo qingnian chubanshe, 1960), 1-33. A complete listing of the author's works to 1974, with a literary biography and some articles and talks by Hao Ran on his writing, can be found in *Hao Ran zuopin yanjiu ziliao* [Research Materials on Hao Ran's Works] (Nanjing: Nanjing daxue zhongwenxi, 1974). See also Hao Ran, *Wode rensheng: Hao Ran koushu zizhuan* [My Life: Hao Ran's Oral Autobiography] (Beijing: Huayi chubanshe, 2000).

32 The author Ma Feng admitted to me in a May 2002 interview that he had also written a story set during the campaign to produce iron. After the failure of the campaign, he was ashamed of the work, made sure it was not republished, and did not keep a copy for himself.

33 Hao Ran (pen name of Liang Jinguang) was born in 1932 to dispossessed peasant parents in a landlord's manure shed near the Kailuan coal mine in Hebei. After his father's death, he lived with peasant relatives and had three and a half years of schooling before his mother's death in 1945. He had various jobs as a writer of propaganda for the Red Army and as a reporter before becoming a full-time author.

34 Ye Shengtao, "Xin nongcun de xin mianmao: Du *Xique deng zhi*" [The New Face of the New Countryside: On Reading *The Magpie Climbs the Branch*], *Dushu* [Reading] 14 (1958): 109-20.

35 Hao Ran, "Song caizi," story dated 14 August 1960 in the Cultural Revolution collection of the author's early works *Chungeji* [Songs of Spring], 201-9, translated as "Sending in Vegetable Seed," in Hao Jan [Ran], *Bright Clouds* (Beijing: Foreign Language Press, 1974), 40-50.

36 Yao Wenyuan, "Shengqi-bobo de nongcun tuhua" [Vibrant Images of Rural Life], in *Zai qianjin de daolu shang* [On the Road Going Forward] (Beijing: Renmin wenxue chubanshe, 1965), 226-39.

37 I interviewed Hao Ran about his work on a number of occasions between 1981 and 2002 but did not raise the subject of this story with him. By 2002, his mental deterioration was clearly evident. Hao Ran died in 2008.

38 Hao, "Zhaoxia hong si huo," 2.

39 The scene recalls the moment in Jane Austen's 1797 novel *Sense and Sensibility* in which Lucy Steeles reveals to her new friend Elinor Dashwood her secret engagement to Edward Ferrars, the object of Elinor's romantic intentions, and asks, "What would you advise me to do in such a case, Miss Dashwood? What would you do yourself?" See Jane Austen, *Sense and Sensibility* (Ware, UK: Wordsworth Classics, 1979), 89. Jin Huazhen, like Elinor Dashwood, chooses repressed anguish over the revelation of her own feelings.

40 Hao, "Zhaoxia hong si huo," 33.

41 Ibid., 27.

42 The building of the smelters is nostalgically described in William Hinton, *Shenfan: The Continuing Revolution in a Chinese Village* (New York: Random House, 1983), 216-17. Hinton's informants recalled the Great Leap as a time of shared purpose and unity (the chapter in which the description occurs is entitled "Those Were the Days").

43 Li Zhun, "Li Shuangshuang xiaozhuan." See version dated March 1959 in Li Zhun, *Li Shuangshuang xiaozhuan* [The Story of Li Shuangshuang] (Beijing: Renmin wenxue chubanshe, 1977), 332-66; version dated late night, 7 February 1960, *Renmin wenxue* (March 1960): 11-27; abbreviated version translated by Tang Sheng as "The Story of

Li Shuang-shuang," *Chinese Literature* (June 1960): 3-25; a pictorial version that appeared in *Lianhuan huabao* 217 (6 June 1960): 9-17, with text by Bai Zi and illustrations by Hua Sanchuan; and a 1964 comic-book version reissued after the Cultural Revolution entitled *Li Shuangshuang*, with text by Lu Zhongjian and illustrations by He Youzhi (Shanghai: Shanghai renmin chubanshe, 1977). The film version *Li Shuangshuang* was directed by Lu Ren and starred Zhang Ruifang in the title role (Shanghai Film Studio, 1962). Li Zhun told me that Premier Zhou Enlai had remarked to Zhang Ruifang after a showing of the film that, if Li Shuangshuang could become premier, he would step down from the post to make way for her.

44 Li, *Li Shuangshuang xiaozhuan*, 322.

45 Li Zhun, born in 1928 to parents of Mongolian nationality, was the son and grandson of teachers; his grandfather had held the *xiucai* degree. He studied classical poetry with his grandfather, learned various local operatic forms, and read Western fiction extensively in Chinese translation. His story "Bu neng zou neitiao lu" is reprinted in *Li Shuangshuang xiaozhuan*, 1-15, and is translated as the title story in *"Not That Road" and Other Stories* (Beijing: Foreign Language Press, 1962), 1-23.

46 Li, *Li Shuangshuang xiaozhuan*, 350. In the *Renmin wenxue* version, *Lie Ning* (Lenin) has become *En Gesi* (Engels); the peasant couple assume that *Ma Kesi* (Marx) and the others are Chinese, hence the reference to "that Ma guy" (*neige xing Ma de*) and my rendering the names of Lenin and Marx in *pinyin*. The same conversation recurs, almost word for word, in the film version.

47 Li, *Li Shuangshuang xiaozhuan*, 364.

48 Felix Greene, *A Curtain of Ignorance* (London: Jonathan Cape, 1965), 93. Greene takes issue with a 22 April 1962 report in the *New York Times* by Harry Schwartz, who states: "three successive years of poor harvests have reduced the food available to most Chinese to little above the barest subsistence level" (96).

49 Some of the effects of the famine were reported in the internal journal *Neibu cankao* – for example, cases of cannibalism in Gansu (14 April 1960) and famine migration in Henan and Shandong (1 May 1960) – but these reports reached only an elite readership.

50 Thomas P. Bernstein, "Mao Zedong and the Famine of 1959-1960: A Study in Willfulness," *China Quarterly* 186 (2006): 421-45. See also Li Zhisui, *The Private Life of Chairman Mao* (New York: Random House, 1994), 270 (for Mao's state of mind in 1958) and 339 (for his depression at reports of the famine in 1960).

51 Hao Ran, *Wode rensheng*, 263.

52 I learned of this incident while in Vienna in November 2006 for the Great Leap conference, where I visited an exhibition at the Leopold Museum of photographs by Erich Lessing entitled "Revolution in Hungary." One of the images was of that meeting, and a caption explained the context and provided the name of György Szüdi.

53 Zhang Yigong, "Fanren Li Tongzhong, de gushi," 93-115 and 193, translated as "The Story of the Criminal Li Tongzhong," in King, *Heroes of China's Great Leap Forward*, 63-128.

54 Yu Xiguang, *Dayuejin: Kurizi* [Great Leap: Bitter Days] (Hong Kong: Shidai chaoliu chubanshe, 2005).

55 Jasper Becker, *Hungry Ghosts: Mao's Secret Famine* (London: John Murray, 1996).

56 My own contribution to this record is *Renditions* 68, a special edition of the Hong Kong translation journal, containing an introduction, the two stories considered here from 1959, three of the "new folk songs," and two other poems, plus excerpts from two works of fiction from the post-Mao era: Zhang Yigong's short novel *The Story of the Criminal Li Tongzhong*, mentioned above, and Wang Zhiliang's 1993 novel *Ji'e de shancun* [Hungry Mountain Village].

3   The Gendered Politics of Woman-Work: Rethinking Radicalism in the Great Leap Forward

Kimberley Ens Manning

Towards the end of the Great Leap Forward, in a small village in central Henan, a large group of peasants shouting insults and wielding sticks gathered outside of Leader Zhang's door. The group was furious with Zhang's husband, the village accountant, because he abused villagers and, in particular, because he had murdered a man in a neighbouring village. They were also angry with Zhang herself. Since becoming women's head in the village several years before, she had tyrannized women and men villagers – forcing women to carry out heavy field work while pregnant and humiliating people who arrived late to the public dining hall. But while Zhang was always looking for opportunities to criticize others for their lack of adherence to collective principles, she herself was said to have dipped into the grain in the village's storage container kept next to her house. The villagers wanted to strike back against the hypocrisy and the abuse that they had experienced under this couple's leadership as well as to avenge the death of the neighbouring villager.[1]

Cadre abuse of villagers was hardly unknown in the Maoist era; indeed, with the collectivization of land, labour, and tools in the mid-1950s, local cadres had grown increasingly powerful.[2] When collective fever was subsequently whipped up into new heights by the Anti-Rightist Campaign and the Great Leap Forward, some cadres tyrannized villagers outright. But what makes Zhang's story unusual is her sex and her leadership role. Why would a village women's head, a leader charged with the responsibility of protecting the most vulnerable in the village, show no regard for pregnant women? Unlike several male Henan village leaders who also mobilized pregnant and nursing mothers to work in difficult conditions, Zhang never mentioned personal fear to

This chapter was originally published in *Modern China* 32, 3 (2006): 349-84. This revised version of the original publication is reprinted with permission.

explain her behaviour. Whereas these men pitied the women in their charge but felt helpless to protect them out of fear for their own and their family's safety, Zhang showed no remorse. Instead, she criticized women who wanted to get out of hard labour for health reasons as not "upright."

In what follows, I argue that Zhang neglected the health of women and children because of the way in which she was recruited and trained. Many women became politically active in the context of local Chinese Communist Party organizations – organizations that operated on the basis of a revolutionary Maoist ethic, according to which all were expected to struggle equally and, if necessary, to sacrifice their physical health for the cause of socialist construction. But while the leadership of the CCP and the All China Women's Federation (ACWF) endorsed a Maoist vision of activism and labour mobilization for men, they sought to moderate it as it applied to women, especially women who were pregnant, lactating, or the mothers of young children. When it came to women, the central leadership sought to implement what I call a Marxist maternalist conception of sexual equality in the Chinese countryside, a form of women's liberation that stressed physiological gender difference and linked women's equality, maternal health, and family harmony to the larger project of nation- and state-building.

In this chapter, I argue that activist commitments depended in no small part on the grassroots organizations responsible for the recruitment and training of local leaders. Whereas the Peasant Union, Youth League, and local CCP branches reinforced a Maoist approach to local leadership, the local Women's Federation and midwifery training teams were more likely to reinforce a maternalist one. Moreover, the cultivation of informal ties also played an important role in this process. Close relationships with family members in Party organizations – membership in what I call "Party families" – reinforced a revolutionary Maoist conception of equality, whereas close friendships with other local women leaders reinforced a Marxist maternalist conception of equality.

Ultimately, the institutionalization of conceptions of equality through different forms of formal and informal ties generated a broad spectrum of activist identities. On one end stood the maternalist activist, a leader who identified with other women and who sought to maintain family unity and to protect women and children; on the other end stood the egalitarian activist, a leader who identified with revolutionaries and who completely refused to countenance ideas of physiological difference. Trained by local Party organizations and a member of a powerful local Party family, Leader Zhang largely ignored the ACWF's calls to protect women's health because she fundamentally disapproved of providing "special privileges" for women. Other rural women leaders not only disregarded mandates to protect women and children but also actively sought to dismantle local women's organizations.

In this chapter, I explore the discursive and institutional tensions in CCP organizations prior to and after the founding of the People's Republic of China. After discussing my research design and methods, I give a brief overview of previous explanations of rural cadre radicalism – explanations that have underestimated the importance of discourses of sexual equality in motivating rural leaders before and after the establishment of the People's Republic. In the third part of the chapter, I argue that an egalitarian vision of equality proved to be far more compelling for many women soldiers and revolutionaries prior to 1949 than did the Marxist maternalist conception of equality advocated by the CCP leadership. Despite the establishment of a national women's organization, the ACWF, in 1949, the gap between the maternalist goals of the leadership and the egalitarian practices of its grassroots only widened further. In the fourth section, I discuss women leaders in Henan and Jiangsu who questioned not only health care for labouring women but also the need for women's organizations. These women leaders ignored or seriously transformed maternalist mandates during collectivization and the Great Leap Forward, I argue, because of their recruitment and training in formal and informal Party organizations. I end the chapter with a close look at Leader Zhang's recruitment into and participation in village-level activism.

Research Design

In 2001, 2004, and 2006, I interviewed a total of 162 individuals at the village, township, county, prefectural, provincial, and national levels. Altogether I interviewed forty-three retired Women's Federation officials, including twenty-five village-level women's heads.[3] Although not statistically significant and, of course, deeply affected by many factors, including the passage of time, the interviews offer important insight into this period.[4] This is particularly the case as I have triangulated the interviews with documentary evidence, including a number of county-level Women's Federation and ACWF archival reports that have recently been made available.

Grassroots research for this study primarily took place in three counties: two in Henan and one in Jiangsu.[5] As is noted throughout *Eating Bitterness*, Henan played a leading role during the Great Leap Forward, and, as a consequence, many of Henan's farmers were at the epicentre of the movement and some of its most tragic consequences. "Huoyue," a county located in Henan's Xuchang region, was severely affected by food shortages as early as the fall of 1958.[6] And, indeed, Huoyue's rate of population growth declined from 15.0 per thousand in 1958 to -6.6 per thousand in 1960.[7] The residents of "Wenhe," a county located in the Luoyang Administrative District, also suffered from severe hunger and malnutrition during the latter years of the Great Leap Forward.[8] Although edema was rampant in both Huoyue and Wenhe during the Great Leap Forward, residents of both counties apparently avoided the massive death and relocation suffered by villagers in regions farther to the south.[9] Both Huoyue and Wenhe were removed from large cities, and both were "liberated" relatively late. During the 1950s, both counties concentrated largely on growing cotton and wheat.[10]

In addition to the two counties in Henan, I conducted research in the relatively prosperous region of Jiangnan. During the 1950s, "Gaoshan" farmers cultivated mulberry bushes for silkworm production and grew rice, wheat, and corn. Although the Jiangnan region as a whole encompasses several large urban centres, Gaoshan's population suffered a decline similar to that of Huoyue (22.80 per thousand in 1958 to -4.30 per thousand in 1961), and edema was rampant during this time as well.[11]

I chose these three counties to explore whether or not there was a gendered basis to radicalism in different regions and, if so, how it manifested itself. I define "radicalism" as the violation of policies to protect the health of women and children as stipulated by the CCP and Women's Federation leadership. With regard to the interviewees, while the Henan leaders of both sexes were more radical in their approach to mobilizing women than were those in Gaoshan, the differences between the female and male leaders in all three counties were also striking. Indeed, whereas men who were formerly leaders in Henan often discussed their fear of being struggled against, women heads only rarely mentioned fear as motivating their behaviour.[12] And, whereas men who had been leaders in Gaoshan discussed their opposition to the Great Leap Forward, several former Women's Federation officials and women's heads emphasized the ways in which the mobilization of women strengthened women. These differences between female and male leaders, I suggest, attest to the profound influence of grassroots organizational life on the development of women's leadership during the 1950s.

Rural Patriarchy and the Great Leap Forward

The importance of the effort to socialize housework during the Great Leap Forward cannot be understated. The very success of the Great Leap Forward, measured in terms of agricultural and industrial output, hinged in no small part upon the ability of local leaders to gain access to women's labour in an unprecedented way. As Richard King discusses in Chapter 2 of this volume, women were mobilized to take on new agricultural roles both inside and outside the village. Thus, young and childless women were assigned to labour on work teams (sometimes at great distance from their village), while the elderly, infirm, and women with children were expected to stay behind to assume primary responsibility for the crops.[13] As a means of ensuring the full participation of women in the mass mobilization efforts, each brigade was also encouraged to organize child care. In some particularly active communes, women organized sewing and washing circles and staffed newly established maternal health centres and homes for the elderly. The most significant expansion of the socialization of labour, however, was the decision to construct a dining-hall system as part of the new communes.

Contrary to the high expectations of the CCP leadership, the Great Leap Forward disintegrated into one of the most devastating disasters of the twentieth century. By the end of the movement in 1960, both agricultural and industrial production throughout the country had dropped drastically; the health of women, children, and the elderly had been severely compromised; and, as discussed in detail in *Eating Bitterness*, several regions endured large-scale starvation.

There is no question that fear played a significant role in the emergence of grassroots radicalism and that this fear-induced radicalism contributed to the havoc and loss generated during the movement. Specifically, scholars suggest that the crackdown on "rightists" following the 1957 Hundred Flowers Movement led to the zealousness among cadres during the Great Leap Forward.[14] In Chapter 4 of this volume, Wemheuer documents not only how the 1957 Socialist Education Campaign (or Anti-Rightist Campaign) frightened local leaders but also how its discourse regime actually prevented local leaders from articulating many of the problems associated with the Great Leap. Cadres fearful of being labelled rightists therefore hid any doubts they might have had about the establishment of the communes and the massive mobilizations of labour and instead sought to prove their socialist ardour by promising their superiors high output.

Explanations of the behaviour of grassroots cadres as being driven by fear are consistent with the view that the behaviour of cadre peasants was largely conservative during the 1950s and 1960s, especially when it came to questions of women and the family. A number of scholars have noted that Maoist policies and institutions reinforced conservatism among male peasants and village-level male cadres. Because grassroots Party organizations allowed new collective structures to organize on the basis of pre-existing kinship groups, the creation of cooperatives actually enabled traditional familial structures to persist in rural Maoist China.[15] Collectivization reinforced kinship structures not only among villagers but also among local Party leaders – a factor that served to increase the power of "traditional" forms of familial authority over villages.[16] According to Xiaobo Lü, resistance to the revolutionary force of the Party

> arose mainly from the paradox that the regime created for itself, namely, a structure that reinforces traditional ways rather than sustaining new norms, and from the precariousness of revolutionary values that can not successfully transcend, transform, and, more important, maintain even the regime's own rank and file as loyal and dependable agents.[17]

Conservative practices among grassroots Party organizations thus increased the cellularity of rural life and undermined the ideological agenda of the CCP.[18]

Peasant conservatism, scholars argue, especially hampered the spread of notions of sexual equality in the Chinese countryside before and during the Great Leap Forward. Specifically, they suggest that, during the 1940s and 1950s, conservative male peasants and leaders raised such a furor over incipient women's rights campaigns that the CCP leadership reversed course and downplayed discussions of sexual equality.[19] Although passage of the 1950 Marriage Law temporarily reversed this trend, Kay Ann Johnson argues that the subsequent outcry by male peasants and rural male cadres dissipated the strength of the law and the effort put into its implementation.[20] Ultimately, the continuation of strong family units at the base of rural life served to strengthen parochialism and patriarchy in the Chinese countryside.[21] It was only during the Great Leap Forward, when a post-anti-rightist climate of fear drove leaders to political zealotry, that the traditional family temporarily shattered. Indeed, according to Judith Stacey, the Great Leap Forward violated the unarticulated "patriarchal pact" among China's male peasants, male grassroots cadres, and the male-dominated CCP.[22]

The argument that local peasant cadres were largely socially conservative and fear-driven during the most radicalized days of the Great Leap Forward is also consistent with the broader literature on the comparative study of peasants. Scholars have long assumed that, while peasants can and do become revolutionary in intent and organization,[23] revolutions rarely alter peasant allegiance to individual and household welfare.[24] Peasants engage in revolutionary movements in order to preserve their way of life, not to alter it dramatically.[25] And yet recent feminist scholarship suggests that rural women engaged in post-revolutionary and postcolonial social movements have, to differing degrees, incorporated notions of sexual equality into their own lives and politics.[26] This chapter seeks to further deconstruct long-held assumptions about the patriarchal nature of the Chinese countryside by making two arguments about the origin and consequences of local women's activism, especially as it manifested itself during the Great Leap Forward. First, both local Party organizations and kin, including fathers, brothers, and even mothers-in-law, seem to have played an important role in encouraging and enabling rural women's leadership – a surprising finding given that, in the 1950s, many still viewed women engaged in public activity as suspect and as violating important social norms. Second, particular family formations, or what Karen Kampwirth calls "family traditions of resistance,"[27] may have led to the adoption of radically egalitarian interpretations of sexual equality among some women activists. In making these arguments, I do not mean to deny the phenomenon of "patriarchal peasants" opposing the assumption of leadership roles on the part of women kin – a very common occurrence that I also document; rather, I mean to suggest that, under certain conditions, peasant particularism may actually have given rise to radical interpretations of equality at the rural grassroots.

Origins of Marxist Maternalism and Revolutionary Maoism

Since the 1910s, intellectual activists, many of whom later became key CCP leaders, drew on the image of the foot-bound, oppressed Chinese woman as a figure for China's national suffering. Because they were doubly oppressed as workers/peasants and as women, senior Party leaders reasoned, women required special help to advance politically. But special help was also needed for physiological reasons: as "natural" reproducers, women required that their bodies be carefully regulated. The very continuation and stability of the family depended on the capacity of women to fulfill their duties to procreate and to care for the home. The CCP labelled work focused on helping women to struggle for equality and maintain the home "woman-work." I call the discourse undergirding woman-work "Marxist maternalist equality."[28]

Although various maternalist discourses circulated in China during the first decades of the twentieth century, Marxist maternalist equality did not consolidate until the Sino-Japanese War. It was at this time that a coalition of leaders, including leading social gospel reformers, progressive intellectuals, and CCP officials, worked in partnership with the Guomindang to address the crisis of large refugee populations and, especially, the plight of children orphaned or separated from their parents due to war.[29] While the Second United Front would eventually crumble, the ties forged among progressive women intellectuals and CCP leaders did not. Moreover, the particular focus on the health and welfare of children that first brought the women together would continue to inform their cooperation in the years to come.

In 1942, Zhou Enlai articulated the Party leadership's emerging approach to the family and women – an approach that was to remain consistent up to and throughout the Great Leap Forward. In a short essay, he argued that motherhood is a natural duty (*tianzhi*) that is crucial to the well-being of society and the nation. In advocating this concept of "maternal duty," Zhou, like early women Party activists, did not think that the socialization of housework would remove women's special obligation to mother.[30] To the contrary: even if a public daycare system were perfect, he wrote, children would still require their mother.[31] The Marxist maternalism developed and embraced by much of the Party leadership suggested that women would always be ultimately responsible for the welfare of children and the home, regardless of the degree of social development.[32]

From its very foundation as a party, however, the CCP struggled to clarify the role of women and of woman-work within the organizational apparatus. Some of this struggle stemmed from a desire to contain the activity of feminist organizations and their potential threat to the development of a more general class consciousness; some of it stemmed from the desire to pacify conservative male peasants; and some of it stemmed from the revolutionary vision of socialist transformation being espoused at all levels of the Party.

Prior to the founding of the People's Republic, men and women were urged to make heroic sacrifices on behalf of the larger revolutionary cause. They were told that revolutionaries could transform their objective conditions – including class essence and the natural world itself – through violent and concerted struggle. Contained in the revolutionary rhetoric, therefore, was the possibility of actually overcoming one's natural physical limitations – an idea totally at odds with the notion of protecting women's bodies. But perhaps most challenging to the realization of woman-work at the grassroots was the very prevalent and deep-seated disdain for womanly weakness. Women and their need for "protection" distracted the Party from its true revolutionary cause, a cause that required total physical, emotional, and intellectual commitment from its leaders. This "revolutionary Maoist" discourse advocated the violent overcoming of self and enemy while simultaneously condemning women and "their issues" as trivial. I call the women most influenced by revolutionary Maoism "egalitarians."

The pre-1949 interaction of revolutionary Maoism and Marxist maternalism in Party organizations created complex and contradictory outcomes. First, under the demands of a wartime mobilization that often put revolutionaries at risk of capture or death, few women felt that they could commit to marriage, much less give birth to and care for children. Many women revolutionaries consequently forewent or postponed motherhood during the 1930s and 1940s.[33] Second, the recruitment and training of women in military and Party organizations led some women soldiers and cadres to develop a strong aversion to any association with woman-work. On the one hand, many realized that they would have little opportunity to advance were they to commit themselves to women's organizing. Indeed, woman-work was often considered a dead-end job for women cadres. On the other hand, revolutionary Maoist messages about the spirit of true revolutionaries fuelled some women's revolutionary desire – a desire that also caused them to cast off any recognition of their own "womanness."

Such rejection of women's traditional role was particularly common among demobilized soldiers. According to one report from 1939, for example, a former woman soldier refused to do woman-work because she "did not know how to be a woman at all" (*wo genben bu hui zuo nüren*).[34] Other women cadres based their refusal of these assignments on the argument that there was nothing to woman-work and that they were built for more onerous responsibilities than could be found in its miscellaneous preoccupations.[35]

Prior to the founding of the People's Republic of China, women leaders were thus shaped by two contradictory discourses. While the CCP leadership expected female leaders to advocate for and protect women and children, many women were persuaded by their personal experience in Party organizations that woman-work was not valued by their comrades. The inclination of many female leaders towards revolutionary Maoism and away from Marxist maternalism was also rooted in a desire to sacrifice the physical self for the sake of revolutionary emancipation. In other words, egalitarian women's leadership emerged not only because some women were "selfishly trying to get ahead," as some senior Party officials suggested, but also because they believed that woman-work ultimately distracted them from the more fundamental and necessary sacrifices involved in making revolution.[36]

Grassroots Woman-Work during Collectivization and the Great Leap Forward

With the cessation of hostilities and the establishment of the People's Republic of China, it might have seemed likely that the CCP would gain greater control over women's organizing. In the post-revolutionary context, the Party had the capacity to build much stronger institutions, such as the All China Women's Federation, and provide them with greater legitimacy and authority. But egalitarian women's leadership continued to emerge in both the cities and the countryside in the 1950s. In fact, the processes of post-revolutionary state-building that enabled the CCP to build a vast network of Party organizations reinforced, rather than undermined, a highly egalitarian vision of sexual equality.

In the 1950s, the ACWF sought to integrate women into socialist construction according to the basic Marxist maternalist vision of women as both producers *and* reproducers. Recognizing that productive work might interfere with reproductive health and the well-being of the family, however, ACWF leaders took steps early on to protect labouring women at the times when their bodies were perceived to be most vulnerable: during menstruation, pregnancy, birth, and the month following the delivery of a child.[37]

As lower- and higher-stage cooperatives were introduced in the mid-1950s, the ACWF and CCP leadership began to devote increasing attention to the health of rural women. At that time, women's participation in agricultural labour, specifically in field work, began to expand considerably. Huoyue, for example, saw a doubling of women's labour power between 1955 and 1957.[38] As a result of these new demands on women, the CCP and ACWF leadership instructed rural leaders to provide special care to women who were pregnant – for example, by allocating them lighter work.[39] They also admonished collectives to reduce the kinds of work performed and the number of days worked; to care for pregnant, postnatal, and menstruating women; and to aid women with their housework.[40]

In December 1956, Cao Guanqun (ACWF Party general secretary) gave a speech in which she praised the Sichuan Women's Federation for assigning menstruating, pregnant, and lactating women work that was light, dry, and close by.[41] This practice became known as the "three transfers," a phrase taken up as a slogan by county-level Women's Federation leaders beginning in the early months of 1957.[42] ACWF and Party officials also advocated that women *zuo yuezi*, or sit the month out, after giving birth. Specifically, they advocated that women avoid physical exertion (i.e., that they not perform housework, work in the fields, cook, or look after older children) in the month following childbirth.[43]

Women's heads, the leaders in charge of woman-work in villages during the 1950s, were given the responsibility of ensuring that the health of women and children was protected. In some villages, they implemented such policies carefully. Two former women's heads whom I interviewed expressed great concern for the health of women before and during the Great Leap Forward. One told me, for example, that she worried a great deal about the menstruating and pregnant women in her charge.[44] Another actually opposed a work team's decision to send nursing mothers to remote construction sites, arguing that they should work only in the day and not at night.[45] Although this woman was herself already working twelve-hour days, she took on the night shift as well, she said, so that mothers could stay home in the evenings and care for their children. Both of these former women's heads thus not only understood and supported the directives flowing out of Marxist maternalism but also struggled hard to put them into practice among the women in their charge.

A few of the female villagers I interviewed in Wenhe described how their women's head looked after them when they were pregnant or menstruating.[46] One woman even relayed the Party's nationalist justification for health protection: "[Women] were liberated. Chairman Mao called for huge production. Socialism needed successors. [Women] were taken care of."[47] But a number complained about the lack of health protection during the late 1950s and were sharply critical of their women's heads. These complaints mirrored the findings of county-level investigations undertaken in the late 1950s, which suggested that not all grassroots women leaders were implementing health protection policies with equal vigour. According to one Huoyue County Women's Federation study, approximately half of the grassroots female cadres in the region did little more than lead women in production and attend meetings.[48] Moreover, when they did call a meeting for other women, they had little to say.

Beginning in 1957, large numbers of young people, mostly men, were mobilized to work on large construction sites. Although public dining halls and child care became institutionalized as part of the new commune structures in the summer of 1958, the child care was often inadequate, and women worked longer hours at home and in the fields just to keep up with their tasks. For some women, particularly young activists, however, the new challenges inside and outside the village offered an unprecedented opportunity to make heroic sacrifices on behalf of their collective and country. In Wenhe, two former women's heads spoke enthusiastically about the time they spent working on steel production and water conservation projects.[49] In Gaoshan, three young women rose to become the most important leaders in their village and found their village renamed the "Mu Guiying Brigade." The female Party secretary (formerly a women's head),[50] women's head,[51] and accountant[52] all recalled their collective accomplishments during this period with great pride and joy. Specifically, their narratives emphasized their own contributions as pacesetters.

But while these three women spoke of their interest in protecting the health and welfare of women, other women's heads insisted on a work ethic that required total devotion and a Herculean effort that sometimes affected their own health. One former Wenhe women's head, for example, refused to give up working in the fields in the late stages of her pregnancy until ordered to do so by the brigade Party secretary.[53] An ACWF report indicates that, in some cases, women activists elsewhere worked themselves to the point of exhaustion and sickness.[54]

Many women who were not leaders likewise worked themselves to the bone during this time. According to county-level reports from Huoyue, Wenhe, and Gaoshan, many women of childbearing age suffered from sleep deprivation, miscarriages, and illnesses in late 1957 and 1958. Children also were injured and even died during the busiest periods of the year because adequate supervision was unavailable.[55] In Huoyue, a 1961 investigation found that, altogether, 11,170 women (or 4.0 percent of the population of women at the time) had suffered a prolapsed uterus.[56] Although some young women were driven by their own desire to work as well as if not better than men, many became exhausted and sick because they had no choice but to overextend themselves at home, in the fields, and on construction sites.[57]

In part, the problem lay in men's continuing failure to become involved in household management; in part, it stemmed from leaders who felt compelled to increase production and thus forced villagers to work many hours a day. But the widespread exhaustion and illness among women during this period may also be attributable to the enthusiastic expectations of some local women leaders. For example, when I asked Leader Liu,[58] a former women's head in Huoyue, whether anyone asked to be excused from work because of menstruation, she told me that such women were "afraid of hard work." Moreover, she repeatedly denied the existence of health care policies for women – an assertion that stands in stark contrast to the response of her brigade Party secretary, who recited the three transfers to me when I asked him the same question. Other former women's heads, leaders very familiar with the policies of women's health protection, argued that, although women suffered a lot during the Great Leap Forward, they grew stronger as a result. "Without the bitter," one former women's head suggested, "there can be no sweet."[59]

The ACWF undoubtedly contributed to a climate in which struggle and sacrifice were the leading values. During much of the latter half of 1958, ACWF publications were filled with stories of "March 8th" brigades producing previously unheard-of results from irrigation projects and experimental fields. However, neither the ACWF nor the Party leadership ever intended for women to sacrifice their health for the glory of socialist construction. Indeed, the commitment to maintaining women's health is evident in the speeches, publications, and reports of leading ACWF officials at that time as well as in activities organized at the grassroots. While only thirteen books were published on women's liberation in 1958, for example, eighty-five appeared on the topics of women's hygiene, medicine, women's obstetrics, and caring for children – some 55 percent of the total number of books published on women that year.[60] Moreover, both Huoyue and Wenhe counties expanded their reproductive health services substantially during the Great Leap Forward.[61] Finally, ACWF officials continued to stress the importance of child care and maternal health care throughout 1959 – even after the Anti-Rightist Campaign was reignited in the wake of the Lushan meetings.[62] Thus, while ACWF rhetoric emphasized hard work and sacrifice, it also highlighted the importance of maintaining and enhancing the health and welfare of women and children.

At the same time that the ACWF leadership was working to ensure women's reproductive health, it was also struggling hard to maintain its organizational base. Beginning at least as early as 1957, all three counties reported the phenomenon of grassroots women leaders rejecting women's organizations. Senior Party and Women's Federation leaders had sought for years to convince reluctant women cadres that woman-work was glorious and a necessary part of socialist construction. But the advent of collectivization and the mobilization of women into production outside of the home prompted some women leaders to argue that women were now fully liberated and no longer needed special organizations to represent them. According to one Wenhe Women's Federation report from April 1957:

> [Some] think that woman-work is degrading, not glorious, and that it has no future. There is no way, they think, that they will ever be able to achieve anything and that it is not as good as Youth League work. When some comrades come to the county to attend meetings, they don't even bother to go to the Women's Federation. There are also some other cadres who have a self-satisfied and arrogant approach to production. They think that all that matters is their own ability and don't bother to try and learn from

others ... There are some who think that the Women's Federation should simply be disbanded or that it should be amalgamated with other departments. Everyone criticized these ideological errors and agreed that right now women have not yet been thoroughly emancipated, that woman-work will require many years of bitter struggle; and they [also] criticized women who are not willing to do woman-work for forgetting their own past suffering.[63]

Though unrest among women leaders did not translate into the disbanding of local women's organizations in Wenhe, the organizational status of the Women's Federation in Jiangsu fell victim to both local unrest and elite level politics in the summer of that same year. As Wang Zheng documents, senior Women's Federation leaders had to work very carefully to maintain support for the organization at the highest level of the Party in the wake of the Anti-Rightist Campaign.[64] Both the provincial Jiangsu Women's Federation and the Gaoshan City Women's Federation lost their status as independent organizations during the Great Leap Forward, a development preceded by women cadres' complaints echoing those voiced in Wenhe and Huoyue.[65] Ultimately, local tensions in places such as Wenhe, Gaoshan, and Huoyue contributed to an unforeseen crisis in these organizations. Indeed, disregard for women's health, dissatisfaction with woman-work, and the press for organizational change contributed to a nationwide upheaval within the ACWF. During the summer and fall of 1958, many local leaders disbanded women's organizations on the new communes across China. Only active lobbying by senior Women's Federation officials prevented grassroots women's organizations from disappearing altogether during the Great Leap Forward.[66]

In discussing the origins of the extreme radicalism of the Great Leap Forward, several former male leaders in Huoyue and Wenhe pointed to the era's climate of political fear. One Wenhe Party secretary, for example, was sharply sarcastic when I asked about health protection for women:

That was during the Great Leap Forward! You have no idea how extreme things were then; how in the hell could you take care of women's health? It wasn't just the women but also us cadre Party secretaries [who had it rough]. If we said one wrong thing at the commune, we'd immediately get struggled against. At that time the struggle sessions were the most terrifying thing.[67]

It anguished him, he said, to watch the women with children work:

At that time the struggle meetings were really extreme. There was just no way. After eating dinner, women lined up to pick the cotton. Oh my! The women would bring their babies to the fields, and they would also stay at the side of the fields. That really broke our hearts. Some of the women were really strong. After picking they could go home. They needed to pick three rows of cotton – at least 0.8 mu. Some women were really worried that they couldn't finish.

Andors argues that women leaders were more likely to protect the health of women than were male leaders during the Great Leap Forward.[68] And indeed, of the twenty-one women's heads whom I interviewed who were active during the Great Leap Forward, nine of them, including both Zhang and Liu, expressed some kind of sympathy for the burdens women endured at that time. But if none mentioned fear of political reprisal, why did some of these same women's heads (such as Liu) deny the need for health care or insist on an ethic of struggle as the road to women's liberation? In an ironic twist, why was it primarily the grassroots male leaders I spoke with who looked back on their past with a Marxist maternalist regret?

Grassroots Party Building

A resurgence in the revolutionary values of voluntarism and militarism in the late 1950s encouraged some women to believe that they could overcome all odds – including the "natural" physiology of their own bodies. But women's radicalism appeared long before the "leftist" period of the Great Leap Forward. I argue that the desire of some women activists to prove that they were equal to (if not better than) male leaders and, in some cases, to disassociate themselves from woman-work altogether arose from the organizational foundations of rural women's activism and leadership. One of the key reasons that Marxist maternalist policies were ignored, defied, and, in some cases, transformed in Huoyue, Wenhe, and Gaoshan during the late 1950s was because of the way in which grassroots women leaders were recruited and trained in CCP organizations and Party families during the formative first years of the People's Republic.

In the early 1950s, many of the Party's earliest recruits in areas newly "liberated" did not choose to become activists at all, much less activists on women's issues. Instead, the CCP had to persuade individuals to think of themselves and their social world in an entirely new way.[69] Newly formed peasant associations (*nongminhui*) and land reform work teams, as well as visiting upper-level cadres, typically identified young, economically impoverished, and oppressed villagers as possible future leaders for two reasons. First, the oppressed-turned-leaders could serve as living discursive bridges between the injustice of the old society and the possibilities of the new socialist reality; and second, the Party leadership believed that, because they had had to labour for their survival prior to 1949, the most economically "backward" villagers often had the most advanced farming skills.[70] Figures from Wenhe and Gaoshan suggest that most rural women leaders in these areas came from among the poorest and most disenfranchised. In Gaoshan, for example, some 62 percent of women's heads in 1961 were from poor peasant backgrounds.[71] In Wenhe in 1964, 90 percent of commune and county Women's Federation officials originally hailed from poor peasant backgrounds.[72]

Local work teams and Party organizations attempted to recruit not only those oppressed by their economic position but also women who were oppressed by the forces of feudal patriarchy. By encouraging former child brides and battered women to see that familial abuse was a remnant of the "old society" and should be rightfully struggled against, the CCP provided these women with a new language for understanding and politicizing their lot. But while some newly minted activists were able to serve as role models in the fields and meetings and thus meet the Party's expectations, others failed dramatically. Indeed, the Party's strategy of reversal, of bringing the lowest to the most high, was particularly vulnerable to painful collapse.

Xiu, for example, a former Wenhe leader,[73] was recruited by a CCP leader from her natal village shortly after her marriage. The Party leader encouraged Xiu to stand up to her new in-laws, who were beating her, and to become an activist. When Xiu's husband joined the army to fight in the Korean War, Xiu began to attend meetings and eventually became a Party secretary and women's head. But when her husband returned from fighting several years later, he harassed Xiu and attempted to stop her from attending meetings. Denied the right to a divorce (because her husband was a soldier) and receiving no help from the local Party organization, Xiu stopped attending meetings. Not long after, she lost her Party membership.

The CCP carved out a new identity for Xiu in the earliest years of the People's Republic of China. The problem was that this identity could not be sustained without ongoing legal, ideological, or even technical support. In addition to facing hostility within her family, Xiu suffered from extremely poor vision. Unable to read or write, Xiu felt herself inadequate to manage the tasks asked of her.[74] Had Xiu been able to divorce her husband, had other leaders "struggled against" her husband and his family, or had Xiu been provided with a literate assistant to help her with her administrative tasks, she might have been able to continue with her political work.[75] Absent such help, she failed to hang on to her position as

Party secretary. Ironically, Xiu was blamed for this failure. A retired male leader who had served as Party secretary during the Great Leap Forward ridiculed Xiu for having behaved bizarrely during and after her time in office.[76] Moreover, he refused to entertain the idea that Xiu's family troubles had anything to do with her being expelled from the Party.

The case of Xiu lays bare the central conflict between the CCP's recruitment of women leaders and its retention of them. In order to successfully make the transition from victim to a figure of Party authority, cadres had to assert a particular kind of autonomy from all familial attachments. They had to demonstrate selflessness and a total devotion to their political work, particularly that of class struggle. Yet, ironically, many could not become selfless role models without the support of their family or a local organization.

Only women who received key support from Party organizations, from the ACWF, or from relatives who were key Party members were able to serve as "living emblems" of sacrifice and struggle. Xiu lacked these sorts of support. The various challenges that women leaders faced in executing their roles were so immense and diffuse that many could not survive politically without the assistance and reinforcement of organization, family, or both.[77] Leader Liu, for example, encountered fierce opposition from her in-laws. Liu was raised in a politically active family in Huoyue. According to Liu, her siblings and her father encouraged her to become an activist. Liu became a member of the Youth League shortly after marrying her husband and joined the CCP in 1956. But while Liu's natal family was supportive of her activism, her husband's family was not. Because of his own political problems, Liu's husband opposed her entry into the Youth League, and both he and his parents complained about Liu's activism as the village's first women's head.[78] Liu's father-in-law was particularly outraged by his daughter-in-law's "running around wild" and not working. She ignored the criticisms, however, and continued in her position for more than two decades. Liu would probably never have stood up to her in-laws if she had not enjoyed the initial support of her natal family. As a result of what she had learned, she felt she had a right to be a leader in the new China.[79]

Although familial or some kind of state support was necessary for women to become activists, their direct participation in formal and informal Party organizations may have also encouraged women leaders to approach their work with revolutionary enthusiasm. Indeed, the fact that Leader Liu's sisters were Party members and her brother was a commune leader may have contributed to Liu's dismissal of menstruating women as "afraid" of hard work.

Party Organizations

In two separate interviews, a former women's head and a former county Women's Federation leader remarked that "women cadres have always had it tough" (*funü ganbu lao chiku*).[80] Women's heads not only assumed multiple responsibilities in a village and so were preoccupied with a number of competing issues, not all related to woman-work, but they were also often in charge of housework and child care in their own homes. As of 1960, of the twenty-four women's heads for whom I have a record about their children, four had at least one child, and thirteen had two or more. They thus managed their official duties while simultaneously caring for children at home. Women leaders also faced community disapproval. Many, especially in the earliest days of the People's Republic, were scorned for "running around outside" and speaking with male strangers. And several felt that their perceived youth influenced their ability to lead as well. At best, these women were doubted because they were young; at worst, they were called derogatory names.

Despite these formidable odds, a number of women whom I interviewed expressed a deep sense of satisfaction with their work.[81] One of the key factors, I found, that helped these women to make themselves into discursive bridges was the close and constant presence of local and, in some cases, county-level Party organizations. Indeed, Party organizations were crucial in both forming the political subjectivity of women activists and enabling them to realize this identity over an extended period of time.

In the earliest years of the People's Republic, the most important organizations in rural areas were the local Party committee (at the district or township level), the Peasants Association, and the Youth League. Work teams set up peasants' associations in villages during land reform as the first step towards establishing new forms of locally elected government. In addition to identifying the first generation of village leaders, work teams and peasants' associations often played the most important roles in struggling against landlords. Some women who later went on to become responsible for woman-work at the commune and county level started their activism at this time. But not all early women activists followed a maternalist trajectory of advancement. In fact, reports suggest that work teams and new peasants' associations found the leadership styles of some young women activists difficult to accept.[82] Some young women "forced" older women to hand over their crops to the state without providing any kind of rationale, while others led with a "crude" work style and terrorized local men – problems that emerged again during collectivization and the Great Leap Forward.

The Chinese Communist Youth League, established to help young people to study communism and assist the CCP, may have exacerbated egalitarian tendencies among women's heads in all three locations. One Gaoshan County Women's Federation report from July 1957, for example, found that those most unwilling to become women's heads included women cadres who had previously been active in the Youth League or who had been responsible for some aspect of a cooperative's finances or production.[83] According to the report, many of these women leaders held that women were "backward," that there was no glory in woman-work, and that they would much rather be involved with the Youth League while they were young and energetic. Some went so far as to declare that they would rather give up the cause altogether and go home than do woman-work.

In addition to peasants' associations and the Youth League, Party membership had a tremendous impact on the emergence and style of rural women's leadership in the 1950s. Eighteen of the twenty-five former women's heads interviewed became Party members at some point while they were activists. In Gaoshan, about 75 percent of women's heads in 1961 were Party members.[84] But Party membership may have not so much encouraged awareness of Marxist maternalist principles as cultivated revolutionary enthusiasm for hard labour. Whereas the ACWF emphasized the ability of women to overcome oppressive feudal forces by renegotiating familial relationships without confrontation (through both the 1950 Marriage Law and the Five Goods Movement), on the one hand, and by engaging in production, on the other, local Party organizations gave far more weight to women's transformation of production. Exhibiting proper political attitudes, or *biaoxian*, entailed emphasizing the CCP's main line.[85] It is thus not surprising that many of the earliest women models were commended for their pioneering labour, not for their willingness to challenge "local standards of virtuous behavior."[86] Ultimately, the politics of *biaoxian* and the spirit of revolutionary sacrifice central to grassroots Party life directed women leaders towards increasing production output and away from recognizing sexual difference.

Model individuals, brigades, and communes all played important roles throughout the Maoist era in the expansion of the ideals of revolutionary sacrifice and struggle in Huoyue, Wenhe, and Gaoshan. But outstanding women activists and leaders, like "model communes," often achieved and maintained the status of revolutionary exemplar because they received direct state support.[87] Where official organizational support was lacking, particular kinds of informal institutional practices in women's leadership formation proved influential. I found that specific family formations, especially Party families, proved to be sufficient if not necessary for women activists to emerge as pioneers in the construction of socialism. Moreover, these more informal kinds of organizational forums could, and in some cases did, contribute to the expansion of egalitarian leadership in Huoyue, Wenhe, and Gaoshan.

Party Families

Party families have flourished since the foundation of the CCP in 1921. Indeed, they have been hugely influential during the revolutionary, Maoist, and reform periods.[88] My research suggests that they played a particularly important role in the recruitment of local women activists to organizational work in post-revolutionary China. Similar to the findings of scholarship on Latin American guerrilla movements, the presence of family support could positively influence a woman's decision to join "the movement."[89] Lin, for example, one of the three women leaders from the Mu Guiying Brigade and an early Youth League recruit, was named a local "pacesetter" for establishing a successful mutual aid team in the early 1950s.[90] Her accomplishment was all the more extraordinary given that she had been widowed shortly after marrying into the village, where she remained with a small son to raise. Lin's in-laws, rather than undermining her leadership as Xiu's had done, actually made her work possible. She said:

> Back then [right after liberation] when I went out to meetings my father-in-law bought me a flashlight. At that time everyone had to carry a bedroll when they went to meetings. He also gave me a piece of rope. He said, "I'll take care of everything at home, you take care of everything outside." It is because of my family's support that I was able to lead the way so successfully.[91]

Rural women such as Lin were often able to make the leap from being a "victim of the old society" to public leader because they were supported by fathers, husbands, brothers, uncles, and sometimes even in-laws. One former child bride whom I interviewed made her transition to local activist as the result of encouragement from her husband.[92] A total of twelve former women's heads told me that they enjoyed the direct backing of their spouses. At least five had supportive in-laws.[93]

Many of the male relatives who encouraged and supported young women leaders in the 1950s were politically active themselves: they were early Party members, former soldiers in the People's Liberation Army, or members of the Youth League or local Peasants Association. Among the twenty-five former women's heads I interviewed, eleven described at least one family member as having been active in Party organizations prior to their own emergence as activists and leaders.

As several scholars have noted, women's custom of marrying out of their natal village often entailed leaving behind their political connections and, thus, curtailed their opportunities for political activism.[94] In my own study, I found that, while at least one woman forewent activism after marrying out of the village,[95] others were able to build on their natal relations by marrying within their brigade,[96] by maintaining important connections with their natal family after leaving home,[97] or by marrying very late.[98] The former Mu Guiying women's head and Party secretary,[99] for example, was strongly encouraged in her political work by her father and brother – both active village leaders. She chose not to marry until she was twenty-nine (at that time an extraordinarily late age for a rural woman), and, when she did, she married within her own village.

In addition to natal families, in-laws were a decisive factor in the emergence of politically active women. Supportive mothers-in-law not only provided essential help with children and household tasks but also, at times, supplied emotional support. Indeed, I was startled by the intensity of affection expressed by two former women's heads towards their mothers-in-law. One woman told me that her mother-in-law supported her because she "loved her dearly."[100] Another Huoyue women's head explained that her mother-in-law's support for her work was rooted in the political changes that had transpired after the founding of the People's Republic.[101] Her mother-in-law had been widowed at a very young age and had suffered greatly. After having liberated herself and gained enough to eat and drink, she was "very active" and "willing to do anything," including minding her grandchildren.

In the Chinese case, Party family ties may have facilitated not only the emergence of women activists but also the kind of activists they became. A close look at Leader Zhang's story illustrates the role that institutional support played in shaping her own political trajectory. Indeed, local Party networks, both formal and familial, provided Leader Zhang with a new language with which to label her experience, develop a new political subjectivity, and exercise authority over others.

The Gendered Politics of Woman-Work

Leader Zhang, the women's head introduced at the beginning of this chapter, was raised in one very supportive family and married into another. Her father insisted that she attend school during an early literacy campaign, and her mother's brother encouraged her to become a cadre. Recruited by a work team, Zhang joined the Youth League as a teenager, served as a model cotton planter and production leader, and rose to become the women's head in her village a year before she married. According to Zhang, she caught her mother-in-law's eye when she was giving a speech. Impressed by Zhang's courage, the woman urged her son, then at school, to marry Zhang. In the early 1950s, Zhang's brother-in-law, then village Party secretary, trained both Zhang and her husband in their work as village leaders – women's head and accountant, respectively.

Unlike some women leaders, Zhang did not see herself primarily as an advocate for women; rather, she saw herself as building the collective. And, in her eyes, individuals who subverted the collective effort by missing work for health reasons or by taking collective property for private use were not morally "upright." Although not unconcerned about questions of sexual equality, Zhang was far more preoccupied with the success of class struggle and collectivization. Her priorities set her on a collision course with the leadership of the Women's Federation and its advocacy of special protections for women. Indeed, Zhang's formative experiences in Party organizations and a Party family generated a conflict between her role as women's head (protector of women and children) and her role as a Party activist (mobilizer of the masses). Ultimately, Zhang's close Party ties were responsible for her rise and fall as a powerful local women's head.

Zhang's case illustrates the complex impact of revolutionary Maoism as manifested in local Party families and organizations in the 1950s. Zhang's main mentor, her brother-in-law (interviewee 35), was himself so "enthusiastic" in the execution of his duties during the Great Leap Forward that he was criticized and removed from his post as a commune leader. Yet, though he embraced sexual equality, as is evident from his cultivation of Zhang and his support for women's liberation during the Great Leap Forward, he refused to entertain the idea of equality in his home, telling me that he always had "the last word." Similarly, while Zhang's mother-in-law helped with many of the household chores, Zhang herself assumed the majority of the tasks associated with child care and housekeeping – tasks she sometimes combined with her leadership responsibilities:

> I have told all of my children, when I went to meetings in those days, [I would] sit down below twisting hemp into thread, [I] used [thimble and needle] to make shoe soles, I even took care of my natal family's clothing! There was a lot of that work; I didn't sleep until I finished all of the shoe soles, [so] I never slept a whole [night]. [At that time] I had to do it myself; later [you could] tear off a strip of cloth and get them to make

clothing. Back then it was really difficult, twisting hemp thread, [and you could] only get this big a bundle [to] hang out on the wall.

Conflicting messages also abounded in the Party organizations to which Zhang belonged. When I asked another village leader who had been involved in Zhang's training about her political education, he said that there were

> no training classes. We did political work and told [Zhang] how to do woman-work. [We] told [her] that the status of women was raised, women were liberated, women and men were equal. Also, [we told her that] doing woman-work had a future. You could participate in Party organizations. At that time we didn't think about how to get rich. The most important thing was your level of enthusiasm.[102]

Although Zhang insisted that she loved to do woman-work, the comment of this village leader suggests that her superiors were at the very least aware of critiques of woman-work circulating at that time.

The persistence of revolutionary Maoism in Party organizations and families created an environment within which activists were more likely to judge their own political value and the political value of others by their willingness to sacrifice and struggle. Instead of seeing themselves through the eyes of Marxist maternalism, they saw themselves through the eyes of revolutionary Maoism as conveyed by male mentors. In Zhang's case, this stance was to have profound implications. On the one hand, it would seem that Zhang was plagued by self-doubt as a leader. She repeatedly stressed her illiteracy as evidence of her lack of ability. Like Xiu and many other former women's heads whom I interviewed, Zhang could not read or write. She compared herself to her mother-in-law, who, she said, learned how to read in a literacy training class, and to her husband. "I learned from my husband," she said: "If you are illiterate, you are really obedient. I just led people to work, is all." Although Zhang had become politically active before her husband did so, and encouraged him to become a leader, she apparently considered herself less capable than her spouse.

And yet Zhang was not a shy woman. After overcoming an initial reluctance to be seen working publicly (she used to crouch down while hoeing, she said, whenever anyone passed by), she willingly began to stand up and give speeches. Moreover, she exuded pride in her achievements at growing cotton and in struggling against those who did not want to join the collective or sell their grain to the state. Zhang, by all accounts, was a formidable presence in the village. Interestingly, although Zhang's brother-in-law admitted to me that he had come to regret the way in which women had been mobilized during the Great Leap Forward, Zhang articulated no such second thoughts;[103] rather, her views seem to continue to reflect her earlier revolutionary enthusiasm.

Early on in our first interview, when Zhang was speaking about men and women labouring for work points, she said that, although there was care, "upright people didn't want [special] treatment." When I asked her directly whether there were any special measures in place to protect women's health, she said, "No." After I pressed her further, asking specifically about women who were pregnant, she told me: "Back then there was special treatment. For example, there were bonus points. In this village I also specially said that [if there were] people in difficulty that a grandmother should give them clothes and a quilt. My mother-in-law also looked after children." It would seem that, while Zhang knew that "special treatment" was required and that she sometimes provided such care, she didn't look highly on those who took advantage of it. In 1959, Zhang told me in a later interview, she herself worked in the fields right up until she went into labour. The high expectations she held (of herself and others) no doubt, in part, led to the harsh condemnation she received from some of her fellow villagers.[104]

Zhang insisted that women were better workers than men, but she did not suggest that the Great Leap Forward marked an important breakthrough for sexual equality, as did some other Women's Federation leaders whom I interviewed.[105] Indeed, she did not attach any particular gendered significance to liberation, collectivization, or the Great Leap Forward: "Back in the old days, men went to the southern mountains to build a canal. If the men went, all ages in the family, young and small, pitched in. How could she not work? Women worked in the old society, not to mention this new society."[106] When I asked Zhang point-blank whether women's thinking had changed at all during the Great Leap Forward, she told me that she "hadn't heard of it."

Although Zhang's primary interests did not lie with women, Zhang did understand and seek to implement some maternalist policies in her village. She worked to resolve quarrels between married couples (sometimes confronting violent husbands), for example, and she reassigned at least some women to rest or lighter work when their health was suffering. She also described her relationship with her husband as one of mutual support:

He had no [problem] with it, he supported me. If we had to attend a meeting, we went together. We never quarrelled about [my work], we were destined to marry. [He] never said: "You are out of control with your work, [I] forbid you to work." Never! If he went to town to attend a model meeting, we attended the meeting [together], [where] the prize was a cow. I also went if he went to attend the People's Congress meetings.

[Interviewer]: Both of you went together?

Right. He was an understanding [person]. He never got angry and criticized me because I spoke with other men, never. As long as my thinking was pure, I never feared [anything].

Interestingly, when I asked Zhang to define sexual equality, she offered a definition that stood in stark contrast to her brother-in-law's rejection of sexual equality in the home – and that also seemed to contradict her earlier assessment of her own leadership capabilities: "I think that it is [when] you are not [victim] to his anger. He works, I also work. You can't bully me, I [don't have to] fear you. You work. I also work. I'm not worth less than you."

As Zhang's activities demonstrate, Party families and Party organizations could powerfully affect how women came to understand themselves as leaders in the post-1949 period. Women who were recruited and trained by Party organizations at times grew to identify more closely with Maoist values than they did with maternalist policies of protection. Zhang, recruited by a work team and trained in the context of the Youth League and a Party family, ultimately lost her position as women's head as a result of the leadership practices she learned in these organizations – as well, perhaps, as a consequence of her family ties to leaders who had been discredited. But, unlike her brother-in-law, who openly admitted that he made errors at that time, Zhang saw nothing wrong with her earlier mobilization style.

When I asked one former Wenhe village women's head how she felt when the communes were first established, she replied: "Of course I worked towards the establishment of the communes! If my husband joined the Eighth Route Army and wasn't afraid to die, why would I be afraid to die?"[107] This woman, mentioned earlier as having participated in field labour until the late stages of her pregnancy, was married to a retired soldier and county-level bureaucrat. Instead of recalling fears of being criticized and struggled against, as did some male cadres in her county, this woman immediately asserted her willingness to give herself over to the cause of establishing the communes. For her, as for Zhang, the revolutionary ideology outlasted the organizational context within which it had originally taken shape.

The contradictions evident in Zhang's understanding of her rise and fall as a women's head some forty years earlier point to larger contradictions in the polity as a whole. These contradictions include rhetoric about the importance of women in building socialism, a continuing disregard for woman-work in grassroots Party culture, and an increasing emphasis on the revolutionary's ability to overcome all natural obstacles – including women's reproductive capacities. As they became manifest in grassroots Party organizations in Huoyue, Wenhe, and Gaoshan, these contradictions undermined the Marxist maternalist mandate of the ACWF and created havoc among grassroots women's organizations.

Insofar as differing ideological commitments played an important role in the emergence of grassroots conflicts, these findings call into question the notion that peasants only participate in revolutionary movements to preserve their way of life. These findings also call into question the role of the peasant family as an automatic barrier to the inculcation of new values. Indeed, in some cases, sympathetic mothers-in-law and local "Party families" played an influential role in realizing new conceptions of sexual equality at the grassroots. Moreover, and as is evident in the case of Zhang, Party families may have facilitated the implementation of a more egalitarian conception of equality than the CCP and ACWF leadership had intended. Some women and men were quite prepared to transform their way of life and the lives of those around them, and, with the support of key family members and organizations, they did.

These findings suggest that post-revolutionary conflict in rural communities, including incidences of women's radicalism during the Great Leap Forward, can be productively explored through attention to the multiple, variegated, and intersecting enactments of "patriarchy" and "liberation" at the grassroots. What may appear to be new manifestations of rural patriarchy, such as the rise of local Party families, may offer a path to liberation, albeit for a select few. At the same time, what may appear as a new manifestation of women's liberation, such as the rise of local women's activism, may foreclose the realization of differing forms of liberation for others. Accordingly, this study suggests that scholarship of revolutionary and post-revolutionary politics should seek to broaden its understanding of the contexts within which peasant resistance arises, including the radicalized resistance of peasant activists. Indeed, this is one important way we can more fully understand the many gendered dimensions of the modern state project at the grassroots.

Table 3.1

Interviewee list

No.	Position	Location	Date of interview (M/D/Y)
10	Women's head (Leader Liu)	Huoyue Village 1	2/14/01, 2/18/01, 7/10/04
18	Women's head's husband	Huoyue Village 1	2/18/01
14	Female work-point model	Huoyue Village 1	2/17/01
20	Women's head (Leader Zhang)	Huoyue Village 2	2/20/01, 7/7/04
24	Female dining-hall worker	Huoyue Village 2	2/20/01
30	Woman	Huoyue Village 2	7/4/01
31	Women's head	Huoyue (near Village 1)	2/15/01
32	Women's head	Huoyue (nearby commune)	2/19/01
33	District women's head	Huoyue Village 2	7/4/01
34	Male district leader	Huoyue Village 2	7/4/01
35	Male commune administrator	Huoyue (from Village 2)	2/20/01
37	Women's head	Wenhe (neighbouring commune)	3/29/01
41	Woman	Wenhe Village 1	3/31/01, 6/27/01
42	Female team leader	Wenhe Village 1	4/2/01
43	Women's head	Wenhe Village 1	3/31/01, 6/27/01
45	Woman	Wenhe Village 1	4/2/01
51	Female team leader	Wenhe Village 1	4/2/01, 4/6/01
52	Women's head	Wenhe Village 1	4/2/01
53	Party secretary/women's head (Leader Xiu)	Wenhe Village 2	4/4/01
61	Male Party secretary	Wenhe Village 2	4/6/01, 6/28/01
65	County Women's Federation leader	Wenhe	3/30/01
73	Women's head (Leader Lin)	Gaoshan Village 2	5/28/01, 6/1/01, 6/23-28/04
74	Commune Women's Federation leader	Gaoshan	5/28/01, 6/25/04, 6/27/04
82	Female accountant	Gaoshan Village 2	6/4/01
83	Women's head/Party secretary	Gaoshan Village 2	6/4/01
85	Youth League rep/women's head	Gaoshan Village 3	6/6/01
114	Male village leader	Huoyue Village 1	2/22/01

Acknowledgments

Research for this chapter was funded by the Canadian Social Sciences and Humanities Research Council, the China-Canada Scholar's Award, the University of Washington Graduate School Fritz Scholarship for International Exchange, the funds de recherche sur la société et la culture, and Concordia University. Earlier versions of this chapter were presented at meetings of the American Political Science Association, the Association of Asian Studies, and the Berkshire Conference on Women's History. Much of the writing of the chapter was completed at the Center for East Asian Studies, Stanford University. Helpful comments on drafts were provided by Senem Aslan, Tani Barlow, Lauren Basson, Jane Curry, Stevan Harrell, Beverly Hooper, Tamara Jacka, Christine Keating, Kenneth Lawson, Joel Migdal, Jean Oi, Maryjane Osa, Isil Ozel, Ki-young Shin, Shui Jingjun, Felix Wemheuer, Wang Zheng, Nicole Watts, Susan Whiting, and six anonymous reviewers. Colleagues and friends in the field also provided invaluable assistance in carrying out this research.

For purposes of confidentiality, all names referred to in this chapter, unless publicly known, are pseudonyms. The county names have also been changed in order to protect the identities of county officials interviewed. All interview transcripts are currently in the author's possession.

Notes

1 Various versions of this story were told to me by Leader Zhang (interviewee 20), a male former district-level Party secretary (interviewee 34), and two women villagers (interviewees 24 and 30).

2 Jean-Luc Domenach, *The Origins of the Great Leap Forward* (Boulder, CO: Westview Press, 1995); Helen F. Siu, *Agents and Victims in South China: Accomplices in Rural Revolution* (New Haven: Yale University Press, 1989).

3 Twenty-one of the twenty-five were women's heads at some point during the Great Leap Forward. Leader Xiu (interviewee 53), a Wenhe woman whom I discuss in this chapter, lost her position in the early 1950s when she was expelled from the Party. Two other former women's heads (interviewees 83 and 85) assumed new positions during the Great Leap Forward. Despite their loss of position, all three women continued to be involved with women's mobilization. Xiu and interviewee 85, for example, both served as team leaders on construction sites during the Great Leap Forward.

4 For recent discussions on the importance of historical memory in the context of rural women in the 1950s, see Gail Hershatter, "The Gender of Memory: Rural Chinese Women and the 1950s," *Signs* 28, 1 (2002): 43-70; Kimberley Ens Manning, "Making a Great Leap Forward? The Politics of Women's Liberation in Maoist China," *Gender and History* 18, 3 (2006): 574-93; and Kimberley Ens Manning, "Communes, Canteens, and Crèches: The Gendered Politics of Remembering the Great Leap Forward," in *Re-Envisioning the Chinese Revolution*, ed. Ching Kwan Lee and Guobin Yang, 93-118 (Stanford: Woodrow Wilson and Stanford University Press, 2007).

5 My last interviews were conducted in a third county in Henan, north of Zhengzhou (2006).

6 See Gao Hua's discussion of Xuchang in Chapter 7 of this volume.

7 *Huoyue xianzhi* [Huoyue County Annal] (Zhengzhou: Zhongzhou guji chubanshe, 1993), 404.

8 Unfortunately, the *Wenhe xianzhi* does not provide population statistics for the years 1958-60.

9 See Qiao Peihua, *Xinyang shijian* [The Xinyang Disaster] (Hong Kong: Kaifang chubanshe, 2009).

10 In the 1950s, Huoyue specialized in tobacco production, and Wenhe was developing apple horticulture.

11 *Gaoshan xianzhi* [Gaoshan County Annal] (Shanghai: Shanghai shehui kexueyuan chubanshe, 1994), 177.

12 In addition to the explanation that follows, it is important to remember that Party secretaries were likely threatened with reprisals more directly than were women's heads. See Ralph A. Thaxton, *Catastrophe and Contention in Rural China: Mao's Great Leap Forward Famine and the Origins of Righteous Resistance in Da Fo Village* (New York: Cambridge University Press, 2008), 143-47 for his vivid description of public criticism sessions in Da Fo village. Leader Liu, an interviewee whom I discuss shortly, described her fear of being struggled against during the Anti-Five Winds Campaign. This campaign, however, took place at the closure of the Great Leap Forward and was designed to rectify the leftist excesses of the Great Leap itself.

13 In her statistical tabulations of women's labour during the Maoist period, Thorborg finds that, in 1958, some 90 percent of women of working age were engaged in agricultural activity. See Maria Thorborg, "Chinese Employment Policy in 1949-78 with Special Emphasis on Women in Rural Production," in *Chinese Economy Post-Mao: A Compendium of Papers*, 535-604 (Washington, DC: US Government Printing Office, 1978), 570. According to Huoyue Women's Federation reports from the period, women's labour power reached more than 90 percent by late February of 1958. See Huoyue County Archives Women's Federation (hereafter HCAWF), "1957 nian funü gongzuo zongjie" [Summary of Woman-Work in 1957], 25 February 1958.

14 Thomas B. Bernstein, "Stalinism, Famine, and Chinese Peasants," *Theory and Society* 13 (1984): 339-77; Domenach, *Origins of the Great Leap Forward*; Edward Friedman, Paul Pickowicz, and Mark Selden, *Chinese Village, Socialist State* (New Haven: Yale University Press, 1991).

15 Phyllis Andors, *The Unfinished Liberation of Chinese Women, 1949-1980* (Bloomington: Indiana University Press, 1983); Norma Diamond, "Collectivization, Kinship, and the Status of Women in Rural China," *Bulletin of Concerned Asian Scholars* 7 (1975): 25-32; William L. Parish and Martin King Whyte, *Village and Family in Contemporary China* (Chicago: University of Chicago Press, 1978).

16 Domenach, *Origins of the Great Leap Forward*; Friedman et al., *Chinese Village, Socialist State.*

17 Xiaobo Lü, *Cadres and Corruption: The Organizational Involution of the Chinese Communist Party* (Stanford, CA: Stanford University Press, 2000), 24. Lü, whose primary interest is official corruption, argues that traditional norms did not begin to undermine state ideology until the Great Leap Forward. I draw on this quotation to illustrate the theoretical assumption that traditional norms and practices necessarily are at odds with ideology.

18 Vivienne Shue, *The Reach of the State: Sketches of the Chinese Body Politic* (Stanford: Stanford University Press, 1988); Lü, *Cadres and Corruption*; David Zweig, *Agrarian Radicalism in China, 1968-1981* (Cambridge, MA: Harvard University Press, 1989). Although see Jonathan Unger, "State and Peasant in Post-Revolution China," *Journal of Peasant Studies* 17, 1 (1989): 114-36, for an important critique of Shue's analysis of ideology in rural China.

19 Kay Ann Johnson, *Women, the Family, and Peasant Revolution in China* (Chicago: University of Chicago Press, 1983); Judith Stacey, *Patriarchy and Socialist Revolution in China* (Berkeley: University of California Press, 1983).

20 Johnson, *Women, the Family, and Peasant Revolution.*

21 Diamond, "Collectivization, Kinship, and the Status of Women"; Friedman et al., *Chinese Village, Socialist State*; Shue, *Reach of the State*; Stacey, *Patriarchy and Socialist Revolution.*

22 Stacey, *Patriarchy and Socialist Revolution*, 247.

23 Barrington Moore, *Social Origins of Dictatorship and Democracy: Lord and Peasant in the Making of the Modern World* (Boston: Beacon Press, 1966); Eric Wolf, *Peasant Wars of the Twentieth Century* (New York: Harper and Row, 1969); Jeffrey M. Paige, *Agrarian Revolution* (New York: Free Press, 1975).

24 Jack A. Goldstone, "Toward a Fourth Generation of Revolutionary Theory," *Annual Review of Political Science* 4 (2001): 139-87; Lucien Bianco, *Peasants without the Party* (New York: M.E. Sharpe), 2001.

25 Craig Jackson Calhoun, "The Radicalism of Tradition: Community Strength or Venerable Disguise and Borrowed Language?" *American Journal of Sociology* 88, 5 (1983): 886-914; James C. Scott, "Hegemony and the Peasantry," *Politics and Society* 7, 3 (1977): 267-96.

26 Ellen Judd, for example, was among the earliest to highlight women's agency in rural China. See Ellen R. Judd, *Gender and Power in Rural North China* (Stanford: Stanford University Press, 1994). More recently, Neil Diamant has also emphasized the agency of rural women in his study of the 1950 Marriage Law. He also questions the homogeneity of "male patriarchy" by suggesting that male court and district officials in rural townships and counties tended to grant divorces to women more readily than did their village counterparts. See Neil Diamant, *Revolutionizing the Family: Politics, Love, and Divorce in Urban and Rural China, 1949-1958* (Berkeley: University of California Press, 2000). See also Gail Hershatter's recent work on rural women in the 1950s: "Virtue at Work: Rural Shaanxi Women Remember the 1950s," in *Gender in Motion: Divisions of Labor and Cultural Change in Late Imperial and Modern China*, ed. Bryna Goodman and Wendy Larson, 309-28 (Lanham, MA: Rowman and Littlefield, 2005); "The Gender of Memory: Rural Chinese Women and the 1950s"; and "Birthing Stories: Rural Midwives in 1950s China," in *Dilemmas of Victory: The Early Years of the People's Republic of China*, ed. Jeremy Brown and Paul G. Pickowicz, 337-58 (Cambridge, MA: Harvard University Press, 2007). Amrita Basu's work on women's activism in rural India offers an early and significant corrective regarding peasant ideological commitments in the comparative study of peasants. See Amrita Basu, *Two Faces of Protest* (Berkeley: University of California Press, 1992).

27 Karen Kampwirth, *Women and Guerrilla Movements: Nicaragua, El Salvador, Chiapas, Cuba* (University Park: Pennsylvania State University Press, 2002).

28 Following Delia Davin, *Woman-Work: Women and the Party in Revolutionary China* (Oxford: Oxford University Press, 1976); and Ellen Judd, "Feminism from Afar," in *Ethnographic Feminisms*, ed. Sally Cole and Lynne Phillips, 37-51 (Ottawa: Carleton University Press, 1995), I have chosen to translate *funü gongzuo* as "woman-work" rather than "women's work." For an excellent discussion of woman-work, see Judd, "Feminism from Afar."

29 See Helen Schneider, "On the Homefront: Women's Work Corps and Social Welfare in the Sino-Japanese War," paper presented at the Southeast Conference of the Association for Asian Studies, Lexington, Kentucky, 2005; M. Colette Plum, "Unlikely Heirs: War Orphans during the Second Sino-Japanese War, 1937-1945" (PhD diss., Stanford University, 2006); and Kimberley Manning, "The Sino-Japanese War and the Second Maternalist Front," paper presented at the Historical Society for Twentieth Century China, Honolulu, 2008.

30 Gilmartin has observed that while early female Chinese Communist leaders "looked forward to the day when a socialist state would relieve them of some of their responsibilities through the establishment of daycare centers and canteens, they adhered to the sanctity of *muxing* (maternal instincts) and thus failed to agitate for a re-division of household responsibilities with their husbands." See Christina K. Gilmartin, *Engendering the Chinese Revolution: Radical Women, Communist Politics, and Mass Movements in the 1920s* (Berkeley: University of California Press, 1995), 58.

31 Zhou Enlai, "Lun 'xianqi liangmu' yu muzhi" [On Good Wives, Loving Mothers, and the Duties of Motherhood], in *Zhongguo funü yundong lishi ziliao (1937-1945)* [Historical Materials of the Chinese Women's Movement, 1937-1945], ed. Wang Menglan, 608-11 (Beijing: Zhongguo funü chubanshe, 1991 [1942]), 611.

32 Cao Guanqun, a senior Women's Federation leader, explicitly argued that women were more suited to housework than were men. See Cao Guanqun, "Guanyu heli zuzhi yu shiyong funü laodongli wenti" [The Problems Regarding Reasonably Organizing and Using Women's Labour], in *Zhongguo funü yundong wenxian ziliao huibian* [A Compilation of Historical Documents of the Chinese Women's Movement], 272-75 (Beijing: Zhongguo funü chubanshe, 1988 [1957]).

33   For example, Cai Chang, future chair of the ACWF, gave her daughter to her mother to raise in the 1920s. Deng Yingchao, future vice-chair of the ACWF, never had children.

34   Zhu Chengxia, "Dabieshan yi nian lai de funü gongzuo" [A Year of Woman-Work in Dabieshan], in *Zhongguo funü yundong lishi ziliao* [Historical Materials of the Chinese Women's Movement, 1937-1945], ed. Wang Menglan, 214-27 (Beijing: Zhongguo funü chubanshe, 1991 [1939]), 225.

35   Xiong Mengjue, "Yi feng gongkai de xin – tan Dongbei funü gongzuo" [An Open Letter to Discuss Women-Work in the Northeast], in *Zhongguo funü yundong lishi ziliao* [Historical Materials of the Chinese Women's Movement, 1945-1949], ed. Hu Lipei (Beijing: Zhongguo funü chubanshe, 1991 [1947]), 128; Zhu, "Dabieshan yi nian lai de funü gongzuo," 225.

36   Zhu De, "Zai jiefangqu funü gongzuo huiyi shang de jianghua" [Speech Given at the Woman-Work Meeting in the Liberated Areas], in *Zhongguo funü yundong lishi ziliao* [Historical Materials of the Chinese Women's Movement, 1945-1949], ed. Hu Lipei, 276-80 (Beijing: Zhongguo funü chubanshe, 1991 [1948]).

37   For discussions of prenatal health care campaigns during the earliest years of the People's Republic, see Joshua S. Goldstein, "Scissors, Surveys, and Psycho-Prophylactics," *Journal of Historical Sociology* 1, 2 (1998): 153-84; and Hershatter, "Birthing Stories."

38   HCAWF, "1957 nian funü gongzuo zongjie" [Summary of Woman-Work in 1957], 25 February 1958.

39   *Renmin ribao* [People's Daily], 9 March 1956.

40   Ibid., 16 May 1956; ibid., 7, 8, 12 August 1956.

41   Cao, "Guanyu heli zuzhi yu shiyong funü laodongli wenti."

42   Women's Federation reports in the Wenhe County Archives refer to the "three transfers"; reports in the Huoyue and Gaoshan County Archives discuss the practices involved in the three transfers but do not mention the slogan directly. HCAWF, "Huoyue xian 1957 nian zuo hao you'er fuli weisheng gongzuo yijian" [Huoyue County Suggestions on Improving Work on the Living Conditions and Health of Children], 17 April 1957; Wenhe County Archives Women's Federation (hereafter WCAWF), "Minzhu funü lianhehui guanche zhuanqu fugong huiyi zongjie, Wenhe xian fulian hui guanyu guanche zhuanqu fu-gong huiyi mingque qingkuang zongjie huibao" [Summary of the Democratic Women's Federation's Implementation of the Woman-Work Prefecture Meeting, Wenhe County Women's Federation's Clarified Summary Report on the Implementation of the Woman-Work Meeting], 7 April 1957; Gaoshan County Archives Women's Federation (hereafter GCAWF), "Gaoshan xian 1957 funü gongzuo yijian" [Gaoshan County's Suggestions for Woman-Work in 1957], 14 March 1957.

43   "Sitting the month out" is just one example of a custom that predated the Chinese Communist Party but that was subsequently incorporated into the scientific discourses advocated by the Party leadership and medical community. See Harriet Evans, *Women and Sexuality in China: Female Sexuality and Gender since 1949* (New York: Continuum, 1997). It is important to note that the maternalist ethic pervading the mobilization of women during collectivization and the Great Leap Forward did not translate into a pro-natalist policy. In fact, during collectivization the Women's Federation urged families to use prophylactics and to delay childbearing. See Tyrene White, "The Origins of China's Birth Planning Policy," in *Engendering China: Women, Culture, and the State*, ed. Christina K. Gilmartin, Gail Hershatter, Lisa Rofel, and Tyrene White, 250-78 (Cambridge, MA: Harvard University Press, 1994). The nationalist framework within which sexual equality was embedded in the mid- to late 1950s emphasized the quality of offspring over the quantity.

44   Interviewee 32.

45   Interviewee 85.

46   Interviewees 42, 45, 51. An activist and team leader in the same brigade told me how she managed the health of women she led: "Women would stay behind after the village

meetings to talk. The women would say if they had any difficulties – for example, [if they] were menstruating and couldn't work for three days and wanted to request leave. The women would speak with the women's head, and the women's head would speak with me. I wouldn't call her out to work" (interviewee 51).

47 Interviewee 41.

48 HCAWF, "Huoyue xian fulianhui guanyu kaizhan 'wu hao'xuanchuan he heli diaopei shiyong funü laoli de zongjie baogao" [A Summary Report on the Huoyue County Women's Federation's Launching of "Five Goods" Propaganda and the Reasonable Allocation and Use of Women's Labour], 10 April 1957.

49 Interviewees 43 and 52.

50 Interviewee 83.

51 Interviewee 73.

52 Interviewee 82.

53 Interviewee 37.

54 Quanguo fulian funü yanjiusuo, ed., "Zhuanfa Ningxia Huizu Zizhiqu fulian: 'Guanyu funü laodongli baohu qingkuang de diaocha baogao" [Distribution of the Investigative Report from the Ningxia Minority Autonomous Region Women's Federation: "The Situation of Women's Labour Protection"], reprinted in *Zhongguo funü wushi nian* [Fifty Years of Chinese Women] (Beijing: Zhongguo funü chubanshe, 1999 [1959]).

55 WCAWF, "Minzhu funü lianhehui guanche zhuanqu fu-gong huiyi zongjie, Wenhe xian fulianhui guanyu guanche zhuanqu fu-gong huiyi mingque qingkuang zongjie huibao" [Summary of the Democratic Women's Federation's Implementation of the Woman-Work Prefecture Meeting: Wenhe County Women's Federation's Clarified Summary Report on the Implementation of the Woman-Work Meeting], 7 April 1957; HCAWF, untitled [Huoye Women's Federation speech], 9 January 1957.

56 *Huoyue xianzhi*, 392. A 1959 Henan Provincial Women's Federation investigation in Xinfeng County found that, in a brigade of 4,861 people, 4.4 percent of women had suffered a prolapsed uterus. The investigators attributed this problem to old midwifery practices as well as to inappropriate working conditions. Specifically, the investigators concluded that women were either not given enough time to rest after giving birth or had been assigned work that was too heavy for them. See "Guanyu kaizhan nongcun funü zigong tuochui de fangzhi gongzuo de tongzhi" [A Notice Regarding the Commencement of Prevention Work on Prolapsed Uteruses (among) Rural Women], *Funü gongzuo* [Woman-Work] (7 August 1959): 12.

57 For example, one woman I interviewed, a work-point model (i.e., someone who had won recognition for the number of work points she was able to accumulate), was extremely proud of her family's accomplishments during the Great Leap Forward (interviewee 14). But many others harboured great bitterness about their experiences during that time. For a discussion of the contradictory demands placed on women villagers during the Great Leap Forward, see Thorborg, "Chinese Employment Policy in 1949-78"; Manning, "Communes, Canteens, and Crèches"; and Xiaoxian Gao, "'The Silver Flower Contest': Rural Women in 1950s China and the Gendered Division of Labour," *Gender and History* 18, 3 (2006): 594-612.

58 Interviewee 10.

59 Interviewee 31. Other former women's heads who mentioned the importance of struggle and sacrifice in their interviews include 57, 73, 83, 97, and 131.

60 Zhang Lihua, Ru Haitao, and Dong Naiqiang, "Jianguo sishi nian funü tushu gaikuang," [A Survey of Forty Years of Books on Women since the Founding of the State], in *Zhongguo funü lilun yanjiu shinian, 1981-1990* [Ten Years of Research on Chinese Women's Theory, 1981-1990], ed. Xiong Yumei, Liu Xiaocong, and Qu Wen, 592-605 (Beijing: Zhongguo funü chubanshe, 1992), 59. In their major writings and speeches of late 1958 and early 1959, both Cai Chang (chair of the ACWF) and Li Dequan (a senior Women's Federation representative and minister of public health) stressed the importance of

protecting women's health. Cai Chang, for example, suggested that some leaders' thinking about women's health protection was "conflicted," a condition that needed to be rectified. See Cai Chang, "Tigao juewu xue hao benling wei jianshe shehui zhuyi fenyong qianjin" [Raise Consciousness and Study Skills Well in Order to Forge Ahead Courageously in the Construction of Socialism], *Zhongguo funü* [Chinese Women] 18 (1958): 6-11; Cai Chang, "Guanxin funü jiankang baochi wangsheng ganjin" [Take Care of Women's Health in Order to Protect Their Exuberant Spirit], *Zhongguo funü* [Chinese Women] 3 (1959): 1-2; and Cai Chang, "Quanguo fulian Cai Chang zhuxi zai shoudu gejie funü jinian 'san-ba' jie dahui shang de jianghua" [The All China Women's Federation Chair Cai Chang's Speech at the Capital's Women's Meeting Commemorating the "March Eighth" Holiday], *Zhongguo funü* [Chinese Women] 6 (1959): 4.

61 In 1958, Huoyue County had a total of 473 trained midwives and 285 maternity clinics. See *Huoyue xianzhi*, 392. In Wenhe, 115 maternity clinics, 26 maternity stations, and 53 maternity groups were consolidated or newly established in 1959. Altogether, 533 birthing beds were available. See *Wenhe xianzhi* [Wenhe County Annal] (Zhengzhou: Zhongzhou guji chubanshe, 1992), 824.

62 See, for example, *Funü gongzuo*, 7 August 1959.

63 WCAWF, "Minzhu funü lianhehui guanche zhuanqu fugong huiyi zongjie: Wenhe xian fulian hui guanyu guanche zhuanqu fugong huiyi mingque qingkuang zongjie huibao" [Summary of the Democratic Women's Federation's Implementation of the Woman-Work Prefecture Meeting: Wenhe County Women's Federation's Clarified Summary Report on the Implementation of the Woman-Work Meeting], 7 April 1957.

64 Wang Zheng, "Dilemmas of Inside Agitators: Chinese State Feminists in 1957," *China Quarterly* 188 (2006): 913-32.

65 GCAWF, "Gaoshan xian minzhu funü lianhehui (gongzuo jianbao)" [Gaoshan Democratic Women's Federation (Simplified Work Report)], 31 July 1957.

66 Dong Bian, Cai Asong, and Tan Deshan, eds., *Women de hao dajie Cai Chang* [Our Good Elder Sister Cai Chang] (Beijing: Zhongyang wenxian chubanshe, 1992), 312-13; Yang Nanying, ed., *Zhonghua quanguo funü lianhehui sishi nian* [Forty Years of Chinese Women: Forty Years of the All China Women's Federation] (Beijing: Zhongguo funü chubanshe, 1991), 114-15. See also Cai Chang's report to the Central Committee on the disbanding of grassroots women's organizations ("Quanguo fulian dangzu dui xian fulian zuzhi cunzai wenti de yijian") and the Central Committee's response. See also Naihua Zhang, "The All-China Women's Federation, Chinese Women, and the Women's Movement: 1949-1993" (PhD diss., Michigan State University, 1996).

67 Interviewee 61.

68 Andors, *Unfinished Liberation of Chinese Women*.

69 For examples of the process by which labour heroines were produced, see Hershatter, "Local Meanings of Gender and Work"; and Xiaoxian, "'The Silver Flower Contest.'"

70 The Party also targeted more privileged community members, including those who had some form of education. Indeed, despite its desire to mobilize the poorest individuals in a village, the CCP often relied on those with some education. See Anita Chan, Richard Madsen, and Jonathan Unger, *Chen Village under Mao and Deng: The Recent History of a Peasant Community in Mao's China* (Berkeley: University of California Press, 1992).

71 GCAWF, untitled, 1961. This archival document lists women who were active in various leadership and professional positions in 1961, of whom 178 were women's heads.

72 WCAWF, "Xuanju Wenhe xian funü lianhehui disi jie zhixing weiyuan houxuanren mingdan" [The Name List for the Candidates Running for the Fourth Executive Committee for the Wenhe Women's Federation], 22 July 1964.

73 Interviewee 53.

74 Xiu commented on her illiteracy repeatedly throughout our interview. She told me of a time when she had to sign her name on the application of an individual joining the

Party: "I was supposed to sign my name, but I didn't know how [she laughs]. I gave him my chop. He used my chop."

75 During this era, many rural Party leaders, men and women alike, were illiterate. In some cases, illiterate cadres were provided with administrative assistance. A former commune women's head in Gaoshan, for example, began her activism when she was brought in to assist an illiterate commune leader (interviewee 74). Of the twenty-five former women's heads for whom I have data, six were illiterate, four had some literacy training, eight had some primary school education, and four were graduates of primary school.

76 Interviewee 61. Specifically, the interviewee accused Xiu of being superstitious. He also told me a story of how Xiu once became so angry with another villager that she climbed a tree so that she "could continue to yell at them after they retreated to their own yard."

77 *Huoyue xianzhi*, 266, reveals that, while CCP membership among men increased by nearly 10 percent (from 1,770 to 1,958) between 1951 and 1953, women's Party membership declined by 18 percent (from 361 to 295) during those years. It is possible that the anti-corruption campaigns of the period may have aggressively targeted women – who perhaps came under attack for some of the same reasons as did Xiu.

78 Because Liu's husband (interviewee 18) was a good friend of the son of the local landlord, he was unable to become a Party member, although he had served as village head during land reform. The way Liu's husband explained it, he opposed his wife's entry into the Youth League because he was upset that he could not join the CCP or the Youth League himself. Liu's husband also admitted holding some "feudal" attitudes.

79 Like Xiu (and unlike Liu), many women leaders quit their positions because they could no longer withstand the criticism, taunts, and even beatings they received when they returned home. One Huoyue women's head (interviewee 31) remarked: "There were also some women cadres who once they got married had [to face] their mother-in-law. If something came up, they would go out and then would get criticized when they came home. These women would [have to] quit. In my situation, two old people supported me. I had six kids and never had to give up my work."

80 Interviewees 31 and 65.

81 Fourteen discussed their leadership experience in positive terms, four with some ambivalence, and two negatively.

82 HCAWF, "Huoyue xian funü ganbu zhengfeng xunlianban zongjie" [A Summary of the Rectification Training Class of Women Cadres in Huoyue County], 24 October 1950.

83 GCAWF, "Gaoshan xian minzhu funü lianhehui (gongzuo jianbao)" [Gaoshan Democratic Women's Federation (Simplified Work Report)], 31 July 1957.

84 GCAWF, untitled [list of women active in various leadership and professional positions], 1961.

85 For discussions of the impact of *biaoxian* on relations of authority in the countryside, see Jean Chun Oi, "Communism and Clientelism: Rural Politics in China," *World Politics* 37, 2 (1985): 238-66.

86 Hershatter, "Local Meanings of Gender and Work," 87.

87 Friedman et al., *Chinese Village, Socialist State.*

88 Gilmartin, *Engendering the Chinese Revolution*; Qiu Jin, *The Culture of Power: The Lin Biao Incident in the Cultural Revolution* (Stanford: Stanford University Press, 1999); Helen Praeger Young, *Choosing Revolution: Chinese Women Soldiers on the Long March* (Urbana: University of Illinois Press, 2001).

89 Kampwirth, *Women and Guerrilla Movements*, 6; Jocelyn S. Viterna, "Pulled, Pushed, and Persuaded: Explaining Women's Mobilization into the Salvadoran Guerrilla Army," *American Journal of Sociology* 112, 1 (2006): 1-45.

90 Interviewee 73.

91 Subsequent discussions in 2004 revealed, however, that the early support Lin received from her parents-in-law was subsequently withdrawn. Lin eventually separated from her in-laws and established a residence of her own with her son.

92   Interviewee 33.
93   In six other cases, the in-laws were relatively neutral regarding the activities of their daughter-in-law. A total of five of the women's heads described either conflict within their marital family over their leadership or their in-laws' direct opposition to it.
94   Norma Diamond, "Household, Kinship, and the Status of Women in Taitou Village, Shandong Province," in *Agricultural and Rural Development in China Today*, ed. Randolph Barker and Beth Rose, 78-96 (Ithaca: International Agricultural Program, New York State College of Agricultural Life Sciences, Cornell University, 1983); Ellen R. Judd, "Niangjia: Chinese Women and Their Natal Families," *Journal of Asian Studies* 48, 3 (1989): 525-44.
95   Interviewee 24.
96   Interviewee 20.
97   Interviewee 10.
98   Interviewee 83.
99   Ibid.
100 Interviewee 32.
101 Interviewee 31.
102 Interviewee 114 (emphasis mine).
103 Zhang's brother-in-law told me that, while women suffered too much during the Great Leap Forward, he felt that it did benefit them in some ways, raising their status domestically, politically, and economically.
104 I have suggested elsewhere that Zhang, like many other local leaders, may have favoured friends and close relatives with special treatment. See Manning, "Communes, Canteens, and Crèches."
105 I discuss the nostalgia of local Women's Federation leaders for the mobilization of women in Manning, "Making a Great Leap Forward?"
106 It is important to note the ambiguity in Zhang's usage of the terms "old days," "old society," and "new society." When Zhang uses the phrase *lao ri lai*, she is drawing on a colloquial expression for "back in the day" – in this context, the time of irrigation mobilizations prior to and during the Great Leap Forward. But she often uses the terms *jiu shehui* ("old society") and *xin shehui* ("new society") to mark the historical break between the time before and after liberation. While Hershatter has noted that some farmers have begun to use *xin shehui* with regard to the reform era, I interpret Zhang as referring to the change after 1949. See Hershatter, "Local Meanings of Gender and Work."
107 Interviewee 37.

4 "The Grain Problem Is an Ideological Problem": Discourses of Hunger in the 1957 Socialist Education Campaign

Felix Wemheuer

In September of 1957, the Chinese Communist Party launched the Socialist Education Campaign to crack down on peasant resistance to the grain policy and to extend the Anti-Rightist Campaign to the countryside. Over the course of this campaign, food became a highly politicized topic. The *People's Daily* declared that the grain problem was an "ideological problem" (*sixiang wenti*): the peasants had enough to eat, but some of them were pretending to be hungry so that they could reduce the amount of grain they sold to the state or so that they could request food aid. The CCP attacked such behaviour as selfish and capitalist. This chapter shows the importance of the Socialist Education Campaign as a significant historical backdrop to the Great Leap Forward and the famine.

I draw on the Chinese press and internal party magazines during the Socialist Education Campaign in the summer and autumn of 1957 to analyze discourses about food and hunger. I begin with a brief look at Foucault in order to rethink the campaigns of the Mao era as discourses. In the second part of the chapter, I describe the reasons for and the aims driving the Socialist Education Campaign. In the case study section, I discuss the main narrative frames of both the government and peasants with regard to food. Next I analyze the influence that the campaign had on the way in which the state handled the problems of hunger and famine aid and, in so doing, demonstrate how the questions of food and hunger were linked to criticisms of social injustice. I look specifically at the preferential treatment city dwellers received under the socialist regime and discuss how the topic of hunger became a battlefield between peasants and the socialist state. In the final section, I evaluate the impact of the politicization of hunger on the Great Leap Forward (1958-61).

The Campaign as Discourse
Apter and Saich describe Yan'an as a discourse community and the rectification campaign of 1942 as a discourse that helped to establish the

master narrative and the myths of Maoism.[1] Schoenhals shows the importance of formalized language for ideological control in the People's Republic of China.[2] Following these earlier scholars and, specifically, Foucault, I understand the campaigns in the earliest years of the PRC as discourses whose purpose was to establish the truth by defining right and wrong statements and setting taboos.[3]

Foucault emphasizes the relationship between discourse and power. According to Foucault, a discourse produces rules and disciplines what can be said. A statement will only be considered true if its fits into the rules of the discourse. Consequently, the discourse produces power because it defines the truth.[4] Establishing prohibitions, taboos, exclusions, and borderlines that define what falls within the discourse is a very complicated process in a pluralist society. This is because the "discourse police" are much less visible than they are in an authoritarian society such as the PRC. Even for a one-party dictatorship it is not enough simply to define the truth. Indeed, the statements and policies have to be explained and justified. The CCP, reacting to the fact that the discourses of the Hundred Flower Campaign of the spring of 1957 had spun out of control, published long lists during the Anti-Rightist Campaign to define which statements were inside the socialist discourse and which belonged to the anti-socialist camp. By defining what was wrong and right and assigning political labels, the CCP was able to repeatedly structure all of Chinese society.

As Mao pointed out, the CCP needed feedback and criticism to improve its work style and to keep contact with the masses.[5] In order to avoid an atmosphere of fear in which no one would be willing to speak openly, in early 1957 Mao differentiated contradictions between "us and the enemy" and contradictions among the people. As a consequence, the Party sought to define the parameters of the socialist discourses. In his lecture "The Order of the Discourse," Foucault uses the rules regarding who could participate in a discourse and who could not as an example of a procedure of control.[6] A former landlord could not enter the socialist discourse, for example, because, based on her/his class label, she/he was not qualified. If the masses wanted to speak in this discourse, they had to learn to use the language of the Party and to invest in the symbolic capital of a good class label such as "poor peasant" or "worker."[7] With the commencement of the Anti-Rightist Campaign and the Socialist Education Campaign, however, a good class status was no longer protection against repression.

The 1957 Socialist Education Campaign and the Crisis in the Countryside

Julia Strauss describes the campaigns in the early 1950s as part of a successful regime consolidation.[8] In the PRC, the official Party historiography evaluated the period from 1949 to 1956 as golden years characterized by the successful construction of socialism. Although this idea could be questioned,[9] 1957 was a striking turning point in the history of New China. The rule of the CCP went through a serious legitimacy crisis and was challenged by intellectual dissident and peasant resistance in the aftermath of the revolts in Hungary and Poland. Jean-Luc Domenach describes the situation as a social crisis of Chinese society.[10] In the spring of 1957, a great wave of worker strikes rolled across Shanghai,[11] and university students also went on strike. The Hundred Flower Campaign spun out of control, and many leading intellectuals questioned the rule of the Party.

During the winter of 1956 and the summer of 1957, a great number of peasants tried to resist the collectivization of agriculture in the countryside. Even Mao Zedong himself admitted that high-ranking cadres had lost faith in the idea of collective agriculture.[12] Hundreds of thousands withdrew from the collectives (*tui she*), slaughtered livestock, and sabotaged the state's grain purchase.[13] Compared to the Soviet Union, however, the collectivization of agriculture in China was relatively peaceful. Authors such as Yu Lin explain the success as a consequence of a stronger implementation of the Party state in the villages, tighter social control through the *Hukou* system, and a successful legitimating discourse.[14]

The CCP drew on the Anti-Rightist Campaign to wage a counter-attack against intellectual dissidence; indeed, starting in July 1957, the CCP focused on the cities to punish critical intellectuals. Over the course of the next few months, some 550,000 intellectuals were labelled "rightist" and were sent to the countryside to be re-educated.[15] At the beginning of the campaign, Mao Zedong estimated that there were four thousand rightists in China. The question of which dynamic caused the radicalization and "overdrawing" of the campaign is still open. It seems safe to say, however, that the CCP feared that rightists might raise their voices in the interests of the peasants and thus unify the anti-socialist forces of city and countryside.[16] The Chinese scholar Sun Dongfang points out that the Socialist Education Campaign shifted the spirit of the Anti-Rightist Campaign to the countryside and, in some places, even led to acts of terror being committed against the peasants.[17] While a fair amount of scholarship focuses on the Anti-Rightist Campaign and its intellectual victims, both Western and Chinese scholars have largely ignored the Socialist Education Campaign in the countryside.

The shift in focus to the countryside began on 8 August 1957, when the Central Committee decided to launch the Socialist Education Campaign and to integrate the entire rural population into the Anti-Rightist Campaign. This campaign would last for four months. In the resolution on the

Socialist Education Campaign, the Central Committee explained: "Besides the criticism against the statements and actions of the bourgeois rightist in the cities, the launching of a great debate in the countryside is absolutely necessary."[18] Political education in the Socialist Education Campaign focused on the question of collectivization, the state grain purchase, the relations between peasants and workers, the need for the campaign to wipe out counter-revolutionaries, and respect for the laws and regulations of the central government.[19] The aim of the "great debate" (*dabianlun*) was the initiation of a "two-line struggle" (*liang tiao luxian douzheng*) between socialism and capitalism. The campaign aimed to attack the reactionary positions of "bad" elements, such as landlords, counter-revolutionaries, and rich peasants; to criticize the capitalist thoughts and tendencies of the rich middle-level peasants; and to educate the rest of rural society. To emphasize the success of the collectivization, the Central Committee issued an order that "speaking bitterness" sessions should be held, at which the peasants could speak publicly about life before and after liberation and collectivization. At the same time, the state council decided to prohibit the sale of agricultural products (which were included in the state purchase) on the open market.[20]

In this context, the term "great debate" is a grave misnomer. Indeed, peasants knew that their comments regarding collectivization and state grain purchase could only be framed in terms of socialism versus capitalism. If the people were neither brave enough nor stupid enough to speak openly, the cadres would simply attack statements that they had made before the beginning of the campaign.

Labelling the Enemy and Dividing the People

Regarding the campaigns of the early 1950s, Julia Strauss argues that the mobilization process worked very well when the targeted enemies were clearly visible and the goals of the state had widespread public support.[21] Compared to the land reform or the campaign against counter-revolutionaries, the Socialist Education Campaign attacked statements rather than a particular and clearly defined group of people. The outcome of the campaign shows that it was very difficult to clearly define the campaign's targeted enemies.

The Central Committee ordered that peasants and workers not be labelled as rightists. And this, perhaps, is the main reason why the Socialist Education Campaign is not linked to the Anti-Rightist Campaign in research. With this decision, taken on 4 September 1957, the Central Committee revoked the labelling of peasants and workers who had already been attacked as rightists. According to this decree, while capitalist "thinking" should be attacked, peasants and workers should not wear the rightist cap. Regarding the "four bad elements," the document said, if someone had already been labelled as a rightist, then her or his original bad status could be restored. The decree also stated that such people should be referred to as rightists.[22]

On 17 September 1957, the political department of the People's Liberation Army (PLA) instructed the cadres to differentiate between three wrong positions in the Socialist Education Campaign:

> Rightists are people who reject collectivization and the state grain purchase. They overestimate the temporary problems in the countryside. [They accept] the capitalist ideology of the rich middle-level peasants who prefer the individual economy and demand the expansion of the free market and the rise in prices of agricultural products. [They are] people who take this view and have the illusion that the differences between city and countryside cannot be eliminated in a short period of time. The rightists could easily exploit these people.

The PLA report also found that some people were unsatisfied with the work style of the rural cadres. Most of their objections were valid, the report stated, but their criticism was biased because they exaggerated temporary problems.[23] The Central Committee ordered the political department to isolate and attack the rightists, but, at the same time, it emphasized that it was important not to identify soldiers as rightists.

We can only speculate as to why the Party finally decided against labelling rightists in the countryside. One reason might be that the labelling of the people in the countryside was originally based on class status, which was defined during the land reform. According to the official policy and the land reform law of 1950, class status was based on economic criteria of exploitation rather than on political behaviour. The category "bad element" (*huaifenzi*) was categorized as moral because it was used for thieves, hooligans, or corrupt persons. In contrast, class labels played a less important role in the cities. During the Anti-Rightist Campaign, the Party drew on political criteria to identify a member of a work unit as a rightist, middle rightist, or centrist. A new political labelling of the rural population would have downplayed the role of the economic class labels that were an important instrument for state control of the peasants.

Despite the decision to forbid the labelling of rightists in the countryside, intellectuals and high- or middle-ranking cadres who questioned the agricultural policies of the Party could be punished with this "bad" label. A 15 October 1957 communiqué from the Central Committee on the standards to be used in the labelling of rightists stipulated resistance against the state grain purchase and statements that alienated peasants from workers as two of the definitions of rightism.[24]

The Party published a multitude of articles and held thousands of meetings in 1957 to establish "the truth" about the situation in the countryside and, thus, to try to reclaim control over the Socialist Education Campaign's discourse. Ironically, however, the campaign's discourse would come to reflect the grievances and resistance of villagers and intellectuals with regard to the agrarian policy of the CCP. When the Party attacked incidences of peasant resistance in the public media, for example, it spread the notion of resistance across the whole country. Taking these phenomena into consideration, it could be said that the official discourse included, or even produced, resistance. This might be why, in some cases, the Party decided not to publicly attack dissenting views.

Coping with Violence

Nearly every political campaign in the 1950s and early 1960s led to beatings or even killings. In the mobilization phase of a campaign, the CCP leadership did not want to pour cold water on the masses and activists. After the violence had spun out of control, the leadership passed resolutions to stop "unhealthy tendencies" and to rectify the movement. As we will see below, using violence to keep the "enemies" outside the socialist discourse was an outcome of the campaign rather than its main goal.

It is difficult, drawing on sources currently available, to estimate the extent of this terror. Local examples are only able to provide an impression of the shapes of the conflicts. In the summer of 1957, *Neibu cankao* (Internal Reference) reported various violent conflicts between local cadres and peasants. For example, in Guangdong Province, the state security forces opened fire on rioting peasants.[25] In Linhai County in Zhejiang Province, the army was sent in to stop peasants from resisting the collectives and the procurement policy.[26] In some places, peasants beat up the village cadres after they withdrew from the collectives.[27]

The Socialist Education Campaign was an opportunity for the cadres to strike back and crack down on the peasant resistance. In Guangdong Province, over sixteen thousand people were arrested and convicted on charges in the course of the campaign.[28] In November of 1957, the *People's Daily* criticized the introduction of a household responsibility system (the fixing of farm output quotas for each household) (*baochan daohu*) in Yongjia County in Zhejiang Province as a restoration of the capitalist small farmer economy. The agrarian system, which was implemented nationwide after 1982, was a crime during the Socialist Education Campaign. The struggle sessions against villagers were often violent. For example, in Qingyuan County in Hebei Province, the cadres beat over 230 villagers. In Xianyang County in Shaanxi Province, seventy-nine villagers were tied up and beaten. Over 643 villagers were struggled against in Yiliang County in Yunnan Province: 102 were beaten, and fifteen killed themselves.[29] Most of the victims were villagers of lower-class status, including poor peasants who had questioned collectivization or the grain policy.

In mid-August, some provincial governments made the decision to stop the violence during struggle sessions. The provincial party committee of Shandong Province instructed cadres to differentiate between anti-socialist statements and peasant discontent. Provincial orders decreed that, during the struggle meeting, no one was to be beaten or offended.[30] After 4 September, when the Party ruled against labelling workers and peasants as rightists, the central government emphasized that the political struggles of the Socialist Education Campaign should take non-violent forms. Deng Xiaoping, then general secretary of the Party, stated that the cadres should use their mouths but not their fists during the "great debate" and the struggle meetings.

Hunger as an Ideological Problem

In his short essay about needs, Adorno reminds us that food is a political and social issue.[31] The question of what people accept as food, and how many calories are required to survive, is answered differently in different societies and cultures.[32] In traditional Chinese culture, food is very important and an absolute value.[33] Gang Yue and Judith Farquhar have shown that, since the 1930s, food metaphors have played an important role in both communist propaganda and literature. Social inequality was often expressed in terms of eating and drinking.[34] In these narratives, the CCP represented the hungry peasantry's desire for food and justice.

After the victory of the revolution and the formation of the PRC in 1949, the Party moved its base of power from the countryside to the cities. On the one hand, the CCP promised the Chinese people that no one would starve to death under its leadership; on the other hand, it called upon the people to tighten their belts in the effort to construct socialism and engage in industrialization. As a result, the state constantly reminded its citizens to save grain and not to waste food. In the 1950s, the Chinese government knew that the food problem was far from being solved and that the country suffered from a lack of grain. Until the 1980s, over 80 percent of the consumption in the countryside consisted of grain. The majority of people who lived in rural areas could only consume meat and eggs once or twice a month.

The importance of the state grain purchase must be emphasized. The state monopoly of purchase and marketing played a central role in economic construction. The peasants were forced to sell their products to the state for less than their market value. This "exploitation" of the villages financed the construction of industry. Indeed, worker wages could be maintained at a relatively low level. China was able to import industrial products from the Soviet Union in exchange for the export of agricultural products. Walker demonstrates that this system, with its uneven agricultural production, was also used to keep some kind of balance among the inner Chinese provinces.[35] The state, for example, could use its monopoly of grain to help famine areas. Yet the contradiction in this system is quite clear: if the state allowed the villagers to raise their level of consumption, the speed of industrialization would have to decrease.

It is here that we can begin to understand the role played by the state's discourse on hunger, which surrounded the grain policy during the Socialist Education Campaign. In 1957, provinces such as Hebei, Henan, and Shangdong were struck by natural disasters. As a result of these events and peasant resistance, the state could not fulfill its grain quotas. Grievances regarding hunger were widespread in the countryside. Before the Socialist Education Campaign, the internal periodical *Neibu cankao* published many of these grievances with no political comment or evaluation.

For example, in January 1957, the agriculture and trade section of the *People's Daily* received many letters from readers who complained about the bitterness of peasant life and about hunger. The majority of these letters came from the provinces of Henan and Hebei and were not written by peasants but by cadres and workers. For example, a delegate from a factory in Shanghai reported, upon returning from a trip to his home village in Hebei, that the peasants were afraid that the road to collectivization would be paved with hunger.[36] The cooperatives gave only thirty pounds of grain per month to their members. The cadres did not care whether people lived or died. The peasants said that they had only three choices: to run to the cities, to organize food by themselves, or to wait until they starved to death. One peasant said that the situation was even worse than it had been in the old society because the Republican government at least sent aid during a natural disaster in 1917. A soldier from Zhejiang Province pointed out that the peasants would not understand the grain procurement policy because it meant that the government exported grain to Russia while the Chinese people did not have enough to eat. In Henan Province, peasants even made up a sarcastic jingle: "Chairman Mao is really good, everyone is hungry" (*Mao zhuxi zhen shi hao, renren chi bu bao*).

With the beginning of the Socialist Education Campaign, complaints about the agricultural cooperatives and state purchasing policies became a question of socialism versus capitalism. An article in the *People's Daily* in August issued a warning that every village cadre and peasant should fulfill 100 percent of the grain quotas. The article concluded that strict control of consumption and saving grain are questions of whether you are walking the socialist road or not and whether you love the country or not.[37] The author asked how the urban population, the army, and the people in disaster areas would be fed if the quotas were not met. As a consequence, the question of whether or not the peasants had enough to eat became highly politicized. The *People's Daily* declared that the grain problem was really an ideological problem. As an example, one of its articles criticized the peasants of You County from Hunan Province for complaining that eight hundred to nine hundred *jin* of sorghum were not enough.[38] According to the article, except for a small minority of peasants who really did not have enough to eat, the others pretended to lack grain out of selfish interests. Furthermore, village and cooperative cadres were driven by a selfish departmentalism and helped the peasants to hide grain. For instance, after the education of the grassroots cadres in Cang County in Hebei Province, over 100,000 *jin* of hidden grain were found.

These kinds of reports regarding false complaints about hunger were largely published in magazines such as *Liangshi* (Grain), *Nongcun gongzuo* (Political Work in the Villages), the periodical of the PLA *Bayi zhazhi* (Journal of 1 August), and *Neibu cankao*. The Party established a discourse narrative based on these complaints. Forms of peasant resistance, such as "to report less grain, to divide secretly" (*manchan sifen*), "to divide more, record less" (*duofen, shaobao*), "to record less, take more" (*shaobao, duona*), "false screams" (*jiahan*), and so on were disparaged and attacked.

During the Socialist Education Campaign, Party officials forced peasants and cadres to undertake self-criticism if they were accused of pretending to be hungry. An example of an article pertaining to this ritual, a report about the "great debate" in the Anle cooperative in Anhui Province, shows how the state tried to stop the criticism of poor nutrition. During the debate, "bad elements" claimed that the grain rations were lower than they had been before liberation, that the peasants did not have enough to eat because of state grain procurement and the collectivization of agriculture.[39] The cadres organized "speaking bitterness" sessions to encourage the peasants to remember how much worse the situation was before 1949 and to educate everybody. At these speaking bitterness meetings, poor and middle-level peasants described their bitter life under the rule of the landlords.

They also blamed themselves for their demands for more grain: "If everyone would be like us, the workers, the army, and the soldiers would have
hungry stomachs."[40] The report argued that the grain ration could not be
improved that year. The peasants of one cooperative consumed 280 *jin* of
grain per person in 1956. During the great debate of the Socialist Education Campaign, they had to engage in self-criticism for this "waste" of grain.

The Question of Famine Aid and the Demands of the Peasants

According to Chinese tradition, the state is responsible for assisting peasants in the event of natural disaster, and it must build up a grain storage
system to prevent starvation. Peasants used this moral economy to emphasize their demands for higher grain rations. In 1953, and again in 1955,
the Party faced the problem of the villagers having overestimated the results
of natural disasters to pressure cadres to obtain food relief aid for them.[41]
The Anti-Rightist Campaign had a large impact on the procurement policies of the state because the minister for industry and grain, Cao Naiqi,
was labelled as a rightist. The new leadership of the grain bureau stated:
"We will definitely not withdraw our forces, until complete victory" (*bu
huo quansheng, jue bu shoubing*).[42] This saying became the motto of the
Anti-Rightist Campaign on the grain front. As a result, even provinces hit
by disasters, such as Shandong, had to fulfill their grain quotas.

The discourse during the Socialist Education Campaign shows how the
government tried to curb the demands of the peasants in disaster areas.
The state did not fully refuse its responsibility to help those living in disaster areas, but it pointed out that these areas must "provide for and help
[them]selves by engaging in production." According to this line of thinking, villagers should tighten their belts before requesting food aid from the
state. For example, a report about Shandong in *Liangshi* said that youth
dissatisfaction caused difficulties for the state when it informed peasants
that their grain rations were being cut back to six hundred grams per day.
The author argued that six hundred grams per day translates into 274 *jin*
per year and, supplemented with some vegetables, would be enough to
survive. In Dingtao County, the peasants were not accustomed to eating
wild herbs, but the chairman of the Bureau for Commerce and Trade
himself organized them to pick wild herbs in the fields and to change their
habits.[43] The article emphasized that the government should provide aid
for disaster areas but that grain should not be blindly supplied to the peasants as the supply situation was difficult.

In an instruction delivered on 18 October 1957, the Party committee
of Shandong Province warned that peasants would freeze, starve to death,

or run away if the political work of the Party did not raise awareness regarding "providing for and helping oneself by engaging in production" and reducing grain rations.[44] The provincial newspaper *Dazhong ribao* (Masses Daily) argued that it would be possible to fulfill the quotas in light of the victory in the two-line struggle against capitalist elements. According to the paper, the grain question should be the centre of political education during the Socialist Education Campaign.[45]

The Chinese government expected that the peasants and local cadres would trust it to fix reasonable grain quotas. An article in *Liangshi* acknowledged mistakes in the past, especially in 1954-55, but blamed local cadres for them. It was because of these that peasants did not have enough to eat. The article also noted that, in three counties in Guangxi Province, over three hundred people starved to death. According to this article, everyone knew that the government took these kinds of mistakes very seriously but that the "boundless ocean" of the small and unstable production of the peasants was hard to control. Furthermore, the state lacked experience in grain purchase. As a result, the problem of "surpassing the quotas" was unavoidable.[46] In the case of one incidence of starvation (*esi shijian*) in Guangxi, the provincial, the district, and the county governments took disciplinary action against the responsible cadres. The author asks, rhetorically: "Did any dynasty in history ever protect the interests of the peasants with such a strict attitude?"

The CCP promised to prevent famines in the aftermath of natural disasters, but, at the same time, it was afraid that peasants would use the fear of starvation to emphasize their own demands. The chairman of the grain bureau of Shanxi Province criticized local cadres who were afraid to cut grain rations in famine-afflicted areas because the peasants might make trouble or withdraw from the collectives. These local cadres argued: "If a [situation such as the] Guangxi Incident occurs, then the higher authorities will be responsible."[47] The Party felt that villagers could extort grain from state stores by using the argument of imminent famine. It was not easy for the state to accurately gauge the seriousness of the supply situation.

Two years before the Great Leap Famine, it is very striking that the government treated three hundred deaths as a serious problem and punished the responsible cadres. In 1957, despite the ongoing Anti-Rightist Campaign, the government was still able to handle the famine in Guangxi.[48] Although the topics of hunger and famine became highly politicized in 1957, the internal news system still functioned better than it would during the Great Leap Forward. In *Neibu cankao*, we find more reports about starving peasants in 1957 than in the entire two-year period between 1959 and 1960.

Peasant Grievances: State Discrimination and Food Availability in Rural China

Another very important discourse during the Socialist Education Campaign focused on the disparity between the cities and the countryside. In debates dating back to the 1990s regarding the relationship between urban and rural China, the term "dual society" (*eryuan shehui*) is used to describe the existence of two different societies.[49] While urban areas were subsidized by the state, rural areas relied on their own resources and production. The so-called dual social system had already been established by the early 1950s. In 1955, a supply system involving ration cards was introduced in urban areas. The state council announced several regulations in 1953, 1955, 1956, and 1957, before establishing a strict *hukou* system in 1958 in order to restrict the rural population from moving to cities in search of employment.[50] In 1955, the state also decided to divide its population between urban citizens and rural citizens. As a result, villagers became second-class citizens, a status that continues to this day. They do not have the same rights as urban dwellers when it comes to the social security system, health insurance, food supply, marriage, freedom of movement, planned parenthood, education, or military service.[51]

Nevertheless, the privileges of the cities were not left unquestioned. In 1953, Liang Shuming, former intellectual and leader of the Rural Reconstruction Movement in the Republican era, commented that the workers lived in the ninth heaven and the peasants in the ninth hell. After liberation, the CCP forgot the peasants and the countryside. According to Liang, the biggest problem was not a shortage of resources but, rather, unequal distribution. Mao attacked Liang in one of the most aggressive speeches of his life. He warned that the adjustment of urban and rural wages would lead to the ruin of industry and to the decline of the state. He questioned Liang's right to speak on behalf of the peasants and abused Liang with all the terms that the CCP vocabulary had to offer.[52]

The topic became popular again in the autumn of 1957. In no other period of the Mao era did the Party have to justify the privileges of the cities in so many articles. The complaints of the villagers who came under attack were largely concerned with hunger and food. The question of "who feeds whom" played a very important role in CCP propaganda during the revolution. At that time, CCP propaganda held that the peasants should assume the reins of power because it was they who fed the landlords and rich peasants. The Party emphasized that the Red Army and, later, the PLA would not take any free food but, rather, would plant grain themselves. In 1957, the question of who feeds whom again became important but in a very different way than it had before. The Party had to explain why it also would have advantages for the peasants to deliver grain to the urban population. Once again, discourses against social injustice were riddled with food and hunger metaphors.

The reports in *Neibu cankao* demonstrate that peasants and rural cadres were quite dissatisfied with the preference the grain supply system showed towards the workers. Even after Mao's harsh attack on Liang Shuming in 1953, complaints about discrimination against the peasants continued to be widespread. Most intellectuals who spoke up during the Hundred Flower Campaign did not make the peasant question a central feature of their discourse. Only a few low-ranking intellectuals raised their voices on behalf of the peasants.

One of the most interesting documents consists of a program that four students from the Institute for Agriculture of the Southwest developed and that was reprinted without comment in *Neibu cankao* in June 1957 during the Anti-Rightist Campaign. The four students requested that both the central government and Mao Zedong acknowledge the revolutionary character of the peasants. They criticized the characterization of peasants as selfish and backward, while workers were celebrated as the most revolutionary class.[53] In contrast to the official view, the students considered the peasants to be the most revolutionary class in China. The peasants had tightened their belts in the interests of socialist construction and ate less rice and meat than did the workers. The students demanded to know why the workers had these privileges and why they ate better than the peasants. Given this situation, they argued, the peasants should have the right to found their own political party. The students also criticized the idea that the migration of peasants to the cities would burden the worker-peasant alliance because its motivation was the great gap in the standard of living between city and countryside. The students called for higher prices for agricultural products, expanded plots of land for private use, reduced rice exports, an increase in rural grain rations, cadre participation in manual labour, practical agricultural production lessons in the agricultural institutes, and sending high-ranking cadres to the countryside so that they might understand the real situation.[54]

I do not know what happened to these students or whether or not they were arrested. Nothing is known about their family backgrounds. Their program questioned orthodox Marxism-Leninism and emphasized the fact that the peasants were the real and primary force of the Chinese revolution, even if the CCP later credited the cities and the workers with this honour. The students were not contesting the historical arguments; rather, they were contesting the idea that the peasants should go hungry to save resources for socialist construction while the workers did not. Some of their demands were Maoist in nature (e.g., that cadres should participate in manual labour). The idea of an independent peasant party or organization, however, differed radically from what was desired by the government. In the context of the Anti-Rightist Campaign, the Chinese government treated demands such as the increase of grain rations and grain prices as a form of sabotage of industrial construction.

While these four students merely made suggestions to the central government, one thousand students from middle schools attacked the county government in Hanyang in Hubei Province on 12 June 1957.[55] In this violent riot, thirteen cadres and twenty-six students were injured. The discrimination that rural students faced in the selection process for the universities played an important role. During their demonstration in front of the government buildings, students shouted slogans such as "abolish the difference between countryside and city in the student selection" and "standardize the selection process nationwide." The county government explained that counter-revolutionary forces had misused student grievances. The majority of protesters were of peasant origin, and the most violent rioter was the son of a worker with a poor peasant family background.[56]

It was not only students with peasant origins who felt that the economic system was unfair but also village-level cadres. During the Socialist Education Campaign, criticism of the discrimination against the rural population came under attack. In *Neibu cankao,* critical reports of such "counter-revolutionary" views were published with increasing frequency. Grievances pertaining to the privileges of the workers, especially with regard to the food supply system, were now not only published for the purposes of documentation but also as examples of political incorrectness.

A report regarding cadre conferences in Hubei Province criticized those rural cadres who supported incorrect and reactionary opinions during the "great debate." The cadres demanded the abolition of state-purchased grain, pointing out that the Soviet Union had already abolished the system.[57] The report accused local cadres of using baseless excuses to argue for the downsizing of the grain quotas. One village official said that the CCP should abolish the state grain purchase so that the peasants would have enough to eat. In some regions, the cadres demanded the government raise the grain ration to eight hundred or even one thousand *jin* per person per year. One village official warned: "If the grain ration does not rise, the masses will make trouble, and I will lead it."[58] A cadre of the women's association complained that the pigs had more to eat than the people.

And so the preferential treatment of the cities was called into question. Some people argued that the grain, oil, and meat policies of the state made it clear that the Party loved the cities and workers but that it treated the countryside and the peasants unfairly (*kuidai nongcun he nongmin*). A cadre said: "The industrial products are expensive, but the agricultural products are cheap. The workers get a fixed salary per month, but the peasants are suffering every day. The workers and cadres enjoy all the fruits of production. The Communist Party just takes care of the cities and workers and does not care about the countryside and the peasants at all."[59] One cadre pointed out that soldiers were allocated more cloth than other people, while another village official made a remark reminiscent of Liang Shuming's 1953 criticism: "Life in the cities is like paradise, [while] life in the villages is like hell. The peasants are not human beings."[60]

The Hubei report demonstrates that some rural cadres spoke up for the interests of the countryside. Despite the fact that the cadres had privileges, they saw themselves as part of the villages and as victims of the state policies of urban preference. The cadres were under pressure from both sides, the state and the peasants, because they had to execute the unpopular grain policies in the villages.

Peasants launched a similar criticism of the dual society. In *Neibu cankao*, a journalist wrote about the "great debate" in an agricultural cooperative in Qingpu city. During the debate, old peasants complained that 520 *jin* of grain per year were not enough to live on. The workers in the city received a ration of forty to fifty *jin* per month. When supply is tight, the peasants noted, the workers could buy *mantou* (steamed bread). In contrast, the villagers had no money to pay for extra food. All that peasants could do was to depend on the supply provided by the cooperative.[61] An older, upper-middle-level peasant argued that, while workers received seven hundred *jin* of grain per year for eight hours of work, peasants had to work from dusk until dawn. A new lower-middle-level peasant even attacked the PRC's entire social security system. He questioned why the workers should enjoy health insurance and other social services, eat in public dining halls, and live in Western-style houses (*yangfang*). The peasants worked much harder, and, as they had to work outside in the fields, their health was dependent on the weather.[62] A peasant woman complained that their situation was even worse than that of women who cleaned the toilets in the streets of cities because the latter got a salary of twenty *yuan* per month and had warm clothes and enough to eat. An older poor middle-level peasant remarked that he pitied young rural men as all of the girls left the villages to look for a husband in the cities, wanting to marry a worker or someone with a cadre background.

Some peasants went beyond complaining and started planning resistance. A rich middle-level peasant argued that the historical foundations of the CCP did not represent the interests of the peasants because it was easier for the workers to unite. He questioned how the workers could lead the country if the peasants refused to sell grain for three years.[63] Based on the experience of the Taiping Revolution, he warned that a revolution would fail without the support of the peasantry. He also pointed out that, after liberation, Mao Zedong moved to Beijing and became a high-ranking bureaucrat, the implication being that Mao could no longer speak as a representative of the peasantry.

The Party Counter-Attacks and Establishes New Taboos on Food and Hunger

Despite the monolithic nature of the CCP's discourse, peasants found unregulated discursive space and took advantage of it. In early 1957, most villagers and city dwellers knew they could not criticize the CCP's agricultural policies because they would be accused of supporting free trade and a market economy. Nor could they reject the state grain purchase without being accused of resisting industrialization. The only possible way for peasants *not* to be excluded from the socialist discourse was to express their criticisms in terms of hunger. By the summer of 1957, the Party leadership felt that this argument had become dangerous. Discourses launched during the Socialist Education Campaign demonstrate how criticism of urban/rural disparity in terms of food could result in a questioning of Party rule. With the argument "who feeds whom," and an emphasis on social injustice, villagers and students attacked the legitimacy of the CCP. Consequently, the Party leadership came to the conclusion that this narrative had to be excluded from the socialist discourse, and it did this by defining criticism of urban privileges as false and wrong. In the tone of its articles, the CCP attempted to establish the "truth" that it did not prefer the cities to the countryside.

Typically, these articles do not mention names, instead using phrases such as "the rightists said." The authors make it clear that criticisms of urban privileges are taboo and that rightists could not in any way speak for the peasants. These articles, which are ideological in nature, use statistics to try to prove that certain opinions are wrong and, in fact, are propaganda created by the enemy. For example, one article, based on an investigation conducted in the city of Baoding in Hebei Province and its rural environment, reports that the income of the workers is twice as much as that of the peasants. However, it explains that these figures mean little because living expenses are much higher in the city. If no natural disasters occurred, the road to collectivization would enable village living standards to catch up with city living standards.[64]

During the Socialist Education Campaign, the *Bayi zazhi* published an entire series under the title "Fair or Not." The "fair-or-not" question is raised in an article written by the political commissar of the "Shao school," who said that the CCP favoured the workers and despised the peasants (*hougong-bonong*). This article served as a negative model and was continuously criticized.

As a result of the politicization of the situation in the countryside, dissenting opinions on it quickly came under attack. During the Socialist Education Campaign, the following statements became taboo, and persons who made them could be criticized or arrested:

"The life of the peasants is bitter."
"The life of the peasants has not improved."
"Collectivization has been implemented in a bad way."
"Collectivization has no advantages."
"The peasants do not have enough to eat."
"The workers live in heaven while the peasants live in hell."
"Grain prices are too low."
"Grain quotas are too high."

Clearly, the CCP was encountering strong opposition to its agrarian policies, especially to its grain policy. If this were not the case, the press would not have published so many articles that attempted to justify Party policies.

With regard to meeting the goals of the Socialist Education Campaign, the CCP was quite successful. It cracked down on peasant resistance to collectivization and halted the retreat of peasants from the collectives. Indeed, it was at this point that the peasants lost the option of leaving the socialist economy.[65] As a result of these measures, the agricultural cooperatives were stabilized, and peasant resistance was forced to assume hidden forms. At the end of 1957, 98 percent of Chinese peasants were organized into socialist collectives, and the crisis of the state grain purchase was solved. In the middle of November 1957, 76 percent of the grain quota of the period between 1957 and 1958 had already been filled.[66]

Despite the apparent success of collectivization, however, the Socialist Education Campaign resulted in serious long-term problems. Scholars such as Frederick Teiwes and Warren Sun (1999) and Gao Huamin (1999) note the important relationship between the Anti-Rightist Campaign and the development of the Great Leap Forward.[67] When famine broke out in 1959, most people were afraid to speak the truth and thus risk being labelled as rightist opportunists. As has now been well documented, the problem of false reporting from below made it difficult for the central government to determine how serious the situation really was.

Despite the CCP's denial of the injustice inherent in the dual society (and its harsh crackdown on its critics), by the end of the Socialist Education Campaign the Party leadership may well have felt that it could no longer ignore some of the arguments put forward by peasants and intellectuals. Pressures internal to China, therefore, may have contributed to the fact that, in 1957, Mao began to question the Soviet way of socialism. In the next section, I discuss the relation between the Socialist Education Campaign and the Great Leap Forward in greater detail.

The Great Leap Forward as a New Deal for the Countryside

In the autumn of 1958, the program of the Great Leap Forward can be seen as both an escape from the legitimacy crisis and a "New Deal" for rural society. In the utopian mood that prevailed after the Beidaihe Conference in August, new discourses on food and urban/rural disparity were established. Instead of defending the status quo, Party propaganda focused on the promise of a new rural life under the system of the People's Communes. The newly established People's Communes were intended to unify industry, agriculture, trade, study, and the military. Abolishing the differences between cities and countryside, manual work and intellectual work, and workers and peasants was a key slogan of the Great Leap.[68] As a result of the steel campaign, peasants became workers, and intellectuals were to be "peasantized" (*zhishifenzi nongminhua*). The newly founded People's Communes promised to bring the welfare state to the villages. It was believed that every commune should establish child-care centres and nursing homes. Model communes in Henan, Hebei, and Shandong introduced a free-supply system for the peasants, through which the peasants in those places were guaranteed free food, clothing, medical care (including pre- and postnatal care), education, housing, and marriage and funeral ceremonies.[69]

During the autumn of 1958, the Party press questioned whether or not the system of distribution according to work performance (*an lao fenpei*) should be replaced by distribution according to need (*an xu fenpei*). The *People's Daily* reported that the villages in Henan Province would complete the grain supply with a wage system. The new distribution system would guarantee the "iron rice bowl" for the peasants and would also save time because it abolished the long discussion pertaining to defining work points and work performance.[70] The leader of the province and radical leftist Wu Zhipu demanded the step-by-step introduction of wages for peasants, which he believed should be similar to those given to urban workers.[71] In 1957, the supply and welfare privileges received by city dwellers had much to do with widespread peasant dissatisfaction. Now the state promised a new equality for those who resided in the countryside.

During the peak of the Great Leap in 1958, the Party had a new solution to the grain problem. With the introduction of public dining halls, the state promised to abolish hunger immediately. The question of "who feeds whom" was to be answered in a new way. The public dining halls took over the management of food and, in some places at the beginning of the Great Leap Forward, instituted an "all-you-can-eat" policy. Mao Zedong used a food metaphor to describe communism: "Eating for free is communism."[72] After a reputed bumper harvest in the summer of 1958, the state established a new discourse focused on the saving of grain (although the discourse focused on the "wasting" of grain did not totally disappear from the public press). The Party press praised the saving of grain, labour, and wood as some of the advantages provided by the public dining halls, thus indicating that eating at the latter was superior to eating at home.[73] The discourse in the Party press focused on how public dining halls served as a way of controlling the supply of food. In Western research, however, the question of dining-hall waste remains a controversial topic. Wen and Chang believe that the waste of food in the public dining halls in the winter of 1958 was a major reason for the famine. Yang Dali rejects this argument, pointing out that the high-water mark of the famine took place in 1960, not in early 1959.

Only a few articles refer to the debates of the Socialist Education Campaign. An article in the *People's Daily* about an investigation of a People's Commune presents a new direction in the narrative depicting the grain problem as ideological. During the summer, "rotten elements" had loafed while working (*mo yanggong*) and complained that they did not have enough to eat. One such person was arrested by state security. After the CCP established the public dining halls, the political consciousness of the peasants improved, and everybody was convinced of the advantages of the new life.[74] The public dining halls were presented as the solution to the "grain problem as an ideological problem." Furthermore, the Party leadership saw public dining halls as key to transforming the ownership structure. An article in the journal *Red Flag* states that, after the public dining halls were established, private plots and private pigs became useless as these halls would now nourish all citizens.[75] Because the public dining halls stored all of the grain for private households, peasants became dependent on the supply of the communes.

How the Topics of Hunger and Famine Were Rendered Taboo

Despite the promise of a new equality between urban and rural society, the Great Leap Forward did not produce a peasant utopia. The government militarized the rural workforce (*laodong junshihua*) in 1958 and led the Chinese peasant in an endless production struggle that has no historical equal. The peasants had to work day and night, following the commands of the production army (*chanyejun*). Villagers quickly learned what it meant when the cadres assumed control of the food. The cadres used the supply system of the public dining halls to discipline and punish people by cutting rations (*kou kouliang*) or even establishing a death ration (*ding siliang*) once famine broke out.[76] The villagers lost their own supply base, and the state was unable to feed them. As Brown notes in Chapter 9 of this volume, the state protected the major cities while millions of peasants starved. The CCP's promise to abolish hunger and eliminate the urban/rural divide was broken.

Although the CCP might have taken heed of some of the criticisms expressed in 1957, the Socialist Education Campaign ended up negatively affecting the way the state dealt with hunger and famine. In the autumn of 1957, the Chinese government came to the conclusion that thousands of peasants pretended to be hungry in order to sabotage state grain policies. It became taboo to express the idea that the peasants were hungry. As noted previously, except for special local cases (such as the famine in Guangxi Province), in 1957 the food supply in the country was certainly limited, but it had not reached the point of resulting in starvation. When real famine struck in 1959, Mao Zedong did not believe that it was a nationwide disaster but, rather, that it was due to some local faults.[77] Perhaps he believed that this crisis was another instance of temporary food shortages, such as had occurred in 1953, 1955, and 1957.[78] Furthermore, the government might have believed that the peasants were expressing false grievances. As previously noted, the topic of hunger had become very sensitive because it was linked to the criticism that held that social injustice was a feature of the urban/rural divide. With the discourses of the Socialist Education Campaign and its definition of what counted as truth, the Party destroyed the tools that could have successfully prevented a nationwide famine before 1958.

During the peak of the famine in 1960, the CCP started new campaigns to save grain and to promote food subsidies (*daishipin*).[79] In October 1960, the citizens of Beijing were forced to publicly recall the bitterness of their lives before liberation.[80] These were the same methods that, during the Socialist Education Campaign, led to the taboo surrounding hunger.

In conclusion, I argue that the campaigns in the Mao era were not only about mass mobilization and the perpetration against the "enemies" of the Party. They also contained a discourse that defined what was true and defined which statements were "wrong" and which were "right." The Socialist Education Campaign of 1957 established the narrative that peasants were pretending to be hungry so that they could sabotage the state grain purchase. Consequently, the CCP treated hunger as a problem of political education and initiated campaigns during which people were required to publicly recall the hunger they had experienced prior to liberation. Without a doubt, the Great Leap Famine demonstrates that discourses can sometimes have deadly consequences.

Notes

1 David Earnest Apter and Tony Saich, *Revolutionary Discourse in Mao's Republic* (Cambridge, MA: Harvard University Press, 1994).
2 Michael Schoenhals, *Doing Things with Words in Chinese Politics* (Berkeley: University of California Press, 1992).
3 Michel Foucault, *Die Ordnung des Diskurses* [The Order of the Discourse] (Frankfurt: Fischer, 2003), 11.
4 Achim Landwehr, *Geschichte des Sagbaren: Eine Einfürung in die Historische Diskursanalyse* [The History of What Can Be Said: An Introduction to Historical Discourse Analysis] (Tübingen: Edition Discord, 2001), 84.
5 Mao Zedong, *Ausgewählte Werke, Band V* [Selected Works, Volume 5] (Beijing: Verlag für Fremdsprachige Literatur, 1977), 464.
6 Foucault, *Die Ordnung des Diskurses*, 26.
7 Xiaojun Zhang, "Land Reform in Yang Village: Symbolic Capital and Determination of Class Status," *Modern China* 30, 1 (2004): 3-45.
8 Julia Strauss, "Editor's Introduction: In Search of PRC History," *China Quarterly* 188 (2006): 862.
9 For a more critical view of the early 1950s, see Jeremy Brown and Paul Pickowicz, *Dilemmas of Victory: The Early Years of the People's Republic of China* (Cambridge, MA: Harvard University Press, 2007).
10 See Jean-Luc Domenach, *The Origins of the Great Leap Forward* (Boulder, CO: Westview Press, 1995).
11 Elizabeth Perry, *Challenging the Mandate of Heaven: Social Protest and State Power in China* (New York: M.E. Sharpe, 2002).
12 Zhonghua renmin gongheguo guojia nongye weiyuanhui bangongting, ed., *Nongye jitihua zhongyao wenjian huibian* [Important Documents Regarding the Collectivization of Agriculture] (Beijing: Zhongyangdangxiao chubanshe, 1981), 665.
13 Gao Huamin, *Nongye hezuohua yundong shimo* [The Whole Story of the Collectivization of Agriculture] (Beijing: Qingnian chubanshe, 1999), 358.
14 Yu Lin, "Why Did It Go So High? Political Mobilization and Agricultural Collectivization in China," *China Quarterly* 187 (2006): 742.
15 Many would remain in the countryside for two decades. See Bo Yibo, *Ruogan zhongda juece yu shijian de huigu (xiuding ben)* [Reflections on Certain Major Decisions and Events] (Beijing: Renmin chubanshe, 1997), 2:618.
16 Zhu Di, *1957: Da zhuanwan zhi mi - zhengfeng fanyou shilu* [1957: The Puzzle of the Great Turn: A True Record of the Rectification and Anti-Rightist Movement] (Taiyuan: Shanxi renmin chubanshe, 1995), 238.
17 Sun Dongfang, "Dui 1957 nongcun shehuizhuyi jiaoyu yundong de lishi kaocha" [Historical Investigation of the Rural Socialist Education Campaign in 1957], *Beijing dangshi* [Beijing Party History] (2006): 11.

18 Zhonggong zhongyang wenxian yanjiushi, ed., *Jianguo yilai zhongyao wenxian xuanbian* [Selected Important Documents since the Founding of the People's Republic of China] (Beijing: Zhongyang wenxian chubanshe, 1996), 10:529.

19 Ibid., 528.

20 Ibid., 531-35.

21 Strauss, "In Search of PRC History," 862.

22 Ye Yongjie, *Fanyoupai shimo* [The Whole History of the Anti-Rightist Campaign] (Wulumuqi: Xinjiang renmin chubanshe, 2000), 2:801.

23 *Bayi Zazhi* [Journal of August 1], 26 September 1957, 1.

24 Ye, *Fanyoupai shimo*, 2:803.

25 *Neibu cankao* [Internal Reference] (hereafter *NBCK*), 17 May 1957.

26 Ibid., 18 May 1957.

27 Sun, "Dui 1957 nongcun shehuizhuyi jiaoyu yundong de lishi kaocha," 11.

28 Dangdai Zhongguo nongye hezuohua bianjishi, ed., *Zhongguo hezuohua lishi ziliao* [Materials Regarding the History of Collectivization] (Beijing: Dangdai Zhongguo nongye hezuohua bianjishi, 1987), 34.

29 Sun, "Dui 1957 nongcun shehuizhuyi jiaoyu yundong de lishi kaocha," 10.

30 Ibid.

31 Theodor W. Adorno, *Soziologische Schriften*, *Band I* [Sociological Writings, Volume 1] (Frankfurt: Suhrkamp Verlag, 2003), 392.

32 See James Vernon, *Hunger: A Modern History* (Cambridge, MA: Belknap Press of Harvard University Press, 2007).

33 Gang Yue, *The Mouth that Begs: Hunger, Cannibalism, and the Politics of Eating in Modern China* (London: Duke University Press, 1999), 33.

34 Judith Farquhar, *Appetites: Food and Sex in Post-Socialist China* (London: Duke University Press, 2002), 36.

35 Kenneth R. Walker, *Food Grain Procurement and Consumption in China* (Cambridge: Cambridge University Press, 1984).

36 *NBCK*, 3 January 1957, 39.

37 *Renmin ribao* [People's Daily], 10 August 1957.

38 Ibid., 5 August 1957.

39 *NBCK*, 13 September 1957, 4.

40 Ibid.

41 Tian Xiquan, "Liangshi gou-xiao zhidu de xingcheng ji qi zai Tanghe xian de yunzuo" [How the System of Unified Purchase and Sale of Grain Was Set Up and How It Was Run in Tanghe County] (PhD diss., Fudan University, 2004).

42 *Liangshi* [Grain], 7 (1957): 2.

43 Ibid., 11 (1957): 4.

44 "Shandong tonggoutongxiao shouce" [Shangdong's Handbook for the State Monopoly for Purchase and Marketing] (Jinan: Shandong sheng liangshiting, 1957), 38.

45 Ibid., 46.

46 *Liangshi* 7 (1957): 4.

47 Ibid. 9 (1957): 4.

48 See *NBCK*, 17 July 1957.

49 Guo Shutian, *Shiheng de Zhongguo: Nongcun chengshihua de guoqu, xianzai yu weilai* [Unbalanced China: The Past, Present, and Future of the Urbanization of the Countryside] (Shijiazhung: Hebei renmin chubanshe, 1990).

50 Xiao Donglian, "Zhongguo eryuan shehuijiegou xingcheng de lishikaocha" [A Historical Investigation of the Dual System of the Chinese Society], *Dangshi yanjiu* [Research in Party History] 1 (2005): 8-11.

51 Ke Jiadong, "Cheng-xiang eryuan shehui shi zenyang xingcheng de?" [How Did the Dual Society Take Shape?], *Shuwu* [Book Room] 5 (2003): http://www.360doc.com/.

52 Mao, *Ausgewählte Werke*, 138.

53 *NBCK*, 19 June 1957, 9.
54 Ibid., 12.
55 Ibid., 22 June 1957, 3.
56 Ibid., 5.
57 Ibid., 17 September 1957, 9.
58 Ibid.
59 Ibid., 14.
60 Ibid., 10.
61 Ibid., 16 September 1957, 8.
62 Ibid., 10.
63 Ibid., 11.
64 *Bayi zazhi*, 24 July 1957, 49.
65 Justin Yifu Lin and Dennis Tao Yang, "On the Causes of China's Agricultural Crisis and the Great Leap Famine," *China Economic Review* 9, 2 (1998): 125-40.
66 Sun, "Dui 1957 nongcun shehuizhuyi jiaoyu yundong de lishi kaocha," 11.
67 Frederick Teiwes and Warren Sun, *China's Road to Disaster: Mao, Central Politicians, and Provincial Leaders in the Unfolding of the Great Leap Forward, 1955-1959* (London: M.E. Sharpe, 1999); Gao, *Nongye huzuohua yundong shimo.*
68 Wu Ren, *Renmin gongshe he gongchanzhuyi* [People's Communes and Communism] (Beijing: Gongren chubanshe, 1958), 19.
69 *Hongqi* 10 (16 October 1958): 5. For more details, see Chapter 5 in this volume.
70 *Renmin ribao*, 29 September 1958.
71 Wu Zhipu, "Lun renmin gongshe" [On the People's Communes], *Xuanchuan jianbao* [Propaganda Presentation], 25 August 1958.
72 Luo Pinghan, *Daguofan: Gonggong shitang shimo* [Eating out of the Big Pot: The History of the Public Dining Halls] (Nanning: Guangxi renmin chubanshe, 2001), 56.
73 *Hongqi* 7 (1 September 1958): 22.
74 *Renmin ribao*, 3 September 1958, 3.
75 *Hongqi* 7 (1 September 1958): 23.
76 Felix Wemheuer, *Steinnudeln: Ländliche Erinnerungen und staatliche Vergangenheitsbewältigung der "Großen Sprung": Hungersnot in der chinesischen Provinz Henan* [Stone Noodles: Rural and Official Memory of the Great Leap Famine in the Chinese Province of Henan] (Frankfurt: Peter Lang, 2007), 161.
77 Thomas B. Bernstein, "Mao Zedong and the Famine of 1959-1960: A Study in Willfulness," *China Quarterly* 186 (2006): 438.
78 Huang Jun, "60 niandai chu liangshi kuifa kunjing xia de chengzhen jingjian renkou: yi Jiangsu sheng wei ge'an" [The Reduction of the Urban Population against the Background of the Lack of Grain in the Early Sixties: Jiangsu Province as an Example], paper from the Second Annual Graduate Seminar on China, Hong Kong, 2006.
79 See Gao Hua in Chapter 7 of this volume.
80 See *NBCK*, 14 October 1960.

5 On the Distribution System of Large-Scale People's Communes

Xin Yi

Translated by Jiagu Richter and Robert Mackie

The purpose of this chapter is to examine the system of distribution (*fenpei zhidu*) implemented in rural communes – a system that combined both free supply (*gongjizhi*) and distribution by wage (*gongzizhi*), during the time of the People's Commune movement.[1] At present, investigations regarding this unique system are dispersed throughout related research articles and teaching materials, but there are very few articles or books specifically devoted to this topic.

According to Bo Yibo, the free-supply system "mainly meant [the provision of] free meals or meals in public canteens [i.e., public dining halls] for commune members." The wage system was limited by economic conditions at the time; therefore, "it contained only negligible elements of a concept of distribution according to work." This distribution system "led to a general decline in commune member productivity and efficiency. This was not solely the problem of a single county or commune. It was an inherent defect in the commune system itself."[2]

Deng Zhiwang analyzes in fine detail the origin, development, and final stages of the commune distribution system. He holds that this distribution system "had mistaken actual egalitarianism for communism" and "caused a tremendous waste of food. It was completely divorced from the actual situation in China and from the level of political consciousness of the people." It was, therefore, doomed to failure.[3]

Luo Pinghan believes that this distribution system was developed to meet the requirements of the new Large-Scale People's Communes. Although the Central Committee did its utmost to popularize and maintain the system, and was convinced it possessed communist elements, the new

This chapter was originally published in Chinese as "Jianlun dagongshe de fenpei zhidu" [On the Distribution System of the Big Commune] in *Zhonggong dangshi yanjiu* [Studies in the History of the CCP] 3 (2007): 22-27. It is reprinted with permission.

system did not account for the reality China was facing and quickly became obsolete.[4]

Besides the theoretical studies mentioned above, some scholars have recently discovered the widespread phenomenon of concealing production and private distribution outside of the formal commune distribution system. Based on his own fieldwork, Gao Wangling demonstrates that, during the period of the People's Communes, there existed a general practice of keeping "outside accounts" ("concealing production and private distribution," "grain theft," "borrowing grain," etc.) in rural areas. These outside accounts made up between 14 percent and 24 percent of total grain statistics kept in official accounts, and they were at their peak during the time of Large-Scale Communes.[5] Commune members' concealment and private distribution of grain was not only a means of opposing[6] the distribution system but also a means of adjusting and supplementing its excessive egalitarianism. The importance of keeping outside accounts for peasants struggling at the subsistence level cannot be understated. Such findings have opened the door for new research possibilities into the distribution system of People's Communes.

Based on the research mentioned above, I seek to demonstrate that there was no nationally consistent model for the distribution system and that it was under constant modification. It developed from a system of distribution according to "necessity" (free distribution of primary necessities) into one of distribution according to work. It was characterized by instability, disunity, low pay, and the pursuit of absolute egalitarianism – an egalitarianism mistaken for communism. Overall, the implementation of the distribution system resulted in a great reduction in productivity in rural areas, fundamentally subverting the existing social order and the driving force behind society. It led directly to the failure of the People's Commune movement and was one of the reasons for the "Three Years of Economic Difficulty."

"Communism Is Paradise, and the People's Commune Is the Bridge"

After the rise of the People's Commune movement, the Central Committee was convinced that People's Communes were the most appropriate organizational means by which to make the transition to communism. Moreover, the free-supply system, widely promoted within the communes, already possessed communist elements. In practice, this distribution system with "communist elements" was, in essence, a system that, free of charge, provided basic necessities such as grain in an egalitarian manner. No doubt, this had a great deal of influence on those peasants who were struggling at a subsistence level.

In the latter half of 1958, national enthusiasm for a "quick transition to communism" resulted in the extension of the distribution system into rural areas throughout the country. At the Beidaihe Conference held in August of the same year, Central Committee resolutions on the establishment of People's Communes in rural areas stated: "The realization of communism in our country is not far off. We should actively exploit the People's Commune model and discover a concrete means by which to make the transition to communism."[7]

At the end of 1958, during the Sixth Plenary Session of the Eighth Central Committee of the Chinese Communist Party, a resolution on several issues concerning People's Communes stated: "At present [we] can predict that People's Communes will speed up the development of socialism in our country and will serve as the best model through which to achieve, firstly, the transition from collective ownership to public ownership in rural areas and, secondly, the transition from a socialist society to a communist one."[8] Evidently, the Central Party planned to exploit People's Communes in order to help with the gradual transition to communism in a relatively economically and culturally underdeveloped China.

There were two means by which the swift transition to communism through People's Communes was achieved. The first was "public" – that is, it involved artificially increasing the degree of public ownership; merging approximately thirty higher agricultural producer cooperatives (HAPCs) into one People's Commune; implementing a unified accounting system within the commune; establishing ownership at the commune level; and preparing for the transition to public ownership and, eventually, communism. The second involved either fully or partially implementing communist distribution principles (i.e., distribution according to need) within specified areas.

At the Beidaihe Conference in August 1958, Mao Zedong discussed his understanding of the relationship between distribution according to need and communism: "In approximately ten years, production volume will be more than sufficient, the morale of the people will be high, and from the food we eat, to the clothes we wear and to the homes we live in, we will achieve communism. When the people can eat in public dining halls and not be charged for food, this is communism."[9]

The *People's Daily* commented on this statement, claiming that a free-supply system that attempts to provide commune members with basic necessities "has certainly not achieved the communist [principle] of 'each taking what one needs.' It has, however, completely broken free from the privileges of distribution according to work and, suiting the need for further development, has advanced towards public ownership. Therefore, it belongs within the scope of, and is in fact the foundation of, communism."[10] The reason people established Large-Scale Communes, public dining halls, and a system of distribution according to need with such passion rested largely on these points. According to Central Committee regulations, distribution within the communes should have been allocated on the basis of work performance. However, when local governments ignored this regulation and began carrying out distribution according to a free-supply system, the Central Committee not only consented to but also supported this system because it was considered more communist.

In the Central Committee's resolution on the establishment of People's Communes in rural areas, it was stipulated that, although a distribution system that combines free supply and salary "contains the sprouts of communism, its basic characteristics are still socialist – from each according to one's ability, to each according to one's work."[11] In the uproar following the claim that "the realization of communism in our country is not far off," two well-known People's Communes regulated a system of distribution according to need. The Draft Constitution of the Qiliying People's Commune stated: "With increased productivity and heightened communist consciousness, communist elements should be gradually extended. When conditions are suitable, a distribution system based completely on the principle of 'from each according to one's ability, to each according to one's needs' should be implemented immediately."[12]

Recommended several times by Mao Zedong, the "Trial Constitution of Chayashan People's Satellite Commune (Draft)" also proposed that, "under conditions of accelerated grain production and unanimous agreement among commune members, a free-supply system will be implemented."[13] At a later conference in Lushan, Mao Zedong admitted: "When I went to investigate [the situation] in Henan Province, I discovered the Chayashan Constitution and kept a copy for myself. What a treasure indeed!"[14]

During its initial stages, the Large-Scale Commune distribution system was basically a combination of the free-supply and wage systems. Localized versions of the free-supply system differed in that some communes supplied grain, others supplied meals, and yet others supplied basic necessities. The "free-grain" supply system provided commune members with free grain rations based on a fixed standard of grain supply and provided free meals in public dining halls. The "free-meal" supply system provided commune members with free grain, vegetables, oil, salt, and firewood for cooking, along with covering any other costs incurred in the preparation of food. The systems that supplied basic necessities took into account economic conditions and member consumption to determine how much food, clothing, and lodging was to be supplied free of charge. In other words, the commune took care of all basic necessities.[15]

There were also a few Large-Scale Communes that were less productive and that, consequently, provided lower salaries. These communes implemented a semi-free-supply system in which a portion of one's grain rations was provided while the remainder was deducted from one's salary. At the end of October 1958, of the 5,254 communes in Henan, Shandong, Hebei, Liaoning, and Anhui, 21 percent planned to implement the free-grain system, 61.3 percent the free-meal system, 15 percent the free-basic-necessities system, and 2.7 percent a system in which everything was supplied.[16]

The communes in Henan Province that implemented the free-grain system, the free-meal system, and the free-basic-necessities system accounted for 35.7 percent, 31.1 percent, and 33.2 percent, respectively, of the total number of communes nationwide adopting such practices.[17]

A Central Committee communist "pilot project," Xushui County of Hebei Province was the first to implement a system in which everything was supplied. On 6 August 1958, the deputy minister for rural works, Chen Zhengren, travelled to Xushui to personally guide the project. At a conference held on 8 August, he claimed:

> With the second Five Year Plan [the transformation] to socialism will be almost complete, and through the third Five Year Plan [we] will be well on our way to communism. We did not anticipate that the Great Leap Forward would be so effective ... This has forced us to reconsider [the situation]. We needed a "pilot project" to make the transition to communism. Comrade Liu Shaoqi instructed us to conduct such a project in Xushui. General labour, agriculture, the military, the academy, and commerce will be combined into one body, and the villages, public and private organizations, and schools will all participate.

On 15 September, the People's Greater Commune of Xushui was established (later renamed the Xushui People's Commune), and the county and commune merged into one. On 20 September, the Draft Resolution of the Communist Party Committee of Xushui County on the Adoption of a Free Supply System stipulated that "each worker's, peasant's, merchant's, student's, and soldier's need for food, clothing, and basic necessities shall be provided for, in moderation and in accordance with the principle of equality, by the People's Commune." In accordance with this resolution, the county implemented the "15 Provisions," whereby many basic necessities (such as food, clothing, medical treatment, soap, matches, etc.) as well as entertainment (such as movie tickets) were covered by the county government. Not only did all county citizens eat free of charge, but those from outside the county were not even charged at commercial restaurants.[18]

Many counties followed the example of Xushui and adopted similar free-supply distribution systems. Qiliying People's Commune, the first People's Commune established in the country, adopted the "16 Provisions,"[19] Aiguo People's Commune in Ju County, Shandong, adopted the "9 Provisions,"[20] and Shidao People's Commune in Rongcheng County, Shandong, which held its fishery as its main source of production, adopted the "11 Provisions."[21]

The Large-Scale Commune distribution system was a system of equal distribution limited to those items necessary to maintain a basic standard of living. At the time, this was the understanding of "communism" nationwide. Even up until the end of 1958, the Central Committee still insisted that, "between socialism and communism, there is no, and there will never be, a Great Wall."[22] After it was advertised that a free-supply system would be implemented in Xushui, the peasants rejoiced: "[We're] taking real action to speed up the transition to communism!" Such support could also be found in Mao Zedong's praise of the "four-dishes-at-every-meal" style of communism found in Fan County, Shandong.

At the time, this was the Party and peasants' understanding of socialism, communism, and the social development of China.

The Retreat from the System of Free Distribution to "Distribution According to Work"

When the basic needs for food and clothing were not met,[23] the free-supply system, in whichever form it took, was difficult to maintain. Under pressure from economic difficulties and famine, Large-Scale People's Communes transformed their distribution system from one based on free supply to one based on labour. Just three months after the implementation of this new communist distribution system, which promised to fill the stomachs of its participants, it was already showing signs of failure nationwide. Limited by economic conditions, the system mutated, became compromised, and eventually collapsed.

At the time, the county was the basic accounting unit, yet county finances were often insufficient to meet the demands of free supply. In August 1958, Xushui County implemented the free-supply system. By September, cadres stopped receiving salaries and were provided instead with insufficient subsidies. Some cadres displayed their "communist spirit" by refusing their subsidies and eating only in the public dining halls – which survived just over three months before being forced to shut down. In November, commune members received a one-time salary and a few daily necessities, at a cost of 5.5 million *yuan*.

The promise to supply all basic needs was never realized. For example, according to the county regulations, each member should have received two towels when in reality he or she received only one. Other daily necessities were distributed only to some in elderly homes or kindergartens. As for entertainment or bathing costs, no provisions were supplied. At the time, the county's total revenue was less than 20 million *yuan* and it simply could not support the free-supply system. The county was forced, therefore, to misappropriate 7 million *yuan* of commercial capital, which led to a cash shortage and left the county facing bankruptcy. Just over three months later, the farce that was the free-supply system of Xushui County came to an early end.[24]

Henan's Suiping County spent all of its money in the first month after adopting the wage system. With no cash to distribute by the second month, it began providing interest-free savings accounts.[25] Free supply accounted for the bulk of a commune member's revenue. As a result, the "distribution-according-to-labour" wage system was rendered meaningless and difficult to implement.

After the 1958 harvest in Hebei Province, three problems regarding the distribution system arose: first, since food supply could not be guaranteed, the communes had to ask the state for relief; second, if food could be supplied, salaries could not be provided; and third, in some cases, food could be supplied, but only a small salary could be provided – some communes could offer a few *jiao* a month, some provided one *yuan* a month, and some provided two to four *yuan*. However, those communes that were able to pay a small salary could not continue this practice for more than a month or two.[26]

In Xin township's Qiliying People's Commune, free supply accounted for 75.4 percent of total distribution, while salary in cash accounted for only 24.6 percent. The labour force was divided into five different grades: the first grade earned three *yuan* a month, while each grade lower earned 0.5 *yuan* less, respectively. The fifth grade earned barely one *yuan* a month.

After the free-grain supply system was implemented in Chayashan People's Satellite Commune, the average monthly salary for a labourer was only four *yuan*.[27] In some counties in Shanxi Province, commune members received little cash in hand as the cash they should have received was transferred directly into a savings account. Even more serious situations could be found in those counties that invested too much in capital construction: 16 percent of accounting units could not pay commune members even the slightest amount more than their allotted grain rations.[28]

The general application of a free-supply/wage-distribution system brought temporary happiness to the large number of peasants who had hardly enough food or clothing. However, the result of this short-lived illusion was heavy damage to the collective economy and an impending famine.

On 26 April 1959, the Hubei Provincial Committee reported that, "since the Spring Festival, a number of demonstrations regarding grain rations have been held." Some places had to deal with spring famines: "Wuhan municipality, which had a population of 2 million, was once in short supply [of grain]."[29] In Hebei Province, grain was in short supply: "More than thirty counties complained of a lack of grain, ten of which [experienced] serious shortages."[30] In May 1959, Guangdong Province's Yaxian, Nanxiong, Luoding, and Qinxian counties all reported that "a number of people were suffering from edema, but most cases were reported before April (according to incomplete statistics, 10,930 people suffered from edema, 134 of which died)."[31] In fact, grain shortages were appearing in other parts of the country as early as the winter of 1958/59. In more serious instances, people were fleeing from famine-stricken areas in which cases of edema were appearing.

Facing a tense economic situation, yet unwilling to completely give up a system of distribution according to need, the CCP leadership, along with a number of provinces, adopted a series of remedial measures. First, there was a gradual reduction in the free-supply system and a restoration of distribution according to labour as the main distribution principle. At the Extended Conference of the Central Committee Political Bureau in March-April 1959, the Central Committee stated: "The principle of distribution according to labour means calculating payment according to the amount of labour one does. The more work done, the more one will earn." As a result, various distribution strategies were recommended, including fixing standards while allowing flexible assessments, fixing quotas for management, recording work points, calculating distribution according to days worked, and so on.[32] In keeping with the "spirit" of the conference, the Central Committee issued the "Instructions for Summer Harvest Distribution in People's Communes": "During distribution of the summer harvest, the salary to free-supply ratio must be adjusted accordingly. One must strive to achieve a salary of approximately 60 to 70 percent [of total distribution], with the remaining 30 to 40 percent provided as free supply."[33]

The second measure taken was to make clear the main distribution policies and distribution ratios issued by the Central Committee, the communes, and the lower levels of administration within the communes. In April 1959, the Central Committee announced that it had "fixed the national grain tax quota and determined the final amounts to be allotted to each province (including amounts added at the local level). Each province shall distribute down, level by level, to the communes and basic accounting units." The committee went on to reiterate: "The government (both central and local) shall not levy agricultural tax. Except in circumstances of extreme disaster, the state shall not increase purchase quotas for grain." At the same time, the CCP regulated commune distribution ratios: production expenses could not exceed 19 to 24 percent of the annual production quota; administrative expenses (including cadre subsidies) should total 2 percent; public welfare funds, 2 percent; and the amount distributed to commune members (less state grain quotas and taxes), 50 to 60 percent.[34]

The third measure taken involved adopting more flexible policies regarding public dining halls. In May 1959, the Central Committee stated:

Public dining halls may be established for all commune members or may be established only for certain members; they may be run throughout the year or only during the busy farming season; they may be open for longer hours during busy seasons and shorter hours during slack times, as operators see fit; dining halls extended beyond their means may reduce their size accordingly. Grain rations shall be distributed to each household and each commune member in an amount determined on an individual basis. Grain rations may be submitted to dining halls in exchange for meals. Unused rations may be retained by the individual. Those who choose not to eat in dining halls may also retain the entirety of their grain rations.[35]

Following this, Hubei Province stipulated:

The free-grain supply system should allocate grain on a per person basis with meal tickets distributed accordingly. Tickets may be exchanged for meals in dining halls. Grain may be sent directly to dining halls or member's homes. Members may freely choose to eat in dining halls or at home; they should not be forced to choose either way. If requested by the people, dining halls are permitted to run only during busy farming seasons, or as the situation requires.[36]

Hebei Province stipulated: "A uniform meal ticket system will be implemented for eating in public dining halls. Unused grain rations may be retained by the holder or sold for cash. Those willing to cook their own meals will be allotted their grain ration accordingly. Those willing to take less grain than their allotted ration may receive the balance in cash."[37] Thus, although the free-supply system was not completely abolished, it transformed from an "all-you-can-eat" system into one limited by meal tickets.

Certain places began allocating meals according to attendance at work or making those who failed to show up for work pay for their own meals. This was devised as a means of punishing those who took advantage of the free-supply system without doing any work. A similar strategy involved distributing basic grain rations according to work points.

The fourth and final measure involved returning to the commune members the private plots and livestock that had been taken away during the People's Commune movement. In May 1959, the Central Committee decreed: "Private plots should be returned to commune members. According to the original HAPC Constitution, private plots must neither exceed nor be less than 5 percent of the average per capita land allotment."[38] In June of that year, the Party's instructions became clear: there would be no restrictions on raising poultry, and all income earned could be retained by individual commune members; where possible, all private plots taken away from members during the HAPCs were to be returned; farming would not be excessively restricted, and all income earned would be retained by individual commune members to use as they saw fit.[39]

The Lushan Conference, held in July-August 1959, almost brought the distribution system reforms to a halt and renewed interest in running public dining halls and restoring the free-supply system. On 15 October, the Central Committee circulated the Ministry of Agriculture's "Report on Rural Developments since the Lushan Conference," which pointed out that, "during May, June, and July of this year, some perverse right-wing trends have appeared in rural areas, partially eroding the free-supply system and doing away with public dining halls. These are in fact reckless and adverse activities that run counter to the path to socialism."[40] At the same time, the *People's Daily* published an article entitled "The Bright Future of Public Dining Halls," which pointed out that "public dining halls have deep social and economic roots and enjoy the support of the Party as well as the people. They were not blown into existence by a gust of wind, nor will they be blown away."[41] With support from the Central Committee, the free-supply system and public dining halls were partially restored. By the end of 1959, 3.9 million public dining halls had been established throughout the country, feeding 400 million people – 72.6 percent of all commune members. Seven provinces saw 90 percent of commune members eating in public dining halls, with the highest rate found in Henan at 97.8 percent.[42] The struggle against "right opportunism," which had spread throughout the country, had not only led to the complete loss of recent leftist successes but also caused the economic situation in rural areas to deteriorate further.

Under pressure from the threat of widespread hunger at the end of 1960, the commune distribution system was once again forced to undergo reform. On 3 November, the Central Committee issued its "Emergency Instructions on Present Problems with Commune Policies," a comprehensive document indicating leftist practices for restoring the rural economy. The instructions dispense with free supply as the main principle of distribution: "For at least the next twenty years, the commune distribution system will be based on the principle of distribution according to labour. When allocating commune member consumption quotas, free supply should be kept under control, while amounts for salary should be increased."[43] In June of the following year, the "Labour Regulations in People's Communes (Revised Draft)" was issued, demonstrating clear opposition to the egalitarianism of the distribution system: "Production teams must conscientiously implement a system of distribution according to labour, with more pay for more work, in order to avoid the egalitarianism currently found in distribution to commune members. Regardless of gender, age, status as cadre, or commune member, [a system] of equal pay for equal work [shall be strictly applied]."[44]

By this point, the commune distribution system had moved from an ideal system of total free supply, to a system of half free supply/half wage, to a system of higher wage/less free supply, and, finally, to a system that restored the principle of distribution according to labour. In less than three years, the entire country went from an infatuation with the free-supply system (the very "sprouts of communism") to a clear-cut opposition to the egalitarianism of this system. The swiftness with which this transformation came, the destructive force it wielded, and the profound influence it had on Chinese society find no equal in the history of China or, indeed, that of any other country.

The Characteristics of the Distribution System of the Big Commune

The "communist" free-supply system that blossomed during the People's Commune movement sprang from the soil of poor, small-scale, rural economies. Lacking the power and means to change their circumstances under natural economic conditions, peasants often transform their hopes to change their "backward" situations into fantastic yearnings for a better future or into unrealistic, reckless acts – to the point of deceiving themselves and others. Often such "fantastic yearnings" cannot be achieved in existing social conditions and call for idealistic and radical social planning or old, backward, even reactionary egalitarianism in order to be realized. Without exception, in modern or ancient times, in China or elsewhere, this leads to self-inflicted chaos and widespread starvation. The various "communist" distribution systems that appeared during the People's Commune movement may also be viewed in this light.

The Large-Scale People's Commune distribution system, the heart of which was the public dining hall, had very distinct features. First, it was fantastic – that is, it was implemented in an attempt to make a hasty transition to a more advanced social form while disregarding current social conditions. In 1957, the average peasant income in China was 72.92 *yuan*, living expenditures were 70.86 *yuan*, grain consumption was 227 kilograms, cooking oil consumption was 1.59 kilograms, and meat consumption was 4.53 kilograms.[45] When unable to meet basic food and clothing requirements, a free-supply system exists only in rhetoric. The transition to a more advanced social form based on such a system was, in reality, a "transition to poverty."[46]

The system's second defining feature was its instability: it was constantly undergoing reform. Mid-1958 saw the appearance of public dining halls; next was the widespread implementation of various free-supply systems; then came a gradual decrease in free supply in favour of distribution according to labour; and, finally, the system ended up being based solely on distribution according to labour.

The system's third defining feature was its lack of uniformity: the Central Committee had no clear or uniform requirements for distribution. The free-supply system took on different forms in different locations. In some cases, half of one's necessities were covered by the free-supply system, while the other half had to be earned through labour. At the same time, there existed numerous Large-Scale Communes that had always enforced the distribution-according-to-labour system as their main form of distribution. In a country as large as China, however, it was natural for local governments to make appropriate amendments to official policy based on local conditions.

The system's fourth defining characteristic was its pursuit of egalitarianism: the "communist" experiment promoted by the Central Committee coincided with the demands of the people and created unprecedented enthusiasm for egalitarianism. Both the free-supply system and the "all-you-can-eat" public dining halls demonstrated an absolute egalitarianism that was characteristic of peasant socialism – the most fundamental characteristic of the Large-Scale People's Commune distribution system.

As long as social inequalities exist, there will be demands for egalitarianism. Generally speaking, the desire for equal distribution of wealth comes from those at the lower level of the social scale. In a period of great social change, egalitarianism is not only the mobilizing flag of the people; it is also a source of energy with which to carry out social reform. This helps us to understand why the free-supply system enjoyed such enthusiastic support from certain villagers. In reality, the People's Commune movement was a consolidation and redistribution of social resources in the rural areas of China; and, in essence, the free-supply system was the takeover of the wealth of the richer teams and households by the poorer – the so-called "egalitarian and indiscriminate requisition of resources." Without the requisition of production teams' means of production, ownership at the commune level would never have been established; and without the requisition of commune members' cooking equipment, public dining halls would never have been realized.

The commune distribution system was based on the requisition of production teams and commune members' means of production, and it was characterized by equal distribution. Implementation of the requisitions resulted in the destruction of the rural moral and social order, and it caused tremendous damage to the economy – which caught commune planners and egalitarian distribution system supporters off guard.

First, in the process of realizing the commune's basic accounting and distribution practices, many locations experienced surges in trends to "go communist," exaggerations of production achievements, commandism, the privileging of cadres, and the issuing of arbitrary and impractical instructions. At will, communes deprived commune members of private property and deprived production teams of collective belongings. In order to realize "organizational militarization, militancy in production, and collectivization," many locations engaged in large-scale village mergers. In many cases, meals were taken collectively, husbands and wives lived separately, and many commune members were deprived of fundamental rights and personal freedoms.[47]

Second, while the distribution system centred on running public dining halls provided everyone with the right to dine free of charge, it also eliminated inequalities in wealth between individuals. Demonstrating contempt for basic human values, this nearly absolute egalitarianism destroyed the driving force behind society and undermined the social order.[48]

Third, the establishment and implementation of the commune distribution system gave low-level cadres the power to allocate and control wealth in rural areas. Thus, they essentially held the fates of ordinary people in their hands. Such power inevitably led to the breeding of privileges and corruption and, in some cases, even to cruel oppression. In public dining halls, commune cadres of all levels generally ate larger portions or applied force or trickery for their own gain. Some cadres would commit serious crimes to benefit themselves, even at the cost of other commune members' lives.[49]

Finally, the implementation of the commune distribution system proved time and again that absolute egalitarianism can never be achieved. Historically, all attempts to achieve absolute egalitarianism have failed due to the high costs of implementing such a practice – the same may be said of the Chinese commune distribution system that held egalitarianism as its defining feature.

Even today, the Large-Scale People's Commune distribution system is scarred by the crime of attempting to implement an egalitarian distribution plan. The public dining hall remains the best "negative" example from which to better understand reactions to egalitarianism.

Notes

1 Late 1958 saw the rise of People's Communes, which were formed through the merger of approximately thirty higher agricultural producer cooperatives (HAPCs). At the commune level, ownership was collective, and these communes were considered the basic accounting units. In this chapter, I call them "Large-Scale Communes" in order to distinguish them from the "three-level ownership" system that appeared after 1962 and held the production team as the basic accounting unit. See Zhang Letian, *Gaobie lixiang: Renmin gongshe zhidu yanjiu* [Farewell to Idealism: A Study of the People's Commune System] (Shanghai: Dongfang chuban zhongxin, 1998), 6; and Xin Yi, "Guanyu nongcun renmin gongshe de fenqi" [A Timeline for the People's Commune], *Shandong shifan daxue xuebao* [Journal of Shangong Normal University] 1 (2000): 23-27. In fact, at the Beidaihe Conference in 1958, Mao Zedong also called the early People's Communes "Large-Scale Communes": "The People's Communes are characterized firstly by their great size, and secondly by collective ownership. I think they should be called Large-Scale Communes." See Bo Yibo, *Ruogan zhongda juece yu shijian de huigu* [Reflections on Certain Major Decisions and Events] (Beijing: Renmin chubanshe, 1997), 2:767.
2 Bo, *Ruogan zhongda juece yu shijian de huigu*, 786-87.
3 Deng Zhiwang, "Jianlun renmin gongshe chuqi de fenpei zhidu" [A Short Analysis of the Initial Phase of the People's Commune Supply System], *Ershiyi shiji* [Twenty-First Century] 32 (2004).
4 Luo Pinghan, "Renmin gongshe gongjizhi tanxi" [Analysis of the People's Commune Supply System], *Dangdai Zhongguoshi yanjiu* [Research on Modern Chinese History] 3 (2000): 38-46.
5 Gao Wangling, *Renmin gongshe shiqi Zhongguo nongmin "fanxingwei" diaocha* [An Investigation of Peasant "Resistance" during the Time of the People's Communes] (Beijing: Zhonggongdanshi chubanshe, 2006), 37-38. See Gao in Chapter 11 of this volume, as well.
6 Mao Zedong said: "Apart from a few disastrous areas, there exists almost everywhere in the country universal unrest in the form of reporting less output and private distribution, and of claiming insufficiency in grain, oil crops, pork, and vegetables. The scale of the unrest is no less widespread than the grain unrest of 1953 and 1955." See Mao Zedong, "Zai Zhengzhou huiyishang de jianghua" [Speech Given at Zhengzhou Conference], in *Mao Zedong wenji* [Collected Works of Mao Zedong], vol. 8 (Beijing: Renmin chubanshe, 1999), 9.
7 Zhonggong zhongyang wenxian yanjiushi, ed., "Zhonggong zhongyang guanyu zai nongcun jianli renmin gongshe wenti de jueyi" [Central Committee Resolution on the

Establishment of People's Communes in the Countryside], in *Jianguo yilai zhongyao wenxian xuanbian* [Selected Important Documents since the Founding of the People's Republic of China] (Beijing: Zhongyang wenxian chubanshe, 1995), 450.

8   Zhonggong zhongyang wenxian yanjiushi, ed., "Guanyu renmin gongshe ruogan wenti de jueyi" [Resolution on Several Issues Concerning People's Communes], in *Jianguo yilai zhongyao wenxian xuanbian* [Selected Important Documents since the Founding of the People's Republic of China] (Beijing: Zhongyang wenxian chubanshe, 1995), 601.

9   Bo, *Ruogan zhongda juece yu shijian de huigu*, 767.

10 "Fanhao caiyehao" [Rice Is Good, but Vegetables Are Also Good], *Renmin Ribao* [People's Daily], 10 November 1958.

11 Zhonggong zhongyang wenxian yanjiushi, "Zhonggong zhongyang guanyu zai nongcun jianli renmin gongshe wenti de jueyi," 611-12.

12 Dangdai Zhongguo nongye hezuohua bianjishi, ed., "Qiliying renmin gongshe zhangcheng cao'an" [The Draft Constitution of Qiliying People's Commune], in *Jianguo yilai nongye hezuohua shiliao huibian* [Compilation of Documents on Agricultural Cooperativization since the Founding of the People's Republic of China] (Beijing: Zhonggong dangshi chubanshe, 1992), 485.

13 Zhonggong zhongyang wenxian yanjiushi, ed., "Chayashan weixing renmin gongshe shixing jianzhang (caogao)" [Trial Constitution of Chayashan People's Satellite Commune (Draft)], in *Jianguo yilai zhongyao wenxian xuanbian* [Selected Important Documents since the Founding of the People's Republic of China] (Beijing: Zhongyang wenxian chubanshe, 1995), 11:393-94.

14 Li Rui, *Lushan huiyi shilu, zengding ben* [Memorandum on the Lushan Conference, Revised and Enlarged Edition] (Zhengzhou: Henan renmin chubanshe, 1995), 137.

15 Wu Ren, ed., *Renmin gongshe he gongchanzhuyi* [People's Communes and Communism] (Beijing: Gongren chubanshe, 1958), 12.

16 Bo, *Ruogan zhongda juece yu shijian de huigu*, 775.

17 Li Lin and Ma Guangyao, eds., *Henan nongcun jingji tizhi biangeshi* [A History of the Economic Transformation of Rural Henan] (Beijing: Zhonggongdangshi chubanshe, 2000), 106.

18 Zhao Yunshan and Zhao Benrong, "Xushuixian gongchanzhuyi shidian shimo" [A History of Xushui County's Communist Pilot Project], in *Dangshi tongxun* [Communiqué of Party History] 6 (1987).

19 Wu Lengxi, *Yi Mao zhuxi: Wo qinshen jingli de ruogan zhongda lishi shijian pianduan* [Remembering Mao Zedong: Several Important Historical Events that I Personally Experienced] (Beijing: Xinhua chubanshe, 1995), 99-101.

20 These nine items included the costs for birth, lodging, food, education, entertainment, weddings, medical treatment, elderly care, and funerals. See Lü Hongbin, "Wo dui aiguo nongye shengchan hezuoshe de huiyi, xia" [My Memory of the Aiguo Agricultural Cooperative, Part Two], in *Zhongguo nongye hezuohuashi ziliao* [Documentation on the Agricultural Cooperativization of China] 3 (1986): 1.

21 These eleven items included the costs for birth, raising children, lodging, food, education, entertainment, weddings, medical treatment, funerals, hair-care, and sewing. See Wu Deyong, "Dayudaocun yuye hezuohuashi" [A History of the Cooperativization of Dayudao Village Fishery], in *Zhongguo nongye hezuohuashi ziliao* [Documentation on the Agricultural Cooperativization of China] 6 (1989): 55.

22 Zhonggong zhongyang wenxian yanjiushi, "Guanyu renmin gongshe ruogan wenti de jueyi," 607.

23 In 1958, per capita consumption in rural areas was 83 *yuan* and 201 *jin* of commercial grain. See Zhonghua renmin gongheguo nongyebu jihuasi, ed., *Zhongguo nongcun jingji tongji daquan, 1949-1980* [Comprehensive Statistics of China's Rural Economy, 1949-1980] (Beijing: Nongye chubanshe, 1989), 574, 576.

24 Zhao and Zhao, "Xushuixian gongchanzhuyi shidian shimo."

25 Kang Jian, *Huihuang de huanmie: Renmin gongshe jingshilu* [The Death of Glory: An Alarming Account of a People's Commune] (Beijing: Zhongguo shehui chubanshe, 1998), 345.

26 Bo, *Ruogan zhongda juece yu shijian de huigu (xiuding ben)*, 786-87.

27 Du Runsheng, *Dangdai Zhongguo de nongye hezuozhi* [The Agricultural Cooperative System of Contemporary China] (Beijing: Dangdai Zhongguo chubanshe, 2001), 530-31.

28 Zhonggong zhongyang wenxian yanjiushi, ed., "Zhonggong zhongyang pizhuan Shanxi shengwei 'Guanyu liuji ganbu huiyi qingkuang de baogao'" [Central Committee Commentary on the Shanxi Provincial Committee's "Report on the Six Levels Cadres Council"], in *Jianguo yilai zhongyao wenxian xuanbian* [Selected Important Documents since the Founding of the People's Republic of China] (Beijing: Zhongyang wenxian chubanshe, 1996), 13:245-46.

29 Zhonggong zhongyang wenxian yanjiushi, ed., "Hubei shengwei guanyu shengwei kuoda huiyi de qingkuang baogao" [Hubei Provincial Committee Report on the Proceedings of the Provincial Committee's Expanded Conference], in *Jianguo yilai zhongyao wenxian xuanbian* [Selected Important Documents since the Founding of the People's Republic of China] (Beijing: Zhongyang wenxian chubanshe, 1996), 12:300-1.

30 Dangdai Zhongguo nongye hezuohua bianjishi, ed., "Zhonggong Hebei shengwei guanyu guanche bajie qizhong quanhui jingshen de baogao" [Hebei Provincial Committee Report on Carrying on the Spirit of the Seventh Plenary Session of the Eighth Central Committee], in *Jianguo yilai nongye hezuohua shiliao huibian* [Compilation of Documents on Agricultural Cooperativization since the Founding of the People's Republic of China] (Beijing: Zhonggongdangshi chubanshe, 1992), 565.

31 Dangdai Zhongguo nongye hezuohua bianjishi, ed., "Guangdong shengwei guanyu muqian nongcun gongzuo qingkuang he bushu de baogao" [Guangdong Provincial Committee Report on Present Labour Conditions in Rural Areas], in *Jianguo yilai nongye hezuohua shiliao huibian* [Compilation of Documents on Agricultural Cooperativization since the Founding of the People's Republic of China] (Beijing: Zhonggongdangshi chubanshe, 1992), 565.

32 Zhonggong zhongyang wenxian yanjiushi, ed., "Guanyu renmin gongshe shiba ge wenti" [Eighteen Questions on People's Communes], in *Jianguo yilai zhongyao wenxian xuanbian* [Selected Important Documents since the Founding of the People's Republic of China] (Beijing: Zhongyang wenxian chubanshe, 1996), 12:171-72.

33 Dangdai Zhongguo nongye hezuohua bianjishi, ed., "Zhonggong zhongyang guanyu renmin gongshe xiashou fenpei de zhishi" [Central Committee Instructions for Commune Summer Harvest Distribution], in *Jianguo yilai nongye hezuohua shiliao huibian* [Compilation of Documents on Agricultural Cooperativization since the Founding of the People's Republic of China] (Beijing: Zhonggongdangshi chubanshe, 1992), 567.

34 Zhonggong zhongyang wenxian yanjiushi, *Guanyu renmin gongshe shiba ge wenti*, 170.

35 Dangdai Zhongguo nongye hezuohua bianjishi, "Zhonggong zhongyang guanyu renmin gongshe xiashou fenpei de zhishi," 567.

36 Zhonggong zhongyang wenxian yanjiushi, ed., "Zhonggong Hubei shengwei kuoda huiyi 'Guanyu renmin gongshe de shiba ge wenti' de taolun jiyao" [Hubei Provincial Committee's Summary of the Extended Conference on the "Eighteen Questions on People's Communes"], in *Jianguo yilai zhongyao wenxian xuanbian* [Selected Important Documents since the Founding of the People's Republic of China] (Beijing: Zhongyang wenxian chubanshe, 1996), 12:309.

37 Dangdai Zhongguo nongye hezuohua bianjishi, "Zhonggong Hebei shengwei guanyu guanche bajie qizhong quanhui jingshen de baogao," 565.

38 Zhonggong zhongyang wenxian yanjiushi, ed., "Zhonggong zhongyang guanyu nongye de wutiao jinji zhishi" [Central Committee's Five Emergency Measures for Agriculture], in *Jianguo yilai zhongyao wenxian xuanbian* [Selected Important Documents since the Founding of the People's Republic of China] (Beijing: Zhongyang wenxian chubanshe, 1996), 12:293.

39   Zhonggong zhongyang wenxian yanjiushi, ed., "Zhonggong zhongyang guanyu sheyuan siyang jiaqin, jiachu he ziliudi deng sige wenti de zhishi" [Central Committee Instructions on Raising Poultry, Keeping Livestock, and Cultivating Private Plots], in *Jianguo yilai zhongyao wenxian xuanbian* [Selected Important Documents since the Founding of the People's Republic of China] (Beijing: Zhongyang wenxian chubanshe, 1996), 12:382-84.

40   Dangdai Zhongguo nongye hezuohua bianjishi, ed., "Zhonggong zhongyang pizhuan nongyebu dangzu guanyu Lushan huiyi yilai nongcun xingshi de baogao" [Ministry of Agriculture's Report on Rural Developments since the Lushan Conference, Circulated by the Central Committee], in *Jianguo yilai nongye hezuohua shiliao huibian* [Compilation of Documents on Agricultural Cooperativization since the Founding of the People's Republic of China] (Beijing: Zhonggongdangshi chubanshe, 1992), 572.

41   *Renmin ribao* [People's Daily], 22 September 1959.

42   Dangdai Zhongguo nongye hezuohua bianjishi, ed. "Niandi quanguo nongcun gonggong shitang fazhan qingkuang (1959)" [The Development of Public Dining Halls in Rural Areas throughout the Country at the End of 1959], in *Jianguo yilai nongye hezuohua shiliao huibian* [Compilation of Documents on Agricultural Cooperativization since the Founding of the People's Republic of China] (Beijing: Zhonggongdangshi chubanshe, 1992), 602.

43   Zhonggong zhongyang wenxian yanjiushi, ed., "Zhonggong zhongyang guanyu nongcun renmin gongshe dangqian zhengce wenti de jinji zhishixin" [Central Committee Emergency Instructions on Present Problems with Commune Policies], in *Jianguo yilai zhongyao wenxian xuanbian* [Selected Compilation of Important Documents since the Founding of the People's Republic of China] (Beijing: Zhongyang wenxian chubanshe, 1996), 13:668.

44   Zhonggong zhongyang wenxian yanjiushi, ed., "Nongcun renmin gongshe gongzuo tiaoli (xiuzheng cao'an)" [Work Regulations in People's Communes (Revised Draft)], in *Jianguo yilai zhongyao wenxian xuanbian* [Selected Important Documents since the Founding of the People's Republic of China] (Beijing: Zhongyang wenxian chubanshe, 1997), 400.

45   Zhonghua renmin gongheguo nongyebu zhengce faguisi, Zhonghua renmin gongheguo guojia tongjiju nongyesi, eds., *Zhongguo nongcun 40 nian* [Forty Years in Rural China] (Beijing: Zhongyuan nongmin chubanshe, 1989), 567, 571, 577.

46   At the Wuchang Conference in November 1958, Peng Zhen said: "After the land reforms, we will begin cooperativization, followed by [the establishment of] People's Communes. When per capita income reaches 150 to 200 *yuan*, we may proceed with the transformation ... The earlier the transformation begins the better. In three to four years, it will be carried out." Mao Zedong also stated: "According to the opinions of Shaoqi and Peng Zhen, we must transform while we are still poor. It will be beneficial to transform while we are poor; otherwise, it will become difficult." See Xu Quanxing, *Mao Zedong wannian de lilun yu shijian (1956-1976)* [Mao Zedong's Theory and Practice in His Later Years (1956-1976)] (Beijing: Zhongguo dabaike chubanshe, 1995), 189.

47   After the public dining halls were established, commune members were not allowed to cook for themselves. The Shanhe production brigade of Xiaoxi River, Fengyang County, Anhui Province, organized an "expert investigation team." It searched village after village and household after household without fail, sometimes searching a single home more than four times. If they were the least bit dissatisfied, they would publicly warn: "What is yours? Only the teeth in your mouth belong to you!" During searches, team members used iron rods to rummage through chests and cupboards, poking through this and that. In the beginning, they searched only for grain, but later they ate whatever they could find and took whatever they set their eyes on. In June 1960, Mei Shuhua, the Party secretary-general of Xiaoxi River People's Commune, forced commoners to form into six villages and destroy more than three hundred homes within half a day. Party members who refused were expelled from the CCP, Communist Youth League members who refused

were expelled from the league, and commune members who refused were deprived of food. One hundred commune members fled as they were left with no homes. They were apprehended, and forty people from fourteen families were forced to live in a single home with three linked rooms. At night the front gate was locked and watched by armed guard. Inside they were forced to relieve themselves with no privacy. See Wang Gengjin et al., *Xiangcun sanshi nian: Fengyang nongcun shehui jingji fazhan shilu (1949-1983)* [Thirty Years in the Countryside: A Record of the Social and Economic Development of Fengyang Village, 1949-1983] (Beijing: Nongcun duwu chubanshe, 1989), 180-81.

48 One production team member from Shujiafan Administrative Region, Baigao People's Commune, Macheng County, Hubei Province, said: "Right now nothing is yours or mine, everything belongs to the state. Even people belong to the government. Only the food in our stomachs is ours." Other commune members said: "Since communization, there is no more rich or poor, you can't earn more for more work, food is free, and no matter what you do you get three *yuan* a month." In Tangyu Commune in the same county, there appeared what came to be known as "Five More and Two Less": "Five More" refers to there being more people sick, more people on the street, more people paying visits to their relatives, more people going to school, and more pregnant women asking leave; "Two Less" refers to decreased rates of work attendance and decreased productivity. See Wang Yanni, "Cong Machengxian kan gongshehua de ABC" [Introduction of the People's Commune in Macheng County] (MA thesis, Renmin University of China, 2004).

49 Chen Rongfu, secretary of Shanhe Production Brigade, Fengyang County, Anhui Province, had no firewood for cooking, so he dismantled the home of commune member Ren Guangheng. Mei Shuhua (secretary of Qiaoshan Production Brigade) and Mei Rushan (brigade accountant) satisfied their sexual desires by staging a "Women's Day" competition in which eight of the brigade's most beautiful women were selected – seven of whom were raped at will, with one able to escape due to her being less desirable. See Wang Gengjin et al., *Xiangcun sanshi nian*, 184-85.

6 An Introduction to the ABCs of Communization: A Case Study of Macheng County

Wang Yanni

Translated by Sascha Mundstein and Robert Mackie

According to most accounts, "the clamour of gongs, drums, and fireworks" and "the hanging of lanterns with coloured silk and posters spreading the good news" accompanied the establishment of People's Communes in late summer of 1958. These scenes of great congratulatory commotion were followed by descriptions of vast numbers of peasants showing support for the communes and expressing their desire to voluntarily join them. However, just over two months after communization, the national economy had devolved into chaos, and the free-supply system was suffering from shortages. As a consequence, the CCP leadership initiated a major reorganization and rectification of the new commune structure at the first Zhengzhou Conference held in November 1958. By December 1958, at the eighth session of the Sixth Central Committee, Mao Zedong himself admitted that he had been a "dare-devil" and that the country was in disorder. He subsequently stressed the need to relentlessly "rectify errors."[1] Soon both central and local governments were no longer discussing how to build communes but, rather, how to repair them.

Why would such a drastic change have occurred in such a short period of time? How could communes that had once received so much support from the people suddenly require reorganization? This chapter examines life in Macheng County in Hubei Province during the first months of the Great Leap Forward. Specifically, it focuses on the period from the Beidaihe Conference in August 1958 to the second Zhengzhou Conference in April 1959, which can also be called the first reform of the communization movement. I argue that the rapidity with which the central leadership sought to reform the commune system can best be understood in light of the original goals of the movement: the establishment of an industrial army. Indeed, while some would argue that a misguided belief in communist ideals propelled the Great Leap Forward, evidence from Macheng County suggests that Mao Zedong and many local authorities primarily sought to create an efficient workforce modelled on a modern military machine. Ultimately, the strong objection of peasants and rapid declines in production caused the central leadership to rethink its commitment to turning peasants into soldiers.

To date, the majority of PRC-based analyses of this period limit their focus to high-level Party policies and policy implementation and specifically link the establishment of the People's Communes to the excesses of communism.[2] The CCP leadership initiated commune reform, this literature suggests, because the boundary between socialism and communism and between public and commune ownership had not been clearly established. The lack of clear boundaries resulted in an excessive eagerness to "transform," which, in turn, led to a series of problems characterized by a trend to "go communist." For example, Bo Yibo points out that "at the time People's Communes actually took advantage of their administrative power, established [their administration] on a natural or semi-natural economic basis, and were a combination of ideas that included elements of egalitarianism, militant communism, and fantasies of a post-socialist society."[3] Li Rui, Mao Zedong's former secretary, similarly argues that the Lushan Conference "was a struggle conducted for the purpose of safeguarding the fantasy of a socialist ideal."[4]

The tendency to focus on elite-level decision making and policy implementation, however, has meant that the behaviour and reactions of the peasantry have largely been ignored.[5] While Liu Lian has published an article on her experiences on Xushui (the Central Party's communist "pilot project" at the time),[6] for example, many questions about local-level dynamics remain outstanding. Similar to several authors in *Eating Bitterness,* I draw upon local archival material and oral interviews to reinterpret local social economic history and the history of the masses. In doing this, I seek to illustrate a clearer understanding of the dynamic relationship between Party policy and policy formulation and peasant reaction.

I was born and raised in Macheng County. Although the Great Leap Forward and famine occurred several years before my birth, the extraordinary historical background of my rural home prompted me to learn more about it. Macheng is located in the northeast of Hubei Province and belongs to the border region of the three provinces of Hebei, Henan, and Anhui. Macheng is a well-known old revolutionary area, having been the site of the famous "Macheng Uprising" in 1927, when the Chinese Communist Party organized an armed peasant revolt. Although liberated relatively late by the CCP (in 1947), Macheng continued to exhibit some of its earlier revolutionary tendencies after the foundation of the People's Republic of China. Indeed, it became famous for bearing the "red flag" of the mass line in the months leading up to the Great Leap Forward.

In January 1958, the first secretary of the Hebei provincial party committee, Wang Renzhong, wrote an article entitled "Emulate Macheng
County," praising the vigour of its cadres and citizens. At the time, posters
could be seen throughout the province calling on the people to "Learn
from Macheng," "Emulate Macheng," and "Catch up with Macheng." That
year Zhou Enlai, Chen Yi, Li Xiannian, and other leaders from the Party's
Central Committee visited Macheng to inspect and guide production (Mao
Zedong was unable to join them for technical reasons); Wang Renzhong
visited three times; more than 400,000 people from various provinces came
to visit and learn; and experts and delegations from twenty-eight countries
worldwide also came to observe. The March 1959 mass meetings and
Chairman Mao's "Three Official Comments" turned Macheng into a
national model for emulation.[7]

Macheng was clearly a national model during a key period of the Great
Leap Forward. But what did this mean for the people of Macheng? How
was it that communization directly affected the commune members themselves? And how did their response, and the response of peasants across
China during this period, affect the central leadership? I begin with an
examination of the demolition of private homes in Macheng during the
earliest weeks of the Great Leap Forward – an aspect of communization
previously unexplored in great detail by either Chinese or Western scholarship. I go on to examine an equally troubling aspect of communization
during the Great Leap Forward: the destruction of gravesites. I then consider the impact of the militarization of communities on family life before
concluding by more fully developing my primary thesis, which is that the
Great Leap Forward was a movement far less concerned with building a
communist utopia than it was with constructing an industrial army.

Home Demolition and Communal Living

One very common, but little understood, phenomenon of the earliest days
of the Great Leap Forward is the demolition of individual homes in favour
of communal residences. In order to realize the "Three Changes" (i.e.,
"organized militarization, active militancy, and collectivization"), and in
order to become "communist" as soon as possible, the entire country competed in the effort to destroy houses and to build "new" villages. Men and
women, old and young, husbands and wives all lived separately, while often
several families were forced to live under one communal roof. A system
was implemented that organized villagers into regiments, battalions, companies, platoons, and squads. This is all well documented in local archives,
including those of Macheng County, but what was the real reason for
tearing down homes? Moreover, what effect did this rapid transformation

have on the peasantry? I would argue that home demolition was prompted by three goals: to facilitate the collection of fertilizer, to facilitate communal living, and to improve production efficiency.

It would seem that the initial purpose behind the demolition of homes was to aid the collection of fertilizer. Indeed, the mud of the old-fashioned houses could be used as very good fertilizer. While reading through local archival material, I discovered that, in April, June, and July of 1958, the local authorities initiated a movement to collect fertilizer. Documents describe both the accounts of those who complained about the movement as well as those who willingly took part. In one township, for example, the demolitions created a veritable "tide" of fertilizer collection. The townspeople removed the mud from 49 ponds, tore down 200 buildings, destroyed 632 cooking stoves, and, in the end, managed to collect 265,000 tons of fertilizer.[8] In three days, Mingshan's Number Four Commune moved eleven *yuanzi* (small villages) and destroyed two thousand tons of old mud structures.[9]

After a debate held in Liangjiafan township's Liaoyuan Number One Commune, members decided they would destroy six hundred mud homes in order to collect nine thousand tons of old clay – within one week, they had destroyed more than two hundred homes.[10] In order to deal with a widespread shortage of fast-acting fertilizers, many people voluntarily demolished their own homes so the material could be used in the fields – countywide, 13,951 homes were demolished and 6.97 million tons of fertilizer collected.[11]

There is also material documenting the "conversion of old walls" and the "five clean-ups," which also seemed to be for the purpose of collecting fertilizer. Dingjia'ao township collected fertilizer in four different ways. The first was through the "Five Conversions": townspeople converted 1,611 houses, 75 cattle pens and pigsties, 83 toilets, 244 henhouses, and 169 semi-finished homes. Second was the "Five Excavations": townspeople manually dug up hard-packed earth, cattle pens, the area around wells, workshops, and manure dikes. Third, townspeople produced homemade chemical fertilizer. Countywide, there were 39 factories producing 1,100 *jin* of fertilizer per day, with a five-day output of 214,500 *jin*. Last, they collected small remnants of manure and green vegetation. Using these four methods, 106,125 tons of various fertilizers could be collected in five days.[12]

Communal Living

Regarding "two families living under one roof" and "commune members living together on their own initiative to share a stove," it seems that, apart from collecting fertilizer, the greater objective was, in fact, to "live together and share a stove." "Abandoning possessions" and establishing "communal property" and "communal living" were additional reasons behind the demolition of private homes in favour of communal residences during communization. One of the most important factors behind the moving and centralization of family residences, in particular, was the convenience of eating in public dining halls.[13] As the dining halls were all very large and centrally located, those who did not live near one found them very inconvenient, which created an incentive to move. In order to establish a large dining hall, a significant number of people from small villages were forced to relocate and reside collectively.[14] The result, however, was that many small villages became deserted, while the large communal quarters became overcrowded. With old and young forced to live in the same room, people began to long for their home villages.[15]

The "Rules and Regulations for Joining Communes" in the Huangguang region were very clear: "The widespread scattering of homes in our region does not suit collectivized production. In order to unify commune work units, plans regarding living quarters must be implemented. Villages must merge ... Distribution must be uniform and ... centralized."[16] Some locations hoped to establish new villages with modernized road systems to make things better organized. Communes called for the construction of new villages: "Commune members' homes must be demolished, no one will live in uncertainty."[17] To this end, Baigao Commune destroyed more than 1,165 of the commune members' 1,910 old homes. Commune unification was organized by constructing new homes or by combining households. At the time, there were 874 households living in communal residences.[18]

After returning from an inspection in Xiaogan, local authorities decided that many households had to be moved. The streets of Minji (an administrative district) were demolished at every turn so houses could be built along the road. Those without a place to live were forced to live in the pigsties. According to statistics, tens of thousands of homes were demolished.[19]

Improving Production "Efficiency"
Although collecting fertilizer and facilitating communal living were important reasons behind home demolition, the most important objective seems to have been the centralization and militarization of communal residences. Communal residences were organized like the military so that the local authorities could prevent holdups in production due to a lack of organization.[20] In fact, although the so-called new villages were designed with this purpose in mind, much of the destruction rendered very few improvements in efficiency.

During the earliest months of the Great Leap Forward, a number of homes were designated for public use. Baigao Commune designated 391 households and 382 buildings for communal use.[21] Countywide, there were 1,772 homes in use by commune members, while 54,386 had been destroyed.[22] In the latter half of 1958, after Songbu Farm had moved, 250 structures were demolished. Among those, seven protective embankments were removed, and eighteen homes were completely evacuated to allow for the construction of a massive pig farm.[23] In this case, the collection of fertilizer was clearly not the goal. As one commune member named Zhang said: "Of our twelve houses, eight were built only two years ago and so could not be used for fertilizer, but we still demolished them with the others."[24]

The situation regarding demolition differed according to location. In certain places, mid-sized and smaller teams tore down up to 130 houses. One mid-sized team consisting of 621 households destroyed 186 houses. At the time, people were saying that everyone was really exhausted from destroying houses and the "Three Eliminations" (i.e., cutting down all the trees, tearing down all the homes, and extracting all the labour).[25]

One person said: "After communization, I had no idea how long I could bear it. We tore down the houses of two villages, but they were never rebuilt. Nobody cared. The tiles were all broken, and the beams and boards were scattered all about."[26] Regarding the demolition of homes in favour of communal residences, a seventy-four-year-old man from Zougongfu told me:

> It was pretty serious here [a certain village in Dianshan]. We destroyed about 40 percent of our homes. The smaller buildings [two or three family homes] were all torn down. My family home was not demolished, but after we moved out they moved the cattle in, and it became a cattle-pen. People with no place to live were all squeezed into the homes of those whose houses had not been destroyed. You had to live like that for two years, and there was no use in complaining about it.[27]

It is clear that, at the time, the demolition of homes countywide was quite common, and in some places it was more serious than in others. As for the total number of homes destroyed, according to a statement made in March 1959 by the first secretary of the county party committee, Wu Dejian: "In Macheng, 41,000 homes were occupied without compensation. The situation can be described as 'returning homes to the people' and 'those who disagree will still join in to clean up all the bricks and beams.'" The provincial party committee secretary, Wang Tingchun, said: "Macheng demolished its houses to make fertilizer. Last year, in many places, almost one-third of homes were destroyed, but nothing new was built. This upset the people greatly."[28] According to the county party committee, more than eighty thousand houses were demolished (however, some reports claimed only forty to fifty thousand were actually destroyed). According to statistics compiled at the Zhengfeng Conference of Third-Level Cadres at the end of 1960, 47,535 buildings were destroyed countywide.[29]

Besides just the demolition of homes, it seems that even private manure stores were "communalized" or destroyed. The entire county was faced with the dilemma of eighty thousand destroyed buildings, while 98,555 manure stores had to be returned to private owners.[30] Nearly 100,000 private manure storage facilities had to be recovered.[31]

Discontentment and Resistance

One must be suspicious of exaggeration when regarding the "voluntary," or "self-initiated," behaviour of the peasantry during the early months of the Great Leap Forward. For example, when the "East Is Red" Commune attempted to mobilize the masses to tear down their homes to make fast-acting fertilizer for the early rice, there was disagreement among the people. During a commune meeting, the commune cadre warned: "Disagree if you will, but these houses do not belong to you,[32] they belong to the government. If you do not tear them down, we will organize people to come and tear them down." One commune member reacted by saying, "so this is the Great Leap Forward, we can't even live in a house."[33] In Licheng township, the masses balked when pressed to demolish their homes, leading to a warning from the commune cadre: "If you don't move, you will not be given your food rations."[34] Four small production teams in Shujiafan, managing steel production, irrigation, demolition, and fertilizer collection, occupied sixty-four houses, leaving eleven households with no place to stay and seven crowded into a dilapidated temple with water dripping from the ceiling and wind blowing through the walls. Song Qixiang, a poor peasant, once owned a row of houses but was forced to leave to make space for a grain shop and ended up living in a pigsty. It was discovered that the shop's occupation of the homes had been organized by a cadre, something the commune members were unwilling to accept. The cadre told them: "If you don't get out, you won't get anything to eat." Grudgingly, they removed the furniture on their own initiative, but in reality they were forced out.[35]

What does it mean to withhold food rations in a time of free supply? Is this not, in fact, a coercive means by which to force the masses to tear down their own homes? Indeed, the masses had no choice but to destroy their own homes and live communally – these were not "voluntary" or "self-initiated" acts. Once, when conducting village-level interviews, I mentioned the time when "the small streams combined into one big stream" (n.b., this was another way to refer to the demolition of homes in favour of communal residences), and an elderly man of over seventy years told me in exasperation: "It was impossible not to obey; otherwise, you would be assigned to the 'shock troops,' and the militia would come and knock down your house."[36]

According to the interviews I conducted, many people threw away any objects they could not take with them. Some individualistic peasants even purposely destroyed their own things. At that time, your house did not necessarily belong to you, so you could not voice your discontent. Some documentation indicates that the building material taken from the demolished homes was either returned to individual commune members or used by the commune at a discounted price. However, it seems that only five *yuan* was given for the demolition of a home. In some cases, members were compensated with the wood that had been originally used to build their homes.

There were reports at the time that claimed that a large portion of the material left over from demolished buildings was either burned, sold, wasted, or destroyed. This greatly upset homeowners, one of whom complained: "They have been saying for a year they would provide compensation. But we'll still have to wait and see if it is true or not."[37] Another said: "Everybody is talking about compensation. In three years, they have scrapped so much material, how can they come up with money for compensation?"[38]

Later, during the ongoing campaign to rectify commune organization, new rules emerged regarding the housing problem: "Commune members will be given 30 to 40 *yuan* per demolished home, and 100 *yuan* for moving expenses."[39] Another rule was later added: "When the state demolishes a home in order to produce steel, repair irrigation or transportation systems, owners will be provided standard compensation: for an average mid-sized home, 30 *yuan*; for better homes made with new bricks, 40 *yuan*; for inferior homes made with mud bricks, 20 *yuan*."[40]

At the time, there were not only communal residences but also separated residences – a phenomenon that also upset some people. It was said that short-term separation was required for production needs: "In military style, men and women will sleep separately; one company will be transformed into two different companies, and two different companies will merge into one; this village's women will report to that village for sleeping, and if they are late they will be criticized. This is the militarization movement, it is 'commandism.' When the masses' stomachs are full, there will be no more complaints." One reaction to this militarization was to point out that there were "twelve big wrongs, one of which is that the women are too concentrated."[41] There were also youth "shock teams" who slept together and undertook all activities together. It was guerrilla warfare in which no one was responsible. Work output was low, and the quality was poor.[42] A member of the county party committee aired his grievances as follows: "The reform has left husbands, wives, and children separated."[43]

The deputy director of the Chengguan Commune in Hongzhuan district said: "There were ten things people did not want to part with in the communes: one, they did not want to leave their homes; two, they did not want to part with their gardens; ... four, they did not want to part with their private possessions; ... nine, they did not want to part with the fowl they had raised." It was also said: "One family sleeps in four different places, the children sleep alone, the parents cannot see each other, and husbands and wives are broken-hearted."[44]

Discussing communal and separated living conditions, one seventy-three-year-old secretary of a village branch of Dianshan Commune told me: "In 1958, during the fall harvest, labour was centralized, and men and women had to live together. They found a big room, covered the floor with rice and straw, and everyone had to sleep on the same plank bed. The place I was overseeing back then had three centralized plank beds for sleeping." The seventy-four year-old former accountant of a large team described his experience:

> Back then men didn't live in their homes. Wherever they went that day was where they would sleep. Many slept in the work sheds, either beside the stove or beside the elevated paths in the fields. During production they would carry a flag. Some called them the "red flag company," the "sharp knife company," or the "shock team." Back then they had absolutely no home. The entire day was spent thinking only of work and production.

In other places, these "shock teams" and base-level cadre militiamen forced men and women to live together in one big shed simply for the sport of "making war."[45]

Towards the end of 1958, the editorial office of the provincial party committee's *Qiyi* magazine initiated an inquiry into peasant thought within Lingjiaxiawan (a mid-sized team from the Zhongyi Commune). Because at the time of this investigation communization was still relatively new and the first reforms had not yet been completely carried out, the report constituted a collection of rare oral accounts. To a certain degree, this document can be viewed as a manifestation of the peasantry's true sentiments.

Among these accounts are many that refer to peasant dissatisfaction with the demolition of homes and the construction of new villages. For example, a poor peasant named Ling Shengbao (fifty-six years old) complained about the way new villages were being built by the communes:

> Building a new house is good, but destroying an old home to build a new one is not. Also, the costs for building a new house are never negotiated with the people. Two cadres will just come along, not even enter the house or say a word, and just point out the order like [the Taoist god] Taishang Laojun, and that's the end of it. The "higher-ups" said that in "new" villages we shouldn't worry about travelling a bit farther to the fields because next year there will be cars to pick us up. But this was just the supervisor's wife fantasizing, like the [Taoist] celestial troops and generals who never came.

Lin Shengqi (forty-two years old) said: "From the beginning, we disagreed with destroying homes to build a 'new' village. After working my entire life to be able to scrape together these few family possessions, [now] we were supposed to demolish everything. We always felt uncomfortable with that. [But] my wife told me that tearing down your home is not as bad as burning up all your strength." Lin Shengqi went on to comment: "Constructing a 'new' village and centralizing living quarters – is our village not big enough already? How big a village do they want?"

According to the *Qiyi* report, a lower-middle-level peasant named Lin Shibin (twenty years old) was the secretary of a brigade branch and very much in favour of joining a commune. When his mother strongly resisted demolishing their home, he tried to persuade her. He did, however, also sympathize with the people. For example, there were often complaints about tearing down houses as nobody wanted to give up their homes. Commune member Lin Shengcai, for one, said: "If they tear down my house, I would rather build a straw shed on flat ground and live there than live in a 'new' village."

When one *Qiyi* investigator asked then twenty-seven year-old Lin Shibin what he thought of communism, he answered: "Look how great the 'new' village is that Zhongyi [Commune] made near the road. Every house is made with new bricks all the way up to the roof." But his wife said: "They are only single-room homes with no guest space. If we have visitors, we must find a place for them to rest or sit." Lin Shibin's family home was built in the winter of 1957. Li spent 900 *yuan* building it, but the commune gave him only 150 *yuan* for its demolition. I asked him if he did not feel it was a pity that the house was destroyed. He replied: "At first, it seemed like it was a few hundred *yuan* too little. But looking ahead from a socialist perspective, what is public and what is private? Now, there are many things that I would not admit belong to me, but I still take care of them." He added: "The new house is better than this one, I'm not against tearing it down." At the time, however, he was not speaking the truth. Two days later I went again to chat with his mother, who told us:

> We have been preparing for this house for three years. Last year we had 15 *jin* of cotton to use for ourselves and one *jin* left over. We wove it into cloth and sold it for 30 or 40 *yuan*. When we built the house, many people helped us, and we still had to borrow 200 *yuan*. As soon as I realized it was going to be like this, I could not build the [new] house. This house is very cool during the summer.

She added: "Of course, homes should first be built for those who have no home. But now people who have a lot of living space are not so eager to build."

Before liberation, upper-middle-level peasant Lin Shijian (fifty-eight years old) had a rocky piece of land and a large house. However, half of it had been vacated in favour of a large dining hall that could feed three hundred people. When the commune wanted to construct a new village, he was given 910 *yuan* for his home. At first he said: "Everyone is the same! It is right and just, there is no conflict." However, he was still reluctant, and during a later conversation he said: "It took me eight years during the Republican era to build that house, and I spent more than 1,000 *yuan*. The material alone is worth several hundred *yuan*, and now it's already been sold." In Lin's opinion, the homes being built in the new villages were of poor quality. They were so spacious that lighting was never sufficient. There were no sitting-rooms, with the result that visitors had no place to rest. They were far away from the public dining halls, and there was nowhere to get water for washing. Regarding the distance required to travel to work, he said, with irony: "We were supposed to go to work by bus, but there was no bus, and going by plane was too fast." Because his house had been made into a dining hall, he had to live with his sister-in-law, who was unhappy about the situation. He once told her earnestly: "You have been alive for decades, but when you're dead the years don't count. Each year alive counts as one year, so why do you still bother talking about this?" After hearing this, his sister-in-law was hurt: "Hearing your words has brought tears to my eyes. When I die I want to die in my own home!"

Clearly, many peasants were outraged by the destruction of their homes. Some said that tearing down their houses was even worse than digging up their ancestors' tombs.[46] One mid-sized team convinced people to demolish 204 houses belonging to 130 families, leaving 50 families with no place to live. They were forced to crowd into other people's homes – a situation that became very malodorous.[47] Another person said that, when several hundred houses were torn down, the commune members wanted to say something but kept quiet. Every day they went to work, but they were listless and just chatted among themselves.[48] Eight houses belonging to a poor, seventy-year-old commune member named Zhou were torn down, his nine pigs were taken away, two big trees in front of his house were chopped down, and the bamboo garden behind his house was destroyed. It was as though he had been "swept right out of his house" and forced to live in an old cattle-pen.

Ironically, in many cases, the destruction of homes decreased efficiency rather than improving it. Indeed, many peasants were so upset by their losses that they became listless and depressed and, thus, slowed down production efforts. Labour efficiency decreased tenfold, with five commune members able to cultivate only 0.8 *mu* of land in two days. It was estimated that grain production decreased by 420,000 *jin,* which is 2,050 *jin* per family and equal to 112 *yuan*.[49] Due to the moves, communal residences, and labour transfers, only 37 percent of the "Three Responsibilities Fields" were cultivated.[50]

The Number Two production team took up six courtyards, which once held forty households in 180 rooms, forcing commune members to live together in crowded courtyards nearby. For example, a certain commune member named Chen already had a family of seven, yet now there were twenty-eight more people from five families (and a few couples) living in his house. This was obviously very inconvenient, but the local cadre did nothing about it for some time.[51]

Mr. Liu, of the Number Two production team, originally had a three-room home, but it was taken over by the commune. As a result, the family was forced to move to another production team, and his family of five had to live together in a single room. He was normally very diligent, but since this incident he became very despondent and frequently murmured to himself, "I don't understand."[52]

Those with "no homes [and who had to] crowd into the homes of others until they became malodorous"; those who were "swept out of their homes and forced to live in old cattle-pens"; "families and couples living together under one roof"; or "entire families of five living in one room" – what kind of lives were they leading? They could not take their personal belongings with them – apart from a bed and some basic living necessities – so were these things not "confiscated," "communalized," or "abandoned"? Such things are mentioned nowhere in the archival materials.

It can be said that, in the atmosphere of a very vigorous communization movement, peasants were unable to completely reveal their true feelings, and this is fully understandable. But when I read through files from the years 1960 and 1961, it is clear that problems revealed themselves layer by layer through the numerous "rectifications." The archivists seemed to have completely changed positions as well. In discussions regarding the demolition of homes in favour of communal residences, there was no more mention of "voluntary" or "self-initiated" peasant attitudes; instead, commune members expressed only bitterness about losing their homes. For example, in 1958, the masses were extremely dissatisfied with the communal living movement. Zhangguanghe administrative region originally owned 148 *yuanzi*, but commune members were forced to combine these into forty-eight villages. The result was that the nearby fields became difficult to get to, all the good fields went to ruin, and those who originally had a home went homeless.[53] There was not even freedom to sleep as men and women, old and young, were all sleeping together in the same room, which was unacceptable.[54]

Grave Destruction

Ancestor worship has played an important role in traditional Chinese culture for centuries. During the initial period of communization, county and commune authorities mobilized peasants to destroy thousands of ancient gravesites. For many peasants, the movement to destroy graves was as traumatic an event as was losing their homes. Indeed, when the movement began, many peasants experienced it as an additional attack on the traditional family structure. Once again, however, local authorities largely ignored the discontent of the peasantry.

The primary purpose behind grave destruction was to open up new fields for cultivation (including flattening the land and linking fields) and to generate additional material for fertilizer. It was clear from the beginning, however, that many people were opposed. For example, one mid-sized team flattened ten small hills and dug up 120 ancient graves in order to transform the land into agricultural fields.[55] An instruction team from Zhongyi Commune dug up more than thirty thousand graves.[56] Chengguan Commune's Nanhu Number Two production team dug up all the commune members' ancestral graves.[57] Jiangshu administrative region's Chengma Commune dug up more than one hundred coffins to expand their rapeseed fields.[58] County party secretary Wu was quoted as saying: "Visiting representatives from Jingzhou realized that digging up graves in Baiguo Commune was not the will of the masses, and so they criticized us. But we didn't pay any attention."[59]

At a rectification meeting, county party secretary Zhao Jinliang stated:

Houses were demolished in order to procure fertilizer, forcing the masses to live in pigsties. Some families were living eight people of three generations in one room. Regardless of peasant opinion, graves were dug up in order to expand agricultural fields, their ancestors' bones becoming fertilizer. In the past, no one ever dared to offend the dead, but now nobody seems to care. At one time, I proposed that the dead should also be collectivized by constructing a collective martyrs' mausoleum. The masses were against the idea but didn't dare speak out.[60]

Archival reports suggest that many people were devastated by the destruction of ancestral graves. "There is no peace," they said, "even after death. Graves of ancient ancestors, many several decades old, were dug up, and bones were scattered everywhere – the living were driving out the dead. And what were we living for? It was like all we were doing was striking the daily bell like monks, passing the time in a daze."[61] Zhongyi Commune was the worst in terms of grave destruction. Some of the elderly members said they just wanted to be thrown into the river and carried off by the current when they died.[62] The members of Tiemen Commune strongly objected to removing dead bodies from coffins in order to use the wood to make objects for sale. They said this was like digging up the dead just to eat them.[63]

In fact, it would seem that the biggest worry of many commune members concerned the fate of their own bodies after they died. When the graves of Minji Commune member Lin Xiaozhou's father, mother, and elder brother were all dug up, not a single bone could be found. Cheng Youzong, who was more than seventy years old at the time, asked a cadre for a favour before his death: "Please bury me deep enough so I don't interfere with the crops growing above me."[64] When the provincial governor, Zhang Tixue, visited Macheng and was chatting with some of the elderly, they all told him that their greatest worry was being dug up from their graves.[65]

During the many interviews I conducted, I realized that grave destruction was not only a very real occurrence but also very common. Over forty years later, the discontent of many peasants could still be heard in their complaints: "There was nothing we could do. In order to expand the fields and increase production, almost all of our ancestral graves had to be dug up." Many cadres also admitted that it was the wrong thing to do. Thinking back after so many years, the eighty-year-old former Chengguan regional committee secretary said, with a sigh: "When the fields were being flattened, the ancestral graves of the peasants were destroyed. It was all a bit inhuman." One former brigade cadre, now seventy-three years old, added: "Graves were unearthed, and many hearts were saddened."[66]

"Production Armies" and Their Impact on Family Life

During the first months of the Great Leap Forward, "production armies," which saw the movement of huge numbers of people for the purpose of building large-scale projects, became common. As a result, in many places only one-half – and sometimes less than one-third – of the labour force remained at home to attend to the fall harvest. Further, the remaining workforce also had to shoulder the burden of looking after the "front lines" of steel and water transport.[67]

The masses reacted strongly to this predicament. Labour force cooperation had the masses constantly on the move, and, as a result, they seemed to do more walking than working.[68] Mid-sized labour teams were transferred to numerous locations as production planning was poorly organized.[69] With the labour force engaged in large-scale cooperation, bureaucratic holdups and losses were especially common. One commune's labour force was allocated to eight different places, making it impossible to finish a single task.[70] The transfer of labour led to an unlikely scene: the weak, old, and crippled taking care of production.

The linking of fields was a success, but with the majority of the workforce away little was grown or harvested. Homes were torn down and their remains scattered about; however, because the communal and the private were indistinguishable, no one cared.[71] Many could be heard complaining: "We're pushed around so much it's like we are floating in space."[72]

Some thought that the communes could be highly productive on account of their large populations, but with everyone being transferred it was, in fact, the opposite. Collectivizing labour on a large scale dampened enthusiasm, decreased efficiency, and led to production mismanagement. Labourers were upset over their lost possessions, and, as a result, "work holdups" occurred on a regular basis. During the rectification campaign of late 1958, the central authorities ordered a halt to excessive collectivization of labour.

In many places, the traditional family lifestyle was destroyed to varying degrees. The first party secretary of Hubei Province, Wang Renzhong, comments in his report:

> Communization had yet to solve a number of problems ... [S]econd, in terms of collectivized living, many policies failed to take into account the reality of the situation, and in fact defied the will of the masses. For example, large dining halls, complete public support, boarding schools for children, etc. ... In many places, communication with the masses was poor,

leading some to say, "even my son has been given to the collective" ...
Regardless of marital status, men and women were separated without
exception, and everyone slept in the same place. What was the point?
This was the end of the family as we knew it."[73]

Some thought that communism destroyed the family to the point that
people no longer cared for one another. Li Yanxi, who opposed separating
husbands and wives, said: "With the arrival of communism, the nuclear
family was destroyed, the elderly were sent to care homes, children were
placed into nurseries and kindergartens, and no one ate or slept together.
There were no feelings between parents and children anymore." It is said
that, in life, there are three especially difficult situations: children having
no mothers, adult men having no wives, and the elderly having no sons.
With the extinction of the family, these three difficulties were very much
a reality.[74]

In sum, both communal residences and separated living conditions were
related to the construction of the new villages, to the elimination of the
family, to the concentration and unification of the labour force, and to the
establishment of production armies. Indeed, these developments all led to
the creation of an industrial-military complex in the countryside.

The Essence of the Communization Movement

The term "commune" originated in medieval western Europe, where it
referred to autonomous cities and towns. The young Engels, who was
influenced by the British utopian socialist Robert Owen, employed it to
refer to the basic unit of organization in a communist society.[75] Marx later
saw the commune as a form of government of the proletariat. Influenced
by their work, Mao Zedong decided to call the combination of Large-Scale
Communes "People's Communes." But was there really a connection between the People's Communes and communism? What did "People's
Communes" really mean to Mao Zedong?

Mao Zedong's own words, perhaps, suggest the best answer. In July
1958, Mao Zedong said that the country must gradually and sequentially
organize labour, agriculture, trade, education, and the military into Large-
Scale Communes that would act as the basic units of Chinese society.[76]
The December 1958 "Resolution on Questions Regarding the People's
Communes" contains the following relevant passage:

> Labour in the People's Communes must be organized through disciplinary
> as well as democratic means. Organized militarization means that labour
> in the communes will be run like that of a factory, or a military unit –

organized and disciplined. This is crucial for large-scale agricultural production. Large-scale agricultural and industrial teams will become one great industrial army.[77]

Later Mao Zedong wrote these famous words:

Today's industrial army is organized on the principle of the bourgeoisie, where the factory corresponds to the military camp. Workers stand in front of a machine following rules no less strict than those in the military. The industrial army of a socialist society is made up of the working class, who rid the system of capitalists exploiting surplus value, vigorously realizing in themselves a self-determined democratic centralist system. We should first apply this system to the countryside in order to establish a socialist, democratically centralized agricultural-industrial army in which there are no exploitative landlords or wealthy peasants and which is divorced from the practice of small-scale production.[78]

The term "industrial army" may be understood as the "industrialization" and "militarization" of the people. On the one hand, Communist Party members called themselves "the governing party of the working class" and advocated a "factory system" in which they employed certain "scientific" procedures that involved concentration, unification of management, division of labour, cooperation, organization, supervision, standardization, monitored rates of progress, and increasing production efficiency to unprecedented rates — none of which traditional agricultural production could ever achieve. On the other hand, the idea of an industrial army was supported by the experiences of the war period.[79]

If workers were an industrial force, peasants were an even greater industrial force. It was thought that, if peasants were organized into industrial armies, they would be more motivated, and production would increase. They could organize themselves into corps, battalions, companies, platoons, and squads.[80] This is why Mao Zedong lauded and hoped for the widespread adoption of Xushui County's "full coverage" labour system (collectivizing labour, pitching camps, and engaging in late-night work parties).[81]

Upon seeing what Xushui County had achieved, Mao asked: "Are they not just like an army? ... [E]ating and starting work at fixed times, organization like this requires discipline ... [A]t once a battalion and a production team ... [O]rganized like an army, labour will become much more efficient." Hence his proposal: "Establishing People's Communes is still the best way to organize ... [T]he combination of industry, agriculture, commerce, education, and the military will be easier to manage."

At the Beidaihe Conference, Mao also noted that many people sacrificed their lives in the revolution without asking for anything in return, and he wondered why the same could not be done now.[82] He suggested that China take the measures it did during the war period. People were meant to forget costs and returns and be willing to sacrifice their lives for the sake of production and the Great Leap Forward. Mao went further, saying that, in the past, armies were run without pay, without weekends, and without eight-hour working shifts but were always united in spirit. The communist spirit flourished as hundreds and thousands of officials and soldiers were motivated and worked together as a team. In the past, the free-supply system was implemented, people lived a communist lifestyle, and they fought a twenty-two-year-long war and won: "Why should we not establish a communist society now?"

I believe this to be an explanation of so-called "communization." If it must be defined as an "-ism," it could be identified as a kind of "military communism." In fact, Mao had been thinking about this much earlier than 1958. He was very concerned about the Soviet Union's experience with socialism, feeling that it had developed there too slowly. He decided to search for a faster route to socialism, one that suited the conditions in China. However, eight years after the establishment of the "new" China, Mao Zedong and other Party leaders still lacked the knowledge and experience required to properly run the economy. They were unwilling to indiscriminately copy the experiences of others; however, because they lacked their own experience, it was easier to apply the economic successes of the revolutionary period to the construction of the current economy. Obvious examples included employing mass movements and administrative orders.[83] There is further evidence that shows that rural collectivization had been Mao's idea from the very beginning, and, indeed, it can be traced as far back as 1953.[84]

Force was used not only against non-proletarian classes but also against the proletariat itself: this included coercion from the barrel of a gun and compulsory labour. Therefore, it is fair to say that the Great Leap Forward followed in the footsteps of the "Leninist-Stalinist model." It was a return to "militant communism" and "labour armies." Moreover, by utilizing labour armies in the countryside – something the Soviet Union was unable to do – the state managed to realize what Marx noted in his *Communist Manifesto* as "measures that almost all of the most advanced states are able to adopt" after seizing power – that is, "the implementation of universal, compulsory labour and the establishment of an industrial army, especially in terms of agriculture."[85]

For exactly this reason, Mao added a special passage concerning "industrial armies" to the 1958 "Resolution on Problems Regarding People's Communes." Therefore, regardless of which perspective we take, I feel it is inappropriate to call the communization movement of 1958 a "great communist experiment."

What exactly was this "agricultural-industrial army"? The original works of Marx, Lenin, and Mao Zedong offer no further explanation. Thus, we must turn to the situation in Macheng to determine its meaning. At one county committee meeting concerning whether or not the "great steel drive" had influenced agricultural production, committee member Chen Guochang criticized himself: "At the time, our knowledge regarding the organization of the new industrial army was insufficient."[86] At a county rectification meeting, county party secretary Chao Jinliang noted:

> The entire county has become one big commune, and peasants have become workers ... [A]ll the land in Macheng County has been combined into production plots of several hundred or several thousand *mu* (the smallest was 500 *mu*, while the largest was several tens of thousands) ... [P]roduction was like an army at war, tens of thousands of people [working] together. All the rice in the fields was neatly transplanted and separated from the grain and cotton – the fields of grain a sheet of yellow, the fields of cotton a sheet of white. The entire county looked like this.[87]

The "Three Transformations" were implemented throughout Macheng's Huanggang region, organizing the masses into military units ready for "battle." Thirteen militia contingents, 134 regiments, 1,084 battalions, and 7,892 companies were established in the region. Also set up in the region were 44,521 public dining halls, 36,163 nurseries, 3,462 kindergartens, 4,304 sewing groups, 526 old people's homes, and 21,758 grain-processing facilities, all tapping a great deal of labour to be invested in production.

Demolishing homes, living in communal residences, working in labour camps (with men and women separated) – was this not the life of an industrial army? "Collectivized living," no fear of "losing your family," rejecting the "one family, one household lifestyle,"[88] "each person needing only a bed and blanket, a few items of clothing, a pair of chopsticks and a bowl, eating wherever they happen to be"[89] – was this not the mentality of an industrial army? "Sharing property," "rushing production," being equally poor, wholeheartedly taking part in the political movement, "forcing the wealthy into a desperate battle,"[90] "selling all possessions except for a marching pack"[91] – were these not the practices of an industrial army? A free-supply system, public dining halls, "having few personal belongings,"[92] reliving past war time experiences – were these not the aspirations of an industrial army?

Do the previous comments really suggest a desire to establish "communism"? I would argue no: the focus of all of the previous statements is on the establishment of an industrial army. After communization, peasants began to "resist" and "take a firm stance" (Mao Zedong's words). As Gao Wangling notes in Chapter 11 of this volume, the main means of peasant resistance were "slacking off at work" or simply "not producing,"[93] which often resulted in decreased output and lower production efficiency, neglect and destruction of fields, and, ultimately, lower cultivation levels. Therefore, the CCP was forced to "rectify" the situation. In light of this, I would like to ask just what the "rectification campaign" of late 1958 and early 1959 actually solved.

From the perspective of this chapter, the campaign seemed to first of all undermine the industrial army. Of course, the industrial army was one of Mao's ideas and could not easily be "rectified." For example, methods such as "large formation warfare" reappeared shortly after the Lushan Conference in July 1959. But the "production army" and the Three Transformations were no longer mentioned or emphasized. To a certain extent, "communal property" was even rejected. At the same time, the free-supply system was undergoing changes. For a number of years, salaries decreased, and the work-point system was poorly administered. But the People's Communes were no longer relying on militarization or the free-supply system to sustain themselves: they now had public dining halls upon which to rely. This is likely the reason public dining halls became so important in the second half of 1959 and in 1960. Further, the earlier spirit of idealism was lost. The peasants now had to struggle for their survival.

Notes

1 *Neibu cankao* [Internal Reference] (hereafter *NBCK*), "Dang nei tongxin" [An Internal Party Letter], 12:283-86.

2 Song Liansheng, *Zongluxian, dajuejin, renmingongshehua yundong shimo* [The General Line, the Great Leap Forward, and the People's Commune Movement] (Kunming: Yunnan renmin chubanshe, 2002), 149.

3 Bo Yibo, *Ruogan zhongda juece yu shijian de huigu (xiuding ben)* [Reflections on Certain Major Decisions and Events] (Beijing: Renmin chubanshe, 1997), 2:757.

4 Li Rui, *Lushan huiyi shilu* [Memorandum on the Lushan Conference] (Zhengzhou: Henan renmin chubanshe, 1995), 9.

5 Regarding the Great Leap on the local level, see Ralph Thaxton, *Catastrophe and Contention in Rural China: Mao's Great Leap Forward Famine and the Origins of Righteous Resistance in Da Fo Village* (New York: Cambridge University Press, 2008); Erik Mueggler, *The Age of the Wild Ghosts: Memory, Violence, and Place in Southwest China* (Berkeley: University of California Press, 2001); and Jia Yanmin, *Dayuejin shiqi xiangcun zhengzhi de dianxing: Henan Chayashan weixing renmin gongshe yanjiu* [A Typical Example of Rural Politics during the

Great Leap Forward: A Study of Henan's Chayashan Satellite Commune] (Beijing: Zhishi chanquan chubanshe, 2006).

6 Zhang Zhanbin, Liu Jiehui, and Zhang Guohua, eds., *Dajuejin he sannian kunnan shiqi de Zhongguo* [China in the Age of the Great Leap Forward and the Three Difficult Years] (Beijing: Zhongguo shangye chubanshe, 2001), 109.

7 For details, see *NBCK*, "Jifei yundong zai ge xiang rehuo chaotian de kaifa" [The Development of the Campaign to Store Fertilizer Is in Full Swing in Every Village], 2-3 April 1959.

8 These notes refer to the archives found in the Macheng City Archive building. Macheng County Party Committee Archives (hereafter MCPCA), no. 1-310, 11 April 1958, "Jifei yundong zai ge xiang rehuo chaotian de kaifa" [The Development of the Campaign to Store Fertilizer Is in Full Swing in Every Village].

9 MCPCA, no. 1-310, 11 April 1958, "Jifei yundong zai ge xiang rehuo chaotian de kaifa."

10 Ibid.

11 Ibid.

12 Ibid., no. 1-331, 15 July 1958, "Xianjin dianxing shiji baogaohui cailiao huibian" [Edited Documents of the Report Conference on the Achievements in Advanced Models].

13 For research regarding public dining, see Li Chunfeng, "Jinnian lai 'dayuejin' shiqi gong-gong shitang yanjiu zongshu" [The State of the Art Research of the Last Years Regarding the Public Dining Halls during the Period of the "Great Leap Forward"], *Gaoxiao sheke dongtai* [Trends of Social Science in Higher Education] 2 (2007): 17-22; and Luo Ping-han, *Daguofan: Gonggong shitang shimo* [Eating out of the Big Pot: The History of the Public Dining Halls] (Nanning: Guangxi renmin chubanshe, 2001).

14 MCPCA, no. 1-428, 23 May 1959, "Xianwei shuji jianghua" [Speeches Made by the Secretary of the County Party Committee].

15 Ibid.

16 Ibid. no. 1-357, 28 September 1958, "Huanggang diqu rushe gui'an [Regulations for Communization of the Huanggang District].

17 Ibid., no. 1-371, 19 March 1959, "Xianwei quantihui jilu" [Record of the Plenary Session of the County Party Committee].

18 Ibid., no. 1-419, 27 January 1959, "Xianwei quantihui jilu."

19 Ibid., no. 1-454, 10 December 1960, "Xianwei shuji cankao xuexi huibao cailiao" [Report Material for Consultation and Learning of the County Party Secretary].

20 Ibid., no. 1-502, 11 December 1960, "Xianwei shuji cankao xuexi huibao cailiao."

21 Ibid., no. 1-419, 27 January 1959, "Xianwei quantihui jilu."

22 Ibid., no. 1-370, 13 April 1959, "Xianwei quantihui jilu."

23 Ibid., no. 1-502, 15 December 1960, "Xianwei shuji jianghua."

24 Ibid., no. 1-408, 20 April 1959, "Xianwei quantihui jilu."

25 Ibid., no. 1-336, 25 January 1959, "Xianwei quantihui jilu"; ibid., no. 1-401, 2 November 1959, "Xianwei shuji jianghua."

26 Ibid., no. 1-371, 22 March 1959, "Xianwei quantihui jilu."

27 Interview notes 2004.

28 MCPCA, no. 1-371, 22 March 1959, "Xianwei quantihui jilu."

29 Ibid., no. 1-454, 24 December 1960, "Xianwei shuji jianghua."

30 Ibid., no. 1-416, 24 July 1959, "Zhonggong Macheng xianwei wenjian" [Documents of the Communist Party of Macheng County].

31 Ibid., no. 1-383, June 1959, "Zhonggong Macheng xianwei wenjian."

32 This point is supported by an interview in which one elderly peasant said to me: "At the time, yours and mine were indistinguishable, and your house did not necessarily belong to you" (interview notes, May 2004).

33 MCPCA, no. 1-299, 20 April 1958, "Xianwei quantihui jilu."

34 Ibid., no. 1-378, 20 January 1959, "Xianwei quantihui jilu."

35 Ibid., no. 1-568, 27 December 1960, "Xianwei shuji jianghua."

36 Interview notes 2004.
37 MCPCA, no. 1-568, 27 December 1960, "Xianwei shuji jianghua."
38 Ibid., no. 1-568, 28 December 1960, "Xianwei shuji jianghua."
39 Ibid., no. 1-454, 20 December 1960, "Xianwei shuji jianghua."
40 Ibid., no. 1-534, 18 February 1961, "Xianwei quantihui jilu."
41 Ibid., no. 1-371, 5 April 1959, "Xianwei quantihui jilu."
42 Ibid., no. 1-378, 25 July 1959, "Zhonggong Macheng xianwei wenjian."
43 Ibid., no. 1-401, 2 November 1959, "Xianwei weiyuan Zhu Zhangkai jianghua" [Speech Made by a Member of the Party County Committee, Zhu Zhangkai].
44 Ibid., no. 1-376, 5 December 1959, "Xianwei shuji jianghua."
45 Interview notes 2004.
46 MCPCA, no. 1-383, 16 April 1959, "Xianwei quantihui jilu."
47 Ibid., no. 1-371, 22 March 1959, "Xianwei quantihui jilu."
48 Ibid., no. 1-371, 19 March 1959, "Xianwei quantihui jilu."
49 Ibid., no. 1-384, 23 May 1959, "Zhonggong Macheng xianwei wenjian."
50 Ibid., no. 1-416, 17 May 1959, "Zhonggong Macheng xianwei wenjian."
51 Ibid., no. 1-378, 25 July 1959, "Zhonggong Macheng xianwei wenjian."
52 Ibid., no. 1-406, 20 August 1959, "Zhonggong Macheng xianwei wenjian."
53 Ibid., no. 1-536, 22 January 1961, "Xianwei quantihui jilu."
54 Ibid., no. 1-502, 11 December 1960, "Xianwei shuji jianghua."
55 Ibid., no. 1-294, 8 December 1958, "Xianwei shuji jianghua."
56 Ibid., no. 1-300, 26 June 1958, "Zhonggong Macheng xianwei wenjian."
57 Ibid., no. 1-502, 13 December 1960, "Xianwei shuji jianghua."
58 Ibid., no. 1-545, 18 December 1960, "Xianwei shuji jianghua."
59 Ibid., no. 1-416, 11 July 1959, "Zhonggong Macheng xianwei wenjian."
60 Ibid., no. 1-454, 10 December 1960, "Xianwei shuji jianghua."
61 Ibid., no. 1-379, 22 March 1959, "Xianwei quantihui jilu."
62 Ibid., no. 1-502, 11 December 1960, "Xianwei shuji jianghua."
63 Ibid., no. 1-502, 14 December 1960, "Xianwei shuji jianghua."
64 Ibid., no. 1-534, 4 October 1961, "Zhonggong Macheng xianwei wenjian."
65 Ibid., no. 1-556, 14 December 1961, "Xianwei shuji jianghua."
66 Interview notes 2004.
67 MCPCA, no. 1-382, 2 January 1959, "Xianwei quantihui jilu."
68 Ibid., no. 1-371, 19 March 1959, "Xianwei quantihui jilu."
69 Ibid.
70 Ibid.
71 Ibid.
72 Ibid., no. 1-463, 10 September 1960, "Zhonggong Macheng xianwei wenjian."
73 Ibid., no. 1-443, 15 January 1959, "Xianwei quantihui jilu."
74 Ibid.
75 Bo, *Ruogan zhongda juece yu shijian de huigu*, 2:735.
76 Zhonggong zhongyang wenxian yanjiushi, ed. *Jianguo yilai Mao Zedong wengao* [Writings of Mao Zedong since the Establishment of the People's Republic of China] (Beijing: Zhongguo wenxian chubanshe, 1995), 7:317.
77 Zhonggong zhongyang wenxian yanjiushi, ed. *Jianguo yilai zhongyao wenxian xuanbian* [Selected Important Documents since the Founding of the People's Republic of China] (Beijing: Zhonggong zhongyang wenxian chubanshe, 1996), 11:618.
78 Zhonggong zhongyang wenxian yanjiushi, ed. *Jianguo yilai Mao Zedong wengao*, 7:573.
79 Regarding the relationship between communization and militarization, see Franz Schurmann, *Ideology and Organization in Communist China* (Berkeley: University of California Press, 1968).
80 Bo, *Ruogan zhongda juece yu shijian de huigu (xiuding ben)*, 2:744.
81 Li, *Lushan huiyi shilu*, 35-36.

82 Recording of a speech made by Mao Zedong during a regional leaders' conference, 21 August 1958.

83 Pang Xianzhi and Jin Chongji, *Mao Zedong zhuan (1949-1976)* [Biography of Mao Zedong (1959-1976)] (Beijing: Zhonyang wenxian chubanshe, 2003), 843.

84 Gao Wangling, "Guanyu Du Runsheng huiyi de huiyi" [On the Recollection of the Memory of Du Runsheng], unpublished manuscript.

85 For more on this, see Gao Wangling, "1956 nian de xiaoyuejin" [The Minor Leap Forward of 1956], unpublished manuscript; and "Wo yan zhong de dayuejin" [The Great Leap Forward in My Eyes], unpublished manuscript.

86 MCPCA, no. 1-375, 6 February 1959, "Xianwei quanti huiyi jilu."

87 Ibid., no. 1-454, 24 December 1960, "Jianding lichang chedi fandiao 'wufeng,' wei baowei sanmian hongqi er douzheng: Chao Jinliang tongzhi zai zhengfeng dahui shang dierci baogao" [The Report of Comrade Chao Jinliang at the Second Conference for Adjustment].

88 Ibid., no. 1-509, 16 April 1960, "Shengwei shuji Wang Renzhong jianghua" [Speech Made by Provincial Party Committee Secretary Wang Renzhong]. In this speech, Wang Renzhong quoted Vladimir Mayakovsky: "Oh, communes / all I have is yours / except for my toothbrush."

89 MCPCA, no. 1-402, 28 October 1959, "Xianwei weiyuan Zhu Zhangkai jianghua" [Speech Made by County Committee Member Zhu Zhangkai].

90 Ibid., no. 1-502, 13 December 1960, "Xianwei shuji Chao Jinliang jianghua" [Speech Made by Secretary Chao Jinliang of the County Party Committee].

91 Ibid., no. 1-502, 14 December 1960, "Xianwei shuji Zhao Jinliang jianghua" [Speech Made by the Party Secretary of the County Zhao Jinliang].

92 Ibid., no. 1-509, 16 April 1960, "Shengwei shuji Wang Renzhong jianghua" [Speech Made by Provincial Party Committee Secretary Wang Renzhong]. In his opinion, "owning few private possessions" and children being "communally raised in a public family" were experiences from "a time when we implemented the free-supply system."

93 The words of Du Runsheng. See Gao, *Guanyu Du Runsheng huiyi de huiyi*.

7 Food Augmentation Methods and Food Substitutes during the Great Famine

Gao Hua

Translated by Robert Mackie

Between 1960 and 1962, two successive campaigns were launched nationwide in response to problems related to grain: the Food Augmentation Methods Campaign and the Food Substitutes Campaign. Initiated by local CCP committees and governments during the spread of the Great Famine (and when the authorities were still convinced grain harvests were plentiful), the former gained the recognition and support of the Central Committee as a means to control grain consumption; the latter, a disaster relief campaign, was instigated once the Party realized the Great Famine was in fact a reality and there was no grain with which to feed the masses. Research related to these two grain-crisis-related campaigns, both domestic and foreign, is relatively scarce. In an effort to fill the void, this chapter seeks to examine the cause, development, and aftermath of each of these campaigns.

Certain of a Plentiful Harvest, the Food Augmentation Methods Campaign Is Introduced

"Advanced rice-cooking methods" and "food augmentation methods" were created early on by local Party committees and governments. In May 1959, a sideline production team from a satellite commune in Santaizi Prefecture, Heishan County, Liaoning Province, came up with the "corn augmentation method," which consisted of first steaming, then grinding, and finally boiling corn. It was reported that, after eating noodles made using the corn augmentation method, "the masses' faces glowed with health, and production was undertaken with renewed vigour." After the Liaoning provincial committee reported its findings, the corn augmentation method was officially approved by the Central Committee and promoted throughout the country. In January 1960, Shanghai's Chuansha County introduced the

This chapter was originally published as "Da jihuang zhong de 'liangshi yong zhengliangfa' yu daishipin" in *Ershiyi shiji* [Twenty-First Century] 72 (2002). It is reprinted with permission.

advanced rice-cooking method, which increased the yield of 1 *jin* of polished rice from 2 *jin* to 2.8 *jin*.

That month Henan Province came up with a more "scientific" term for a similar process: the food augmentation method. Specifically, the process consisted of taking 60 to 70 percent cooked rice, removing it from boiling water, using a water mill to grind it into a paste, adding yeast to the paste, and then, once it began to leaven, steaming it in a basket until cooked. The result was that, while using the traditional method of steaming, *mo* buns consisting of only one or at the most two *jin* could be produced from one *jin* of flour. Using the augmentation method, one *jin* of flour could yield five *jin* of *mo* buns. Commune members in Henan called these *mo* buns "Great Leap buns" and even composed a song to express their excitement:

> Great Leap buns cannot be over-rated,
> They cure your hunger and leave you sated.
> Economical and nutritious,
> For the nation and the people they're more than just delicious.[1]

The experiences of Chuansha County and Henan Province demonstrate how food conservation in the south, where rice is the staple diet, differed from food conservation in the north, where noodles are the staple. After these methods became known, numerous "augmentation methods" began appearing one after another, all claiming that the food produced was "healthy" and "easy to digest." These included:

- Beijing city, Miyun County's "boil, steam twice, and then grind" method;
- Liaoning Province, Fushun city's "oil and water blend" vegetable oil augmentation method, the special technique of which was to use ultrasonic waves to emulsify vegetable oil in water;
- Hunan Province's "fry, scald, and steam" method;
- Sichuan Province, Qionglai city, Pujiang County's "steamed millet" and "thrice boiled" augmentation methods;
- Wuhan city's "steamed rice" method;
- Chongqing city's "cold water" rice-cooking method;
- Lanzhou city's "boiled noodles and steamed buns" method;
- Xi'an city's "basic noodles" and "buns steamed in bowls" augmentation methods;
- Henan Province, Lushan County's "boil, dry, grind, and scald" noodle augmentation method.

All over China various augmentation methods were being invented. Even though, prior to the Lushan Conference, the Central Committee had spread word of the experiences of Liaoning's Heishan County throughout the country, after Peng Dehuai, Huang Kecheng, Zhang Wentian, and Zhou Xiaozhou were criticized, work on this had been put aside. Not until March 1960 did leaders finally begin to truly express interest in and promote these newly invented augmentation methods throughout the country. After March, the number of "meal-units" in Hubei, Hebei, Henan, Anhui, Jiangsu, Shandong, Inner Mongolia, Jiangxi, Guangxi, Shanxi, Sichuan, Liaoning, Beijing, Tianjin, and Shanghai using augmentation methods had risen from 50 to 90 percent.[2]

Did the promotion of augmentation methods mean the leadership finally realized China was facing a serious grain crisis and was thus preparing to adopt the appropriate relief measures? If we review those policies enacted by the leadership in the first few months of 1960, we are unable to formulate a judgment. The facts are as follows. Beijing firmly believed that nationwide harvests were plentiful, that granaries were full, and that they could not only meet domestic grain requirements but also export grain for profit. At the same time, the leadership believed that grain conservation and bumper crops did not conflict: the more crops that were harvested, the more grain it was necessary to save. Naturally, the next question that must be asked is this: what was the leadership's response to the widespread outbreak of edema, the unusual number of deaths, and the population outflow following the Great Leap Forward of 1958?

State Response to Outbreaks of Edema
After the introduction of the Great Leap Forward in 1958, internal reports on cases of edema (except those that occurred in the first few months following the Lushan Conference) maintained, for the most part, that the situation was normal. According to incomplete statistics, in 1958 alone, Henan, Sichuan, Yunnan, Gansu, Shandong, and Hunan reported serious increases in the number of cases of edema.[3]

By 1959, edema had spread over an even larger area at an even faster pace. According to statistics from a number of sources,

• Shandong Province, Heze region, early spring 1959, cases of edema reached 727,000, with 1,558 fatalities;
• Guangdong Province, Hainan Island, July 1959, 43,000 cases of edema in Haikou city and six other surrounding counties.[4]

By 1960, edema had become a common illness throughout the country. In Hubei Province alone, cases of edema, emaciation, and metreptosis reached 39,500 by mid-April. In Jiangsu, 12,600 cases of edema were reported, and by June 89,200 people were suffering from edema and emaciation.[5]

Provincial leaders and the Central Committee spent a considerable amount of time searching for a reason for the widespread outbreak of edema. At first, it was thought that eating unclean food was causing digestive and absorption problems that led to edema. Later, it was thought that consuming too much salt was the cause of edema. Finally, it was decided that poor nutrition led to edema.[6] Beijing then demanded that local governments solve the problem of edema that was afflicting the masses, yet it would not reduce the grain-quota taxes these localities were obligated to pay.

State Response to Population Outflow

In April 1958, great numbers of peasants from Shandong and Gansu began migrating to Inner Mongolia's Hetao region. In 1959, huge numbers of peasants from outlying areas began to move into the cities of Beijing, Shenyang, Hohhot, and Baotou. By April, tens of thousands of peasants had migrated to Shanghai. According to incomplete statistics,

- in Hebei Province the migrant population was 280,000;
- in Shandong Province the migrant population reached 320,000, among which 100,000 were able-bodied youth.[7]

From January to April 1960, the number of migrant peasants "riding the train for free" reached 170,000, three times as many as during the same period the previous year. The majority of these "free-riders" were from Shandong, Hebei, and Henan – 60 percent heading northeast, 20 percent heading northwest, and another 20 percent heading to other cities. Between January and June of that year, 600,000 peasants "blindly" migrated to Inner Mongolia, while another 300,000 fled from Liaoning Province.[8]

Beijing was greatly opposed to the population outflow from rural areas. In March 1959, the Central Committee and the state council issued an "emergency notice on stopping the random outflow of the labour force from rural areas," after which refugee camps were established at all major traffic hubs. Beijing and other major urban centres were able to provide food (even without grain coupons) for this new migrant population, but each person was required to register and, without exception, return to her or his native place.

State Response to the Economic Slide's Effect on the Export of Non-Staple Foods to Hong Kong

Due to a short supply of agricultural secondary products, mainland exports of non-staple foods to Hong Kong decreased sharply after November 1958.[9] Beijing's response was to encourage the masses to eat less meat and eggs, and, by May 1959, the sale of pork and fresh eggs in local mainland markets had been greatly reduced. In the larger urban centres, citizen provisions (other than guaranteed necessities) had been either reduced to the absolute minimum or cut off all together in order to revitalize exports. Henan Province responded to the call of the Central Committee by suggesting: "Prior to the National Day holiday, do not eat meat or eggs, or at least eat fewer eggs." Hubei Province regulations stipulated that, from the county level to the provincial level, without exception (other than special requirements), the provision of meat would cease. In April 1959, the city of Wuhan extended the ban on meat supply to include restaurants, public dining halls, and snack shops. On the rare occasion meat was offered somewhere, people were lined up as far as the eye could see.[10]

State Response to Provision Difficulties in Urban Centres during Holidays

Between January and April 1959, pork provisions for Shanghai residents had been reduced by 35.92 percent; domestic fowl had been reduced by 75.19 percent; eggs had been reduced by 79.56 percent; and chicken, duck, and fish ceased to be provided. The original monthly amount of six *liang* (based on a former weight measurement system) of meat per person could no longer be maintained. Items that once collected dust on supermarket shelves, such as powdered-milk substitute and powdered-lotus substitute, had become bestsellers. Grain shops started distributing sweet potato strips and maize noodles to serve as fixed rations.[11]

The nation's capital was also dealing with provision difficulties during holiday periods. Even with local support from around the country, in 1959 Beijing's food supply was still less than it had been during the previous year's Spring Festival. During the Dragon Boat Festival of 1959, Ma Yin-chu could eat only a few *zongzi* (rice and choice of filling wrapped in leaves and boiled) because there was no chicken or pork. He said that, in all his seventy-eight years, this was the first time he was unable to celebrate the Dragon Boat Festival. Professor Fu Ying from the chemistry department at Beijing University raised fifty small chickens of his own at home.

Compared to challenges regarding provisions in the larger urban centres, those in the smaller cities were far greater. In 1959, the black market in Shandong Province's Zaozhuang city was selling dried yams for eight *mao* per *jin* and acacia leaves for five *fen* per *jin*.[12] From every committee and government level, the state appealed to people to establish the People's Republic of China and to campaign for people to compare the new China favourably with the old China.

State Response to the Sudden Increase in Unnatural Deaths

After 1958-59, the situation became increasingly serious, and, according to *Neibu cankao* (Internal Reference), certain provinces were especially hard hit.

- Henan Province: Between 20 September and 20 December 1958, 152,132 people developed edema and 7,465 died in the four special districts of Nanyang, Xuchang, Kaifeng, and Luoyang. Weishi County of the Xuchang district was affected the worst.
- Sichuan Province: Between late October and November 1958, some 2,078 people developed edema, and 405 died in Ziyang County. In August, leg edema occurred in ten counties and cities, including Meishan, Dazu, and Jiangjing. Three thousand one hundred and five people developed edema, and 405 died.
- Yunnan Province: Between February and October 1958, 334,000 developed edema, and 4,500 died. The death rate among the sick was 13.77 percent. The situation was most serious in Qujing and Yuxi special districts, which accounted for 58.6 percent of the sick and 63.4 percent of the deaths for the whole province.
- Gansu Province: After December 1957, edema appeared in the Tianshui district. In Qin'an County, 1,026 people developed edema, and in An County 1,113 people died as a result of edema, while 327 people died because they were so "skinny."
- Anhui Province: Between October 1958 and 14 February 1959 in the two districts of Fuyang and Fengbu, 23,992 people developed edema, and 365 died.

In 1959 edema was widespread on a large scale. According to unverified sources,

- Shangdong Province, Heze district: After the arrival of spring in 1959, 727,000 people developed edema, and 1,558 died.
- Guizhou Province: Between January and April 1959 in the Xijiang Commune in Kaili County, twenty-four people "starved to death," twenty-nine people died as a result of starvation and disease, 248 people died as a result of disease, and 627 ran away. The Party secretary of the county

proclaimed that the people died because of an "infectious disease" and that the escapees were engaging in "counter-revolutionary destruction."[13]
- Between the winter of 1959 and April 1960, the number of deaths in Jiangsu Province's Baoying County reached 35,391, the majority of which were the result of starvation. Also, in Baoying, 927 abandoned babies were found, 153 of whom had died.[14]
- Between January and February 1960, there were 1,171 unnatural deaths in Jiangsu's Gaochun County.[15]

Beijing felt that the reason for these unnatural deaths was the fact that the "democratic revolution was incomplete,"[16] and it demanded that class struggle be employed to counter-attack the damaging effects of class enemies. At the same time, local governments were instructed to appropriate proper relief measures for refugees and to fix any problems arising in the aftermath of the famine. Leaders in Beijing held the following beliefs regarding these "negative occurrences."

First, they firmly believed that the national food situation was stable. On 26 January 1960, the state council issued a document that proclaimed that, in 1958 and 1959, particularly large amounts of grain were harvested; that the current grain supply situation was exceptionally good; and that, by the end of June 1960, state granaries would be stocked with 50 billion *jin* of grain (up from the 34.3 billion *jin* from the previous year). In reality, however, by the end of June 1960, state granaries held only 12.7 billion *jin* of grain or even less. The situation was extremely dangerous.[17]

Second, the Beijing leaders firmly believed that these "negative occurrences" were simply "single-finger" problems and that the other "nine fingers" were just fine.

Third, the leaders believed in continuing with the widespread establishment of public dining halls. After the Lushan Conference, private plots were again confiscated by the state; after March 1960, all grain was distributed directly to the public dining halls (not to the people); and by April, 400 million people throughout rural China were eating in public dining halls.

Fourth, the leaders believed that, without exception, all opinions voiced by the people regarding food supply to be reactions to class struggle and the struggle between socialism and capitalism, and they considered any dissatisfaction with the supply system as simply an attempt to "stir up trouble." Further, the adage "socialism will not allow people to starve to death" became an indisputable fact – a fact through which all reality had to be filtered. Wemheuer points to the origins of this "factual discourse" in Chapter 4 of this volume.

As a result of these beliefs, Beijing paid insufficient attention to local government emergency reports on the food crisis. In fact, Beijing believed this so-called "grain crisis" was the result of peasants and low-level production teams engaging in "concealed production and private distribution." Thus, beginning in 1959, the state engaged in a continuous "struggle against concealed production."

In regard to the food crisis, Beijing adopted the following four measures. First, China was to continue to export grain. In 1958, China exported 2.66 million tons of grain. In 1959, exports suddenly increased to 4.15 million tons, and in November alone 1.88 billion *jin* of grain were exported. This 400 million *jin* totalled more than the total fourth quarter exports of 1.5 billion *jin* and set a new record for grain exports. In 1960, exports were expected to reach 2.72 million tons (actual grain exports that year were 2.65 million tons). As a result of China's claim to have harvested bumper crops, Eastern European countries demanded that China supply them with 847,000 tons of grain, an increase of 50 percent over the previous year.[18]

Second, the country was to continue with high grain purchase quotas. In 1958, grain purchase quotas made up 29.4 percent of all grain produced. In 1959, quotas increased to 39.7 percent of all grain produced, and in 1960 they were at 35.6 percent.[19] By 27 November 1959, the state had purchased 107.7 billion *jin* of grain, 24.18 billion *jin* of which were stored in granaries in October of that year – 15.37 billion *jin* (or 1.5 times) more than that from the same period the previous year.[20]

Third, China was to reduce the sale of grain in urban and rural centres. Between July and November 1959, rural grain sales amounted to 12.7 billion *jin*, 4 billion *jin* fewer than the previous year. In the whole country, sales amounted to 34.6 billion *jin*, 4 billion *jin* fewer than the previous years.[21]

Fourth, propaganda was utilized to explain the new concept of "good days make up for the bad ones," which came from the highest level of government. At the Lushan Conference, Mao Zedong stated: "Prosperous times will make up for times of poverty, times of comfort will carry us through times of stress. Control food supply, conserve grain, mix grain with vegetables, eat your fill, and eat well." At the same time, Mao argued that it was necessary to "rectify the thinking of those peasants who wanted more provisions, more land, and more to eat."

The beliefs Beijing held and the measures it took were related to the inaccurate channels of information by which it was served. According to available information, the higher levels of leadership were aware that certain provinces and regions were suffering from starvation. Yet, from the start of the Great Leap Forward, local disaster reporting systems were ineffective, among which Henan's Xinyang region was the worst. In the winter of 1959, the number of victims of natural disasters in Xinyang was staggering, but local leaders were still covering up the truth: "If there is famine due to crop failure, report a bumper harvest."[22] Local leaders in many locations failed to report disasters, which resulted in Beijing's inability to understand the extent of the starvation affecting the nation.

The concealment of disaster reports by local officials was related to the "anti-rightest" trend that arose after the Lushan Conference: to report a disaster meant self-negation. As a result, although many local officials were witness to a large number of deaths, they still would not distribute any grain (even if they had grain stored in the granaries), and they even refused to report the disaster. Of even greater significance was the fact that the highest levels of leadership considered disaster "taboo" and something to be avoided – something many local officials took into consideration in their concealment of disaster reports (again, see Wemheuer in Chapter 4 of this volume).

Finally, according to a number of government officials, grain conservation and the exportation of grain were not contradictory: it had been this way for many years, it was simply "dynamic equilibrium," or it was "overall balance." This is an example of how the leadership steeped itself in its own logic.

However, the food problem became increasingly serious. Against this backdrop, Beijing formally responded to the nationwide food shortage in March 1960 by continuing with the principles of confiscating private plots, distributing grain to public dining halls, continuing to export grain, "organizing the people's economic lives," and promoting "food augmentation methods" so that it would be possible to achieve grain conservation and exportation targets.

What Was the "Organization of the People's Economic Lives"?

In March 1960, the phrase "organization of the people's economic lives" began to appear frequently in various Central Committee documents and publications. In the context of the period, this phrase can be understood on two different levels. First, it was part of the development of a number of various propaganda campaigns meant to explain the rationality and necessity behind current economic policies, especially why "after a bumper harvest it is still necessary to conserve grain."[23] Second, it was indicative of the initiation, on every level of government, of measures meant to increase production but remain economical, control grain consumption, and "counter the destructive activities of class enemies."

The greatest difficulty the organization of the people's economic lives faced was the discrepancy between official propaganda and the decrease in the people's standard of living. After 1960, the *People's Daily* and other publications continued to report that, in 1958 and 1959, unprecedented bumper crops were harvested. People's lives, however, continued to deteriorate, and their dissatisfaction with the "three red banners" had spread from the urban centres to the countryside and border areas.

The following responses to the situation have been taken from various sources. Shenlu fishers from Jinjiang County, Fujian Province, attacked the food policy, saying that, with Mao as chairman, it's four *liang* per meal; with Liu Shaoqi as chairman, it's three *liang* per meal; when the next chairman comes, who knows how many *liang* it will be? An old fisher from the Yangyi Commune said: "We are just afraid that we will not make it to Jinmen. If we can, we will just escape to Jinmen." Eight to nine thousand dependents of overseas Chinese from Jinjiang County were "trying to leave the country or flee to Hong Kong."[24] There were "a few 'bad elements' in Shenyang spreading the word," taking pictures of starving children and sending them to Chairman Mao. Several workers from an iron manufactory in Baotou even wanted to send Chairman Mao millet with grains of sand in it.[25]

In the face of so many complaints from around the country, the Central Committee decided to combine enhanced dictatorship with ideological education. Chief Minister of Public Security Xie Fuzhi demanded that all local "dictatorship offices" hold high the red banner of Mao Zedong thought, commenting: "We must fully take hold of the situation and tighten the struggle against the enemy" and stressing that strong measures must be taken against the "fabrications," "slander," and "reactionary political views" of the five bad elements.[26]

While attacking and striking fear into the hearts of "class enemies," the Central Committee was also employing the following rhetorical strategies to make the masses believe that "in ten years great accomplishments will be made" and that "the future looks very prosperous for many years to come," and it wanted to clarify their "blurry conceptions":

- Were there in fact any bumper crops harvested? The correct response was "maintain the belief that bumper crops had been harvested and show no signs of wavering."[27]
- If bumper crops have been harvested, why the call to conserve grain? If on every "battle front" we have achieved victory, why are we still unable to purchase daily necessities? The correct response was "it is not the case that grain is in short supply, it is that there are too many people

who need to eat. It is not the case that consumer items are rare, it is that there are too many people buying them."[28]

- Small households have small difficulties, and the nation has its own. The masses must be considerate and consider problems from the perspective of the state. Do not begin to complain or express grievances as soon as "grain conservation" is mentioned.

- Socialism will absolutely not allow people to starve to death. To say that people are starving to death in the countryside is complete slander fabricated by class enemies.

The rhetorical strategies outlined above employed the power of the state as a means of obtaining ideological support and were extremely effective in their ability to reinvigorate the masses. At the same time, however, such "coercive ideology" also had a "soft" side: it was able to resort to and manipulate people's emotions using the language of "commoners." For example, things we said, such as "you don't know the value of rice or fuel until you manage your own household," in order to convince people to practise self-constraint. The reality in China had for a long time been grave, but seen through this "ideological filter" it became a "bright and colourful" illusion, a "picture of growing prosperity." This was the very powerful "ideological blinding effect," which informed what the leadership considered "common knowledge" and influenced its ability to make proper judgments.

In May 1960, leaders in Beijing gradually began to realize the very serious nature of the food problem. The situation in Liaoning's industrial base, Tianjin and Shanghai, was already dire, but at that point Beijing was still not fully aware of the depth or scope of the food crisis in the countryside. It understood the problem to be only the result of difficulties with the allocation and transportation of grain. On 28 May, the Central Committee issued emergency grain management instructions nationwide, and on 6 June it further issued "emergency instructions for the allocation and transportation of grain in Beijing, Tianjin, Shanghai, and Liaoning." What is surprising, especially at this stage, is that several officials and cadres continued to conceal crop failure and famine. According to Song Renqiong, as early as the Beidaihe Conference, which was held in the summer of 1960, Zhou Enlai "was already aware that there was a food problem, but everyone was afraid to admit it. The result was a 'cover up' of the actual situation."[29] The "everyone" to whom Zhou Enlai refers includes Party cadres and high-ranking officials at the provincial level. Also during the Beidaihe Conference, Mao Zedong held a meeting with Li Fuchun, Bo Yibo, and Chen Zhenren, demanding that the entire nation form small coastal and inland groups, along with the mobilization of 70 million people that winter, to smelt huge amounts of steel.[30] Mao's instructions quickly became known specifically as the "guaranteed food, guaranteed steel campaign" that arose following July 1960.

At the heart of the guaranteed food, guaranteed steel campaign was a political attempt to increase steel production and to solve the grain crisis in the countryside. Although even at this point the Central Committee was still unaware of the food shortage facing the nation's provinces, it had a general idea of the emerging crisis.[31] It was only then that it "mobilized all party members to focus on agriculture and produce more grain." Without a doubt, there was absolutely no way 18.6 million tons of steel could be produced by a nation of starving peasants. Further, Beijing continued under the premise that the public dining hall system would somehow oppose the "five winds" (*wufeng*)[32]; however, mobilizing commune cadres throughout the countryside had no effect on the crisis.

While the guaranteed food, guaranteed steel campaign was being launched, starvation in the countryside was becoming increasingly severe. On Huanghe Commune in Shandong Province, in Zhangqiu County, alone, 642 people died between early June and 15 August 1960, and 229 people died between 1 and 15 August – a rate of 15.2 per day.[33] It was under these abnormal circumstances that the upper levels of government in Beijing finally became fully aware of the situation. On 7 September, the Central Committee issued the "instructions on lowering rural and urban grain quotas," which stipulated that, other than a few heavy labourers, all city and town citizens would have their monthly grain quotas reduced by two *jin* per month. It was at this point that documents began to contain admissions that, "after the summer harvest, occurrences of edema, unnatural deaths, and population outflow continued."

With Famine and Crop Failure Becoming Increasingly Serious, the "Food Substitute" Campaign Is Initiated Nationwide

With food supply at an unprecedented low, many peasants were not getting enough to eat. Even the citizens of the relatively wealthy region of Yangzhou in Jiangsu Province were forced to "eat gruel with no vegetables on a daily basis." In the ninety-six days between 10 May 1960 and 15 August 1960, citizens of Taixing County were provided with grain rations amounting to only eighty-two *jin* per person.[34] By late 1960, grain rations for citizens living in the three northeastern provinces had been reduced to 232 *jin*, 55 percent fewer than the previous year.[35] As for the rural areas of Henan, Anhui, Sichuan, Shandong, Gansu, Qinghai, Guangxi, and Guizhou, death from starvation was already commonplace, and many places were deserted. State granary stores had already reached their absolute lowest limits: in July and August 1960, granaries held 10 billion *jin* fewer than they held at the same time the previous year.[36] As a means of dealing directly with the imminent food crisis, Beijing formally addressed the nation, demanding that all levels of the Central Committee, government offices, and schools do their utmost to solicit and develop "food substitution" activities.

During a speech on 10 August 1960, at the Beidaihe Central Committee Working Conference, Mao Zedong said that every effort must be made to reap as much as possible from the fall harvest. Regardless of province, county, or commune, more grain must be harvested, more vegetables grown, and more "food substitutes" found (from wild sources). In sum, as Han-xin said regarding the number of troops he could command, "the more the better."[37] Although Mao Zedong never actually asked why more grain was not being harvested, his message to "find more food substitutes" was clear and, as such, provided the media with a new working objective.

The drastic change from ubiquitous claims of bumper crops to urging the population to search for food substitutes left ideological administrators unable to explain the situation to the people. Instead, they developed an empty campaign promoting the "three forevers" (the General Line, the Great Leap Forward, and the People's Communes). It was not until October 1960 that a National Day editorial in the *People's Daily* offered a new explanation for the current state of affairs: "In the last two years or so, the nation has been continuously subject to a number of serious natural disasters which have led to a severe decrease in food production." The editorial further asserted that "the People's Communes have allowed the nation's peasants to be forever free from the fate of having to starve, flee, or die as a result of natural disaster."[38] Of course, editorial writers were aware of the great degree of starvation that was being experienced throughout the nation's rural areas while this piece was being issued; but, despite the facts, they chose, against their better judgment, to "bite the bullet" and stay within the Party line.

However, in the face of alarming reports of starvation nationwide, a means of solving this problem had to be realized. On 3 November 1960, Zhou Enlai took charge of drafting the "Central Committee Emergency Instructions" (composed of twelve articles). Through continuing the public dining halls, allowing the peasantry some leniency, and making policy adjustments, it was hoped that occurrences of starvation would quickly abate. On 14 November, the Central Committee issued the "emergency instructions on immediately developing a large-scale campaign for the gathering and manufacturing of food substitutes" and, based on the opinions of the Chinese Academy of Sciences, recommended a number of these substitutes. The "emergency instructions" stipulated that Zhou Enlai would be head of the Central Committee's leading group on "melon and vegetable" substitutes, that an administrative department would be established, and that a formal call to "eat melon and vegetable substitutes, and decrease grain provisions," would be issued. Provinces nationwide established leading groups to "eradicate illnesses" and created "people's livelihood information networks" specifically to carry out tasks related to melon and vegetable substitution.

So-called melon and vegetable substitution referred to substituting fruits and vegetables for grain as the main source of one's diet. In 1960, however, a large number of famine-stricken villages had consumed all their melons and fruit, forcing peasants to substitute bark, roots, wild plants, and clay (*guanyintu*) for grain. Thus, the melon and vegetable substitution group's main task was to initiate the development of food substitutes.

In modern Chinese, the term "food substitute" (*daishipin*) first appeared in 1955. During the "state monopoly for purchase and marketing of grain" campaign, thousands of people from Guangxi's Lingshan County went into the hills to gather wild fruit and tree bark to supplement the lack of grain in their diet. These kinds of "non-grain foods" were given the scientific name "food substitutes," a term that then began appearing in official documents. The reason wild vegetables and tree bark were called food substitutes has to do with an ideologically required political stance. From the "political stance of the proletariat," the rough grain and vegetables workers had to swallow in the old society could not be called "edible food substitutes"; yet, during socialist collectivization and the People's Communes movement, it was mandatory to refer to the rice millet, tree roots, and corn stalk pith peasants ate as "food substitutes." Later, through customary usage, the term "food substitute" gradually entered the modern Chinese lexicon.

Those items deemed food substitutes generally fell under two different categories:

1 Naturally grown animals and plants
   • Chlorella, or any other aquatic plants (such as red duckweed)
   • Stalks from various crops (corn, rice, wheat, sorghum, etc.)
   • Stalks, roots, or parts of plants hidden beneath the soil (broad beans, peas, potatoes, etc.)
   • Cold tree bark
   • Various wild vegetables and fungi (wild melons, goose grass, loach straw, wild celery, wild pond rice, *mao* mushrooms, bean segments, etc.)

- Limbs and stems from various crops (sweet potato seedlings, kidney bean husks, etc.)
- Various wild fruits (acorns, sweet oak, plantains, etc.)
- Various insects

2 Synthetic foods (made from bacteria cultures)
- Artificial meat extract and powdered artificial meat extract
- Artificial meat (also called "fake" meat), artificial meat balls, artificial meat soup
- Artificial milk
- Artificial cooking oil

Among the substitute foods listed above, chlorella, an alga that grows on water, received the most attention from the Central Committee and local leaders. In the earlier half of 1960, Shanghai and other places were using it as pig fodder. Because food supply was at an unprecedented low, pig and livestock farming decreased sharply, and exports as well as the people's non-staple food supply were seriously affected. Chlorella was quickly recognized for its ability to increase the amount of nutrition in pig fodder while at the same time alleviating the problem of pig fodder shortage. The results of Shanghai's "invention" quickly gained popularity, and by late July 1960 twenty-seven provinces, cities, and regions nationwide (excluding Tibet) had, to varying degrees, already begun experimenting with chlorella cultivation and large-scale chlorella production.

Alternate Secretary Hu Qiaomu of the Central Party Secretariat proposed a crucial application for chlorella: in October 1960, he submitted an official document to Mao Zedong suggesting that chlorella be employed nationwide as a food substitute. Thus, chlorella instantly went from being a food supplement for pigs to a food source for people. Hu claimed that, widely used, it could cure edema and "guarantee that people would not starve to death." Mao had heard that chlorella possessed this capability and thus, on 27 October, transmitted Hu Qiaomu's suggestion throughout the CCP ranks, demanding it be promoted on all fronts.[39]

Immediately after Mao's instructions and Hu's report were issued, a vigorous mass campaign for the large-scale cultivation of chlorella arose nationwide. The main objective behind cultivating chlorella was to collect the liquid culture. There were numerous ways that the liquid culture of chlorella could be diluted, but the most common involved the use of human or animal waste. In Beijing and Hunan, it was discovered that diluting chlorella with 1 to 2 percent human urine provided the best results.

At administrative offices, schools, factories, and even on the streets, small ponds were built to cultivate chlorella. Urban residents were using the pitchers and pots in their homes to do the same. In many households, parents fed their children one or two spoonfuls of liquid chlorella culture a day before meals, believing it had rich nutritional value. In reality, however, this was only the desire of a people living in a time when food was in extreme shortage, and it could not be substantiated by scientific fact.

While large-scale chlorella cultivation was under way, Beijing invented a means to "accelerate the growth of Chinese cabbage." It was said that, by taking the "knot" of the cabbage carrying the sprout, planting it in a pot, and keeping it in a room at fifteen degrees, it was possible to accelerate its growth.

Among all the food substitutes, the most practical was probably "artificial starch." Artificial starch was made by grinding processed stalks, roots, leaves, stems, and spores into a powder. Often this powder was added to corn or sorghum flour and used to make *mo,* or corn buns. Once eaten, these buns gave the stomach a "full," or "swollen," feeling, unlike after eating liquid chlorella, after which it felt like nothing at all had been eaten.[40]

Organization, Ideology, and the Popularization of Food Substitutes

The development of the campaign to popularize food substitutes was meticulously arranged by Party organizations of various levels. After the latter half of 1960, solving the food problem of the masses became the priority of all Party committees and governments. While maintaining the People's Commune system and public dining halls, committees and governments rigorously employed conventional political mobilization methods to carry out Central Committee measures regarding melon and vegetable substitutes. Party committees of various levels were continuously setting quotas for the gathering of food substitutes. Each province had to report to the Central Committee the amount of food substitutes it expected to collect.

In early 1961, Qinghai Province made two promises: (1) that annual peasant grain rations would not be less than 180 *jin* per year and (2) that, in late August 1961, the production of artificial meat and powdered chlorella would amount to 3 million *jin,* foliage protein to 150 million *jin,* and artificial refined starch to 200 million *jin.* In late 1960, the northeastern bureau of the Central Committee planned to organize peasant lives in all regions between January and September 1961 so that each person would receive 120 *jin* in grain rations and two *liang* of dry starch (substitute) daily.[41] In Hubei Province's Chongyang County, 250,000 people were sent into the hills to gather wild fruit. The Insect Research Institute at the Chinese Academy of Sciences came up with more than 1,200 *jin* of edible insects in a short period and promoted its results nationwide, claiming that: "gathering and eating insects is one way more nutrition can be added to [our] diets."[42]

Through great promotional efforts made by every level of the local Party committees, the commercial production of artificial meat extract achieved great progress. According to incomplete statistics from the ministries of Light Industry, Commerce, and Chemical Industry, by 15 April 1961, 479 tons of powdered artificial meat extract had been produced, among which the Ministry of Light Industry's "experimental" factories (e.g., Jinnan distillery, Shenyang brewery, and ten other major factories) produced 446 tons. Beginning in March 1961, seventeen second-level restaurants in Tianjin began selling "artificial meat stir-fry." In Yunnan Province, seventy tons of chlorella were used to produce popsicles, rice gruel, and soup for market supply. Heilongjiang, Jilin, Liaoning, and ten other cities provided their residents with 1.95 million *jin* of "fake meat." Sichuan Province's Tongliang County used food substitutes to produce 330,000 *jin* of candy and 190,000 *jin* of pastry, and it still managed to provide foliage protein balls, chlorella stew, and meat extract dumplings.[43]

In order to further promote the development of the food substitute movement, CCP committees and governments at all levels called various meetings. These included "conferences on food" and "meetings to commend advanced units and individuals on grain conservation," which publicized the superiority of food substitutes and cleared up the "blurry understandings" of cadres inside and outside the Party during the promotion of this campaign.

The keys to popularizing substitute foods were the cadres, yet many of them expressed negativity during the campaign. At first they doubted "green water" (the masses referred to chlorella as green water) could be used as a substitute for pig fodder, and, later, they had even more doubts that it could be used to feed people. In accordance with the arrangements made by the Central Committee's northern bureau and the Hebei County committee, the Longhua County committee held a "conference on food" to popularize substitute foods. During this conference, leaves from elm and oak trees were mixed with corn flour to make corn buns for the county's fifth-level cadres to eat.[44] Naxi County in southwestern China's Sichuan Province also held a "conference on food." County committee secretaries had dining hall cooks prepare a number of substitute foods for the county cadres to taste, and they asked, loudly, "are these substitute foods not great?" Of the many county and commune cadres who attended the conference, only a few managed to say with any conviction that these substitute foods were indeed "great."[45]

During the campaign to popularize substitute foods, the Departments of Scientific Research and Propaganda were of critical importance. The "tendency to exaggerate" during the Great Leap Forward had weighed heavily on the disaster-stricken area of Henan Province, forcing it to the nation's forefront with regard to promoting the superior aspects of food substitutes. The provincial scientific research department conducted tests to determine the "nutritional content" of corn husks and sweet potato stems, the results of which are as follows:

- Corn husks: moisture content 7.09 percent, protein 3.92 percent, starch 33.36 percent, sugar 1.6 percent, unrefined fats 0.44 percent;
- Sweet potato stems: moisture content 39 percent, ash 4 percent, starch 63.17 percent;
- Final conclusion: corn husks and sweet potato stems are quality foods suitable for human consumption.[46]

Henan Province's Electrical Institute invented a kind of steamed bun made from equal parts powdered rice straw and flour, claiming that "medical tests show that the nutritional value of [our] buns exceeds that of standard Beijing noodles." In Hunan, Sichuan, and Guangxi, people boiled rice straw in limewater and then ground it into paste, claiming that the starch content in rice straw could reach 30 to 80 percent. This kind of starch was given the scientific name "rice straw starch."[47] For a short period after November 1960, the Ideological Propaganda Department promoted substitute foods to the highest possible degree, claiming that "their nutritional value was even greater than that of real grain." They said that "twice-steamed rice" was easy to digest and that it was even easier to absorb nutritional value from – a revolutionary contribution of great importance to people's diet structure. As well, neither chlorella nor refined starch contained cholesterol, which was beneficial for the prevention of cardiovascular disease.

Despite the exaggerated efforts of the media to praise the superiority of substitute foods and twice-steamed rice, frequent reports of many people getting sick from eating inedible food substitutes were being made nationwide. In April 1960, the Ministry of Health issued a nationwide notice banning the promotion of the achene of Siberian cocklebur. Prior to this notice, 5,900 people in Lankao County, Henan Province, mistakenly ate the achene of Siberian cocklebur, which led to 1,100 poisonings and 38 deaths. During this period, poisonings and deaths from eating inedible poisonous plants were occurring in rural areas nationwide. In May, 3,800 people in Shandong Province were poisoned from eating the achene of

Siberian cocklebur, 54 of whom died. Peasants nationwide were also suffering from cyanosis from having eaten rotten vegetables. Because poisonings were becoming more common, in the latter half of 1960 medicine factories nationwide quickly began manufacturing the "No. 60" antidote, and a promotional campaign for the prevention of cyanosis was immediately developed.[48]

During the campaign to promote food substitutes, work was under way to prevent an epidemic of cyanosis. This demonstrated the CCP ideology's inability to explain the very real problems currently facing China. This contradiction was nowhere more apparent than in the public and private opinions of leading cadres.

In public forums, Party and government heads attempted to mobilize the masses to produce large amounts of substitute foods, yet rational sense left them doubting the propaganda surrounding food substitutes. Liu Ren, the second secretary of the Beijing Party Committee, who was assistant bureau chief of the Beijing Bureau of Commerce and at one time in charge of food substitute production, asked, "how did we come up with such a 'moth' (a Beijing colloquialism meaning bad idea), is it all right to tell people to eat this?" He was also dissatisfied with twice-steamed rice, saying, "steam one *liang* of grain once or twice, it's still one *liang* of grain isn't it?"[49] Liu Ren was already making such comments in 1961. At the ninth plenum of the eighth CCP Central Committee, the committee advocated an "investigative research and fact-finding spirit." As a result, propaganda related to the superiority of food substitutes began gradually to subside. The Department of Scientific Research also made new determinations related to the nutritional value of food substitutes. In Sichuan Province, forty kinds of food substitutes tested positive for poison. The Institute of Physiology at the Chinese Academy of Sciences tested the nutritional content of powdered acorn and rice straw and found that there was basically no nutritional value to these foods. The latest research results from the Organic Chemical Research Institute at the Chinese Academy of Sciences, the Biochemical Research Institute, and the Chinese Medical Academy of Science showed that the nutritional value of rice straw, corn stalks, corn pith, and corn straw was very low: "They do not provide energy, they are difficult to digest, difficult to absorb, and are unsuitable for consumption in large amounts." Further, the actual starch content in "unrefined starch" was shown to be only 0.8 to 2.96 percent, and protein was 0.27 to 0.6 percent. When fed to mice, it was found that the latter's body weights dropped by 31 percent within three days. Autopsies on the mice showed that their stomachs had expanded and that the walls of their stomachs had thinned.[50]

While Liu Ren and others were privately criticizing these practices, and scientific research departments were internally re-evaluating the nutritional value of food substitutes, average "proletariats" were more directly and more clearly expressing their dissatisfaction with food substitutes and food-substitute-related policies.

Students: A student majoring in medicine in Shenyang said: "Building up the country through hard work and frugality is truly great, and now we get to eat wild vegetables and straw." Children of cadres at Taiyuan's number five, three, and ten middle schools refused to eat wild vegetables, saying, "this is pig food." University students at Guangzhou University grumbled: "If the situation is so good then why do we have to eat 'seamless steel tubes' [i.e., water spinach] everyday?" The students further "attacked" state aid policies for "trying to do something they were incapable of doing just to look good, like a skinny dog trying to pass a hard stool."[51]

Workers: In the latter half of 1960, when grain rations were reduced, workers at the Fushun generating station were forced to eat only corn buns made from almond flour: "This is chicken food, and chickens wouldn't even eat it. But it fills you up, and if you don't eat this what are you going to eat?"[52] A few workers in Angang said: "In the past, working as a farm labourer for a landlord you never had to worry about not getting enough to eat." And: "The old society was no good – fish, shrimp, liquor, meat – you could have them all. The new society is better: you can't buy anything, but it's still not as good as working as a hired-hand for a landlord, and [life] is certainly nowhere near as good as it was for pigs and dogs back then."[53]

Peasants: Peasants in Shanghai's Qingpu County said: "Life was tough under Chiang Kai-shek, but you could eat rice. Life under Chairman Mao is easy and comfortable, but we have to eat gruel." Dissatisfied farmers from Xuancheng County in Anhui Province complained: "Chairman Mao indeed: he's more foul than an outhouse toilet seat! He's ruined our crops, so we have nothing to eat."[54] Village children in Hai'an County, Jiangsu Province, sang a song about Mao Zedong: "Chairman Mao with his big fat face, doesn't seem to care commune members are starving to death all over the place!"[55]

Senior intellectuals: After experiencing the Anti-Rightest Campaign of 1957, most senior intellectuals were careful with their words and cautious in their actions. But, in 1960-61, as a result of the widespread shortages in grain and non-staple foods, a few scientists from the Chinese Academy of Sciences formally applied to leave the country to visit relatives.[56]

Of all the widespread dissatisfaction being expressed at all levels of the social strata, that of low-income urban residents was the most prominent.

Beginning on 15 January 1961, provincial capitals nationwide took the lead in executing Liao Chenyun's instructions on producing large amounts of high-grade snacks and candies in order to withdraw currency from circulation. On 20 January in Beijing, 122,000 *jin* of high-grade snacks, 19,000 *jin* of high-grade cookies, and 121,000 *jin* of high-grade candies were sold. High-grade pastry sold for as much as 7.6 *yuan* per *jin* or as little as 3 *yuan* per *jin*, but sales were low. High-grade candy sold for 5 *yuan* per *jin* and as much as 16 *yuan* per *jin*, and high-grade cookies brought in 4 *yuan* per *jin* or 5 *yuan* per *jin* for two different types. Although many consumers of these types of high-grade foods were average urban residents, most of those purchasing these foods were cadres and senior intellectuals. After a meeting attended by seven thousand people held in early 1962, the state extended the scope of the "preferential non-staple food supply," stipulated in November 1960, from high-level cadres, prominent democrats, and scientists who have made significant contributions to society to also include cadres ranked at the seventeenth level and up. Regulations stipulated that cadres ranked at the seventeenth level and up would receive monthly provisions subsidies of one *jin* of sugar and one *jin* of beans per person; high-level cadres ranked level thirteen and up were provided with an extra monthly supply of two *jin* of meat and two *jin* of eggs per person. Although this act was supported by mid- and high-level cadres nationwide, it caused great harm to average cadres as well as to the masses.

Average cadres in Beijing said, mockingly, "high-income earners get to eat pork and fried eggs, low-income earners get a pot of vegetable leaves and boiled rice gruel. There are currently three grades of cadres, the first grade eats meat, the second grade eats sugar and beans, and the third grade sips broth."[57] In a short time, all kinds of "trouble-making words" surged through China like tidal waters.

The granting of subsidy provisions to high- and mid-level cadres ranked at the seventeenth level and up reflected the Central Committee's concern for the cadre class, the official line being that "cadres are valuable state property."[58] In early 1962, other forms of "care for the cadre class," besides the provision of non-staple foods such as sugar, beans, meat, and eggs, were introduced. In Beijing, "the Central Party decided to hold study classes for Party cadres ranked at the seventeenth level and higher," the main purpose of which was (1) to "unify Party thought" and (2) to allow cadres to supplement their diets. These study classes had a certain "nurturing" quality: "Each semester was two months"; daily meals were made up of "steamed buns made from enriched flour, steamed rolls, rice, market rarities such as pork, eggs, and sausages, and other rare delicacies"; and "daily meals cost only one yuan."[59] (At the time, the minimum cost of living for an average family member in a provincial capital was eight to ten *yuan* per month; in Shanghai, where salaries were the highest in the nation, the relatively high salary of a textile factory worker was on average only forty or more *yuan* per month.)[60] The provincial committee of Liaoning Province cared for its cadres by having them take turns "staying in a hotel, reading Marxist-Leninist texts, and improving their meals."[61] The provisional aid that county- and commune-level rural cadres received was far less than what their urban counterparts received.

Meetings were often held in county cities in order to allow county and commune level-one cadres to supplement their diets in county dining halls: "While attending two- to three-day meetings in the city, one meal of pork will be provided; for four- to five-day meetings, meat will be served twice ... For several days, there was no need to take medicine, and swollen bellies disappeared." As a result, many rural base-level cadres "looked most forward to attending county meetings."[62] Because cadres were eating and staying at meetings held in county cities, peasants were unaware of the "health-replenishing activities" in which they were engaging.

Looked at from a practical point of view, it is obvious that leaders were systematically "caring" for cadres ranked at the seventeenth level and higher, with the hope that they would work hard and so better "lead the masses in the fight against and relief from natural disasters, as well as restore production." However, certain regions became deeply interested in borrowing from the revolutionary force of "caring for the level-seventeen cadres" and exploited it to greater and greater degrees. According to relevant reports, in the early half of 1962, Tangshan, Chengde, and seven other prefectures in Hebei Province greatly increased the degree of caring for level-seventeen cadres. It was stipulated that each cadre ranked at the seventeenth level and higher would receive monthly provisions of 1 *jin* of sugar, 3 *jin* of soybeans, 0.5 to 3.5 *jin* of cooking oil, 0.5 to 3.5 *jin* of meat, 0.5 to 2 *jin* of eggs, 2 cigarettes, 2 to 3 *jin* of pig entrails, 3 to 5 *jin* of aquatic products, 3 to 5 *jin* of starch noodles, and 3 to 5 *jin* of bean curd. Fengnan County took a different approach and divided the county's more than two hundred cadres into "three grades and nine levels." A level-one secretary from the county committee secretariat was able to eat forty or more *jin* of chicken, duck, pork, and lamb a month, and a number-one county committee secretary was provided with more than seventy *jin* of meat a month.[63]

Although cadres ranked at the seventeenth level and higher ate better and more than the masses, this practice indicates that there was in fact food available at the time. In late 1961, the state increased standard grain rations for urban residents. Early the following year, although there were still "negative occurrences" (e.g., in Henan's Shangqiu, Kaifeng, Xinxiang, Anyang, Xinyang, and six other prefectures alone, up to 320,000 people fled for fear of starvation),[64] the nation's economic situation showed signs of recovery. For example, in early 1962, cases of edema in Jiangsu Province reached 393,000, and although this was up by eighty thousand cases from late 1961 there were still considerably fewer than what had been reported for the same period in the previous year.[65] Following the gradual economic recovery, non-staple food provisions for urban residents also improved, and food substitutes gradually disappeared from people's lives.

The key factor in the improvement of food provisions was not actually food augmentation methods or food substitutes; rather, it was the fact that the Central Committee decided in November 1960 and June 1961 to return private plots to the peasantry, to dismantle public dining halls, and to import large amounts of grain from outside the country. According to statistics, in 1961 alone 5 million tons of grain were purchased from outside the country, and in 1962 another 3 million tons were imported. Augmentation methods and food substitution also helped to alleviate the food crisis. By the time of the 1962 National Day celebrations, obvious improvements had been made to holiday food provisions in urban centres nationwide. Between 25 September and 2 October, markets in Beijing alone had sold 300,000 chickens, a rare commodity during the previous two years. During this time, residents of Beijing were each provided with three *liang* of fresh meat (normally, residents were provided with meat coupons limiting them to only two *liang*, and most of it frozen), and residents altogether purchased 1.6 million *jin* of fresh meat.[66] A number of famous restaurants in Beijing, which had been cold and empty for many years, began to prosper once again. The Clay Pot Restaurant was back to employing its roasting, scalding, boiling, and thirty-two other cooking variations. Also back in supply were Menkuang Lane's flash-fried stomach and *naobai* bean curd; Caishikou's *baishui* mutton head; and Jinshenglong Restaurant's jellied bean curd and deep-fried meatballs. High-income earners' favourites – such as Yushengzhai Restaurant's beef braised in soy sauce; Putianlou Restaurant's stewed chicken, roasted pork on a skewer, and baked pork; and Fuyulou Restaurant's pork braised in soy sauce – were all in great supply.

However, although there was excellent food available, not everyone was able to indulge. While high-income earners were enjoying their fill, many lower-class residents of Beijing could not afford holiday supply coupons for non-staple foods, and, as a result, many items that normally would not last on market shelves were selling poorly. Between 25 September and 5 October 1962, the city of Beijing put 800,000 chickens and ducks into market circulation to ensure that each resident household could purchase one. However, by 2 October, only 300,000 had been sold.[67] Regardless, the many years of extreme economic difficulty had finally, "[and] through great effort, managed to pass."[68] The leadership's greatest concern had, for the most part, never actually occurred: for several years, despite "food shortages and a number of deaths, no great problems arose, no new 'emperor' rose to power (in the words of Song Renqiong)."[69] The food substitute nightmare of urban centres nationwide was also, for the most part, over by the early half of 1962.

In sum, the initiation of the campaign to promote the food augmentation program and food substitutes in the face of the Great Famine was unavoidable. Throughout Chinese history, governments have all had their own ways of dealing with famine. By the time of the Qing dynasty, a relatively well-developed disaster-reporting and relief system had been established, by which the court would supply grain, cease taxation, supply goods, relocate people to where food was available, and provide work-relief and other measures to lessen the hardships of the masses.[70] In the early 1950s, after the establishment of the People's Republic of China, the government also made great gains in terms of disaster evaluation and relief. However, the Great Leap Forward and the subsequent Anti-Rightist Campaign of 1957 caused great damage to disaster-reporting and relief mechanisms, the consequences of which were difficult to bear.

After the latter half of 1960, leaders gradually began to face reality. However, they were distressed by the fact that there was no longer any grain remaining with which to relieve the situation. As a result, ideology and state power were employed to initiate a food substitute campaign nationwide – a campaign that proved to be extremely effective. During these difficult years, the great majority of cadres shared in the hardship of the masses. But, unfortunately, the resilience of and sacrifices made by the commoners, especially China's numerous peasants, were unable to shame the country's leaders into "changing their tune," and, due to the latter's concerted efforts to maintain the construction of "a new socialist countryside," peasants suffered through an extended period of food shortage. The food problem in the countryside was not truly alleviated until 1980, when Deng Xiaoping initiated the rural reforms. The lessons learned during this period are forever etched in the minds of the common people.

Acknowledgments
Source material for this chapter comes from the Archives of Contemporary Chinese History, kept in the China Studies Centre at the Chinese University of Hong Kong, and for the use of which I express my most sincere gratitude.

Notes

1 *Neibu cankao* [Internal Reference] (hereafter *NBCK*) 2958 (12 January 1960): 23; ibid. 2964 (20 January 1960): 9.
2 Ibid. 3017 (29 March 1960): 16.
3 Ibid. 2681 (10 January 1959): 9-10.
4 Ibid. 2805 (23 June 1959): 7; ibid. 2842 (9 August 1959): 6.
5 Zhonggong Jiangsu shengwei dangshi gongzuo bangongshi, ed., *Zhonggong Jiangsu difangshi, di er juan* [History of the CCP in Jiangsu] (Nanjing: Jiangsu renmin chubanshe, 2001), 2:365.
6 *NBCK* 2468 (29 April 1958): 16; ibid. 2467 (28 April 1958): 23.
7 Ibid. 2467 (28 April 1958): 22; ibid. 2461 (21 April 1958): 12.
8 Ibid. 3089 (27 July 1960): 12; ibid. 3091 (3 August 1960): 20.
9 Ibid. 2691 (22 January 1959): 10-11, 15-17; ibid. 2730 (17 March 1959): 12.
10 Ibid. 2715 (24 February 1959): 13; ibid. 2756 (22 April 1959): 18.
11 Ibid. 2788 (3 June 1959): 3; ibid. 2761 (28 April 1959): 13-14.
12 Ibid. 2797 (16 March 1959): 13; ibid. 2807 (25 June 1959): 10.
13 Ibid. 2791 (6 June 1959): 16.
14 Zhonggong Jiangsu shengwei dangshi gongzuo bangongshi, *Zhonggong Jiangsu difangshi*, 2:365.
15 *NBCK* 3006 (17 March 1960): 20.
16 Ibid. 2996 (5 March 1960): 6.
17 Zhonggong zhongyang yanjiushi, ed. *Zhou Enlai zhuan* [Biography of Zhou Enlai] (Beijing: Zhongyang wenxian chubanshe, 1998), 4:1558.
18 *NBCK* 2920 (November 1959): 21.
19 Bo Yibo, *Ruogan zhongda juece yu shijian de huigu (xiuding ben)* [Reflections on Certain Major Decisions and Events] (Beijing: Renmin chubanshe, 1997), 2:884.
20 *NBCK* 2909 (14 Novemeber 1959): 13.
21 Ibid. 2929 (8 December 1959): 16.
22 Chen Minzhi and Ding Dong, eds., *Gu Zhun riji* [The Diary of Gu Zhun] (Beijing: Jingji ribaoshe, 1997), 57.
23 *NBCK* 3112 (21 September 1960): 14-16.
24 Ibid. 2721 (5 March 1959): 16; ibid. 2781 (26 May 1959): 7.
25 Ibid. 2697 (29 January 1959): 17; ibid. 2704 (6 February 1959): 15.
26 Ibid. 2995 (4 March 1960): 3-4; ibid. 3116 (30 September 1960): 14.
27 Ibid. 3109 (14 September 1960): 9.
28 Ibid. 3149 (16 December 1960): 15.
29 Song Renqiong, *Song Renqiong huiyilu* [Song Renqiong's Memoirs] (Beijing: Jiefangjun chubanshe, 1994), 369-70.
30 Bo, *Ruogan zhongda juece yu shijian de huigu*, 2:872. See also Du Hong, *20 Shiji Zhongguo nongcun wenti* [Issues in 20th-Century China's Countryside] (Beijing: Zhongguo shehui chubanshe, 1998), 450.
31 Zhonggong zhongyang wenxian yanjiushi, *Zhou Enlai nianpu (zhong juan)*, 2:365.
32 The winds of communism, exaggeration, cadre privilege, force and command, and blindly emphasizing production.
33 *NBCK* 3103 (31 August 1960): 11.
34 Zhonggong Jiangsu shengwei dangshi gongzuo bangongshi, *Zhonggong Jiangsu difangshi*, 2:368.
35 Song, *Song Renqing huiyilu*, 368.
36 Xie Chuntao, *Dayuejin kuanglan* [The Raging Tide of the Great Leap Forward] (Beijing: Zhongguo shehui chubanshe, 1990), 202.
37 Du, *20 shiji Zhongguo nongcun wenti*, 458.
38 *Renmin ribao* [The People's Daily], 1 January 1960.

39 Zhonggong Zhongyang wenxian yanjiushi, ed., *Jianguo yilai Mao Zedong wengao* [Writings of Mao Zedong since the Establishment of the People's Republic of China] (Beijing: Zhongguo wenxian chubanshe, 1995), 327.

40 Zhu Zheng, *Xiaoshu sheng dashidai* [The Little Book that Gave Birth to a Great Generation] (Beijing: Beijing daxue, 1999), 195.

41 *NBCK* 3158 (4 January 1961): 9; Qiang Xiaochu, Li Li'an, and Ji Yeli, *Ma Mingfang zhuanlüe* [The Brief Biography of Ma Mingfang] (Xi'an: Shaanxi renmin chubanshe, 1990), 86.

42 *NBCK* 3019 (31 March 1960): 19; ibid. 3154, "Daishipin zhuankan" [Special Issue on Food Subsidies] (27 December 1960): 6.

43 Ibid. 3215, "Daishipin zhuankan" (10 May 1961): 2-3.

44 Ibid. 3148 (14 December 1960); 10.

45 Deng Zili, *Kanke rensheng* [Rough Human Life] (Chengdu: Sichuan wenyi chubanshe, 2000), 156.

46 *NBCK* 3019 (31 March 1960): 18.

47 Ibid. 3215, "Daishipin zhuankan" (10 May 1961): 12.

48 Ibid. 3153 (26 December 1960): 12; ibid. 3154 (27 December 1960): 15.

49 Zhonggong Beijingshiwei bianxiezu, ed., *Liu Ren zhuan* [The Biography of Liu Ren] (Beijing: Beijing chubanshe, 2000), 409-10.

50 *NBCK* 3215 (10 May 1961): 11-12.

51 Ibid. 3145 (7 December 1960): 22.

52 Zhou Weiren, *Jia Tuofu zhuan* [The Biography of Jia Tuofu] (Beijing: Zhonggong dangshi chubanshe, 1993), 197.

53 *NBCK* 3149 (16 December 1960): 15; ibid. 3150 (19 December 1960): 16.

54 Ding Xueliang, "Geming huiyilu zhiwu: Wo zuizao yudao de 'chi butong zhengjian zhe'" [Five Recollections from the Revolution: My Earliest Encounter with a "Dissident"], *Xinbao caijing xinwen* [Hong Kong Economic Journal], 13 February 2001, 24.

55 Wang Juefei, *Shizhe rusi* [Time Passes Like the Flow of Water] (Beijing: Zhongguo qingnian chubanshe, 2001), 426.

56 *NBCK* 3282 (18 October 1961): 16.

57 Ibid. 3327 (2 February 1962): 6-7; ibid. 3340 (12 March 1962): 7.

58 Shao Hua, *Shuo jiahua niandai* [A Generation of Liars] (Changchun: Changchun wenyi chubanshe, 1999), 60.

59 Jin Feng, *Lishi de shunjian: Yige xinwen jizhe de huiyi* [A Glimpse of History: Memoirs of a Journalist] (Beijing: Zhongguo wenlian chubanshe, 1986), 116.

60 Xiong Yuezhi, ed., *Shanghai tongshi* [A Comprehensive History of Shanghai] (Shanghai: Shanghai renmin chubanshe, 1999), 11:170.

61 Shao, *Shuo jiahua niandai*, 61.

62 Deng, *Kanke rensheng*, 157.

63 *NBCK* 3351 (6 April 1962): 9.

64 Ibid. 3340 (12 March 1962): 8; ibid. 3351 (6 April 1962): 3.

65 Zhonggong Jiangsu shengwei dangshi gongzuo bangongshi, *Zhonggong Jiangsu difangshi*, 2:380.

66 *NBCK* 3421 (9 October 1962): 11-12.

67 Ibid., 12.

68 Wei Junyi, *Sitong lu* [Recollections of a Bitter Past] (Beijing: Beijing shiyue wenyi chubanshe, 1998), 89.

69 Song, *Song Renqing huiyilu*, 385.

70 Li Xiangjun, *Qingdai huangzheng yanjiu* [A Study of the Failed Government of the Qing Dynasty] (Beijing: Zhongguo nongye chubanshe, 1995), 23-25. See also Yuan Lin, *Xibei zaihuang shi* [A History of Famine in Xibei] (Lanzhou: Gansu renmin chubanshe, 1994), 304, 307; and Cao Xingsui et al., *Minguo shiqi de nongye* [Agriculture during the Republican Era] (Nanjing: Jiansu wenshi ziliao bianjibu, 1993), 295-302.

8   Under the Same Maoist Sky: Accounting for Death Rate Discrepancies in Anhui and Jiangxi

Chen Yixin

This chapter examines why the provinces of Anhui and Jiangxi experienced different death rates during China's Great Leap Forward Famine between 1959 and 1961. Located in inland China, these two agricultural provinces are neighbours along the Yangzi River, and many of their villages are separated only by a few kilometres. However, their death rates during the Great Leap Famine varied greatly. As the Chinese population historian Cao Shuji's recent research has shown, between 1958 and 1961, there were 6.33 million excess deaths in Anhui, or 18.37 percent of Anhui's population, whereas in Jiangxi the excess deaths were 0.18 million, or 1.06 percent of its population.[1] Furthermore, tens of thousands of Anhui famine refugees fled to Jiangxi, where they were able to survive. Given that the CCP leader Mao Zedong had promoted a uniform set of policy programs during the Great Leap Forward, it is quite striking that famine death rates varied so dramatically between the two provinces.

In the past decade, five theories have attempted to interpret, as they have claimed, "the variations in the death rate across provinces" or "cross-province differences in death rates." The first theory, relying on classical economics, contends that food availability decline was the cause of death and the regional difference in death rates. In 1959-60, this theory suggests, when an area had a decline in grain output and a reduction in caloric intake below the minimum threshold required for subsistence, famine occurred, and the responsive death rate was higher.[2] The second theory, adopting Amartya Sen's entitlement approach to famine studies, contends that the cause of death was the peasants' lack of rights to food. This theory holds that famine occurred more seriously in agricultural provinces because the Chinese government procured grain from the agricultural sector to guarantee subsistence consumption for urban populations in times of food shortage, leaving the agricultural population with inadequate grain supplies.[3] The third theory argues that the government's resource distribution policies, as they played out with regard to the diversion of labour and food, accounted for the collapse of grain output in 1959 and the consequential famine because they resulted in labour and food shortages in rural regions when resources were redirected to provinces that had modern industry and a larger number of urban centres.[4] The fourth theory suggests that communal dining under the People's Commune system affected the death rate because the compulsory public dining halls first encouraged excessive food consumption, which aggravated food shortage, and then led the peasants to starvation.[5] The last theory advocates a thesis of political radicalism: the degree of political loyalty of provincial leaders, together with Party membership density or percentage of population who were Chinese Communist Party members, decided the difference in death rates. A lower Party membership density meant that a larger portion of cadres without Party membership would be more eager to adopt radical policies in hopes of demonstrating their political loyalty and advancing their own careers. According to this theory, the more zealous a province's leaders, and the lower its Party membership density, the more likely it would be to have a higher public dining hall participation rate among rural people and, therefore, a higher rate of death.[6]

All these theories are illuminating, but each is flawed in one way or another. The theories of food availability decline and food entitlement, as Gene Chang and James Wen point out, do not explain why no famine occurred in 1962 and 1963, when the annual per capita food availability was at an identical level to that of the famine years.[7] The same criticism can be applied to the third theory. Since per capita food availability at the national and provincial levels had not changed by any significant degree between the famine and the post-famine years, one can hardly argue that the diversion of food and labour resources to urban and industrial centres during the famine years had decisively affected the life and death of rural populations. The communal dining theory is also criticized because it fails to explain why the famine was at its most severe in 1960. As James Kung and Justin Lin point out, the excessive consumption of food occurred in late 1958. By spring 1959, most public dining halls had become unpopular, and many of them only operated on a seasonal rather than on a year-round basis.[8] In other words, the famine in 1960 could not have been the consequence of excessive consumption since there had been no such consumption in 1959. The theory of political radicalism, Kung and Lin indicate, cannot explain the regional difference in death rates because the range of Party membership density among the provinces was "exceedingly narrow." To better construct the theory, Kung and Lin add a new variable: the time of liberation – the actual month and year that a province was declared "liberated" by the CCP. This new variable means that the later a province was liberated and the shorter its revolutionary history, the more likely it would be to have a shallower Party base. This, in turn, heightened the chances that radical policies would be pursued and followed by a higher death rate.[9]

The preceding criticism aside, these theories have not really explained why the death rates differed across provinces. Relying on the national demographic and food data published by the Chinese government in the 1980s, the aforementioned scholars have been more interested in building econometric models for general interpretations of the Great Leap failure and famine, even though the official data themselves, as both Carl Riskin and Cao Shuji point out, are not reliable and should be carefully readjusted before being put to use.[10] Political radicalism has long been considered an important reason why some provinces, particularly Sichuan, Anhui, and Henan – which were ruled by notoriously radical leaders – suffered heavy human losses during the Great Leap Famine.[11] However, this view has never been able to explain why some other provinces, which were not labelled "radical," also suffered a high rate of death. In Shandong and Gansu, whose leaders political scientist Dali Yang characterized as being not the "most zealous," and whose public dining hall participation rates were significantly lower than those in other provinces, the death rates were among the highest of the nation.[12] Furthermore, advocates of the political radicalism theory have never provided a concrete account as to how provincial leaders, zealous or not, made policy decisions that either augmented or reduced the number of deaths in their provinces. Chang and Wen notice that Jiangxi had not closely followed Mao's radical policies because "[its] leader, Shao Shiping, a well known pragmatist, resisted imposing the communal dining system on peasants."[13] Yet they provide neither details nor references regarding Shao's pragmatism or his resistance to communal dining. Actually, Shao was Jiangxi's governor and one of Jiangxi's Party secretaries, but it was Yang Shangkui, Jiangxi's first secretary of the Party, who was the more important person in terms of policy decision making.

Through a detailed study of provincial stories, I try to interpret the difference in the number of Great Leap Famine deaths in Anhui and Jiangxi. I rely predominantly on provincial data and recently available biographies and memoirs of provincial leaders. Unlike any of the aforementioned theories, I do not seek, nor have I discovered, a single cause to explain the famine and the consequential deaths. Instead, I argue that a combination of three factors – agricultural conditions, the in-kind agricultural tax, and the political attitudes of the provincial leadership – was crucial to determining the severity of the Great Leap Famine and the difference in death rates between the two provinces.

The Agricultural Factor

At first glance, Anhui and Jiangxi show a striking difference in human-land ratio. Anhui is located at northern latitude 29°41' to 24°38', with a total area of 139,600 square kilometres. In 1851, Anhui had about 37,630,000 people, but the number declined to 27,865,411 by 1949 due to warfare, epidemic diseases, and famines throughout the Late Qing and Republican eras, particularly during the Taiping Rebellion between the 1850s and 1860s. At the end of 1957, Anhui's population was at 33,370,244 people, of which the rural population comprised 91.8 percent.[14] In 1949, Anhui had a total cultivated acreage of 76,380,000 *mu* (1 *mu* = 0.165 acre). The acreage increased to its highest at 86,730,000 *mu* by 1952 and then decreased to 85,550,000 *mu* by 1957 and to 72,760,000 *mu* by 1965.[15] The decrease starting from 1952 meant that, in the early People's Republic, Anhui did not have any potential in land resources, while facing an increase in population. On average, in 1957, Anhui had a per capita 2.56 *mu* of agricultural land, and Anhui's farmers, at a total of 13,270,000 people, cultivated per capita 6.45 *mu* of land.

Jiangxi, to the south of Anhui, has a total area of 166,600 square kilometres, 17 percent larger than Anhui. However, in the 1950s, Jiangxi's population was 47 to 53 percent less than that of Anhui. In 1851, Jiangxi had about 24,516,000 people. The number shrank to 13,140,400 by 1949, mainly as a result of the Taiping Rebellion and the communist warfare in the 1920s and 1930s. At the end of 1957, Jiangxi had 18,514,500 people, with 87.8 percent of them residing in rural areas.[16] In 1949, Jiangxi's cultivated acreage was at 35,480,000 *mu*,[17] and it increased to 41,220,000 *mu* by 1952 and then to 42,190,000 *mu* by 1957. After that the amount slightly decreased to 41,000,000 *mu* by 1965.[18] On average, in 1957, Jiangxi had a per capita 2.28 *mu* of agricultural land, and Jiangxi's agricultural labourers, at a total of 7,140,000 people, each cultivated 5.9 *mu*.[19]

It appears that, on a per capita basis, Jiangxi had slightly less cultivated acreage than did Anhui; however, in reality, Jiangxi had a larger amount of land reserves. The total acreage of land resources suitable for crops in Jiangxi is 208 million *mu*, or 83 percent of Jiangxi's land, whereas in Anhui that figure is 140 million *mu*, or 68 percent of the province's total acreage.[20] Historically, the richness in land resources gave Jiangxi's people something to fall back on when starvation occurred; it also enabled Jiangxi, at the peak of the Great Leap Famine, to absorb half a million famine refugees, mostly from its neighbour Anhui.[21] More significant are the better quality of Jiangxi's soil and the province's better water supply for crop growing. In the 1950s, the majority of land in Jiangxi had fertile soil, and over 70 percent of cultivated acreage was effectively irrigated.[22] In Anhui, over 78 percent of cultivated acreage was low-yield land, and the problem of water loss and soil erosion was always very serious. As late as the mid-1980s, irrigation systems were only able to water 40 percent of Anhui's agricultural land.[23] As a result of soil and irrigation conditions, Jiangxi always had a higher crop yield than did Anhui. In 1949, Anhui's unit output of grain per *mu* was 63 kilograms, whereas Jiangxi's was 150 kilograms.[24] By the mid-1980s, when Anhui's unit output increased to 200 kilograms, Jiangxi's increased to 301 kilograms.[25] In the 1950s, a Jiangxi farmer, working on a nearly identical size of land acreage, harvested 50 to 100 percent more than his counterpart in Anhui. He or she did not need to work on as large a piece of land to sustain the family's livelihood as did the typical Anhui farmer.

Natural geography has also benefited Jiangxi farmers more than it has Anhui farmers. Anhui consists of plains, which take up about 49.6 percent of its geographic size; mountains take up 15.2 percent; hills, 14 percent; terraces, 13 percent; water surface, 3.4 percent; and the rest is marshland and low-lying land.[26] As a result of its geographic types and the human use of lumber, in the early 1950s forests covered only 12.5 percent of Anhui's land. In north Anhui, which shared 49 percent of Anhui's population and 36 percent of its area, forest coverage equalled only 0.1 percent of its land.[27] Overall, historically, more than 87 percent of Anhui's population was concentrated on plains, low hilly regions, and terrace areas in northern and central Anhui, while the mountainous and hilly southern and western regions, which make up 28 percent of the province, were inhabited by only 13 percent of its people.[28] In Jiangxi, mountains make up 36 percent of its geography; hills, 42 percent; terrace and plains together, 12 percent; and water surface, which includes many lakes, rivers, and Lake Poyang (China's largest freshwater lake), 10 percent.[29] Because of its many mountains and hills, in the early 1950s Jiangxi's forests covered 40.3 percent of its land.[30] About 37 percent of Jiangxi's people lived in the central to north area – where plains, Poyang Lake, and Jiangxi's capital Nanchang are located – and the rest were pretty evenly diffused throughout the mountainous and hilly regions.[31] The two provinces' geographic conditions and patterns of population distribution visibly suggest that, when the Great Leap Famine occurred, a larger portion of Anhui people were easily victimized because they, unlike people living along mountains or lake sites, could not resort to consuming wild vegetation or fish as alternative sources of food. As Gao Hua points out in Chapter 7 of this volume, wild vegetation was one of the major reasons that many peasants survived starvation. At the worst time of the Great Leap Famine, even the CCP's Central Committee had to call for a nationwide "food substitute" campaign, requiring both urban dwellers and rural peasants to eat various kinds of wild vegetation – as a substitute for grain – in order to survive the so-called "serious natural disaster," the communist term for the Great Leap Famine.

Ecological elements further disadvantaged Anhui agriculture. Shaped by natural geography, over 60.1 percent of Anhui cultivated acreage is dry land, whereas the rest is composed of small rice fields. In such a pattern, wheat and rice are two major food crops. However, with an annual rainfall of between 750 and 1,700 millimetres, Anhui does not have a sufficient amount of water for rice growing. Moreover, located in the tangled zone of the dry monsoon from the north and the wet monsoon from the south, both of which arrive in late spring and early summer, northern and central Anhui are easily influenced by changes of climate. While the gradual northward retreat of the cold monsoon makes the temperature too cool for double cropping of rice, the advance of the warm monsoon sometimes moves too quickly and leads to an early end of rainfall in summer, with subsequent droughts. When the wet monsoon hangs over Anhui for too long, it brings too much water, leading to flooding and thus damaging the wheat crop, which is supposed to be harvested in early summer.[32] Such ecological considerations not only render Anhui unfavourable for rice cultivation and wheat harvest but also render it susceptible to bad weather.

Finally, historical events significantly augmented the negative influence of ecology on Anhui's agriculture, especially in north and central Anhui. In 1128, the Yellow River, after breaking through its levees, rushed into the Huai River, which runs from west to east across northern Anhui, and then entered Hongze Lake in Jiangsu, which has no exit to the Yellow Sea. This event made the Huai into a notorious "flood river" because the route alteration of the Yellow River not only brought a huge amount of sediment into the Huai – whose riverbed was already much higher than the northern Anhui plain – but also caused the Huai to flow in reverse when Hongze Lake became too full. More negatively, the route alteration led to desertification and the alkalization of the Huai River regions in north and central Anhui, and greatly affected the output of crops, particularly wheat. Then, in 1938, Chiang Kai-shek exploded the Yellow River levees to block the advance of the Japanese military. The levee explosion turned most of north Anhui into part of the so-called "Yellow River Inundated Area," an area that was experiencing great soil erosion.[33]

The consequences of these historical events have proven catastrophic. In 1949, the Huai River broke through its levees, flooded 12.9 million *mu* of land, and affected over 8 million people; in summer 1950, the Huai River flooded again, covering more than 31.6 million *mu* of land and affecting 9.98 million people; and, in 1954, the Great Huai River Flood affected 49.45 million *mu* of land and 15.37 million people. Between these floods, northern and central Anhui suffered from droughts.[34] In the meantime, the Yangzi River in the central to southern part of Anhui also caused large floods in 1949 and 1954, respectively.[35] The floods and droughts occurred so frequently that the Anhui people summed up the situation with a saying: "Great rainfall, great flood; small rainfall, small flood; and no rainfall, then drought."[36] As a result of these natural disasters, not only were crops often damaged, but also the unit output of crops and the per capita agricultural production both remained very low. In 1950, Anhui's unit output of rice per *mu* was 131 kilograms; and, in 1952, its unit output of wheat was 37 kilograms.[37] In 1950 and 1954, due to the Huai and the Yangzi floods, Anhui's per capita grain production was lower than 200 kilograms.[38] This kind of unit output of crops and agricultural production resulted in the larger portion of Anhui being under nearly permanent famine conditions.

In contrast, except for the Great Yangzi River Flood of 1931, large natural disasters seldom plagued Jiangxi in modern times. During that flood, 7,227 people died in Jiangxi, while 112,288 people died in Anhui.[39] The Yangzi is the only river that poses a potential threat to Jiangxi but only to a small region in the northern part of the province. As Jiangxi's topography is high in the south and low in the north, the Yangzi, which runs a short way along Jiangxi's northern border, can hardly generate flooding in inland Jiangxi. Furthermore, Poyang Lake, which connects to the Yangzi at its northern end, functions as a reservoir to absorb the water from the Yangzi's overspill. In 1950, Jiangxi contained the Yangzi flood very well. In 1954, Jiangxi again successfully withstood the Yangzi flood without turning peasants into famine refugees, while, by contrast, Anhui suffered dearly from this same flood.[40]

It would thus seem that, under favourable ecological conditions, Jiangxi's agricultural production was in better shape than was Anhui's. Jiangxi has an annual rainfall that ranges between 1,300 and 1,900 millimetres, about 200 to 550 millimetres more than Anhui receives. With a longer period of sunshine and of warm weather, plus a large water surface, Jiangxi peasants plant mainly rice on 90 percent of the province's cultivated land.[41] As Jiangxi does not have the problem of soil erosion, its unit output is high. Due to the state's desire for more food, in 1953 Jiangxi started to promote the practice of double-cropping its rice. By 1957, the double-cropping had been extended to 33.7 percent of the province's rice acreage and significantly increased the total output of grain.[42] Anhui, on the contrary, only started promoting double-cropping of rice in 1956, and the result was disappointing. Since the larger part of Anhui was not appropriate for double-cropping of rice, the 1956 promotion of double-cropping in many areas resulted in a failure of rice cultivation that year.[43]

All the aforementioned conditions – human-land ratio, natural geography, ecological elements, and historical events – together formed an important agricultural factor in the Great Leap Famine: the diversion of the agricultural labour force. Many scholars believe that Mao's steel-making campaign in late 1958 caused a labour shortage in the agricultural sector, but the truth is that the campaign's impact was not particularly devastating in Anhui or in Jiangxi. On 8 August 1958, Anhui built its first backyard furnace in the court of the provincial government. By the end of September, the number of backyard furnaces in Anhui reached 19,322, but 99 percent of them were smaller than 1.5 cubic metres and did not require many labourers. Although there were 2.4 million people working in a variety of ways on those furnaces in September and October, a larger portion of this labour force was dismissed by the end of October because Anhui's CCP first secretary Zeng Xisheng did not think that the steel produced by those furnaces was of good quality.[44] The same can be said of Jiangxi. After the kickoff of the steel-making campaign in August, Jiangxi designated September as the "rush-work month." From September to October, the province built nearly fifty thousand backyard furnaces and mobilized over 2.1 million people to work on them. However, after the province declared the successful completion of the target output of steel on 3 November, enthusiasm for the campaign faded away, and the peasants returned home.[45]

The most crucial difference between Anhui's and Jiangxi's agricultural production during the Great Leap lay in each province's different need regarding a labour force available for irrigation engineering projects. To be sure, Jiangxi completed many irrigation projects during the Great Leap, but the overwhelming majority of them were village-level reservoirs, requiring only a small number of labourers to work a very short time. The only large project was the Gan-Fu Plain irrigation project, which started in May 1958 and finished in April 1960. The project needed to complete a total of 54 million cubic metres of earth- and stonework, and it required 140,000 labourers annually.[46] This amount of labour force, diverted from agriculture, did not greatly influence farming. Simply put, Jiangxi did not need to construct many large irrigation projects.

Anhui's story was different. Starting from 1951, Anhui had already undertaken large irrigation projects to cope with the overspill problem of the Huai and Yangzi Rivers. Inspired by *The Outline of the National Agricultural Development*, issued by the central government in October 1957,

Table 8.1

Grain output, state requisition, and export, Anhui, 1957-62 (in 1,000 tons)

Year	1957	1958	1959	1960	1961	1962
Reported projected output[a]	–	22,500	27,000	23,100	–	–
Actual output[b]	10,270	8,850	7,010	6,750	6,290	6,710
State grain requisition[c]						
Amount	2,980	2,760	2,730	1,970	1,340	1,290
As percent of output	29.02	31.19	38.94	29.19	21.30	19.23
Amount after requisition	7,290	6,090	4,280	4,780	4,950	5,420
Grain exported[c]	47	73	43	23	-9	17

Notes and sources:

a This row indicates the amount of grain output the provincial leaders reported to the central government each year. Su Hua et al., *Dangdai Zhongguo de Anhui* [Anhui in Contemporary China] (Beijing: Dangdai Zhongguo chubanshe, 1992), 1:85-89.

b Guojia tongjiju zonghesi, ed., *Quanguo gesheng, zizhiqu, zhixiashi lishi tongji ziliao huibian, 1949-1989* [A Compilation of Historical Statistical Data on Provinces, Autonomous Regions, and Municipalities, 1949-1989] (Beijing: Zhongguo tongji chubanshe, 1990), 416.

c Shangyebu dangdai chubanshe liangshi gongzuo bianjibu, *Dangdai Zhongguo de liangshi gongzuo shiliao* [Historical Data on Food Work in Contemporary China] (Baoding: Hebei sheng gong-xiaoshe Baoding yinshuachang, 1989), 1800-5, 1832-37.

Anhui initiated a campaign to build large irrigation projects that winter. Starting on 6 November, Anhui organized a labour force of 4.98 million peasants to work on irrigation projects. When the campaign was over on 24 February 1958, the labourers had moved a total of 2.43 billion cubic metres of earth.[47] Although this campaign took place during the agricultural slack season, it caused labour fatigue because peasants did not have the traditional stress-free period in which to recover their physical strength. As Anhui historians point out, the irrigation projects in the late 1950s often resulted in "the overwork and decline in physique of the peasants."[48] After returning home, the irrigation peasants would also have to manage various household affairs, which would then add to their peak season workload. Due partially to this irrigation campaign, Anhui's grain output in 1958 decreased by 13.83 percent from its 1957 level (see Table 8.1), despite the fact that Anhui had good weather in 1958.

The story took a turn for the worse in 1959. After the Great Leap started in May 1958, Anhui ambitiously undertook several large projects to deal with the Huai and Yangzi Rivers, in addition to the buildup of tens of thousands of medium-sized and small reservoirs. Of the large projects, two gigantic ones were significant. One was the Canal-Network Project in north Anhui, which included digging 10 large canals and over 100,000 smaller and shorter canals and ditches at a total length of 125,000 kilometres. This project needed to complete 10 billion cubic metres of earthwork. The other was the Pi-Shi-Hang Irrigation Project, a comprehensive project to connect three rivers in order to create an irrigation-shipping system that could irrigate 12,280,000 *mu* of land, equal to 14.35 percent of Anhui's cultivated acreage. The project was located in the central-western part of Anhui, and to complete it would require 530 million cubic metres of earth and stone. This project had a very high degree of difficulty. As the project was largely situated in hilly and terrace regions, it involved a great deal of engineering.[49] When he saw the blueprint, An Zhiwen, a deputy director of the State Council of Economic Planning, exclaimed, "this is the largest irrigation engineering project [and is] unprecedented in the world!"[50]

Great as these projects were, tens of thousands of Anhui peasants, overwhelmingly from north and central Anhui, left home in November 1958, travelling on foot, to labour at the engineering sites that were ten to one hundred kilometres away, on the principle that the would-be beneficiary areas should supply labour forces for a project. Throughout most of 1959 to mid-1960, over 5 million peasants worked on these projects. A number of these peasants, particularly those at the Pi-Shi-Hang and at a few large reservoir projects in the Yangzi regions, worked there for a whole year or longer, while the people working on the other projects were continuously employed on a slack season basis. As the Pi-Shi-Hang and the Yangzi projects were approved by the State Council and subsidized by the appropriations jointly made by the central government and the Anhui provincial government, the leadership of these projects was able to afford to employ the peasants for a longer time than was the case with the other projects.[51] At the Pi-Shi-Hang alone, more than 800,000 peasants worked from August 1958 until spring 1960.[52] These irrigation peasants, in effect, created a great diversion of agricultural labour forces. In 1958, Anhui had about 11.25 million agricultural labourers.[53] When nearly 44 percent of the labourers, essentially the most able-bodied, were continuously away from home between 1958 and 1960 – and many of them were permanently away for a year and a half – agricultural production in 1959 turned out to be a great failure, decreasing 20.79 percent from 1958 (see Table 8.1). Crop failure occurred disproportionally in northern and, especially, central Anhui. It is not a coincidence that the worst year of the Great Leap Famine in Anhui took place in spring 1960, following the agricultural failure of 1959. Nor is it coincidental that the worst famine regions in Anhui were in the northern and central parts of the province.

The In-Kind Tax Factor

The difference in agricultural conditions between Anhui and Jiangxi probably would never have led to the great variation in the Great Leap Famine
deaths between these two provinces had the state not taken an excessive
amount of grain away from the peasants. Under favourable natural conditions, historically Jiangxi was known as a great tax contributor to dynasties,
while most of the time Anhui, frequently devastated by famines, could
just hold itself together at the level of subsistence.[54] The Great Leap altered
this precarious dynamic in several ways. First, the so-called "winds of exaggeration" (*fukuafeng*) took a severe toll on grain output. As a consequence
of the optimistic enthusiasm of local cadres and/or hierarchically induced
pressure from Mao himself, the winds of exaggeration prevailed in both
Anhui and Jiangxi at the beginning of the Great Leap. In August 1958, a
commune in Anhui's Fanchang County reported having launched a large
"sputnik" of rice output of 21,537 kilograms for one *mu*; and, in November, a commune in Jiangxi's Poyang County launched "a giant sputnik"
consisting of 114,000 kilograms of rice for one *mu*.[55] Provincial leaders
inspired lower-level cadres to exaggerate. As is shown in both Table 8.1
and Table 8.2, in July 1958, when projecting grain output to the central
leadership, the leaders of both provinces nearly doubled or tripled the
actual grain output.

Table 8.2

Grain output, state requisition, and export, Jiangxi, 1957-62 (in 1,000 tons)

Year	1957	1958	1959	1960	1961	1962
Reported projected output[a]	–	12,000	–	–	–	–
Actual output[b]	6,550	6,620	6,270	6,060	6,100	6,040
State grain requisition[c]						
Amount	1,320	1,510	2,000	1,800	1,530	1,350
As percent of output	20.15	22.81	31.90	29.70	25.08	22.35
Amount after requisition	5,230	5,110	4,270	4,260	4,570	4,690
Grain exported[c]	54	39	58	57	44	30

Notes and sources:
a This row indicates the amount of grain output the provincial leaders reported to the central
   leadership each year. Li Xiwen and Wei Rengzhang, *Liu Junxiu zhuan* [Biography of Liu Junxiu]
   (Beijing: Zhongyang wenxian chubanshe, 1996), 265.
b Guojia tongjiju zonghesi, comp., *Quanguo gesheng, zizhiqu, zhixiashi lishi tongji ziliao huibian, 1949-
   1989* [A Compilation of Historical Statistical Data on Provinces, Autonomous Regions, and
   Municipalities, 1949-1989] (Beijing: Zhongguo tongji chubanshe, 1990), 475.
c Shangyebu dangdai chubanshe liangshi gongzuo bianjibu, *Dangdai Zhongguo de liangshi gongzuo
   shiliao* [Historical Data on Food Work in Contemporary China] (Baoding: Hebei sheng gong-
   xiaoshe yinshuachang, 1989) 1800-5, 1832-37.

As understood by scholars, the problem of exaggeration lies in the fact that the reported figures became the basis of the state's grain requisition. In 1953, the CCP state created the grain requisition system (*tonggou tongxiao*) in order to control the food supply. Indeed, the CCP used the grain requisition system to feed an increasing urban population and to increase exports to the Soviets and Eastern Europeans in exchange for industrial equipment. Under the grain-requisition system, the peasants not only had to pay "public grain" (*gongliang*, or in-kind agricultural tax) but could only sell their "surplus grain" (*yuliang*) to the state according to prices upon which the state decided.[56] The system, which combined the in-kind tax and the surplus grain into one requisition, aimed to absorb all of the surplus grain of the peasants, leaving them a per capita amount to meet their basic needs for annual food consumption. The troublesome part of the system was that the annual amount of grain to be collected was planned in advance, based on the estimation of the grain output by local officials. When the leaders of Anhui and Jiangxi exaggerated the anticipated grain output for 1958 and 1959, as documented in Table 8.1 and Table 8.2, the state correspondingly increased its amount of requisition in 1959 and 1960.

Exaggeration had a negative impact on both Anhui and Jiangxi but particularly on the former. In 1959, Anhui's agriculture failed after the great diversion of the agricultural labour force to irrigation works. However, in contrast to the consecutive decline in grain production from 1958 to 1960, as shown in Table 8.1, the rate of the state's grain requisition in those three years increased, most noticeably in 1959, to 38.94 percent of that year's output. This increase resulted in the reduction of grain available to the Anhui people to its lowest level of the 1950s. As the state's requisition target was too high to realize, the province had to drain grain from its food reserve. Between 1958 and 1960, Anhui depleted a total of 2,093,000 tons of grain from its granary to meet the central government's yearly requisition targets.[57]

Consequentially, Anhui became severely impaired in its ability to supply food to peasants, and the provincial government had to cut back on the amount of food rations provided to the rural public dining halls. To be sure, the government also reduced the ration to urban residents, but only by 0.5 to 1 kilogram per month. It was the peasants who suffered dearly. In 1959 and 1960, the annual food consumption allocated to each rural individual dropped lower than 100 kilograms, less than half of the amount the state had defined for an individual's annual consumption – 250 kilograms.[58] At Laoqu, a village in Dingyuan County in central Anhui, the daily food ration at the local public dining hall was 600 grams per person in early spring 1959. This ration was subsequently reduced to 250 grams by May and to 100 grams by November. The local commune finally stopped supplying grain for fifty-three days between late January and March 1960, resulting in massive deaths: 101 of the 198 villagers perished.[59] The same situation occurred in the central Anhui village of Xiaogang, which later became famous for its initiation of China's economic reform in 1978. In 1959 and 1960, 67 of Xiaogang's 120 people died of starvation, and a total of six households perished.[60] Located in the barren central Anhui plains, neither the Laoqu nor the Xiaogang villagers, after their grain was requisitioned, could find enough wild vegetation upon which to survive.

Hunger occurred among Jiangxi peasants as well, but it was less severe than among those living in Anhui. In the spring of 1960, when Liu Junxiu, the province's Party secretary in charge of agriculture, conducted a field survey of thirty-three brigades in a broad region in southern Jiangxi, he discovered that many peasants did not have enough food to consume on a daily basis. In several of these brigades, two-thirds of the peasants did not have enough rice gruel for meals and so had to resort to eating wild vegetation and rice bran. After months of such malnutrition, many of these peasants developed edema and were left with no energy to work. Furthermore, the number of edema patients was growing rapidly, and mass starvation was imminent.[61] When he conducted a field survey at the Hunan Commune of Linchuan County in 1960, Yang Shankui, Jiangxi Party's first secretary, discovered that the peasants there cooked sweet potato leaves to supplement their daily meals.[62] The significant increase in the amount of the state's grain requisition in 1959 and 1960, as is shown in Table 8.2, explains why peasants in some regions of Jiangxi were starving. Everyday hardship and a depletion of physical strength indicate why, in these two years, Jiangxi experienced a decline in food production, although at relatively small percentages.

As a whole, Jiangxi was not really threatened by famine. After visiting the thirty-three brigades, Liu immediately earmarked fifteen thousand tons of rice to those southern counties. Yang also quickly ordered tens of thousands of kilograms of rice to be delivered to the Hunan Commune. Such stories indicate that there was enough grain in Jiangxi, and the statistics in Table 8.1 and Table 8.2 clearly prove the point. In 1958, Jiangxi had 19.13 million people, equal to 56.4 percent of Anhui's population, yet its amount of grain after the state's requisition equalled 83.9 percent of Anhui's. More striking was the identical amount of grain retained by the two provinces in 1959: Anhui had 4.28 million tons, whereas Jiangxi had 4.27 million tons. Similar conditions existed in 1960. In that year,

Anhui's retained grain increased by 4.78 million tons, while Jiangxi's increased by 4.26 million tons, which equalled 89.1 percent of Anhui's (see Table 8.1 and Table 8.2). Without a doubt, the state's requisition led to the scarcity of food in Jiangxi villages; however, at the provincial level, grain was available.

The availability of grain in Jiangxi can be attributed to the state regulations on agricultural tax, or the in-kind tax factor. Although the central government had practically combined the public grain and the surplus grain into one requisition, in theory it still regarded the two as different categories. The public grain remained as the in-kind tax that all people engaged in agricultural production had to pay, whereas the extraction of the surplus grain occurred only among rural peasants. Derived from the theoretical distinctions between these two kinds of grain, in June 1958 the central government proclaimed The Agricultural Tax Regulations of the People's Republic of China, which, in effect, was a set of laws on how to collect, reduce, or exempt the agricultural tax. The regulations contained the following rules, which are relevant to understanding why Jiangxi had sufficient food.

- The rate of the state tax is based on 15.5 percent of the agricultural output of normal years;
- Provinces, for causes of the public good, can collect an additional tax, whose rate should not exceed 15 percent of the amount of the state tax;
- A state farm or a local state-owned farm is regarded as a taxpayer;
- A taxpayer who lawfully reclaims wastelands, starting from the year the taxpayer begins earning agricultural income, is exempted from agricultural taxation for one to three years;
- A migrant who lawfully reclaims wastelands, starting from the year the migrant begins earning agricultural income, is exempted from agricultural taxation for three to five years;
- The old revolutionary bases remaining backward and the poor and barren mountainous regions are allowed tax reductions, pending decisions by their provincial government.[63]

There is no record available that would allow one to calculate how many peasants in Jiangxi, in light of the aforementioned regulations, enjoyed agricultural tax reductions. However, it is reasonable to assume that many of them did benefit from those regulations as more than two-thirds of Jiangxi could be characterized as "the old revolutionary bases" or as "poor and barren mountainous regions."

What one can accurately calculate are Jiangxi's state farms. In order to reduce the size of governmental bureaucracy and to assist the development of old revolutionary bases, in December 1957 Jiangxi mobilized over fifty thousand state cadres, headed by Governor Shao Shiping and Deputy-Governor Fang Zhichun, to move to mountains, hills, and lakesides in order to start land reclamation projects and to organize state farms. These farms began to produce in 1958 and developed rapidly thereafter. They recruited demobilized soldiers, urban youth from Jiangxi and other provinces, migrants from other provinces, and local peasants. In 1959, there were 349 state farms in Jiangxi that engaged in agriculture, forestry, and fishing and aquatic production. The provincial government directly managed the large farms, while the prefectural (*diqu* or *zhuanqu*) and county governments managed the medium-sized and small ones. The entire state-farm system had 1.46 million people, divided into so-called "state-farm workers" (who received a salary paid by the state) and "state-farm peasants" (whose level and manner of income were decided by the managerial authority of each farm). These people cultivated a total of 2.3 million *mu* of land, of which 0.64 million *mu* were newly reclaimed, and they produced 1,125,000 tons of grain.[64] They also produced aquatic products.

Under the state's agricultural tax regulations, these state farms did not need to pay any agricultural tax for one to three years, nor did the Jiangxi government have the obligation to report the grain output these farms produced. Yet the amount of grain from these farms was so large that it was able to offset a larger portion of the grain that the state requisitioned between 1959 and 1961. Possessed and managed by the provincial government, the state-farm grain enabled Jiangxi to prevent a general famine among the peasantry and to supply additional amounts of grain to other provinces – especially to Shanghai – when the central government requested it.[65] The existence of the state-farm system was the chief reason why the Jiangxi government could control a large amount of grain, and it is why many Great Leap Famine refugees from Anhui and other provinces found farm jobs in Jiangxi and were able to survive there.

Anhui also tried state farms. However, due to the lack of land resources, it had never been able to create a large state-farm system, nor had all of its farms been started for the purpose of agricultural production. Anhui began its state-farm reclamations in 1952. By 1957, it had sixteen state farms engaging in agriculture: they employed 21,500 people and possessed 273,000 *mu* of land. The majority of those farms were founded in the marshlands around several large lakes in remote regions, with the exception of a couple of farms that were located in the mountains. Nearly half of these farms were so-called "criminal labour-reform farms," which were apparently trying to make use of their geographic settings to deter criminals from escaping. When the Great Leap popularized the so-called "winds of communism" (*gongchanfeng*), the farms and their nearby communes, expecting the realization of a communist society in a few more years and confused by the theory of public ownership, decided to form joint units by pooling their land. As a consequence of the creation of these joint units, the divide between state property and collective property was effectively erased. In August 1958, the provincial government decided to relinquish all of the farms to prefectural and county governments. Soon the farms and communes ran into disputes over a number of issues regarding who ought to be the overall leader, which side had land property rights, whose land had privileges to use irrigation facilities, and even how the farm workers and commune peasants should dine at the public dining halls. In the end, in 1959 the provincial government decided to break up these units and take back eleven state farms and ten criminal labour-reform farms.[66] In the confusion that came with the changes in leadership and organization, Anhui's state farms neither developed into a functioning system during the Great Leap nor made any noticeable contribution to the province's grain production.

The Leadership Factor

Had Jiangxi's leadership been very enthusiastic in trying to achieve Great Leap goals or to please Mao, Jiangxi might have ended up in as unfortunate a situation as did Anhui. The different Great Leap Famine experiences between Anhui and Jiangxi clearly indicate that the two provinces had two different sets of leadership, one being radical and the other being moderate. This does not mean that Jiangxi's leadership was politically less loyal to Mao than was Anhui's. While Zeng Xisheng, Anhui's first secretary, was certainly a radical and a close follower of Mao, some of Jiangxi's leaders were also radical and close to Mao. The difference lies in the leadership structure, the leaders' local ties, and their attitude towards Mao's programs.

Anhui had a hierarchical leadership structure headed by the dictatorial Zeng Xisheng. Born in 1904 to a bankrupt gentry family in Hunan, Zeng attended a local teacher's school and then, in the mid-1920s, the Whampoa Academy. He joined the Northern Expedition in 1926 and the Communist Party in 1927. Because of Zeng's family and student origins, historian Yung-fa Chen labels Zeng "a petty bourgeois intellectual," implying Zeng's enthusiasm for radical ideas.[67] In the 1930s, Zeng worked for years as the head of the Red Army's intelligence services. In 1949, Zeng became the paramount leader of Anhui. His intelligence service work at the Red Army headquarters enabled him to know Mao personally, and he also earned high praise from Mao.[68] Prior to the Great Leap, other important leaders in Anhui included Huang Yan, Li Shinong, and Zhang Kaifan. Both Huang and Zhang were Anhui natives, and all three were several years junior to Zeng and had taken part in communist activities in the late 1920s to early 1930s, working in Anhui for a number of years.

In the communist cadre system, which valued revolutionary seniority (*geming zige*) and glory, Zeng's experiences, achievements, rank, age, and, especially, personal ties to Mao placed Zeng well above the others and awed them. Further to this, his dictatorial nature was partnered with a famous temper: he was known as a "tiger" who would explode at the slightest criticism.[69] In January 1958, Zeng purged Li because the latter, as a Party secretary and a deputy-governor of the province in charge of judicial affairs, had spoken against a series of decisions that labelled too many people as "Rightists." Even though Li had been Zeng's colleague for ten years, Zeng expelled him from the Party with little hesitation.[70] The story that best exemplifies Zeng's dictatorial impact on the province involves his series of proposals on how to achieve Anhui's irrigation projects during the Great Leap. In a Central Committee conference from November to December 1958, Zeng first proposed that Anhui could complete 800 million cubic metres of earthwork and stonework in irrigation projects for the coming year; then, in just a few days, he doubled that number several times – all the way to 6.4 billion cubic metres – without consulting any of his colleagues or considering what such an increase would mean for the people of Anhui. Mao, on the other hand, lavished praise on Zeng's proposals and exhorted the Central Committee to learn enthusiasm from Zeng.[71] Zeng pleased Mao with his proposals, but they ultimately resulted in 5 million peasants working on large-scale irrigation projects and, consequently, produced the terrible failure of Anhui agriculture in 1959.

Unlike the case in Anhui, Jiangxi's four primary leaders co-existed in a collaborative structure. In the mid-1950s, Yang Shangkui, who was of peasant origin and had five years of elementary education, served as the Party's first secretary. Shao Shiping, the Party's second secretary and provincial governor, was more senior in age and was the most well known because he had studied at the Beijing Normal University in the early 1920s and had co-founded the Tenth Army of the Red Army in 1930. The other two, Fang Zhichun and Liu Junxiu, both originated from peasant families and were several years Shao's junior. All four were Jiangxi natives and had joined the Red Army in the late 1920s. In the mid-1930s, when Shao and Liu followed the Red Army on the Long March to northern Shaanxi, Yang and Fang stayed behind to continue waging Red Army guerrilla warfare in northeastern and southern Jiangxi, respectively. They all had a glorious revolutionary past. In addition, they had all known Mao in person during the Red Army period.[72]

There were subtle differences that held Jiangxi's four leaders in a sort of balance of power. Theoretically, Yang was the chief of the province, but practically he needed to respect Shao because Shao had seniority in revolutionary accomplishments as well as in age and education. Furthermore, owing to their geographic origins during the Red Army period, Yang and Liu naturally led a loose-fitting group of cadres who came from southern Jiangxi (*Gannan pai*), whereas Shao and Fang led a group from the northeastern part of the province (*Gandongbei pai*).[73] Probably as a result of these subtle differences, in 1953-54 Yang formally proposed to the provincial Party committee that he and Shao would only oversee general affairs of the province and not be responsible for any routine, detailed work.[74] The proposal, soon approved, further shaped the provincial leadership into a well-balanced collaborative structure. After that, Liu was appointed to be the Party secretary in charge of agricultural affairs. Being loosely watched by the two more senior leaders, Liu, despite his radicalism, needed to genuinely take criticism and be willing to readjust his policies. In 1958, Jiangxi organized 180,000 public dining halls, in which over 93 percent of Jiangxi's peasants ate daily. After receiving many complaints, including one from Shao, Liu dissolved more than eighty thousand dining halls in 1959 in an attempt to make the communal dining system more functional.[75] This dissolution saved many troubles that might have led to widespread starvation in Jiangxi villages.

Practically, the division of cadre groups was not a bad thing because it permitted Jiangxi leaders to tie themselves closely to local people and to become better informed about local realities. It is apparent that all four leaders had genuine feelings for Jiangxi. During their Red Army years, each leader had seen the sacrifice of his relatives and friends and had been fed, assisted, or saved by the local peasants. In September 1956, at China's Eighth National Party Congress, Yang made an emotional speech appealing to the CCP authority for more support and a reduction of the tax burden since Jiangxi, as the most glorious "old base," remained backward after it had greatly contributed to the revolution.[76] When the Great Leap began, Shao and Fang led a large group of state cadres to the Damao Mountains in northeast Jiangxi – where they had conducted guerrilla warfare in the 1930s – to start state-farm reclamations.[77] Yang, wanting to better understand what was happening in villages, visited all of the province's eighty-two counties.[78] Staying calmly away from the Great Leap and dedicating themselves to the economic programs that could assist the development of the old base areas, Yang, Shao, and Fang effectively desisted from promoting the Great Leap. In the meantime, their visits to the counties and old bases enabled them to become aware of local realities as well as to hear the truth from the old-time supporters among the local peasants and cadres.

Zeng, who was in Anhui, did not have these local ties. In a letter to Mao written in March 1959, Zeng complained that many local cadres did not understand his speeches, likely because of his Hunan accent or because his words were too abstract.[79] He did not seem to care much for maintaining a good relationship with native Anhui cadres. When he purged Li in 1958, Zeng also dumped a large group of Anhui cadres – 3,300 people – along with him.[80] Between March and April 1959, when Zhang, then a Party secretary and a deputy-governor of the province, disagreed with Zeng about the public dining hall system, Zeng accused Zhang of always looking on the dark side of things. In fact, Zhang had heard of hunger and deaths when his visiting relatives brought him the news. In July, when Zhang, conducting a field survey of his hometown, Wuwei County, decided to dissolve all the public dining halls of that county, Zeng, then attending the Central Committee's Lushan Meeting, reported the event to Mao. Unhappy to see a provincial challenge to his Great Leap programs, Mao labelled Zhang a member of the "Peng Dehuai anti-Party military clique." Implicated along with Zhang was a large group of Anhui cadres at the provincial level, as well as 28,741 local and grassroots cadres in Wuwei, who were then dismissed, imprisoned, or criticized at the public struggle sessions.[81] Intimidated by Zeng, even Huang, Anhui's governor and a Party secretary, dared not express any disagreement.[82]

Zeng's lack of local ties had fatal consequences. In late 1958, Zeng made himself the concurrent Party secretary of Feidong County, a county about twenty kilometres away from Anhui's capital Hefei, in an attempt to enhance the local leadership. In 1960, 81,550 people died in Feidong as a consequence of starvation.[83] Later Zeng claimed that he had not been aware of the occurrence of hunger and deaths in Feidong until mid-1960.[84] This was probably a lie. By any measure, as the concurrent Party secretary, he was supposed to know the details of every important event in Feidong, not to mention the massive deaths happening under his nose. At the very least, if he had established a genuine local connection with Feidong's cadres and people, he would have had a sense of what was happening in Feidong.

Since Jiangxi leaders worked together collaboratively, they took a realistic approach to Mao's Great Leap. With the exception of Liu, the Jiangxi leaders did not seem excited about it. In early 1959, Shao stated in a public speech to the provincial cadres, "socialism will never succeed if the public dining continues," thus showing his disgust with the public dining hall system. He was able to evade any political difficulties that might have been caused by his remark only because Yang Shangkun, the chief of the General Office of the Central Committee, did not report the remark to Mao.[85] Yang Shangkui and Fang Zhichun chose to focus on their own agendas. While Yang spent three years travelling to all eighty-two counties during the Great Leap, Fang travelled to his reclamation farm in the Damao Mountains four times between 1958 and 1959.[86] By either publicly opposing some of the Great Leap programs or quietly making themselves unavailable, the Jiangxi leaders appeared to take a passive attitude towards the Maoist economy. Even Liu, who was enthusiastic about Mao's Great Leap in agriculture, could not have done too much once the other leaders either revealed their dislike of it or remained largely silent about it. Make no mistake, they were all politically loyal to Mao, but they were realistic about the rural societies under their governance. Their moderate politics kept Jiangxi from being damaged by the Great Leap.

Anhui's Zeng was a blatant political radical who almost single-handedly damaged Anhui. In March and April 1959, in one of Mao's meetings with provincial Party secretaries regarding various production targets, almost all of the secretaries were stunned by his unrealistic goals but were unwilling to say a word against them when Mao called upon them. Zeng, however, told Mao and the other secretaries that Anhui would accept the high targets because lower targets would not inspire the enthusiasm of the cadres and masses. As long as the people had spirit and energy, Zeng argued, all of the high targets could be achieved.[87] It was with this radical attitude that Zeng not only proposed Anhui's unrealistic targets for the irrigation projects but also supported the hugely exaggerated target for grain output. The result of his radicalism was the failure of Anhui's agricultural production and a massive number of peasant deaths.

When one compares the leadership structures, local ties, and political attitudes of leaders in Anhui and Jiangxi, it is clear in which area the leadership factor made the most fundamental difference with regard to Great Leap Famine death rates – famine relief work. In Jiangxi, the leaders could not have rejected Mao's Great Leap or prevented the peasants from suffering, but they did their best to minimize the damages that it caused. As evidenced by Liu Junxiu's and Yang Shangkui's earmarking of rice to areas suffering food shortages, the Jiangxi leadership prevented a large-scale famine from occurring in its province.

In Anhui, Zeng's leadership augmented the damage caused by the Great Leap. Zeng's ignorance of the truth permitted the occurrence of massive deaths. It is hard to imagine that, by 1959, Zeng, already the chief of

Anhui for ten years, could not tell what was true from what was false in the province under his governance. He first got word of Anhui's food shortages from his colleagues in early February 1959. But, after receiving Mao's instruction in late February 1959 regarding the widespread problem of grain concealing on the part of the peasants, Zeng ordered a round of house searches in Anhui villages without bothering to travel to the countryside to observe local conditions for himself. When widespread deaths began to take place in Anhui in early summer of 1959, Zeng denied it and chose to listen only to positive reports. At the same time, he defeated Zhang over the issues of hunger and public dining halls in July 1959, and he ignored evidence from Zhang's field investigation in Wuwei County as well as a report on Anhui's food scarcity, which Zhang had obtained from Ding Zhi, the head of the province's food bureau.[88]

After defeating Zhang, Zeng could never admit the occurrence of famine in Anhui because that would have proven that he had been wrong. He did not make any trips to the countryside, not even to Feidong County, nor did his Anhui cadres, even his close followers, dare to report bad news to him, especially after seeing the fall of Zhang and so many provincial and local cadres. When massive deaths occurred in Anhui in early 1960, Zeng was recuperating from stomach problems in Guangzhou and Shanghai. Although one of his secretaries reported the bad news to him in person, he failed to respond. Moreover, after he returned to Anhui in March, he continued to sit on his hands. It is even more difficult to understand why, even after the Central Committee had issued a document dated 9 September 1960 pointing out the large number of abnormal deaths in Anhui and other provinces, Zeng still failed to provide anything in the way of famine relief.[89] On 25 September, when Premier Zhou Enlai flew to Anhui to request a contribution of grain to help solve the nationwide food problem, Zeng promised that Anhui would do its best.[90]

On 9 October 1960, Zeng moved to Jinan, the capital of Shandong Province, after Mao appointed him as the concurrent first secretary of the Party in Shandong. Immediately after arriving in Jinan, Zeng adopted a series of policies to deal with Shandong's famine, but he continued ignoring the serious situation in Anhui – the province that remained under his leadership. In mid-December, by which time Zeng was definitely aware of Anhui's massive number of deaths (as he had listened to the report from his visiting Anhui colleagues), he still had not come up with any policy on famine relief. Only on the last day of December did Zeng, by telephone, instruct the Anhui provincial government to take emergency measures to start famine relief. These included distributing food quotas of 250 grams of grain per day per head to rural areas and dissolving public dining halls.[91]

By 7 February 1961, Zeng returned to Anhui to lead Anhui's famine relief work himself, blaming the massive number of deaths on cadres at the lower levels.[92] The famine occurred, he said, "mainly because the cadres at the lower levels [*xiamian*] had not dared to report the truth to us."[93]

Zeng's efforts at famine relief in Anhui, however, arrived too late. In 1960, Anhui experienced a net loss of 3.84 million people.[94] Surprisingly, in early February 1962, at the Seven Thousand People Conference of the Central Committee, Zeng continued to deny mass starvation in Anhui and reported to Liu Shaoqi, then the deputy chairman of the CCP, that only 400,000 deaths had transpired. The reported number was so small that Liu lost his temper because, having previously read a report written by a field investigation team of the Central Committee on Anhui's famine conditions, he knew that Zeng was lying.[95] Zeng was indeed lying. At this conference, the Anhui delegation was ready to report to the Central Committee a large number of Anhui's deaths for the year 1960, but it was Zeng who reduced the death toll to 1.17 million after having at first reported only 400,000.[96] After being criticized by Liu, Zeng finally admitted that the death toll in Anhui was 4 million.[97] Yet it is likely he only made this admission in order to evade more severe criticism or even punishment. Zeng himself never thought that the famine in Anhui was terribly serious. In May 1967 in Beijing, when Zeng received the visiting Liang Shoufu, the leader of Anhui's Red Guards in the early days of the Cultural Revolution, he told the latter: "At the Seven Thousand People Conference, Anhui's problem was made so serious because Liu Shaoqi wanted to give me a hard time. I could not shirk responsibility and thus alone took the blame."[98]

Under Mao's enormous pressure for his Great Leap Forward, perhaps no provinces could have completely avoided some damage, but the provincial leaders could have at least tried to save lives, as did Jiangxi's leadership. In late 1960, Zeng briefly adopted famine relief policies in Shandong, probably because he was not the one who had created the Great Leap mess there and so would not have to take responsibility for it. Yet, in Anhui, where Zeng ruled for over a decade, he simply denied the truth of the Great Leap disasters. Had Zeng admitted the reality and adopted famine relief measures slightly earlier, tens of thousands of Anhui peasants would have been saved. It is famine relief work that makes the leadership factor so important in understanding the Great Leap Famine deaths.

Conclusion

This chapter does not point to a single cause for the cross-province difference in death rates; rather, it argues that this difference was decided by a number of intersecting factors: specifically, whether a province experienced a sudden shortage of agricultural labourers, had a sufficient amount of available food, and had a set of famine relief measures. In Anhui, the sudden shortage of agricultural labourers, generated both by Anhui's need to reconstruct its infrastructure for the purposes of agriculture and its unrealistic pursuit of Great Leap irrigation projects, first caused agricultural failure in 1959 and predisposed the province to food scarcity. Then the hunger problem worsened after the state, based on Anhui's exaggeration of the amount of grain output, extracted excessive quantities of grain from the peasantry and emptied the province's food reserve. However, it was Anhui's dictatorial leadership that, by enforcing Maoist programs and stubbornly refusing to admit reality and take famine relief measures, permitted a massive number of deaths to take place. Having favourable natural conditions, Jiangxi had never needed to divert great numbers of its agricultural labour force towards irrigation projects. Thanks to the large quantity of "hidden" grain reserves resulting from its state-farm system, which offset the state's requisition of food, Jiangxi never experienced a general famine. Finally, Jiangxi's collaborative leadership, with its accurate sense of local realities and passive attitude towards the Great Leap, successfully pre-empted the conditions that might have led to a famine.

The experiences of Anhui and Jiangxi may shed light on the Great Leap Famine in other provinces. For instance, in Sichuan, another province that was devastated by hunger during the famine, the Party's first secretary Li Jingquan, a Jiangxi native, also started as a sort of "petty bourgeois intellectual," much like Anhui's Zeng. Li also ruled a province that he neither knew well nor with which he had strong local ties. His leadership style was dictatorial, and he often denied the truth of Sichuan's Great Leap Famine and was careless regarding the massive number of deaths. In Maoist politics, Li was sometimes even more radical than Zeng.[99] Under Li's governance, between 1958 and 1961 Sichuan lost 9.4 million people, or 13.07 percent of its population.[100]

Like Jiangxi, Heilongjiang had plentiful land resources and favourable agricultural conditions; like Jiangxi, during the Great Leap, it also underwent a period of land reclamation for the purpose of building state farms. Between 1956 and 1958, Heilongjiang received the so-called "100,000 demobilized soldiers" to start reclamation. By 1959, these former soldiers, dealing with a high level of agricultural mechanization on their state farms, had reclaimed 6.42 million *mu* of land.[101] There is no doubt that the abundance of land resources and the tax privileges for newly reclaimed land enabled Heilongjiang not only to offset the Great Leap Famine but also to become a major food supplier to the nation during the famine years.

In re-examining Great Leap Famine scholarship, I find that the communal dining theory does not explain the experiences of Anhui and Jiangxi. The theory identifies communal dining as the single cause of famine deaths by pointing to a collateral relationship between the time span of the famine deaths and that of the public dining halls. Yet, and as is evident in Anhui and Jiangxi, the deaths were closely related to the level of per capita food ration, not to the public dining system. In fact, Anhui stopped its communal dining hall system in January 1961, and Jiangxi stopped its system in May 1961, but the longer length of communal dining in Jiangxi did not cause more deaths in that province. From another perspective, Great Leap Famine deaths did not end in Anhui as a result of the demise of its communal dining system; rather, as is shown in Table 8.1, they ended because the province reduced the amount of the state's grain requisition and imported food from other provinces. The end of Great Leap Famine deaths in Anhui was also the result of the provincial leadership's having adopted famine relief measures.

It seems even more inappropriate to causally connect the Great Leap Famine death rates to the public dining hall participation rate, Party member density, and the time of a province's liberation. As this chapter reveals, the theories of "public dining hall participation rate," "Party member density," and "time of liberation" were not the causes of deaths in Anhui and Jiangxi. Jiangxi was liberated in January 1949 and Anhui in May 1949, but Anhui's number of Great Leap Famine deaths (6.33 million) was thirty-five times larger than that of Jiangxi (0.18 million). One would certainly question how five months' difference in the time of liberation could result in such a great variation in the number of deaths one decade later. Without taking into account natural conditions, the public dining hall participation rate and Party member density are meaningless. For instance, Liaoning's dining hall participation rate was 23 percent at the end of 1959, the second lowest in the nation, and its Party member density was 1.75, the fourth highest in the nation.[102] Yet, as is shown in Alfred Chan's study, Liaoning normally had severe winter weather, which continuously covered the countryside with snow and completely prevented agricultural activities from late November to March.[103] It is hard to imagine how a Liaoning farmer, Party member or not, walked a half kilometre in snow and below-zero temperatures with his or her family members to eat in a public dining hall. Under these circumstances, the public dining hall participation rate and Party member density are irrelevant.

The same kind of criticism can be applied to both the "food availability decline" and the "entitlement" theories that have tried to build econometric models on the national data. As this chapter demonstrates, by relying solely on the national data, no econometric model, no matter how mathematically perfect, is capable of accounting for Jiangxi's "hidden" store of food, nor is it capable of explaining why food was available in Jiangxi but not in Anhui. Nor can such models tell why the massive number of deaths in Anhui occurred mainly in the central and northern parts of the province, despite Anhui's appearing in the national data as a "bad" famine province. In short, what this chapter shows is that, at the provincial level, the Great Leap Famine was a complex event and is better explained through a detailed study of the stories and data belonging to each province.

Acknowledgments
This chapter was first presented at the biennial conference of the Historical Society for Twentieth-Century China, in Singapore, 26-28 June 2006. I would like to thank Wang Shuobai and Liu Jigang for their assistance to my research in Anhui, and Xiao Tangbiao for assistance to my research in Jiangxi. I am grateful to Lu Junping, a Jiangxi native, for the conversations with him that enabled me to have a better understanding of Jiangxi's agricultural conditions. I would also like to thank Ramon Myers and R. Mark Spaulding for their criticism and suggestions and Nina le Ferla for editing this chapter.

Notes

1 Cao Shuji, "1959-1961 nian Zhongguo de renkou siwang jiqi chengyin" [The Death Rate of China's Population and Its Contributing Factors from 1959-1961], *Zhongguo renkou kexue* [Chinese Population Science] 1 (2005): 14-28.
2 Justin Yifu Lin and Dennis Tao Yang, "Food Availability, Entitlements, and the Chinese Famine of 1959-61," *Economic Journal* 110 (2000): 136-58.
3 Ibid.; James K. Kung and Justin Y. Lin, "The Causes of China's Great Leap Famine, 1959-1961," *Economic Development and Cultural Change* 52 (2003): 51-73.
4 Wei Li and Dennis Tao Yang, "The Great Leap Forward: Anatomy of a Central Planning Disaster," *Journal of Political Economy* 113 (2005): 840-77.
5 Dali Yang, *Calamity and Reform in China: State, Rural Society, and Institutional Change since the Great Leap Famine* (Stanford: Stanford University Press, 1996), 55; Guanzhong James Wen and Gene Chang, "Communal Dining and the Chinese Famine of 1958-1961," *Economic and Cultural Change* 46 (1997): 1-34.
6 Yang, *Calamity and Reform*, 56-59.
7 The annual per capita grain consumption in 1959, 1960, and 1961 was 183, 156, and 154 kilograms, respectively; and, in 1962 and 1963, it was 161 and 160 kilograms, respectively. See Gene Hsin Chang and Guanzhong James Wen, "Food Availability versus Consumption Efficiency: Causes of the Chinese Famine," *China Economic Review* 9, 2 (1998): 157-65.
8 Kung and Lin, "Causes of China's Great Leap Famine."
9 Ibid.
10 Carl Riskin, "Seven Questions about the Chinese Famine of 1959-61," *China Economic Review* 9, 2 (1998): 111-24; Cao, "1959-1961 nian Zhongguo de renkou siwang jiqi chengyin."
11 Kenneth Lieberthal, "The Great Leap Forward and the Split in the Yenan Leadership, 1958-1965," in *Cambridge History of China*, Vol. 14, ed. John K. Fairbank and Roderick MacFarquhar, 293-359 (Cambridge: Cambridge University Press, 1987), 293-359.
12 Dali Yang sees a causal relationship between a high mortality rate and political radicalism. He argues that Henan, Hunan, Sichuan, Yunnan, Guizhou, and Anhui, the provinces that suffered heavy human losses, all had zealous political leaders, low Party membership

density, a high public dining hall participation rate, and a high mortality rate. However, Shandong and Gansu reverse Yang's model. These provinces did not have the "most zealous" leaders and had high Party membership density and low public dining hall participation rate, but their human losses were heavy too. See Dali, *Calamity and Reform*, 57; Cao, "1959-1961 nian Zhongguo de renkou siwang jiqi chengyin."

13 Wen and Chang, "Communal Dining and the Chinese Famine."

14 Anhui difangzhi bianzhuan weiyuanhui, ed., *Anhui shengzhi: Renkouzhi* [Anhui Provincial Gazetteer: Population Volume] (Hefei: Anhui renmin chubanshe, 1995), 6, 20, 27.

15 Guojia tongjiju zonghesi, ed., *Quanguo gesheng, zizhiqu, zhixiashi lishi tongji ziliao huibian* [A Compilation of Historical Statistical Data of Provinces, Autonomous Regions, and Municipalities, 1949-1989] (Beijing: Zhongguo tongji chubanshe, 1990), 405-6, 418.

16 Ma Juxian, Shi Yuan, and Yi Yiqu, eds., *Zhongguo renkou: Jiangxi fence* [Chinese Population: Jiangxi Volume] (Beijing: Zhongguo caizheng jingji chubanshe, 1989), 57, 61. For Jiangxi's population, please also see Lu Fangshang, "Kangzhan qian Jiangxi de nongye gailiang yu nongcun gaijin shiye, 1933-37" [Agricultural Reforms and Rural Improvements in Jiangxi Prior to the War against Japan, 1933-37], in *Jindai Zhongguo nongye jingjishi lunwenji* [Symposium of Rural Economic History of Modern China], ed. Zhongyang yanjiuyuan jindaishisuo, 517-56 (Taipei: Zhongyang yanjiuyuan jindaishisuo, 1989).

17 Ma et al., *Zhongguo renkou*, 32.

18 Guojia tongjiju zonghesi, *Quanguo gesheng, zizhiqu, zhixiashi lishi tongji ziliao huibian*, 477.

19 Ibid.

20 Huang Zhiquan et al., eds., *Zhongguo ziran ziyuan congshu: Jiangxi juan* [A Series on China's Natural Resources: Jiangxi Volume] (Beijing: Zhongguo huanjing kexue chubanshe, 1995), 12, 20; Zhou Benli et al., eds., *Zhongguo ziran ziyuan congshu: Anhui juan* [A Series on China's Natural Resources: Anhui Volume] (Beijing: Zhongguo huanjing kexue chubanshe, 1995), 31, 81.

21 Yang Peijin, *Yang Shaokui zhuan* [Biography of Yang Shangkui] (Beijing: Zhongyang wenxian chubanshe, 2000), 414.

22 Huang et al., *Zhongguo ziran ziyuan congshu*, 28, 105.

23 Zhou et al., *Zhongguo ziran ziyuan congshu*, 18-19, 73-74.

24 Su Hua et al., comps., *Dangdai Zhongguo de Anhui* [Anhui in Contemporary China] (Beijing: Dangdai Zhongguo chubanshe, 1992), 1:238; Fu Yutian et al., comps., *Dangdai Zhongguo de Jiangxi: Shangjuan* [Jiangxi in Contemporary China] (Beijing: Dangdai Zhongguo chubanshe), 1:120.

25 Huang, *Zhongguo ziran ziyuan congshu*, 30.

26 Su et al., *Dangdai Zhongguo de Anhui*, 1:3.

27 Ibid., 262; Zhou et al., *Zhongguo ziran ziyuan congshu*, 279, 393.

28 Anhui difangzhi bianzhuan weiyuanhui, *Anhui shengzhi: Renkouzhi* [Anhui Chronicle: Population Volume], 31-32.

29 Fu et al., *Dangdai Zhongguo de Jiangxi*, 1:154-55.

30 Huang et al., *Zhongguo ziran ziyuan congshu*, 353.

31 Ma et al., *Zhongguo renkou*, 165-67.

32 Zhou et al., *Zhongguo ziran ziyuan congshu*, 5, 17, 21, 33, 223-25.

33 Ibid., 130-38.

34 Ibid., 225.

35 Su et al., *Dangdai Zhongguo de Anhui*, 1:37, 216-17.

36 Ibid., 225; Zhou et al., *Zhongguo ziran ziyuan congshu*, 134-35.

37 Anhui difangzhi bianzhuan weiyuanhui, ed., *Anhui shengzhi: Nongyezhi* [Anhui Provincial Gazetteer: Agriculture Volume] (Hefei: Anhui renmin chubanshe, 1996), 35, 58.

38 Ibid., 34-35; Anhui difangzhi bianzhuan weiyuanhui, ed., *Anhui shengzhi: Liangshizhi* [Anhui Provincial Gazetteer: Food Volume] (Hefei: Anhui renmin chubanshe, 1991), 1-2.

39 Li Wenhai et al., *Zhongguo jindai shida zaihuang* [Ten Great Famines in Modern China] (Shanghai: Shanghai renmin chubanshe, 1994), 230.
40 Fu et al., *Dangdai Zhongguo de Jiangxi*, 1:225-26.
41 Ibid., 2, 119-20.
42 Li Xiwen and Wei Rengzheng, *Liu Junxiu Zhuan* [Biography of Liu Junxiu] (Beijing: Zhongyang wenxian chubanshe, 1996), 251-52.
43 Anhui difangzhi bianzhuan weiyuanhui, *Anhui shengzhi: Liangshizhi*, 37.
44 Hou Yong et al., eds., *Dangdai Anhui jianshi* [A Brief History of Contemporary Anhui] (Beijing: Dangdai Zhongguo chubanshe, 2001), 195-96.
45 Fu et al., *Dangdai Zhongguo de Jiangxi*, 1:54.
46 Ibid., 226.
47 *Anhui ribao* [Anhui Daily], 27 February 1958.
48 Su et al., *Dangdai Zhongguo de Anhui*, 1:201.
49 Zhou Jun, "Caifang Pi-Shi-Hang guangai gongcheng zhuiyi" [Recollection of My Reporting the Pi-Shi-Hang Irrigation Engineering Project], *Jianghuai wenshi* [Anhui Cultural and Historical Records] 3 (1999): 121-34.
50 Su et al., *Dangdai Zhongguo de Anhui*, 1:231.
51 Ibid., 1:85.
52 Guo Weilian, "Pi-Shi-Hang gongcheng xingjian shi de Liu'an diwei shuji Du Weiyou" [The Liu'an Prefectural Party Secretary Du Weiyou during the Construction of the Pi-Shi-Hang Engineering Project], *Jianghuai wenshi* [Anhui Cultural and Historical Records] 4 (1999): 77-82.
53 Anhui had 13.25 million agricultural labourers in 1957, but the data for 1958 and 1959 are not available. Since 1.95 million peasants were recruited to urban enterprises in late 1958, and people began to die from the Great Leap Famine in 1959, one may guess that Anhui's agricultural labour force in 1959 was about 11.25 million people. See Guojia tongjiju zonghesi, *Quanguo gesheng, zizhiqu, zhixiashi lishi tongji ziliao huibian*, 405, 418; Anhui difangzhi bianzhuan weiyuanhui, *Anhui shengzhi: Nongyezhi*, 3.
54 Fu et al., *Dangdai Zhongguo de Jiangxi*, 1:5; Su et al., *Dangdai Zhongguo de Anhui*, 2:3-4.
55 Su et al., *Dangdai Zhongguo de Anhui*, 1:79; He Youliang, "Dangdai Jiangxi nongye shilüe" [A Brief Agricultural History of Contemporary Jiangxi], *Nongye kaogu* [Agricultural Archaeology] 3 (2003), http://www.guoxue.com.
56 Jin Chongji and Chen Qun, eds., *Chen Yun zhuan* [Biography of Chen Yun], (Beijing: Zhongyang wenxian chubanshe, 2005), 836-60.
57 Anhui difangzhi bianzhuan weiyuanhui, *Anhui shengzhi: Liangshizhi*, 2.
58 Su et al., *Dangdai Zhongguo de Anhui*, 1:85.
59 Yixin Chen, "When Food Became Scarce: Life and Death in Chinese Villages during the Great Leap Forward Famine," *Journal of the Historical Society* 2, 2 (June 2010): 117-65.
60 Han Fudong and Lei Min, "Xiaogang cun dabaogan daitouren: Yan Junchang jiangshu gaige kaifang 30 nian" [Xiaogang Village's Pioneering of the Household Responsibility System: Yan Junchang Talks about the Thirty Years of Reform and Opening], http://news.xinhuanet.com/.
61 Li and Wei, *Liu Junxiu zhuan*, 271.
62 Yang, *Yang Shaokui zhuan*, 409.
63 "Zhonghua renmin gongheguo nongyeshui tiaoli" [The Agricultural Tax Regulations of the People's Republic of China, 3 June 1958], in *Jianguo yilai zhongyao wenxian xuanbian* [Selected Important Documents since the Founding of the People's Republic of China], ed. Zonggong zongyang wenxian yanjiushi, 11:354-61.
64 Li and Wei, *Liu Junxiu zhuan*, 271.
65 Liu Mianyu and Hu Shaochun, *Fang Zhichun zhuan* [Biography of Fang Zhichun] (Nanchang: Jiangxi renmin chubanshe, 2005), 401-2.
66 Su et al., *Dangdai Zhongguo de Anhui*, 1:263, 299-302.

67   Chen Yung-fa, *Zhongguo gongchan geming qishinian, xiajuan* [Seventy Years of the Chinese Communist Revolution] (Taipei: Lianjing chubanshe, 2001), 2:723.

68   Anhui xinsijun lishi yanjiuhui, comp., *Jinian Zeng Xisheng wenji* [Collected Writings Commemorating Zeng Xisheng] (Beijing: Dangdai Zhongguo chubanshe, 2005), 56-68.

69   Shui Jing, *Teshu de jiaowang: Shengwei diyishuji furen de huiyilu* [Unique Interactions: The Reminiscences of the Wife of a Provincial First Party Secretary] (Nanjing: Jiangsu wenyi chubanshe, 1992), 232-49.

70   Su et al., *Dangdai Zhongguo de Anhui*, 1:67-68.

71   Zonggong zongyang wenxian yanjiushi, ed., *Jianguo yilai Mao Zedong wengao* [Writings of Mao Zedong since the Establishment of the People's Republic of China], vol. 7 (Beijing: Zhongyang wenxian chubanshe, 1992), 636-42.

72   Shao Shiping, *Shao Shiping riji* [The Diary of Shao Shiping] (Nanchang: Jiangxi renmin chubanshe, 1983), 1-3; Liu and Hu, *Fang Zhichun zhuan*, 105-13; Yang, *Yang Shaokui zhuan*, 119-20; Li and Wei, *Liu Junxiu zhuan*, 36-38.

73   Yang, *Yang Shaokui zhuan*, 380.

74   Ibid., 379.

75   Liu and Hu, *Fang Zhichun zhuan*, 420; He et al., "Dangdai Jiangxi nongye shilüe."

76   Frederick Teiwes, "Provincial Politics in China: Themes and Variations," in *China: Management of a Revolutionary Society*, ed. John Lindbeck, 116-89 (Seattle: University of Washington Press, 1971).

77   Liu and Hu, *Fang Zhichun zhuan*, 362-67.

78   Yang, *Yang Shaokui zhuan*, 407-8.

79   Zhonggong Anhui shengwei bangongting, ed., *Zhonggong Anhui shengwei wenjian xuanbian, 1958-1962* [Selected Documents of the Anhui Provincial Committee of the Chinese Communist Party, 1958-1962] (Hefei: Anhui shiyou kantan gongsi yinshuachang, 2004), 155-57.

80   Liu Yanpei, "Li Shinong fandang jituan shijian de zhenxiang jiqi lishi jingyan" [The Truth and the Historical Lessons of the Incident of the Li Shinong Anti-Party Clique], *Jianghuai wenshi* [Anhui Cultural and Historical Records] 1 (2006): 168-76.

81   Zhang Kaifan, *Zhang Kaifan huiyilu* [Memoir of Zhang Kaifan] (Hefei: Anhui renmin chubanshe, 2004), 340-68, 388.

82   Gui Yingchao, ed., *Cong fangniuwa dao shengzhang: Huang Yan zhuanlüe* [From Child Cowherd to Provincial Governor: A Short Biography of Huang Yan] (Hefei: Anhui renmin chubanshe, 1994), 98, 114, 135.

83   Anhui difangzhi bianzhuan weiyuanhui, *Anhui shengzhi: Renkouzhi*, 99.

84   Zheng Rui, *Zhengcheng huimou* [My Journey in Retrospect] (Beijing: Renmin chubanshe, 2005), 499.

85   Liu and Hu, *Fang Zhichun zhuan*, 420.

86   Ibid., 362-75.

87   Tao Lujia, *Mao zhuxi jiaodao women dang shengwei shuji* [Chairman Mao Taught Us to Be Provincial Party Secretaries] (Beijing: Zhongyang wenxian chubanshe, 2003), 98-102.

88   Zhang, *Zhang Kaifan huiyilu*, 343-49.

89   Zheng, *Zhengcheng huimou*, 34-35.

90   Zhonggong zhongyang wenxian yanjiushi, ed., *Zhou Enlai nianpu* [Chronicle of Zhou Enlai] (Beijing: Zhongyang wenxian chubanshe, 1998), 2:350-51.

91   Su et al., *Dangdai Zhongguo de Anhui*, 1:86-81.

92   Hou et al., *Dangdai Anhui jianshi*, 233-34.

93   Zheng, *Zhengcheng huimou*, 35-36.

94   Guojia tongjiju zonghesi, *Quanguo gesheng, zizhiqu, zhixiashi lishi tongji ziliao huibian*, 405.

95   Zhang Suhua, *Bianju: Qiqianren dahui shimo* [The Change: The Beginning to End of the Seven Thousand People Conference] (Beijing: Zhongguo qingnian chubanshe, 2006), 268-73.

96 Liu, "Li Shinong fandang jituan shijian de zhenxiang jiqi lishi jingyan."
97 Zhang, *Zhang Kaifan huiyilu*, 344.
98 Liang Shoufu, "Chaoqi chaoluo" [The Tide Came In, the Tide Went Out], *Huaxia wenzhai zengkan* [China News Digest Supplementary Issues] 682 (29 December 2008), http://www.cnd.org.
99 Tao, *Mao zhuxi jiaodao women dang shengwei shuiji*, 100-1.
100 Cao, "1959-1961 nian Zhongguo de renkou siwang jiqi chengyin," 14-28.
101 Heilongjiang sheng difangzhi bianzhuan weiyuanhui, ed., *Heilongjiang shengzhi: Guoying nongchan zhi* [Heilongjiang Provincial Gazetteer: The State Farm Volume] (Harbin: Heilongjiang renmin chubanshe, 1992), http://www.zglz.gov.cn/.
102 Yang, *Calamity and Reform in China*, 57.
103 Alfred Chan, "The Campaign for Agricultural Development in the Great Leap Forward: A Study of Policy-Making and Implementation in Liaoning," *China Quarterly* 129 (1992): 52-71.

9 Great Leap City: Surviving the Famine in Tianjin

Jeremy Brown

In 1959, in response to food shortages in Wuqing County just northwest of Tianjin, a member of an opera troupe in the village of Zaolin composed a "clappertalk" (*kuaiban*) routine called "Suffering from Famine" (*Nao liang huang*). The piece was performed openly in the village. The composer charged that there were many obstacles to getting sufficient food and that no matter how good the crops were there was never enough to eat. In contrast, he continued, people in Beijing and Tianjin always had plenty to eat. After hearing the performance, villagers proposed organizing a caravan to Tianjin. Some peasants expressed doubt that food was more abundant in the city and did not want to go, but the clappertalk composer, insinuating that certain families might be hoarding grain secretly, said, "whoever does not go to Tianjin must have food in their house." Persuaded by this argument, more than 180 villagers clambered on to eight large carts and embarked for Tianjin. When the villagers arrived in the city, they begged for food on the streets.[1] They were indeed correct in their impression that food was more plentiful in Tianjin.

As the preceding chapters make abundantly clear, the Great Leap Famine was primarily a rural tragedy. The utopian promises described by Richard King (Chapter 2) and Kimberley Ens Manning (Chapter 3) were mainly directed towards the countryside; the bureaucratic failings exposed by Wang Yanni (Chapter 6) and Xin Yi (Chapter 5) occurred in rural communes; and, as Gao Wangling (Chapter 11) and Ralph Thaxton (Chapter 10) show, peasant resistance played an important role in finally ending the disaster. Yet the Tianjin-bound caravan of desperately hungry peasants from Wuqing – most of whom suspected that cities were better off than villages during the famine – reminds us that cities must be brought back into the picture if we are to fully comprehend the Great Leap.

Focusing on the city does not mean discounting the rural nature of the famine. But in order to understand how the famine struck China so unevenly, we cannot ignore cities. In this chapter, I draw on newly accessible archival materials to describe how the northern port city of Tianjin weathered the famine. The Great Leap's call for rapid urban industrialization drew many peasants away from communes and into Tianjin factory jobs. This rural-to-urban population transfer contributed to an imbalance in the supply system that exacerbated food shortages because there were fewer agricultural workers in the countryside and more people eating state grain in cities.

We now know without a doubt that, as early as 1958, Mao Zedong and other top leaders in Beijing were aware of famine conditions caused by Great Leap policies.[2] The view from Tianjin's offices and neighbourhoods confirms that it is not plausible to claim that urban officials were unaware of famine in the countryside. Average Tianjin residents knew about rural starvation because they saw beggars on the streets or hosted hungry relatives in their homes. City leaders, including top Party secretary Wan Xiaotang, had an even clearer picture of the problem. They received daily reports on deaths and illnesses caused by the famine, and they travelled to villages to assess the situation first-hand. They knew how bad it was but were more vigorous in fighting for food for urban residents than in addressing the rural famine.

Urban residents did feel the pinch. Food rations were cut, and hundreds of thousands of Tianjin people were malnourished. Tensions ran high as urbanites fought over food at grain shops, and urban crime – from illicit market activity to petty theft to brazen armed robbery – escalated as people struggled to stay afloat. Overall, a perspective that takes urban-rural relations into account allows for a fuller picture of the famine years. Most important, it helps to explain why people in villages were allowed to starve in massive numbers while city residents tightened their belts but survived.

"We Want Peasants"

By the early twentieth century, Tianjin had become north China's financial and trade centre and was home to eight foreign concessions. But after the founding of the People's Republic of China in 1949, the city faced uncertainty and found its role diminished.[3] The First Five-Year Plan funnelled resources to interior cities, while coastal Tianjin's existing industrial infrastructure was to be "fully exploited but not further developed."[4] Even so, economic recovery following the Chinese Communist Party's takeover made the city a magnet for rural migrants seeking jobs. This was especially true as the Great Leap kicked off in 1958.

One of the ironies of the Great Leap Forward was that a movement aimed at radically increasing rural production ended up draining the countryside of some of its most productive labourers. In addition to rural

Table 9.1

Population moving in and out of Tianjin's urban districts, 1956-63

	Moved in	Moved out	Net change
1956	221,038	161,046	59,992
1957	168,968	83,823	85,145
1958	· 136,937	102,647	34,290
1959	132,070	57,112	74,958
1960	118,186	64,859	53,327
1961	42,476	91,232	-48,759
1962	25,910	107,483	-81,573
1963	28,329	29,349	-1,020

Source: Tianjin shi dang'anguan, ed., *Jindai yilai Tianjin chengshihua jincheng shilu* [Record of the Process of Urbanization in Modern Tianjin] (Tianjin: Tianjin renmin chubanshe, 2005), 715.

communization and miraculous bumper harvests, the Great Leap also called for rapid urban industrialization. Recently promulgated household registration (*hukou*) regulations restricting rural-to-urban migration were ignored as city factories and workshops scrambled to hire workers.[5] According to official counts, Tianjin's population swelled as rural people moved into the city during the Great Leap (see Table 9.1).

The dramatic increase in temporary residents during the leap (not counted in Table 9.1) is even more striking. New industrial contract labourers were often given temporary *hukou* permits. The increase in temporary urban *hukou* holders in 1958 and 1959 was especially significant:

- 1956: 74,000
- 1957: 102,000
- 1958: 232,000
- 1959: 168,000
- 1960: 73,000[6]

Other new arrivals did not have any urban *hukou* at all because city factories were in such a rush to hire peasant labour in 1958. One Tianjin government bulletin criticized factory managers who clamoured, "we want them from villages, we want peasants," and who complained that "city people are useless" when it came to the Great Leap's exhausting construction projects and production blitzes. The bulletin acknowledged that all city enterprises needed more labour because of the "new situation" brought about by the Great Leap, but it ordered officials to limit hires from villages.[7]

The demands of urban production swept aside bureaucratic obstacles to migration and hiring. An internal report notes that 195,000 villagers from the twelve rural counties under Tianjin's jurisdiction in 1958 had received official sanction to transfer to urban jobs – a full 6.6 percent of the total labour power in Tianjin's hinterland. Almost as many people left their villages without permission: 127,506 in 1958, including 13.2 percent of the labour force in Cang xian, a county south of Tianjin. One major problem, the report continues, was that urban factories continued to recruit workers in villages without permission from city labour officials: "The peasants do not move their *hukou* or grain card, they simply leave. The work unit then writes to the commune asking it to cancel the peasant's *hukou*."[8]

What kind of work were these new employees doing? Evidence suggests that new arrivals in Tianjin in 1958 and 1959 did not quickly become regular workers in major urban industries. Rather, many rural migrants to Tianjin during the Great Leap obtained temporary or contract positions in small workshops, generally on the outskirts of the city. They were paid less than their counterparts in larger urban factories.

Of the fifteen factories under the aegis of Tianjin's Hexi District Handicraft Industry Bureau (*shougongyeju*) in 1960, nine were situated within the city, and six were on the outskirts (Hexi, south of the city centre and home to the former German concession, was one of the least densely populated of Tianjin's urban districts). The well-established city enterprises included machine equipment, printing, carpet, metal, and cooking utensil factories, and they employed a total of 1,984 workers. Although the number of workers at the city factories increased significantly after the Great Leap began in 1958, most of the new employees were from within Tianjin, not from outside villages. After 1958, the nine factories within the city limits hired 728 urban residents but only 54 villagers. Coveted urban factory jobs were out of reach for many rural people during the Great Leap.

While Hexi's urban enterprises were already in operation when the Great Leap began, most of the suburban factories were established during the big industrial push of 1958. The six suburban factories included a small brewery, an agricultural machinery plant, and brick and cement factories. Of the 634 workers hired on at the district's six suburban enterprises since 1958, 304 were classified as "agricultural population" and 302 as "idle population" from the suburbs.[9] At the brick factory, almost all of the labourers were from the suburbs, while the cement plant mainly employed people from rural Hebei and Shandong whom police had detained in Tianjin because they were part of the "blindly flowing population." But city industry needed them. Instead of being returned to their villages, Tianjin's Public Security Bureau sent them to make cement in the suburbs in early 1959.[10] One man named Li had been exiled from Tianjin to Xinjiang for the crime of protecting a counter-revolutionary in 1949. In 1958,

Li returned to Tianjin to visit his mother but failed to report back to his labour reform unit. Instead, he worked at odd jobs until police officers arrested him and assigned him to the cement factory.[11]

Cement workers like Li were not granted Tianjin *hukou* or regular positions. Their employment status remained temporary, and, without official residence permits, their presence in the Tianjin area was semi-legal at best. For a time during the Great Leap, increased production trumped the household registration system, and some people moved around in search of the best deal. During the first half of 1960, when cement factory workers' demands for better wages and urban *hukou* were met with silence, 19 of the plant's 171 workers left to pursue better opportunities. Ten workers left to find jobs in the northeast, five got better-paying positions at a nearby chemical plant (1.5 *yuan* a day versus the 1 *yuan* they had been making), and four disappeared without a trace.[12] While rural migrants were excluded from the best city jobs during the Great Leap, those dissatisfied with low pay and instability in marginal enterprises had some room to manoeuvre.

Famine in Tianjin's Hinterland: The View from the City

Wage-paying jobs drew people from villages to Tianjin during the Great Leap. This drain on the agricultural labour force contributed to worsening conditions in the countryside, which, in turn, compelled more peasants to flee villages. The desperate situation in rural Hebei during the winters of 1959 and 1960 pushed many villagers towards the city. Their first priority was to find food. Malnourished beggars on the streets and visiting relatives who stayed for longer than usual were signals to city residents that something was horribly wrong in the countryside.

Hungry members of the Wuqing County opera troupe took advantage of their proximity to the city and had the energy and resources to make it to Tianjin. People who lived farther away had more difficulty in fleeing desperate famine conditions, but they tried anyway. Starving peasants strained China's railway system during the crisis. An internal article sent to top central leaders in June 1960 reported that, during the first quarter of the year, more than 176,000 "blindly flowing peasants" had taken trains without paying for tickets. Most of the fare-jumpers were from Shandong, Hebei, and Henan, and they were heading for the northeast, northwest, or to large cities. Peasants also regularly looted freight trains, according to the report: "They eat anything that seems edible and steal whatever they can, and even wilfully destroy and stomp on goods, urinate and defecate on things, and use high-grade women's socks as toilet paper."[13] Some of the famine victims who managed to board trains ended up in Tianjin.

During the first ten days of January 1961, city authorities at the Tianjin train station detained almost three thousand passengers arriving from the northeast, Shandong, and Henan. Most had edema, a swelling condition caused by malnutrition, and many were so weak that they fainted as they stepped off the trains. Fourteen of those who fainted never woke up.[14]

Tianjin residents who saw sick and dying beggars on the streets or who sheltered hungry rural relatives knew about the massive disaster in the countryside. Claims of ignorance by officials like Sidney Rittenberg, an American member of the CCP who worked at the national Broadcast Administration in Beijing ("Because the worst devastation was in the countryside, far from our view, most of us in the city knew nothing about it"), are unconvincing and certainly did not apply to most people in Tianjin.[15] By mid-1959, Tianjin residents had an idea of the scale and causes of rural problems. An internal report noted that quite a few people in Tianjin were critical of key aspects of the Great Leap Forward, including the commune system and the massive nationwide push to forge steel. These city dwellers "cried out about the peasants' hardship, exaggerating the degree of grain shortage in villages. Some cadres and employees requested decreasing the urban standard of living and increasing peasants' food and oil supplies." This generous proposal was not rewarded but, instead, was written up by informers and reported as a "thought problem."[16] As we shall see, a year later, food supplies dwindled so low that decreased urban grain rations would become a necessity.

In study sessions, residents who had bad official class labels were asked for their opinions about the Great Leap. At one such meeting in December 1959, in Tianjin's Chentangzhuang neighbourhood, a "bad element" named Wang offered his explanation of the Great Leap's failures. "Ever since the People's Communes became totally screwed up," Wang said, "all villagers are unenthusiastic about work, the fields are desolate, and production has been affected. Villagers have no income, all they get is a little bit of grain. Villagers in the suburbs do not work because they think that even if they work a lot they will only get two corn buns."[17] Wang was correct about failed harvests and disillusionment with the unmet promises of the commune system. But he was overly optimistic in assuming that peasants were guaranteed at least two buns a day.

Famine in Tianjin's hinterland was not as bad as it was in Anhui and Henan Provinces, where entire villages were virtually wiped off the map.[18] But for many the difference between Tianjin and its hinterland during the famine was the difference between life and death. City residents also went hungry, fell ill, and suffered the psychological effects of food shortages, but they still received regular – albeit diminished – grain rations. Rural people had no such safety net, and urban leaders considered them more expendable than city dwellers. That top policy makers rushed to save city people while villagers starved was the clearest proof of the socialist command economy's anti-rural bias.

Tianjin's top authorities were not necessarily callous, but they were overwhelmed with problems. Their first priority was protecting vital urban industries and the well-being of city residents, not rural counties that had only recently been dumped into their laps. Over the course of 1958, bureaucratic reshuffling presented a host of new challenges to Tianjin leaders such as first Party secretary Wan Xiaotang. Early in the year, in a political tug-of-war over scarce resources in the socialist command economy, Tianjin lost its status as a special municipality and became part of Hebei Province. Tianjin became the provincial capital, and, rather than answering directly to Party centre as they had before, city leaders now had to deal with another layer of bureaucracy. At the time, Tianjin's industrial output was almost double that of the rest of Hebei Province. Provincial authorities who moved their offices to the new capital in 1958 saw Tianjin as a cow that might nourish the rest of relatively destitute Hebei. Central economic planners in Beijing still allotted more resources to Tianjin than to Hebei, but, because provincial authorities had the final say in how to allocate Tianjin's part of the plan, they appropriated funds and materials for projects elsewhere. Tianjin leaders complained to Premier Zhou Enlai that the slow dismembering of their cow was making it difficult to meet yearly production targets, and, in January 1959, Party centre required Hebei number crunchers to wall off Tianjin's resources from the rest of the province's budget.[19]

Tianjin's headache of being subordinate to Hebei Province was aggravated in late 1958 when the rural areas under the city's control drastically expanded. Cities had been centres of political and economic authority since the founding of the People's Republic. This meant that urban officials were ultimately responsible for setting rural policy. During the Great Leap, village cadres answered to commune officials, who answered to county leaders, who reported to agricultural bureaucrats in prefectural headquarters and provincial capitals.

In 1957, Tianjin leaders were responsible only for suburban villages surrounding the city. In 1958, as part of the Great Leap's "bigger-is-better" principle, Tianjin Prefecture (which had been headquartered in Yangliuqing and was directly subordinate to Hebei, not Tianjin) merged with Cang xian Prefecture and was then completely dissolved and put under the jurisdiction of Tianjin municipality. Tianjin leaders now had to manage twelve rural "super counties" (formed in 1958 by merging thirty counties

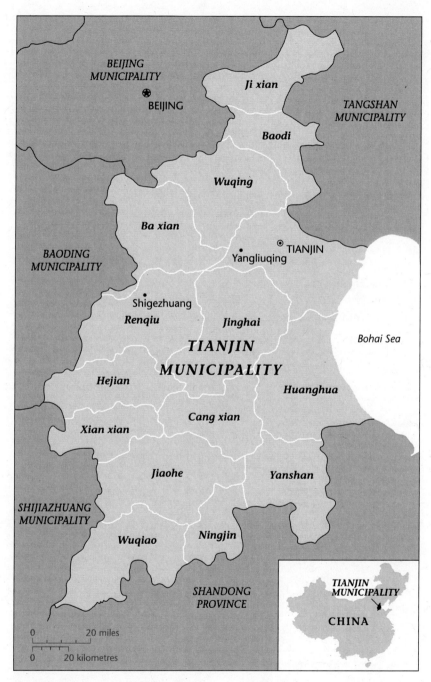

Tianjin Municipality, 1960

into larger entities) with a combined population of 7,832,226. The rural population under Tianjin's control now greatly exceeded the number of people living in the city itself (3,500,690 in 1958).[20] In mid-1960, two more counties were added to Tianjin's portfolio, and land under the city's control spanned the area between the Great Wall at Huangyaguan in the north and the boundary with Shandong Province in the south. By the time vast rural areas were transferred to Tianjin at the end of 1958, Great Leap policies had already pushed them to the brink of disaster. Tianjin's leaders, who had spent the past ten years in the city, were unable to shift course in 1959. They were ill equipped to handle the famine. They knew what was happening but were not sure what to do about it.

As hunger worsened in rural Hebei during 1959 and 1960, Tianjin leaders received regular reports on the extent of the disaster. They also went on inspection tours of villages. Tianjin vice-mayor Niu Yong and municipal Grain Bureau director Liu Pichang travelled to counties in the Cang xian area in mid-1959 and were shocked by what they saw. Commune cafeterias served watery gruel, vegetable stalks, and leaves. Liu turned to Niu Yong and asked, "is this okay?" The vice-mayor shook his head and laughed nervously but said nothing. Later Niu directed Liu to lend wheat bran and dried yams to the afflicted areas, which the grain official did without obtaining permission from the national Grain Bureau or other Tianjin vice-mayors. The Grain Bureau reported this lapse in protocol to Zhou Enlai, who ordered Tianjin and Hebei leaders to stop lending food without prior approval.[21]

In addition to reminiscences by officials like Liu Pichang, archival data and internal documents confirm that municipal and provincial leaders in Tianjin knew full well that peasants were starving. Top officials in Tianjin received detailed reports of rural looting, starvation-related illnesses, and deaths throughout 1959, 1960, and 1961. Nine times over the course of three days in late 1960, farmers looted granaries in Shengfang, directly west of Tianjin.[22] In December 1960, when more than two hundred peasants besieged a rice warehouse in Tianjin's south suburbs, one looter was shot and killed by a militia guard.[23] In other parts of Hebei, including villages in the Tianjin region, commune organizations had completely collapsed, and instances of people abandoning and selling children were "occurring often."[24] In January 1961, Tianjin leaders learned that 217,286 people suffered from edema during the previous year in the fourteen rural counties surrounding the city. More than two thousand had died from the condition, the report noted. Also in 1960, more than 28,000 people had been poisoned because they ate dirt, seeds, or other non-edible items (we do not know how many died, but during two weeks in April, almost nineteen hundred people suffered poisoning in Wuqing County, and twenty-one of them perished).[25]

City leaders dispatched work teams to investigate the perilous situation in villages. In February 1961, the Tianjin Village Livelihood Office (*Nong-cun renmin shenghuo bangongshi*) sent a team to Shigezhuang Commune in Renqiu County. The work team's summary report began: "The main problems are that most cafeterias are doing poorly and the masses' lives are awful. The situation of illnesses and deaths is extremely serious." Villagers were so exhausted that, instead of drawing well water, they drank standing water from fetid pits. "Deaths are increasing by the month," the report continued. In November 1960, 90 commune members died; in December, 190 more perished; and in January 1961, 251 died. Rural cadres hoarded grain and beat or fined villagers who tried to steal it. The work team in Shigezhuang discovered more than seven hundred cases of people being tied up and beaten; ten people had been beaten to death.[26]

Wan Xiaotang, Tianjin's top leader, read such reports and even travelled to villages himself, but he was overwhelmed by the scale of the disaster. The tragedy pained Wan, who had been born and raised in a Shandong village, but even more frustrating was his impotence in the face of calamity. Wan went to Wuqiao County in February 1960, where he saw haggard villagers crying by freshly dug grave mounds. In October, he travelled to Cang xian. There an ill-advised policy to plant paddy rice on dry alkaline soil had doomed the fall harvest. "Do the peasants know how to plant, or do we know how to plant?" Wan asked, referring to officials who made disastrous agricultural decisions during the Great Leap. "We cannot have this type of lunacy ever again," he said. An increasingly fatalistic Wan seemed resigned to the inevitable: people would starve to death in villages. "We cannot just suck crops out of the ground," he said over a meagre meal with Cang xian County leaders: "It looks as if things will only get worse from now on."[27] In speeches to county leaders in November 1960 and April 1961, Wan told cadres that the solution was to explain the situation to the masses and to replace non-existent staples with "food substitutes" (*gua cai dai*).[28] But, as Gao Hua explains in Chapter 7 of this volume, this last-ditch measure came too late for many villagers who were already eating weeds, bark, roots, and dirt.

Tianjin Gets Priority

Wan Xiaotang was defeated by the magnitude of the famine in the countryside. Yet he took drastic measures to help Tianjin when hunger threatened the city. In January 1959, Tianjin leaders realized that food shortages might affect the ability of city residents to enjoy the traditional Chinese

New Year dumpling meal. Wan Xiaotang sent grain director Liu Pichang to Shandong and Anhui to request assistance. Liu remembered, "we knew that these provinces also had difficulties, but if leaders [like us] showed up personally it might help." Shandong officials agreed to provide Tianjin with tons of such dumpling ingredients as wheat, beans, cabbage, onions, and ginger. In the Shandong provincial capital of Jinan, Liu bumped into his counterpart from Beijing, who was also there to procure dumpling supplies. Liu took a stroll through the city's main vegetable market. The only items for sale in the Jinan market were spicy peppers and onions. Liu realized that Shandong was worse off than Tianjin, but he worked to ensure that Tianjin residents would enjoy their holiday dumplings.[29]

Tianjin leaders, all of whom lived and worked in the city themselves, did their utmost to protect urban residents. Central leaders also worked hard to prevent starvation in China's largest cities, even as peasants were dying in the countryside. In the summer of 1960, Liu Pichang attended a meeting convened by central finance minister Li Xiannian about how to guarantee adequate grain rations for China's three largest showcase cities: Beijing, Shanghai, and Tianjin. Liu remembered that, at the time, a remote area in Sichuan Province was the only place in China that had surplus grain that could be transferred to coastal urban centres. Liu travelled to Sichuan as Tianjin's representative and spent a month supervising the grain transfer, which required local women to carry sacks of grain down winding mountain paths.[30] This infusion was not enough to keep urban grain rations at pre-Great Leap levels, however. On 7 September 1960, grain standards for all city residents were slashed nationwide.[31]

Even after this belt-tightening, in late 1960 Tianjin vice-mayor and finance and trade director Song Jingyi informed Wan Xiaotang that the city only had a three-day supply of grain left and that, if the next scheduled food shipment failed to arrive on time, "there would be chaos." Wan sent Song to Beijing to report to central leaders about the imminent threat.[32] It was only at this point, when the food supplies of major cities like Tianjin reached crisis levels in December 1960, that central leaders arranged for foreign grain imports from Australia and Canada.[33] Top leaders in Beijing and Tianjin had been receiving reports about starvation in villages for well over a year and had even personally visited famine-stricken rural areas. Yet they waited until China's largest cities were threatened to take drastic anti-famine measures.

Imports in late 1960 may have saved city residents from starvation, but food was still in short supply. In 1961, Tianjin again clashed with Hebei over scarce resources. On the eve of the central Party work meeting in Lushan in August 1961, Wan Xiaotang called Tianjin's top economic planner Li Zhongyuan, who would be attending as part of the Hebei delegation. Just one month earlier, Tianjin's rural portfolio had been reduced to five nearby counties from the fourteen that had been added in 1958 and 1960. This must have come as a relief to city leaders who had been overwhelmed by rural problems during the Great Leap. In 1961, Wan Xiaotang and Li Zhongyuan continued to prioritize the city.

Wan told Li to make sure central leaders knew that Tianjin's winter grain supply was tenuous. Wan's goal was to secure an increase in the total amount of grain allocated to Tianjin. In Lushan, Li Zhongyuan asked Hebei leaders Liu Zihou and Wu Yuannong to report Tianjin's difficulties to central leaders, but the next day the provincial leaders did not mention Tianjin. When Li asked about this omission, Hebei officials justified their decision, saying that, compared with other areas, Tianjin's situation was not so bad. City leaders had seen with their own eyes that rural Hebei was much worse off than Tianjin. But even though the Hebei officials were correct, Li's job was to lobby on behalf of the city, not the countryside.

Upset, Li Zhongyuan called Wan Xiaotang and asked him to come to Lushan, but Wan demurred because Hebei leaders had left him off the list of meeting participants in the first place and his presence would have violated protocol. Wan told Li that it was up to him to inform central leaders about Tianjin's problems. Li finally got his chance during his previously scheduled address about light industry. Noticing that Zhou Enlai and Li Xiannian were in the room, Li departed from his original talking points. He played up Tianjin's supply shortage and requested more beans. After the meeting, Li learned that his impromptu plea had displeased Hebei officials, but he did not care. "Party centre took measures and helped to solve some of Tianjin's difficulties," Li remembered.[34]

Wan Xiaotang and Li Zhongyuan knew that central leaders were terrified of the prospect of urban starvation. So they made an end run around Hebei provincial leaders and took their request directly to Party centre. The gambit succeeded, and Tianjin was guaranteed enough grain to make it through the winter of 1961.

We have now seen evidence that urban leaders acted helpless when faced with widespread rural starvation but that they moved quickly and decisively when urban food supplies dwindled. Why the difference? Did top city officials view the lives of rural people as somehow less valuable than the lives of urbanites? The different treatment afforded to urban and rural China during the famine can be attributed to a number of factors. Maoist paeans to peasant virtue notwithstanding, the socialist-planned economy consistently prioritized urban heavy industry.[35] Cities held the upper hand in political turf battles. In addition, officials at every point in the chain of command were reluctant to admit and report the mistakes and problems illustrated by Wang Yanni in Chapter 6 of this volume and Xin Yi in Chapter 5 of this volume. Such problems were easier to hide in China's relatively remote countryside.

China's coastal cities were showcases of socialist industry. By comparison, rural areas were invisible to the outside world. With very few exceptions, foreign residents, including journalists, diplomats, teachers, and students, were barred from leaving urban areas. During the Mao era, signs reading "no foreigners allowed beyond this point" were posted on major roads leading out of Chinese cities. If the worst of the famine was confined to the countryside, officials could attempt to perpetuate the lie that there was no mass starvation in China, and they could claim that whatever hunger existed had been caused by natural disaster. Numerous internal reports and first-hand visits by city leaders contradicted this lie. So did the deteriorating situation in cities. Hunger, malnutrition, and anxiety about grain supplies became widespread in Tianjin.

Hunger in Tianjin

> Food became much scarcer in 1959. Rationing began then. There were many discussions about who would get how much. It was decided by how much people ate as a rule. I didn't eat much then, so I had one of the lowest rations. I had about twenty-six catties a month, eight ounces of grain a day (mostly cornmeal). There were not many vegetables. We began pickling parts of the veggies we used to throw away. There [were] only a few ounces of oil a month, maybe two ounces a month. Very little sugar. Coal was also scarce. Once food is scarce, everything is scarce. Each region had its own quota depending upon how much food was available. It was better for us in the big cities than in the countryside.
>
> – Nini Liu, Tianjin Water Works employee[36]

As Nini Liu's remembrance suggests, people in Tianjin knew that they were better off than villagers, but that did not mean that life was easy during the famine years. Many Tianjin residents showed symptoms of edema. Pressing the flesh on co-workers' and neighbours' arms and comparing how long the depression in the skin lasted (a sign of malnutrition) became a common practice in Tianjin offices, alleyways, and schoolyards. Tianjin's leaders received weekly top-secret reports of new edema sufferers in the city. Between 24 and 28 February 1961, 4,871 new cases were reported. This contributed to a total of 673,430 cases since reporting began, meaning that more than one-fifth of Tianjin's urban population was malnourished.[37]

Wan Xiaotang not only read reports about urban hunger, but he also conducted personal spot checks. On the way home from his office one evening in 1960, Wan noticed that the lights were still on at the Public Security Bureau headquarters, where he had served as director during the 1950s. He stopped in and asked the staff why they were still working. He then instructed all the workers to roll up their pant cuffs and to press on their bare legs. No one's skin bounced back: they all had edema. The next day Wan ordered the grain bureau to increase daily rations for public security cadres because they were working late and needed extra meals.[38]

Not everyone in Tianjin was fortunate enough to benefit from Wan Xiaotang's personal intervention. After grain rations were cut in autumn 1960, families struggled to make ends meet. In a survey of 161 households in a central Tianjin neighbourhood conducted by the city's Policy Research Office at the end of 1960, about 60 percent had enough food to get through twenty-seven or twenty-eight days, while 21 percent could make it through to 25 January 1961, but only by watering down their meals. Seven other families were missing a week's worth of grain.[39] Some people quietly suffered, but others made more noise. When the Chentangzhuang neighbourhood in Tianjin's Hexi district cut the rations of its 1,634 residents by a total of 5,500 kilograms, people reacted furiously and fought for more grain, either by protesting or by altering and counterfeiting ration tickets. When residents heard about the reduction, they threatened to stage sit-ins at the neighbourhood police station or told local officials: "You might as well just shoot me in the head."[40]

Tianjin residents smuggled food between city and countryside in order to help both themselves and their rural relatives. At first, in 1958, people sent grain out of Tianjin. On one day in May, city officials set up twenty-six checkpoints on the roads and waterways leading out of the city and discovered 1,800 instances of people carrying grain out of Tianjin, including women strapping grain to their bellies and pretending to be pregnant, and shipments of sealed coffins full of smuggled food.[41] Later, when conditions worsened in the city, urban work units and individuals sought out food in relatively well-off villages. In early 1959, Tianjin factories and elementary schools sent cadres to suburban villages to buy vegetables. The Tianjin city government ordered work units to stop this practice: "Because the cabbage on the market is often delayed and of poor quality, when city residents see cadres carrying vegetables home they all ask about it. This has negative effects."[42] One city dweller who was thirteen years old during the winter of 1960-61 remembered making monthly food supply runs to his uncle's village in Cang xian south of Tianjin. Residents there had created a self-sufficient fortress by resisting state grain requisition and posting armed guards around the fields, a type of defiance similar to what Gao Wangling in Chapter 11 of this volume and Ralph Thaxton in Chapter 10 of this volume describe. The Tianjin teenager's entire family filled up gunnysacks with grain and vegetables to bring back to the city. The boy remembered that the supplement made a big difference. "We were not hungry, and none of us got edema," he said. "We did not eat bark or weeds like other people did."[43]

City people without connections to fortunate villages could rely only on the overstretched urban food supply network. Tensions mounted at neighbourhood grain shops, where harried shop workers squabbled with hungry customers. In June 1962, when one Tianjin woman named Wang purchased dried yam chips (a common substitute food at the time), she forgot to get her ration booklet back from a female clerk named Su. When Wang returned and Su refused to give back the booklet, saying, "I have the authority, and this is the way it is going to be," the two women began to curse and spit at each other. Other people waiting in line took Wang's side and threatened to beat the rude clerk. The grain shop manager had to apologize and hold off the angry crowd until police officers arrived to defuse the situation.[44]

Crime and the Black Market

Police officers had their hands full during the famine years in Tianjin. In addition to disputes caused by frayed nerves at neighbourhood grain shops, urban theft was on the rise. Criminal behaviour ranged from pilfering to armed robbery. In late 1961, nine of the twenty-six employees at a neighbourhood nursery were found to be stealing food that was intended for the children. One woman took food fifty-eight times; she was finally caught when the nursery's chef discovered her stealthily pouring cooking oil into her own container. Another woman stashed twelve pieces of the children's fish in her lunch box. The nursery workers' behaviour was criticized as evidence of "corrosive bourgeois ideology," and they were disciplined by their work unit.[45]

Police did not get involved when nursery workers stole food from children, but they took notice when a thief broke into the home of one of Tianjin's top leaders. In 1960, public security officers informed Tianjin Party secretary Zhang Huaisan that they had caught a burglar stealing flour from his home. They asked Zhang how to handle the matter. The

Party secretary was magnanimous. "People do not have anything to eat," Zhang said. "If this thief has any other illegal behaviour, then deal with him according to the law. But if this grain is the only thing you have on him, then forget it, let him take it."[46] Robbers sometimes got away with much more than a few bags of grain. In March 1962, thieves jumped over the gate of an electrical machinery factory in Tianjin's central Heping district. The intruders killed two employees who were on guard duty, cracked the factory safe, and escaped with ten thousand *yuan* and one thousand ration tickets for food and other goods. They were never caught.[47] Later in the year, a pistol-wielding man wearing a blue coat and a worker's hat walked into a bank on Dali Road in Tianjin's former British concession and demanded cash. When bank employees put up resistance, he killed one and wounded another before fleeing the scene.[48]

Many people engaged in illicit behaviour found small urban inns to be ideal hiding places. In 1961, public security officials inspected residents of more than three hundred inns in Hebei's five largest cities, including Tianjin. Of the 1,200 criminals identified during the investigation, 1,059 were "speculators and profiteers," most of whom had rented long-term rooms at the inns, where they conducted black market trades.[49] During the famine, Tianjin's black markets swelled with goods, including food from rural areas that had weathered the famine without major losses.

Between 1 and 15 January 1961, Tianjin officials counted almost eight thousand cases of black market activity at thirteen different sites within the city. Of the cases, 22 percent involved people selling things they had produced themselves, 27 percent involved people who had transported items between city and countryside, and 33 percent involved speculators reselling goods at a profit.[50] One official investigator counted more than eight hundred people selling goods at one Tianjin market on a single day in January and estimated that two thousand people were milling about, looking at goods, and blocking traffic. "There are no goods that the black market does not have," the report claimed.[51]

Municipal cadres who patrolled the streets fought a losing battle against peddlers, according to Geng Chen, who was director of Tianjin's Finance and Trade Commission during the early 1960s. The crux of the problem was that the city's prohibition on private trade clashed with new central policies, including the Twelve-Article Emergency Directive of November 1960 and the Sixty Articles on Agriculture of March 1961. These measures aimed to ameliorate the rural famine by encouraging family plots and allowing limited markets in villages. Peasants wondered why they could sell their own vegetables at home but were harassed by city officials when they tried to sell cabbage in the city. On several occasions, peddlers punched and drove away Tianjin officials when the latter attempted to stamp out market activity on city streets.[52]

In 1962, Tianjin authorities finally decided to regulate behaviour that they had failed to eradicate. Thirty-seven market sites were legalized in July 1962. By the end of the year, one-quarter of all pork and half of the fruit sold in Tianjin changed hands in peddlers' markets. The Finance and Trade Commission registered more than 7,000 people as peddlers, and, of these, 2,322 were "workers who had been downsized" (*bei jingjian de zhigong*), a full 32.1 percent of the total (most of the rest, 62.2 percent, were unemployed city residents).[53] Top Party theorist Chen Boda came to Tianjin on an inspection visit shortly after the markets were legalized. Chen, who had advocated doing away with money during the Great Leap, toured the sites and was aghast at what looked suspiciously like capitalism. The average peddler earned 125 *yuan* per month, far more than the 50 to 70 *yuan* a state worker would make. Some fishmongers made as much as 700 *yuan*. "Where have you lured the working class off to?" Chen demanded to know.[54] Geng Chen, who accompanied Chen Boda on the tour, might have been fired for telling him the truth: downsizing in the aftermath of the famine had driven workers to the markets. The rustication of workers who had entered the city after 1958 was the final chapter in Tianjin's Great Leap.

Downsizing

In 1961, central policies allowing village markets and family plots began to improve the situation in rural areas. But the basic imbalance between agriculture and industry caused by the Great Leap had yet to be addressed. Wang Man, head of the Hebei Labour Bureau, explained the problem: since 1958, untrammelled urban development had drawn huge numbers of peasants into cities. New city workers depleted grain supplies, so peasants were forced to sell more grain to the state at low prices, exacerbating shortages in the countryside. Too many workers on the job negatively affected productivity in urban factories, which led to declines in state revenues, and the depleted rural labour force was unable to increase agricultural yields.[55]

At a Central Committee work meeting on 31 May 1961, top leaders, including President Liu Shaoqi and economic czar Chen Yun, argued that the only way to address the crisis was to reduce China's "non-agricultural population."[56] This was the official opening of the "downsizing" (*jingjian*) movement, which ordered all urban workers who had come from villages since 1958 to return home, unless they had become "production backbones" or skilled experts.[57] At the meeting, Liu spoke frankly, saying that, in squeezing peasants for grain, the Party was acting even worse than the landlords in the old society. "Currently city people – that means us – are competing with peasants over rice, meat, oil, and eggs to eat," Liu said, "Many things were completely bought up by us, and the peasants are unhappy. If it keeps up like this, a sharp conflict will arise in the worker-peasant alliance." Liu realized that the well-being of city people would continue to be threatened if the Party squeezed peasants too hard.[58] Rural China could not support such a large non-agricultural population, Liu argued. He acknowledged that some workers might resist being cut but held that they would warm to the idea of returning to villages when they heard about official approval of family plots. "When the situation in villages gets better, it will be easy to mobilize workers to return," Liu predicted.

At the same meeting, Chen Yun agreed that family plots were crucial to ensuring that people in both cities and villages had enough to eat. Chen addressed critics of rustication, who said that returned workers would have to eat no matter where they were. He estimated that each returned worker would, on average, need seventy-five fewer kilograms of state grain annually (thanks to harvests from private plots plus savings in grain transport and processing). This meant that a return of 20 million workers would save the state 1.5 million tons of grain, easing supply problems in cities.[59]

Both Chen and Liu stressed that downsizing would be a difficult task and that problems, even protests, were sure to arise. But according to Chen the only other option – increased requisition of villagers' grain – was a non-starter. Villagers had already been pushed past the breaking point. At the 31 May 1961 work meeting, Party leaders proposed a nine-point program specifying how to reduce the urban population.[60] The directive, officially released by Party centre on 16 June, ordered a reduction of more than 20 million urban people over the course of three years: 10 million in 1961, at least 8 million in 1962, and the rest in the first half of 1963.[61] Each province, city, and urban district set numerical targets. On 16 June, the Tianjin Party Committee met and decided to cut the urban population by 300,000 by 1963. A year later, Tianjin's overall target jumped to 400,000.[62]

City authorities now knew how many people to remove, but many confusing logistical questions remained unanswered. Who was supposed to leave the cities? What about their family members? Would people who were downsized receive any compensation? Similarly, villages needed guidance in how to house, feed, and assign farm work to the influx of returned workers. Over the course of 1961 and 1962, a series of official directives addressed these issues. A 28 June 1961 circular tackled the most pressing questions. Workers who had started their jobs after 1958 had to go back, but those who began working before the end of 1957 were to return to villages only if they were genuinely willing to do so. Generally, people who were originally urban residents would not be downsized. Downsized workers would receive severance packages according to the time they had spent on the job and would receive travel and food stipends for their journey home. These funds were to be paid by the workers' original work units.[63]

Workers' responses to the prospect of leaving Tianjin varied greatly. Some welcomed the chance to get sizable severance payments and to reunite with their families. In May 1962, a man named Meng left his job at the Tianjin Glass Meter Factory and returned to his village in the suburbs north of Tianjin. Meng used his severance money to treat local cadres to a banquet and received permission to set up a glass pipe factory in the village. He boasted that he would use his technical skills so that everyone in the village would be able to eat as much corn as they pleased. Over the next two years, Meng earned more than six thousand *yuan* from his enterprise, and people in the village competed to get jobs for their children in the factory. And just because Meng had lost his city job did not mean that he stopped going to Tianjin. He often visited the city, eating at expensive restaurants and spending his profits on consumer goods like watches, bicycles, and radios. If the downsizing policy was a lemon, Meng had squeezed out several gallons of lemonade. Not surprisingly, his ostentatious behaviour got him in trouble later in the 1960s.[64]

In the Hexi District Handicraft Industry Bureau factories, introduced earlier in this chapter, some workers, like Meng, volunteered to return to their villages. At the brick factory, workers complained that their monthly wages were so low that they "could not afford to wear shoes." They requested to be transferred home immediately, before all of the best land for family plots was snatched up. In July 1961, brick factory manager Zheng reported to his superiors that because people wanted to return to their villages, they were no longer working hard. Zheng asked for advice: "Even though we have done lots of [persuasion] work on people who vigorously request to leave and do not work, if the results are minimal, what should we do? These people have a big impact when they say that wages are too low, and some of them stir up trouble." Zheng also wondered how the factory would survive after its second group of return-to-village targets left, and he asked if any new workers might be available for transfer to the brick factory.[65] Table 9.2, adapted from a handwritten document held in the Hexi District Archive, shows that industries like the brick factory, which had opened during the Great Leap and employed recent rural migrants, were decimated by the downsizing order. In order to meet production targets, factory leaders pleaded with their superiors to exempt key workers from downsizing.

Table 9.2

Progress in mobilizing the agricultural population to return to villages, 1961

Factory	Total workers	Return-to-village targets	Skilled workers or production workers who cannot be let go	Number who can return to villages	Already left	Yet to leave
			Workers recruited after 1958			
Hexi brick factory	171	145	21	124	42	82
Jinnan cement plant	158	72	11	61	43	18
Jinnan paper-making factory	120	35	1	34	34	
Hexi pharmaceutical factory	157	39	6	33	33	
Hexi electric machine factory	455	4		4	2	2
Hexi deaf/mute metals factory	232	6		6	4	2
Hexi electroplate factory	118	1		1		1
Hexi cooking utensil factory	232	4		4		4
Hexi printing plant	203	3		3		3
Total	2,196	309	39	270	158	112

Source: Hexi District Archive, 17-1-15C, 108.

Even city factories that were barely affected by downsizing did not want to lose any workers. For example, only four workers at the Hexi Cooking Utensil Factory fell into the category of "return-to-village targets" who had entered the city after the Great Leap began. Even so, factory leaders claimed that none of the four targets, all women in their twenties and thirties, could leave. One woman from Hebei's Fucheng County had just given birth, and one from the Hengshui area had three young children to care for. These family obligations made it impossible for the women to return to villages, factory cadres argued. Another worker, also from Hengshui, needed to stay in Tianjin because her husband was suffering from chronic lung problems and was recuperating at home. The fourth woman was from distant Fujian Province, "not far from the front lines of national defence." Travelling home would take her a month, would cost the factory two hundred *yuan,* and would "also be unsafe." In addition, the woman had three children and was a skilled worker.[66] Factory managers who wanted to maintain production by keeping key employees on the job sometimes won their clashes with district and municipal officials who were under pressure to meet downsizing quotas. Not everyone who was supposed to leave Tianjin for the countryside actually departed.

Although some volunteers left quickly, resistance to downsizing by officials and return-to-village targets meant that the city did not come close to meeting its reduction target of 400,000. As late as May 1962, Tianjin Party secretary Wan Xiaotang was still exhorting city officials to downsize 220,000 employees and shrink the city population by 400,000 in the coming year. But he was frustrated. Wan noted that insufficiently vigilant *hukou* control was allowing almost as many people to enter Tianjin as were leaving it. As we saw in Table 9.1, 222,064 people moved out of Tianjin's urban core between 1961 and 1963, but, because of continued immigration, the net reduction was only 131,352.[67]

Conclusion: City, Countryside, and the Great Leap

People experienced the Great Leap and its aftermath in diverse ways. One of the key variables that affected how people in China weathered the disaster was whether they were in a large city like Tianjin or in a rural commune like Shigezhuang in Renqiu County, where a Tianjin-based work team discovered horrifying starvation and violence in 1961. Certainly, the famine affected rural areas unevenly, and not everywhere was as unfortunate as was Shigezhuang. But, generally speaking, city residents had much greater odds of surviving the Great Leap than did rural people. So did the thousands of migrants who entered cities during the industrialization frenzy of 1958 and 1959. People in Tianjin were not immune from hunger during the lean years, but municipal and central leaders – well aware of the horrific scene in the countryside – went to extraordinary lengths to prevent urban starvation, even brushing off comments from Hebei provincial officials that the city was relatively well-off.

As Chen Yixin argues in Chapter 8 of this volume, understanding complex local conditions is more helpful than are other factors, including leaders' political radicalism or public dining hall participation rates, in explaining why some areas got through the famine better than others. Yet we can still identify nationwide patterns that allow for broader conclusions. Rural-urban difference determined who had the best chance of surviving the famine. Throughout China, systemic urban bias in the socialist-planned economy trumped celebratory pro-peasant rhetoric and policy statements that promised to eliminate the gap between city and countryside. It is tragically ironic that a movement that aimed to dramatically improve living conditions in the countryside did more to poison rural-urban relations than any other event in the history of the People's Republic. The uneven toll of the famine laid bare the human cost of a political and economic system that valued cities – and the people fortunate enough to live in them – more than villages.

Acknowledgments

Research for this chapter was assisted by a Fulbright-Hays Doctoral Dissertation Research Award and a Social Science Research Council International Dissertation Field Research Fellowship, with funds provided by the Andrew W. Mellon Foundation.

Notes

1 The story of the opera troupe is from Zhonggong Hebei shengwei, Hebei si qing tongxun bianjibu, ed., *Hebei nongcun jieji douzheng dianxing cailiao* [Representative Materials on Class Struggle in Hebei Villages] (Shijiazhuang, 1966), 1:169-70.
2 Thomas P. Bernstein, "Mao Zedong and the Famine of 1959-1960: A Study in Wilfulness," *China Quarterly* 186 (2006): 421-45.
3 On Tianjin during the late Imperial and Republican periods, see Gail Hershatter, *The Workers of Tianjin, 1900-1949* (Stanford: Stanford University Press, 1986); Ruth Rogaski, *Hygienic Modernity: Meanings of Health and Disease in Treaty-Port China* (Berkeley: University of California Press, 2004); Brett Sheehan, *Trust in Troubled Times: Money, Banks, and State-Society Relations in Republican Tianjin* (Cambridge, MA: Harvard University Press, 2003); and Tenshin chīki shi kenkyū kai, ed., *Tenshin shi: Saisei suru toshi no toporojī* [Tianjin History: Topology of a Reborn City] (Tokyo: Tōhō shoten, 1999). On the first years of the People's Republic in the city, see Kenneth Lieberthal, *Revolution and Tradition in Tientsin, 1949-1952* (Stanford: Stanford University Press, 1980).
4 Dangdai Zhongguo congshu bianjibu, ed., *Dangdai Zhongguo de Tianjin* [Contemporary China's Tianjin] (Beijing: Zhongguo shehui kexue chubanshe, 1999), 1:100-1.
5 For the official line on Tianjin's role during the Great Leap, see, for example, *Renmin ribao* [People's Daily], 19 August 1958, 7.
6 Li Jingneng, ed., *Zhongguo renkou, Tianjin fence* [China's Population, Tianjin Volume] (Beijing: Zhongguo caizheng jingji chubanshe, 1987), 182.

7 *Tianjin shizheng zhoubao* [Tianjin Municipal Government Weekly] 17 (28 April 1958): 11-13.

8 Ibid. 14 (6 April 1959): 9-10.

9 Hexi District Archive (hereafter HDA), 17-1-15C, 1.

10 Ibid., 17-1-18C, 1, 24.

11 Ibid., 17-1-15C, 32.

12 Ibid., 17-1-18C, 36, 45.

13 *Neibu cankao* [Internal Reference] (hereafter *NBCK*) 3077 (20 June 1960): 11-12.

14 Hebei Provincial Archive (hereafter HPA), 855-6-2232Y, 6.

15 Sidney Rittenberg and Amanda Bennett, *The Man Who Stayed Behind* (Durham: Duke University Press, 2001), 248. For more on the famine denials of foreigners living in China during the early 1960s, see Anne-Marie Brady, *Making the Foreign Serve China: Managing Foreigners in the People's Republic* (Lanham, MD: Rowman and Littlefield, 2003), 117-20.

16 *NBCK* 2817 (8 July 1959): 9-10. This type of censure is not surprising in light of Felix Wemheuer's finding that complaints about hunger and rural-urban inequality had become politically unacceptable by the outset of the Great Leap (see Chapter 4 in this volume).

17 HDA, 43-2-23C, 11.

18 Ralph A. Thaxton, *Catastrophe and Contention in Rural China: Mao's Great Leap Forward Famine and the Origins of Righteous Resistance in Da Fo Village* (New York: Cambridge University Press, 2008), 196.

19 Wan Xiaotang jinian wenji bianjizu, ed., *Wan Xiaotang jinian wenji* [Collected Writings Commemorating Wan Xiaotang] (Tianjin: Tianjin renmin chubanshe, 2001), 120.

20 Hebei sheng minzhengting, ed., *Hebei sheng xingzheng quhua biangeng ziliao, 1949-1984* [Changes in the Administrative Divisions of Hebei Province, 1949-1984] (Shijiazhuang, 1985), 80.

21 Liu Pichang, "Chentong de huiyi" [Painful Memories], *Tianjin wenshi ziliao xuanji* [Collected Historical and Cultural Records of Tianjin] 79 (1998): 114.

22 *NBCK* 3155 (28 December 1960): 14-15.

23 Guo Fengqi, ed., *Tianjin tongzhi: Gong'anzhi* [Tianjin Gazetteer: Public Security Gazetteer] (Tianjin: Tianjin renmin chubanshe, 2001), 43.

24 *NBCK* 3052 (8 May 1960): 5-7.

25 HPA, 878-2-45C, 32-33. On Wuqing, see Guo, *Tianjin tongzhi: Gong'anzhi*, 42.

26 HPA, 878-2-45C, 58, 60.

27 Wan Xiaotang jinian wenji bianjizu, *Wan Xiaotang jinian wenji*, 47.

28 Ibid., 274-76, 288-90.

29 Liu, "Chentong de huiyi," 115.

30 Ibid., 115-16. Liu's story seems especially remarkable because Sichuan was in one of China's hardest-hit provinces during the famine, as mentioned by Chen Yixin in Chapter 8 of this volume. Liu's claim of a grain transfer out of Sichuan may be further evidence of the political primacy of coastal cities over inland, mostly rural, areas.

31 Zhonggong zhongyang wenxian yanjiushi, ed., *Jianguo yilai zhongyao wenxian xuanbian* [Selected Important Documents since the Founding of the People's Republic of China] (Beijing: Zhonggong zhongyang wenxian chubanshe, 1996), 13:565-70.

32 Wan Xiaotang jinian wenji bianjizu, *Wan Xiaotang jinian wenji*, 170.

33 Roderick MacFarquhar, *The Origins of the Cultural Revolution*, vol. 3, *The Coming of the Cataclysm, 1961-1966* (New York: Columbia University Press, 1997), 23.

34 Wan Xiaotang jinian wenji bianjizu, *Wan Xiaotang jinian wenji*, 39-40.

35 Robert Ash, "Squeezing the Peasants: Grain Extraction, Food Consumption, and Rural Living Standards in Mao's China," *China Quarterly* 188 (2006): 959-98.

36 Nini Liu was the daughter of F.C. Liu and Grace Divine Liu, a woman from Tennessee who lived in Tianjin for four decades. See Ellie McCallie Cooper and William Liu, *Grace: An American Woman in China, 1934-1974* (New York: Soho Press, 2002), 284.

37 HPA, 878-2-45C, 57. It is unclear when the tally started.

38 Wan Xiaotang jinian wenji bianjizu, *Wan Xiaotang jinian wenji*, 160.

39 *Hebei jianshe* [Building Hebei] 521 (10 January 1961): 28. I am grateful to Michael Schoenhals for sharing this source.

40 HDA, 43-2-23C, 103.

41 *Tianjin shizheng zhoubao* 24 (16 June 1958): 14.

42 Ibid. 7 (16 February 1959): 9.

43 Author interview, Tianjin, July 2005.

44 HDA, 1-6-15C, 27.

45 Ibid., 45.

46 Zhang Huaisan jinian wenji bianjizu, ed., *Zhang Huaisan jinian wenji* [Collected Writings Commemorating Zhang Huaisan] (Tianjin: Tianjin renmin chubanshe, 1999), 296.

47 Guo, *Tianjin tongzhi: Gong'anzhi*, 44.

48 Ibid., 461.

49 Zhongyang gong'an bu, *Gong'an gongzuo jianbao* [Public Security Work Bulletin] 52 (11 December 1961): 4.

50 *NBCK* 3173 (6 February 1961): 5-6.

51 Ibid. 3167 (23 January 1961): 10.

52 Geng Chen, "Liushi niandai chuqi Tianjin shi kaifang tanfan shichang de qianqian houhou" [The Whole Story of Opening Peddlers' Markets in Tianjin in the Early 1960s], *Tianjin wenshi ziliao xuanji*, 79 (October 1998): 119.

53 Most dictionaries define *jingjian* as "cut" or "reduce. I use "downsize" and "downsizing" because the euphemistic flavour of the English term, which began to be used in the 1980s to sugarcoat reports of corporate layoffs, applies quite well to the Chinese usage in the early 1960s.

54 Geng, "Liushi niandai chuqi Tianjin shi kaifang tanfan shichang de qianqian houhou," 123-25.

55 Wang Man, "Liushiliu nian de huigu" [Recollections of Sixty-Six Years], unpublished memoir, 330-31.

56 Central leaders had been pushing to cut the urban population since issuing a directive on 10 August 1960 urging the entire nation to "do agriculture and grain in a big way." See Zhonggong zhongyang wenxian yanjiushi, *Jianguo yilai zhongyao wenxian xuanbian*, 13:516-26.

57 I discuss the downsizing movement in greater detail in Chapter 4 of my dissertation, "Crossing the Rural-Urban Divide in Twentieth-Century China" (PhD diss., University of California, San Diego, 2008).

58 Renmin chubanshe ziliaoshi, ed., *Pipan ziliao: Zhongguo Heluxiaofu Liu Shaoqi fangeming xiuzhengzhuyi yanlun ji, 1958.6-1967.7* [Materials for Criticism: Collection of Counter-Revolutionary Revisionist Utterances by China's Khruschev, June 1958-July 1967] (Beijing: Renmin chubanshe ziliaoshi, 1967), 175-76. The text of Liu's speech in the above source is more credible than the version in Zhonggong zhongyang wenxian yanjiushi, *Jianguo yilai zhongyao wenxian xuanbian*, 14:357.

59 Zhonggong zhongyang wenxian yanjiushi, *Jianguo yilai zhongyao wenxian xuanbian*, 14:374. See also MacFarquhar, *Origins of the Cultural Revolution*, 3:32.

60 Jin Chongji and Chen Qun, eds., *Chen Yun zhuan* [Biography of Chen Yun] (Beijing: Zhongyang wenxian chubanshe, 2005), 2:1242.

61 Zhonggong zhongyang wenxian yanjiushi, *Jianguo yilai zhongyao wenxian xuanbian*, 14:412-13.

62 MacFarquhar, *Origins of the Cultural Revolution*, 3:33. See also Zheng Zhiying, ed., *Tianjin shi 45 nian dashiji* [Forty-Five-Year Chronology of Tianjin] (Tianjin: Tianjin renmin chubanshe, 1995), 202; and Wan Xiaotang jinian wenji bianjizu, *Wan Xiaotang jinian wenji*, 333.

63   Zhonggong zhongyang wenxian yanjiushi, *Jianguo yilai zhongyao wenxian xuanbian*, 14:505-7.

64   *Jinjiao si qing jianbao* [Tianjin Suburbs Four Cleanups Bulletin] 75 (30 April 1966): 2-3.

65   HDA, 17-1-15C, 45.

66   Ibid., 21-23.

67   This net decrease is 30,943 higher than the one used by Li Jingneng, *Zhongguo renkou, Tianjin fence*, 89, cited in MacFarquhar, *Origins of the Cultural Revolution*, 3:34.

10 How the Great Leap Forward Famine Ended in Rural China: "Administrative Intervention" versus Peasant Resistance

Ralph A. Thaxton Jr.

Although there is a corpus of Western social science literature on how famines begin and on famine prevention, the issue of how famines end, and how their endings affect short- and long-term relations between state and society, is still more or less unexplored academic terrain. Perhaps this state of scholarship, in combination with the Chinese Communist Party taboo concerning research on Mao's Great Leap Forward in the Chinese countryside, explains why the process whereby the Great Leap Forward Famine ended in the remote villages of rural China remains vague and elusive.

This chapter begins with an analysis of how Western journalists and scholars have portrayed the end of Mao's Great Leap Famine in rural China. I then ask how Mao's famine actually ended, paying attention to whether the enlightened Liu Shaoqi-led faction of the CCP was able to forge an anti-famine contract in the process of addressing the politics engendering hunger and starvation. In addressing this second issue, I compare the memories of some Great Leap-era survivors with the official CCP representation of central government efforts to alleviate the famine. Finally, I seek to shed light on how the way in which the Great Leap Famine actually ended seems to have affected the ability of high-level CCP rulers to promote an image of benevolent governance.

In addressing these questions, I draw on interviews conducted in several famine-stricken Chinese provinces, on some of the New China News Agency internal reference reports on the Great Leap crisis in 1959 and 1960, and on recent Chinese and Western scholarship on the Great Leap Famine. A commonly held assumption in the scattered literature on famines is that they are often ended by *administrative intervention*. This assumption is shared by most of the top-rank China scholars who have focused on Mao's Great Leap Famine and its conclusion. They by and large assume that the Great Famine of 1958-61 was brought to a conclusion by the administrative intervention of the reform-minded Liu Shaoqi-Deng

Xiaoping-led opponents of Mao's political extremism and that this intervention rapidly ended hunger, starvation, and death in rural China. This interpretation, which has been put forth in varying degrees by Jasper Becker; Dali Yang; and Edward Friedman, Paul G. Pickowicz, and Mark Selden, is logical and not without considerable merit.[1]

In fact, however, we know only a little about how the famine of Mao's Great Leap actually ended in the villages of China. We are greatly indebted to Becker, Yang, Friedman et al., and to other scholars who have advanced some variant of the "administrative intervention" theory. Still, a careful examination of their writings reveals a number of important gaps in knowledge about the primary causal factors that brought the famine to an end – and about whether and when it actually did end. Before providing an alternative historical and analytical framework for grasping how the Great Leap Famine ended, let us look at how those who espouse the administrative intervention theory have portrayed the politics that resolved the great subsistence crisis of Maoist rule.

Some Cracks in the Administrative Intervention Paradigm

To begin with, the notion that China's enlightened Leninist rulers saved rural people from the Great Leap Famine through administrative efforts is predicated on the a priori assumption that the central government reformers actually had a strategy to address the crisis. However, as Becker (much to his credit) reminds us, just what took place in the famine-related policy struggles between mid-1960 and the end of 1961 remains sketchy.[2] The campaign to save lives by saving food, which started after the closing of the public dining halls in mid-1960, was itself as much a product of the crisis as a solution to it. Referring to this campaign, Ding Hongtian, a villager in Jing County, Anhui Province, says, "the campaign to save food was launched right after the public dining halls closed in mid-1960. Actually, at the time the government did not have any strategy to relieve the famine, so it encouraged people to conceive their own ways of finding food and resolving their hunger."[3]

Ding's wisdom is refreshing. The public dining halls were disbanded in mid-1960, mainly because central government leaders realized the state had almost exhausted its own grain supply. From this point on, panic swept the centre, resulting in hasty, stop-gap measures to stem a pandemic. This dire political situation should provide the context of any scholarly analysis of how the Great Leap Famine ended, but the proponents of the administrative intervention thesis have not fully grasped this *political context:* in reality, in most of the 1960-61 period, the central government did not have either the material resources or the human capital to provide any significant famine relief to remote, starvation-plagued villages. There is little evidence that the centre regenerated such administrative capacity in the period between the time when the Liu-Deng famine alleviation policy was articulated and the time when the spiral of the Great Leap's acute hunger actually began its descent in the towns and villages of rural China – late 1961 to early 1962. Put another way, Liu Shaoqi and Deng Xiaoping did not save villagers through direct administrative intervention because, quite simply, they lacked the administrative capacity to do so: they only articulated policies that allowed rural people to attempt to save themselves by forging their own strategies for finding sufficient food for their families. Furthermore, given the debilitating material devastation of farm households, there was no assurance villagers could do this immediately and effectively, let alone count on government relief to achieve this goal.

Second, we do not know if the policy structuring the Liu-Deng group's famine alleviation schemes was articulated in ways that found an audience with the most vulnerable of famine victims – that is, those rural dwellers who were located in the provinces, counties, and villages making up the deep agricultural interior of north, central, western, and southern China. On the one hand, it is important to keep in mind that the Liu-Deng reformers had to compete with Maoist efforts to maintain a hold on the policy articulation machinery of the centre and the provinces. Hence, the struggle between these two high Party-state factions over Great Leap policy did not result in policy directives that automatically informed the rural poor of the intentions of Mao's opponents to alleviate the famine through issuing food security initiatives on their behalf in 1960-61. Ding Xiehua, a native of Huang Tian village in Anhui Province, suffered hunger and edema in the Great Leap, but she never heard anything about the centre's efforts to fight the famine through grain relief or food substitution campaigns.[4] Many other rural people were not informed, or were poorly informed, about the state policies designed to address the rage of famine-induced hunger and illness.

On the other hand, there is reason to suspect that farmers in some of the interior agricultural provinces, which had served as CCP base areas during the pre-1949 Mao-led insurgency, and which, therefore, had very high densities of die-hard Maoist Party leaders in charge of subcounty administration during the Great Leap Forward, suffered the most from overzealous procurement and extraction during the calamity of 1958-61. Whether the Liuist famine relief program was extended quickly and effectively to these agriculturally depressed, geographically remote, and politically hostile pro-Maoist Party dominions remains to be studied. One cannot help but wonder whether these backward rural places (where the economic costs of delivering famine relief food aid were the highest to the Liu-Deng reformers and where the political pay-off was most likely to be complicated, if not usurped, by the pro-Mao leaders who had imposed the famine) actually were given priority by the Liu-Deng leadership. Even if they *were* given priority, how do we know that pro-Maoist forces did not take over the relief program and, in turn, take credit for it themselves, officially professing support for the Liu-Deng work teams but informally, in oral discourse with villagers, recasting the relief as yet another benevolent act of Mao?

Nor do we know much about the actual delivery of famine relief food by the Liu-Deng Party leadership. To presume that such a process worked by a perfect relief scheme is to overlook two important obstacles and to skirt the difficult question of how the Party-reformers coped with, or possibly overcame, each. For one thing, remote villages were often very difficult to reach in the China of the early 1960s.

If the Liu-Deng reformist groups did strive to reach the rural poor in such remote places, how do we know that their food deliveries, which by and large went to the commune, actually arrived in time to save starving villagers? Apparently, as some of the inhabitants of a village in Jiangsu's Gaoshan County recall, the local village-level Party secretaries sometimes did succeed in appealing to the commune for relief grain loans at the height of the Great Leap crisis, but surely there was considerable variability across counties and communes.[5]

And what of the inferior substitute foods that were delivered to rural villages by CCP-regulated government vehicles (trucks and wagons) in late 1960? Surely the local brigade-level Party leaders and their clients – not powerless farmers – received such items first. The former occupied a privileged position in the Party/state-structured food chain, and they frequently benefited the most from these substitute foods – a pattern that was apparent in Liangmen People's Commune, Henan Province, where Da Fo Brigade Party leaders received substitute foods from Yunnan Province at the height of the famine.[6] Moreover, neither the Leninist centre nor its commune-level administrative arm allocated any funds to ensure the integrity of famine relief efforts, so that, locally, favouritism, abuse, and fraud often enveloped this process, which, in some instances, remained in the hands of old guard Maoists.

Finally, there is the question of political danger. By 1960, popular anger with the CCP ran deep in some of the places where the Great Leap had taken its toll, and there were popular attacks on local Party leaders at the height of the famine.[7] As Jurgen Domes has pointed out, in Hunan and parts of south China, angry rural people torched the homes of cadres and rioted against cadre rule.[8] So the question is this: did rural people distinguish Liu-Deng famine relief work team cadres from pro-Mao cadres, or did they see all Party cadres as "black crows" with predatory intentions? If the latter perception was operative, how did the pro-Liu work teams overcome it to secure popular cooperation for famine relief?

There is yet another question that the administrative intervention thesis avoids: To what extent did worries over the political safety of their famine relief assignments temper the determination of the ground-level agents of the Liu-Deng reform policy group to find ways to reach famine-ravaged farm constituencies? In Henan Province, the official central government famine-investigation teams often had to travel under armed guard, and the tensions between neglected and abused famine victims and even the best-intentioned Party officials were so explosive that even the agents of the Liu-Deng leadership group were at serious risk in rural China.

The Way in which the Great Leap Famine Ended and the Presumption of an Anti-Famine Contract between the Party-State and Rural Society

In his path-breaking work, *Famine Crimes: Politics and the Disaster Relief Industry in Africa*, Alex de Waal writes of "the paramount duty of the state" to assist its rural population during a period of famine.[9] Professor de Waal goes on to stress the importance of forging an *anti-famine contract* between state officials committed to realizing famine relief and rural people who speak up for their basic social rights and demand that the legitimacy of the former be related to their willingness and ability to address the political causes of famine.[10] Whereas we know that the Imperial Chinese state had forged anti-famine contracts with local people, and often relegitimated its presence in the process of addressing famine conditions, the question of whether the CCP-led central government actually established a political contract against future radical food scarcity with impoverished villagers while attempting to alleviate the Great Leap Famine remains to be answered.[11] Implicit in the administrative intervention paradigm is the notion that there was such a contract.

But why assume, a priori, that such an anti-famine contract was established between the Party-state and rural people towards the end of the Great Leap disaster? For one thing, the creation of such a contract would have mandated the conceptualization and implementation of a process to determine the political accountability of local CCP leaders who had had control over the acquisition, delivery, and distribution of relief food and funds at the county, commune, and brigade (village) levels during and after the Liu-Deng-sanctioned relief and recovery effort of 1961-62. If top-level CCP leaders had been able to effectively discipline their subnational, subcounty political base, then perhaps this process would not have required institutional openness and popular accountability in order to be successful. By 1960, however, the national CCP Disciplinary Committee was unable to effect such discipline in rural China. In this situation, the process of determining political accountablility would have more or less required institutionalizing openness and transparency. And it would have required placing regulatory power over food in the hands of farmers who had suffered from the Great Leap debacle so that non-partisan civilians would be involved in enforcing the anti-famine contract. As far as I can determine, the Liu-Deng-led centre actually did little to nurture such a process at the subcounty level. The People's Republic of China, after the Great Leap Famine, seems to have remained a place where there was no anti-famine contract involving either of these two features.

When it came to transparency, the lines of accountability for post-Great Leap Famine relief aid were mainly between the CCP-led centre and its local Party operatives, not between the government and the village people. Perhaps this approach had something in common with late-Imperial China's model of an anti-famine compact, which did not necessarily presume a democratic process of political accountability when it came to the implementation of relief; rather, it only presumed a capacity and a will to carry out such relief. I suspect that the extreme dearth engendered by Mao's famine undercut capacity, while the CCP's strong preference for first provisioning the cities and its national army, not to mention Mao's determination to sustain the state's utopian development scheme at any cost to rural dwellers, worked to weaken the will to carry out relief.

In any event, we can begin to grasp this CCP failure to establish an anti-famine contract by asking a simple question: Who held the keys to the local grain storage bins in rural subcounty China in the decade spanning Mao's Great Leap Forward – roughly from 1958 to 1968? We have little information on this question. To be sure, not all brigade-level Party secretaries were pro-Mao. Still, there is reason to believe that, in the villages where the Maoists prevailed, the Party secretaries and their clients retained the keys to bins, even as the Liu Shaoqi-led reformers crafted policies to alleviate the famine. In reality, these village Party secretaries played crucial roles in deciding whether popular impulses to establish political accountability through Liu-sanctioned mobilization constituted loyal or disloyal opposition: and they were still positioned to crush opposition.

Moreover, these Party secretaries and their loyal political networks were often the very same actors whose lies about food production yields, availability, and distribution had fuelled the subsistence crisis of the Great Leap locally. Their political work style was one of habitual dishonesty, deception, and delusion. Reorienting these local political actors, who had seen that practising deceit in the service of extremism paid off in the form of praise from their superiors, was not at all easy to accomplish in either the short or the long hall – and the Liuists were in a hurry. Hence, these actors remained a problem for would-be centrist reformers. In much of the countryside, they still operated by a code of conduct that was totally at odds with Camus' reminder that the only way to defeat a plague (or, in this case, a famine) is by honesty.[12] Yet honesty was the number one casualty of Mao's Great Leap. There is no convincing evidence that Beijing rulers, Liuists or Maoists, ever systematically corrected the deceitful political habits of subnational Party leaders who perpetrated the Great Leap's horrors. So, even as rural people recovered from Mao's famine, they had no one whom they could trust to negotiate a political contract against future famine.[13]

For yet another thing, the Liu-Deng-led effort to rectify the anti-democratic politics engendering the famine, which took the form of the Anti-Five Winds Campaign of 1960-61, proved incomplete and, often, ineffective. The so-called reformers were more interested in regaining political control and re-establishing the priority of "tolerable procurement" rather than in creating democratic mechanisms of political accountability for leaders or political empowerment for non-Party villagers. Thus, the Anti-Five Winds Campaign failed to provide institutionalized reassurances that the Party's local political base could be trusted to move beyond the politics engendering the Great Leap Famine.

When the central government learned about the magnitude of death by starvation in rural Henan Province in 1960, it sent out work teams to put an end to the edema and acute hunger: this was the start of the Anti-Five Winds Campaign. The mission required the work team cadres to discipline and re-educate local Party leaders who had imposed Mao's famine policies. But two problems repeatedly cropped up, and the work teams never resolved either to the satisfaction of angry famine survivors.

The first problem was that work team members could not effectively prevent old guard Maoist Party leaders from threatening the farmers who exposed their wrongdoings via petitions. In Zhangwulou Brigade, Suiping County, Henan, for instance, Yu Yantang, the CCP militia leader, openly declared that all letters of grievance had to be approved by him before being submitted to work team superiors. And even after this militia commando was sent to a political study camp for discipline and training, his father told villagers: "No matter how many opinions you submit to the upper level, my son will still be the militia commander, and when he returns he will exact revenge."[14] Although the work teams sent many of Mao's Great Leap accomplices to special rectification camps, and encouraged the election of poor peasant representatives to replace them, this was *only a temporary arrangement*. When the disciplined Party leaders returned to their villages, they frequently resumed their old brigade-level positions. Hence, they were positioned to settle scores with the farmers who had identified them as agents of the famine. This reversal quelled the hopes of farmers for a democratically enforced contract that placed the food consumption requirement of tillers before the grain demands of the Party's rural cadre base and its city-based constituencies.

The second problem had to do with work team efforts to discipline the agents of the local Party-state. The leaders of these work teams sometimes punished the local Party leaders in ways that resurrected the political savagery of the Great Leap itself. In Suiping's Luozhuang Brigade, for example, the work team leader punished the local Party agents of the Great Leap by beating them, hanging manure cans around their necks, and stuffing their mouths with feces.[15] In situations like this one, where the discipline of the work team broke down, the Liu-Deng reformers undercut their ability to win villagers over to their attempt to re-establish the moral primacy of the socialist state. The issue of why such abuses had been tolerated by the Maoists was lost to a desire for vengeance, and the political scape-goating of "small fry" Party leaders became the order of the day.[16] Unintentionally, perhaps, the work teams taught villagers a lesson: that the state reformers would use violence to re-establish political control over local society and its food resources and that this – not a contract based on popular memories of righteous governance – was the primary goal. No matter what the reformers said, therefore, their undisciplined violence likely informed villagers that this campaign was primarily about state power and only secondarily, if at all, about addressing popular fears of a re-run of the Great Leap past.

Thus, if the Liu-Deng-led famine relief process of 1961-62 emphasized material incentives, including the paring of compulsory grain quotas and the restoration of small household parcels upon which to grow tubers for family consumption, these significant changes were not accomplished by any institutional political innovations designed to enable pro-reform village people to collaborate in forging specific mechanisms, or a comprehensive plan, to prevent a future disaster.[17] The socialist state plan for rural development did not provide a strategy for resolving any future politically induced food crisis, let alone involve ordinary farmers in creating and carrying out such a strategy. No doubt the Liu-Deng leadership made progress in reconstructing the rural economy around material interests and incentives, but the reform-minded leaders did little to reform the political regulations and political habits that stood in the way of involving poor farm people in creating a nationally sanctioned anti-famine pact. In this political context, China's farmers had little reason to trust that the mechanisms of socialist state power would not fail them again, leaving them to find their own way out of yet another famine. Rural people might have accepted, even endorsed, the Liu-Deng reform. But that reform did not provide them with reason to trust Leninist rulers.

Chiqing and the Unofficial History of the Way the Great Leap Forward Famine Actually Ended

If administrative relief from reform-minded Beijing leaders was not the key to how the Great Leap Forward Famine ended, then how did China's rural people pass over the so-called "three bitter years"? Of course, many villagers turned to ageless family-initiated strategies of survival to stave off hunger and starvation, including concealing grain, pilfering crops from collective fields, begging in the towns of the rural interior, and migrating to cities. These strategies for acquiring the small bundles of food that had been lost to aggressive Maoist state appropriation played a significant role in enabling dispossessed villagers to cope with sharp hunger, emaciation, and skeletonization in the first year of the Great Leap Forward. However, in the fall of 1959, as Mao revved up the Anti-Rightist Campaign, brigade-level CCP secretaries and their political clients came under excruciating pressure to halt the pursuit of these strategies of survival.[18] Subsequently, a new wave of Party-state repression rolled over the Chinese countryside, and rural people who attempted to survive by employing the above-mentioned strategies were publicly criticized, ostracized, and punished.[19]

This Mao-directed Party-state crackdown on the independent strategies of survival of the powerless rural poor, which is barely visible in the works of Becker, Yang, and Friedman et al., was carried out with ferocious violence and brutality. Defining the pursuit of the freedom needed to engage in these attempts to secure enough food to survive as "resistance," the Party cadres who enforced the crackdown struck terror into the hearts of half-starved villagers. Frequently, they stepped up grain-seizing invasions of non-compliant households, and, increasingly, they used food as a weapon against troublemakers, withholding the public dining hall food ration of those who refused to further shrink their bodies for Mao's communal state.

If many of these strategies of survival were closed off by Party-state repression, if this closure was a major factor fuelling the Great Leap Famine between late 1959 and late 1960, and if the Liu Shaoqi-led reform and relief effort commenced only *after* most rural people had found a way to cope with this repression, then the critical question is this: How did rural people actually survive the Great Leap Famine?

Of course, many did not – at least 30 to 55 million died in what became, as Dali Yang has aptly observed, the worst famine in modern world history.[20] Nonetheless, millions upon millions of half-starved rural people managed to survive Mao's Great Leap Famine by relying on a low-profile form of everyday resistance. This so-called resistance, which villagers initiated in response to the cutback in the public dining hall food ration and the repressive crackdown on unauthorized family-based efforts to secure food, was known in local parlance as *chiqing*, or, translated literally, "eating the green crops." In essence, *chiqing* involved going to the collective fields and eating the unripened standing crops before they were harvested and carried to the threshing grounds and then seized for delivery to the commune. In scores of rural places, this was the most effective of all of the hidden forms of popular resistance to the run-away state procurement that had powered the Great Leap Forward Famine. Farmers relied on it to avoid giving up all of their harvest to Maoist procurement agents when the famine intensified between late 1959 and late 1960. This elementary form of popular resistance implicitly challenged the Maoist ideological transcript of the Great Leap, which held that development was dependent on putting production for the big state collective before the basic food security of smaller units of kin and village.[21] To be sure, *chiqing* was not a new strategy of survival. Long before the Mao-led Leninist state invaded the food security of farm households, villagers were accustomed to nibbling a few green wheat spears or a few ears of unripened maize in the periods before they harvested the mature crop. Common in the pre-Mao Republican era, this practice lingered on in the post-1949 period. Villagers augmented it in order to cope with the loss of food entitlement during the Great Leap Forward. Apparently, *chiqing* became more pronounced in 1959 and 1960, the worst years of the famine.[22] Initiated by individuals and families, this practice often had the tacit approval, and even support, of some of the local brigade leaders in villages far removed from the eyes and ears of the CCP-appointed officials in charge of the People's Communes. Reflecting on the activation of this strategy of food acquisition, many villagers say that, as the Great Leap Famine progressed, they ate the standing crops without concern for ruining the collective harvest.[23]

In short, the unfolding process of *chiqing* became a crucial strategy for relieving the starvation brought about by Mao's famine. This particular innovation, employed by countless rural people, not the administrative intervention of the Liu-backed reformers in the central government, spelled the difference between life and death at the height of the famine. Relief initially grew out of this independent, self-initiated attempt to counter the actions of the agents of the socialist state. We can only fully grasp the famine's climax by grasping this strategy of survival.

Several aspects of *chiqing* are worth noting. First, without *chiqing* millions upon millions of China's rural people would not have made it through the Great Leap Famine. Both oral history testimonies and the printed evidence indicate that rural people depended on *chiqing* for survival in the worst months of the Great Leap calamity. In the throes of the famine, they got 50 to 90 percent of their food supply by going to the fields and eating the collective's unharvested wheat and corn crops. In many places, this practice spread to other crops, including vegetables and tubers.[24] The crucial point is that it was this augmented customary practice – in combination with scavenging sweet potato leaves, tree bark, and wild vegetables and sucking the watered-down porridge of the public dining halls – that relieved hunger and saved villagers from Mao's famine.

Second, this practice was widespread in the Chinese countryside of 1960. There are reports of *chiqing* occurring in the villages of Shandong, Henan, Anhui, Fujian, Guizhou, and Gansu, so this local survival practice was nationwide. Subnationally, we might expect that this particular famine-relief practice would be less prevalent in rural settlements that overlapped with the headquarters of the People's Communes as they often received more from the CCP-controlled state, had first dibs on official relief food sent to the countryside, and housed the cadres charged with cracking down on efforts of villagers to keep grain from the state. By and large, *chiqing* escalated in those rural villages that were the most tenuously connected to the space dominated by the Party-state. Thus, it is unlikely that we can fully grasp its dynamic by studying the towns and villages in which the Party-based power networks in charge of the People's Communes were situated: these officially connected and celebrated "model places" most likely were not reduced to the sheer desperation that triggered the wave of *chiqing* activities prevalent in less privileged villages.

Here are a few examples of *chiqing* in widely dispersed rural villages. Fei Xiaoying, of Huangwa Village, Yingshang County, Anhui Province, recalls that,

In the great famine, we strived to find food by any methods we could think of. The public dining hall ran out of food, and the cadres did not provide us with cooked food. So many persons suffered from edema or died ... Since the cadres did not provide cooked food, we had to eat the raw food crops. When we tended the crops in the fields of the collective, we often rubbed out the crust of the wheat and directly put a handful of the raw wheat grain into our mouths.[25]

According to Fei, few people survived the great famine in Huangwa Village without engaging in *chiqing*. Lin Zhimin, a native of Rancu Village in Xianyou County, Fujian Province, has a similar memory of famine and survival. "During the great famine," Lin tells us, "we secretly ate raw food grain crops standing in the crop fields. We also ate raw sweet potatoes while they were still small and in the fertilization period. We also ate sugar cane in the fields. We secretly cut small pieces to imbibe. If the cadres caught us, they deducted our work pints and imposed a fine upon us. But every person secretly ate the raw crops in the fields, because we all were starving."[26]

Third, in comparison to other strategies of survival, the strategy of eating the green crops in the fields persisted in the face of the Party-state crackdown triggered by Mao's Anti-Rightist Campaign of late 1959. Why? For one thing, the decision to eat the green crops was spontaneous, and so it was seldom announced to anyone beforehand. People just did it when the opportunity presented itself, and they often carried it out by employing quick hit-and-run tactics. This strategy was employed at dusk, midnight, and in the early dawn, and it occurred in many different villages simultaneously. Hence, commune officials were often at a loss when it came to designing ways to systematically deflect this mode of resistance.

For another thing, as the Great Leap Famine intensified, the number of people eating the green crops reached a critical mass, straining the capacity of county and subcounty CCP officials to effectively suppress it. In reality, there were so many half-starved, half-mad rural people snatching the green crops in the fields that there was no way that Party leaders could halt this practice. Logistically, it would have literally exhausted Party leaders to try to keep pace with the anarchic rhythms of *chiqing* and to control the secret spaces in which this practice unfolded from one production team field to the next or from one brigade to the next.

For yet another thing, the practice of *chiqing* was, significantly, a product of the extent of the famine itself and of a power lacuna in Party-state requisitioning below the level of the People's Communes. These two factors combined to assure villagers that *chiqing* was relatively safe, feasible, and efficacious. On the one hand, by the spring hunger of 1960, some of the minor brigade-level Party and militia leaders were themselves facing difficulty. Members of their families often had to rely on *chiqing* for survival, so it made little sense for them to rigidly enforce a crackdown on it.

On the other hand, through news gleaned from public spaces and discourses of public dissent, many villagers learned of the spread of *chiqing* and of the alarm of commune authorities who were unable to curtail it, all of which emboldened them to pursue it with audacity.

Fourth, although the CCP-led state attempted to arrest the development of *chiqing* by extending its general crackdown on strategies of survival to this particular one, this often backfired and effectively increased the struggle to avoid state appropriation. The following excerpt on the spread of *chiqing* in Madian People's Commune, Shandong Province, taken from an internal New China News Agency report, warns of this type of blowback during the Great Leap Famine. The CCP Committee of Madian People's Commune in Jiao County, Shandong Province, immediately implemented strategies to adequately address the problems of eating the green crops (*chiqing*) and stealing the crops (*touqing*) of the collective.

Eating and stealing the crops has been widespread throughout thirty-two production brigades of the commune since late July. Over 2,000 *mu* out of 4,843 corn fields owned by the People's Commune have been consumed; 663 *mu* out of 4,843 sorghum lands; 404 *mu* out of 2,532 millet fields; and 507 out of 8,262 *mu* of spring sweet potatoes have been eaten in the entire commune. In seven production brigades where the phenomena were most severe, 70 percent of the crops have been eaten.

On realizing the phenomenon of eating and stealing the crops, some leaders adopted rough methods, some of which even broke the laws and regulations. Some leaders beat and abused the people eating the crops, and some reduced the food supply ration for those who ate the green crops. However, all of these methods could not effectively prevent the people from eating and stealing the crops. Instead, the phenomenon grew more serious, and the situation became rather tense.[27]

It seems, from the evidence pertaining to Madian People's Commune, that the violence perpetrated by unaccountable cadres was linked to their subsequent inability to contain *chiqing* because, at some point, systematic, iron-fisted methods drove more and more individual villagers to devour the standing crops, turning *chiqing* into a concerted popular endeavour and making it more difficult for subcounty authorities to contain it. How this collective resistance affected state policy, and actually resulted in policy change, remains to be studied for a rural China in the throes of the Great Leap Famine.

Nonetheless, it appears that, from mid-1960 on, reports of *chiqing* were sent up the Party-state hierarchy by commune- and county-level CCP secretaries. Many of these reports voiced Party-state panic over cascading losses of grain and revenue, so that from the standpoint of local Party leaders the "criminals" who were perfecting the arts of *chiqing* were literally eating away the fiscal foundations of state power. If *chiqing* were to run amok, then where would the grain for provisioning the cities, feeding the People's Liberation Army, and exporting grain to the Soviet Union come from? Something had to be done to counter this elusive form of popular "everyday resistance" as it constituted an exemption from the Party-state's scheme of grain appropriation and thus threatened the fiscal basis of the socialist state.

But what?

The mechanism proposed by the reform-minded Liu-Deng CCP leadership was known as *baochandaohu* – a "household responsibility system" wherein farmers again took charge of tilling small family plots but were contractually obligated to give up a portion of the harvest to the state. Most scholarship on this arrangement situates it within the context of the popular struggle to escape starvation and death in the Great Leap and thus has treated it as though it were a product of the Liu-initiated *sanziyibao* ("three freedoms, one contract") policy reform (which allowed villagers to freely cultivate small patches of land, engage in animal husbandry, and trade in local markets). What this line of logic (which has been influenced by official CCP historiography pertaining to the origins of the household responsibility system) misses is that, during the long spree of *chiqing*, which, by late 1960, had become pandemic, local CCP leaders could not carry out, or implement, *sanziyibao* because starving villagers did not believe that more work would bring more gain or that more production would result in more food consumption. Further, they had concluded that, if the corrupt local Party leaders were still eating the lion's share of food (just as they had done before the public dining halls were disbanded), then their only chance of survival was to eat the raw, green crops in the fields. They refused to give up *chiqing* and to re-engage the harvest extraction processes of the Mao-led Party-state without a plan that gave them greater control over the harvest and put food in their stomachs before putting it into the granaries of the communes. Such a plan was the quid pro quo for a popular suspension of *chiqing* practices.

Only when the CCP provincial committees, working with the county-, commune-, and brigade-level Party leaders, addressed the issue of *chiqing* and promised to institute a contractual system to improve incentive and initiative did rural people begin to consider the notion of desisting from eating green crops. This consideration was not effected without commune-level CCP secretaries pleading with desperate villagers to give up this practice. These secretaries often had to enlist production brigade and production team leaders to help them persuade farmers of the "benefit" of doing so. We learn, for example, that in Shandong Province "the Caozhuang production brigade encouraged the people to discuss the contract system and ensured the plan of contracting, and [only] then did the masses unanimously promise that, 'in the future, we will no longer eat the crops. Instead, we will work within the framework of the contracting plan.'"[28]

Supposedly, the phenomenon of eating and stealing green crops tapered off substantially after the Party leaders used the *baochandaohu* (fixing of farm output quotas for each household) system to "strengthen the political ideological education of the masses." Such propaganda exaggerated the ease with which the reformers in Beijing moved wretched and angry rural people into this system. It also overstated the extent to which this system actually drew villagers into a mutually agreeable pact with high-level CCP rulers, alleviated tensions and restored mutual trust between cadres and villagers, supplanted *chiqing* as a means of relieving the famine once and for all, and was actively endorsed by farmers as an alternative to independent household agriculture.

In reality, many Great Leap-era farmers struggled to avoid the CCP version of *baochandaohu*, which ultimately resonated with the Liuist *bao*, or so-called "guarantee," in the *sanziyibao* policy. The political history of Nanbai People's Commune near Zunyi, in Guizhou Province, reflects this struggle. Between May and October 1959, formerly affluent farmers in this commune publicly denounced the Party cadres and cursed Party leaders who had mismanaged agriculture and triggered fears of famine. Embittered over the food crisis engendered by the Great Leap's "achievement" of having poor peasants take over leadership of the commune, the angry farmers were so aggressive that Wang Deming, the key Party official in this commune, publicly invited them to beat him and members of his entourage with sticks. In an effort to convince the farmers to accept *baochandaohu* and to refrain from eating the collective's standing crops, he admitted that placing poor peasant activists in leadership positions had been a mistake. Nonetheless, Party work having to do with the formerly affluent landowning farmers subsequently became more difficult to carry out because the leaders of the sub-brigade production teams dared not assign work to them, and "the production contracting could not go through."[29]

Furthermore, these same formerly well-to-do farmers brazenly presented the CCP leaders of Nanbai People's Commune with four choices: (1) disband the production team and work the land on the basis of one family, one household; (2) freely combine this with mutual aid team members on a voluntary basis; (3) separate themselves from the brigade and divide the small teams into smaller groups; or (4) contract with the household, in which case the household would assume responsibility for all profits and losses.[30]

It is clear that the farmers strongly preferred the first choice: they felt the restoration of private family-based farm ownership and land-use rights gave them the best chance to free themselves from hunger. The second and third choices were also acceptable, though the level of freedom was less than in the first choice. The fourth choice, which they equated with the least amount of freedom, was acceptable only if they, not the Party-state, took over responsibility for assessing and dealing with harvest gains and losses. What is important about this fourth choice is that farmers were giving *baochandaohu* a different interpretation than did the Liu-Deng reformist faction, which took the *bao*, or so-called guarantee, to mean that farmers would give up a fixed percentage of the harvest to the government in return for the right to keep the rest for their own use and/or sale in the market. Essentially, the farmers wanted *baochandaohu* to work primarily for them and only secondarily for the state. In other words, they wanted to calculate the harvest, stake their moral claim to it, and *then* decide how much they could give to the government. In this way, they could first stabilize their income and *then* support the state's claim to the harvest.

In short, villagers were looking to renegotiate the state appropriation that had endangered survival during the Great Leap Forward. The communal tip of the Maoist state had taken its gains from, and shifted its losses to, farm people; now, as a precondition for letting go of *chiqing*, the battered survivors of the socialist state's 1958-61 win-win appropriation system insisted that *baochandaohu* be formulated to ensure that they would never again be subjected to the unbridled greed that had introduced famine. Put another way, if the Liuists were saying "trust us, this time we will pare our claims and not let you suffer anymore from hunger," the farmers were saying, "you trust us, this time we will pare your claims, and we will make sure your overzealous local cadres will not drive us to desperation." To villagers, connecting with Liu-led Party-state reformers via *baochandaohu* was not appealing as this system had not succeeded in providing a solution to the problem of food insecurity. Further, it was a mechanism of state domination, designed to again tether them to the administrative pathology of Leninist state power.

In the crisis moments of the Great Leap Forward Famine, China's half-starved farmers equated socialism with CCP-guided deprivation, and they equated the socialist state with death. What, then, was so beneficial about a household contracting system that reintegrated them into the state power system? The household responsibility system required that tillers meet the quota set by the Party-state *before* they deployed whatever was left for their own needs. But what if the harvest was poor and the quota requirement cut into the amount of the harvest needed for family consumption? What if entrenched local Party leaders continued to lie about the precise quota and again took more than the state quota without the knowledge of official superiors? Again, farmers sought to escape the Great Leap Famine via a system of household-based agriculture that freed them from the terrible memory of centre-driven quotas, which, in reality, was a far cry from the household contracting system of which Leninist reformers had conceived.

Whereas official CCP sources suggest that, with the implementation of *sanziyibao* and *baochandaohu,* the phenomenon of *chiqing* stopped and the household responsibility system became the means for ending the Great Leap Famine and, hence, for successfully addressing the issue of food in-security, the fact is that, in some villages in rural China's hinterland, people continued to rely on eating green crops to relieve their hunger well into the fall harvest period of 1962. To be sure, they also relied on sweet po-tatoes grown on small family parcels, on gleaning, and on small gains derived from market exchange, but there is little evidence that, in the last year and a half of the famine, these strategies of food acquisition, which were sanctioned by the Liu-Deng *sanziyibao* reform, actually surpassed in importance the food acquired from *chiqing.* What they did was supplement *chiqing;* it was only in the years to follow that they gradually supplanted its central role in survival.

While data on the phenomena for this period are woefully inadequate, this particular form of resistance to Mao's killer famine became an embed-ded form of inflicting Party-state attempts to appropriate grain production and control producers from above well into the post-Great Leap period. It was principally *chiqing,* not *baochandaohu,* that villagers relied on to compel People's Commune leaders to bring their claims on staple crops in line with what James C. Scott calls the "subsistence first principle" of peasant economy.[31] Some villagers say that *chiqing* also offered an import-ant lesson to local Party leaders, reminding them that they had to take less when the harvest was poor no matter what the central government's procurement policy might be.[32] Not only did rural people resist state claims as they made inch-by-inch progress in the struggle to effectively revive the household strategies of survival lost to state savagery during the Great Leap Famine, but they actually held this "weapon of the weak" in reserve long after the famine ended, just in case the conditions under which the Maoists initially failed them reappeared.[33] Thus, we should not be surprised to learn that a struggle over the renewed upsurge of *chiqing* between hun-gry villagers and some local Party activists erupted during the Cultural

Revolution, partly in response to the attempt of radical pro-Mao militants to recolonize the countryside, which involved returning small household parcels to the collective, compelling farmers to plant mainly grain crops for which there were state-mandated quotas, and curtailing petty trade.[34]

To sum up, the assertion that administrative intervention brought the Great Leap Famine in rural China to an end is an error of attribution anchored in a set of assumptions about the policy intent, the political resources, and the policy implementation process of socialist rulers in a distant, badly split, urban-based system of Leninist state power. No doubt the way in which the Liu-Deng opponents of Mao changed state policy was important. But this policy variable was only one factor in relieving the Great Leap Famine in village China. It was a necessary but not a sufficient condition for ending starvation, especially in rural places where reformist Leninist rulers lacked the protein-rich cereals to quickly and effectively meet the enormous needs of ruined villagers, faced intransigent and wily pro-Mao Party secretaries, and were not fully trusted by farmers who understood the Leninist state as a form of predatory colonization. As this chapter begins to demonstrate, the rural poor, facing hunger, edema, and death, were politically astute: they appreciated Liu and Deng, and they knew Mao had placed them in an unprecedented social predicament, but they also knew that both Liu and Deng were implicated in the Great Leap and its carnage.

The error of the administrative intervention paradigm is also the product of not listening carefully to the rural people who were most directly affected by Mao's toxic system of vigilante socialism. The voices of those who suffered the most from the savagery of Mao's Great Leap Famine cannot be found in the cities, towns, or model villages of Mao-era China because, in these places, where Leninist rulers mitigated and muted the impact of the Great Leap Famine, the memory of the popular struggle both to survive – and to escape – the famine is comparatively dim, fragmented, and sometimes misleading. The life-and-death struggle of which I am speaking unfolded in deep China, in countless villages about which we still have only minimal knowledge. The rural people who waged this struggle played a critical role in relieving their own hunger and, ultimately, in *enabling themselves* to escape the death grip of Mao's great famine, which, prior to 1961, was a high-intensity killer – the equivalent, so to speak, of a level-five hurricane. Thanks in part to Liu Shaoqi and Deng Xiaoping, this level-five famine was significantly downgraded to a level-one famine between 1961 and 1963; however, after 1964 it began another upward turn that locked fearful tillers into deep poverty – a poverty they survived, and began to alleviate in little ways, through informal acts of resistance that were sanctioned neither by Mao nor by his high-level inner-Party opponents.

To be sure, rural people blamed Mao for the famine, but they also blamed the CCP, and they understood that Liu Shaoqi was a key national Party leader: and this understanding made it difficult for Liu to escape blame and for the Liuists to use their *baochandaohu* policy to renew the mystique of benevolent CCP governance. Of course, it is not easy to establish this point empirically, but surely not all of the Great Leap Famine survivors were in the thrall of Becker's interpretation of Liuist reform policy, which equates reform with the restoration of benevolent rule. Listen to Ding Huilin, a rural Anhui villager, on this issue: "Of course Liu Shaoqi did a great thing to distribute lands to the household. But he too was to blame for causing the famine. If we had owned the land privately in the Great Leap Forward, we would not have starved because owning the land means owning the crops, and owning crops means owning food."[35]

Perhaps, therefore, the argument for a Manichean struggle between the Liu-Deng group and Mao is somewhat overstated. Certainly, both Liu Shaoqi and Deng Xiaoping were supporters of the Great Leap, and so it is difficult to ascertain whether and at what point in the unfolding of the Great Leap and its catastrophic failure the Liu-Deng group wanted to alter course and break with Mao. Moreover, the Liu-Deng group had its hands full when it came to reorienting local Party leaders who had pushed the Great Leap to abandon the extremism that had resulted in so much suffering. All of this would explain, in part, why some of the same farmers who praised Liu Shaoqi for doing a great thing by reinstating small private strips of land and restoring incentives to produce were less charitable when it came to placing blame for the Great Leap's outcome. Apparently, they knew that both Liu Shaoqi and Deng Xiaoping were implicated in the disaster of socialist rule. Hence, they recognized that the Liu-Deng reform was first and foremost about saving the CCP, and they saw that the underlying needs of the socialist state still came first.

In short, China's rural people understood that even good communists had failed them and that, in the end, their resistance, which took the form of *chiqing* and threatened the fiscal basis of a socialist state whose major source of primitive capital was a dictatorial form of procurement, had forced the wisest of Leninist-cum-Stalinist rulers to relent and to scurry to find a way to regain credibility and to reconstruct legitimacy in a world in which trust in the Party-controlled state had been shattered. The mandate to govern had been lost, the mystique of benevolent governance had been destroyed, and the local knowledge that the Liu-Deng reformers were only modifying, rather than overthrowing, state tyranny made for an uneasy, deeply suspicious union between rural people and enlightened rulers at the centre.

Notes

1 Jasper Becker, *Hungry Ghosts: Mao's Secret Famine* (London: John Murray, 1996); Dali Yang, *Calamity and Reform: State, Rural Society, and Institutional Change since the Great Leap Famine* (Stanford: Stanford University Press, 1996); Edward Friedman, Paul Pickowicz, and Mark Selden, *Chinese Village, Socialist State* (New Haven, CT: Yale University Press, 1991); Edward Friedman, Paul Pickowicz, and Mark Selden, *Revolution, Resistance, and Reform* (New Haven, CT: Yale University Press, 2005).

2 Becker, *Hungry Ghosts*, 235.

3 Ding Hongtian, Anhui interview no. 1.

4 Ding Xiehua, Anhui interview no. 2.

5 Kimberley Manning, personal correspondence, critique of 23 October 2007; and Kimberley Ens Manning, "Making a Great Leap Forward? The Politics of Women's Liberation in Maoist China," *Gender and History* 18, 3 (2006): 574-93.

6 Ralph A. Thaxton, *Catastrophe and Contention in Rural China: Mao's Great Leap Forward Famine and the Origins of Righteous Resistance in Da Fo Village* (New York: Cambridge University Press, 2008).

7 Li Ruojian, "Dayuejin yu kunnan shiqi de shehui dongdang yu kongzhi" [Social Turbulence and Social Control during the Great Leap Forward and the Period of Difficulty] *Ershiyi shiji* [Twenty-First Century] 4, 62 (2002): http://www.xschina.org/.

8 Jurgen Domes, *Socialism in the Chinese Countryside: Rural Societal Policies in the People's Republic of China* (Montreal: McGill-Queen's University Press, 1980), 38, 69-70.

9 Alex de Waal, *Famine Crimes: Politics and the Disaster Relief Industry in Africa* (Bloomington: Indiana University Press, 1997), 12.

10 Ibid.

11 Pierre-Etienne Will and Bin Wong, *Nourish the People: The State Civilian Granary System in China, 1650-1850* (Ann Arbor: Center for Chinese Studies, University of Michigan, 1991); and R. Bin Wong, *China Transformed: Historical Change and the Limits of the European Experience* (Ithaca, NY: Cornell University Press, 1997).

12 This comparison has been inspired by de Waal's reference to Camus' *The Plague*, in de Waal, *Famine Crimes*, 221.

13 Lu Xiaobo, *Cadres and Corruption: The Organizational Involution of the Chinese Communist Party* (Stanford, CA: Stanford University Press, 2000); and Yan Sun, *Corruption and Market in Contemporary China* (Ithaca, NY: Cornell University Press, 2004).

14 Jia Yanmin, *Dayuejin shiqi xiangcun zhengzhi de dianxing: Henan Chayashan weixing renmin gongshe yanjiu* [A Typical Example of Rural Politics during the Great Leap Forward: A Study of Henan's Chayashan Satellite Commune] (Beijing: Zhishi chanquan chubanshe, 2006), 233.

15 Jia Yanmin, *Dayuejin shiqi xiangcun zhengzhi de dianxing* [Rural Political Models during the Great Leap Forward] (Beijing: Zhishi chanquan chubanshe, 2006), 235-36.

16 See Antjie Krog, *Country of My Skull: Guilt, Sorrow, and the Limits of Forgiveness in the New South Africa* (New York: Random House, 1998), chaps. 1 and 2.

17 As Friedman et al. show was the case for Wugong Village and Raoyang County. The authors of this study found that, even with the state attempting to promote a more comprehensive plan for preventing a slide back towards famine, Wugong farmers had to subsist on "low-quality coarse grains" in 1964, and the state did little to assist poorer outlying villages (which suffered the most from the great famine) to acquire the

agricultural inputs that would boost yields. See Friedman et al., *Revolution, Resistance, and Reform,* 73-74.

18 Thomas B. Bernstein, "Mao Zedong and the Famine of 1959-1960: A Study in Wilfulness," *China Quarterly* 186 (2006): 421-45; and Thaxton, *Catastrophe and Contention.*

19 We still lack a study that compares rural counties and villages where CCP cadres systematically clamped down on independent household strategies of survival with those where they did not. But surely it was better to reside in a village where local Party leaders were not totally beholden to Mao and did not ruthlessly enforce the 1959 crackdown.

20 Compare Yang, *Calamity and Reform in China*; Frederick Teiwes and Warren Sun, *China's Road to Disaster: Mao, Central Politicians, and Provincial Leaders in the Unfolding of the Great Leap Forward, 1955-1959* (London: M.E. Sharpe, 1999); Yu Xiguang, *Dayuejin ku rizi shangshuji* [A Collection of Petitions Made during the Hard Times of the Great Leap Forward] (Hong Kong: Shidai chaoliu chubanshe, 2005), 8; and Li Huaiyin, "The Great Leap Forward and Its Aftermath," unpublished paper, 22.

21 Friedman et al., *Chinese Village, Socialist State*, chaps. 7 and 9.

22 Thaxton, *Catastrophe and Contention,* chap. 6.

23 Ibid., chap. 6.

24 Ibid., 200-7.

25 Fei Xiaoying, Anhui interview no. 3.

26 Lin Zhimin, Fujian interview no. 4.

27 "Shandong Madian gongshe xunsu zhizhi chiqing touqing xianxiang" [The Madian People's Commune in Shandong Province Swift Stoppage of the Phenomena of Eating and Stealing the Green Crops], *Xinhuashe Jinan 20 ri xun* [New China News Agency, Jinan, Day 20 Report], 1960.

28 Ibid.

29 "Yige dangzongzhi shuiji jing xiang fuyu zhongnong 'qingzui'" [A Party Secretary of the Party General Branch Surprisingly Pleads Guilty to Rich Middle-Level Peasants], in *Xinhuashe Guiyang* [New China News Agency, Guiyang], 1959.

30 Ibid.

31 James C. Scott, *The Moral Economy of the Peasant: Rebellion and Subsistence in Southeast Asia* (New Haven, CT: Yale University Press, 1976), 15.

32 Thaxton, *Catastrophe and Contention.*

33 Compare James C. Scott, *Weapons of the Weak: Everyday Forms of Peasant Resistance* (New Haven, CT: Yale University Press, 2005); and Thaxton, *Catastrophe and Contention.*

34 Thaxton, *Catastrophe and Contention.*

35 Ding Huilin, Anhui interview no. 7.

11 A Study of Chinese Peasant "Counter-Action"

Gao Wangling

Translated by Sascha Mundstein and Robert Mackie

Introduction

It has long been assumed that Chinese peasants failed to put up any sort of resistance in the face of collectivization. By way of contrast, scholars have noted that peasant resistance to collectivization in the Soviet Union in the 1930s was so fierce that the Soviet government resorted to massive force to implement it; it brought the country to the brink of civil war and starved millions before managing to subdue the peasants. In China, however, it was as if the country had been hit by a tidal wave that swept the peasants away. Over the course of a quarter century of collectivization, tens of millions of people lost their lives in order to provide the country with large quantities of low-cost grain and some 600 billion *renminbi* in tributes and taxes. Looking back on this period of history, it seems as though Chinese peasants were docile, obedient, resigned to adversity, and well disciplined.

The reality of Chinese peasants under collectivization was, however, quite different, but our knowledge of the role, status, and conduct of the Chinese peasantry (during this period) has been clouded by ambiguity. In this chapter, I argue that peasants were in a constant state of negotiation with the state during the collective era. Indeed, they appropriated collective goods (especially grain) on a regular basis in order to supplement their meagre diet. Although large appropriation efforts were branded as "robbery" by local authorities, the everyday practice of pilfering food was often not characterized as "stealing" either by the peasants or by the local cadres who supervised them; rather, this method of survival was understood as a kind of moral right that could be traced back to before the foundation of the People's Republic of China itself.

For nearly a decade, starting in 1994, I carried out research in villages in Shanxi, Guangdong, Hunan, Yunnan, and Anhui Provinces. I interviewed a large number of peasants and cadres as well as students who had been sent to the countryside to perform labour (of whom I was one). In addition to conducting oral histories, I also analyzed local records and a few restricted materials in order to better understand the phenomenon of peasants' falsifying production figures and privately distributing or stealing collective resources. Although this kind of behaviour is by no means a state secret (it has been mentioned, for example, in novels and memoirs), no one to date has used it as a singular focus of research or considered its cumulative magnitude.[1]

For the most part, past research on collectivization and the collective economy has stressed the elite-level policy-making and implementation process. This was reasonable as collectivization was a top-down movement regulated by the leadership: it was never chosen by the people. The upper levels of government, including Mao himself, were the decisive initiating factors. But history is constructed from multiple vantage points. Moreover, with respect to understanding the rural "collective economy," it is essential that scholars begin to incorporate a grassroots perspective.

Therefore, let us begin by focusing on the reaction of the masses and the behaviour of the peasants. If previous research in China has primarily viewed the phenomenon of village collectivization from the perspective of the government, this chapter views it from the perspective of the peasantry. I begin with a discussion of the concept of "counter-action," which, I argue, peasants exhibited in the face of government-instituted systems. Later I focus on two manifestations of counter-action: (1) "concealed production and private distribution" and (2) outright "theft." I conclude with a call for additional research on peasant behaviour during the collective era.

An Analysis of Counter-Action

In the face of a government-planned system, what kinds of corresponding counter-active or secretive behaviours were adopted by the Chinese peasantry? In general, they can be described as suppressing and limiting production, adopting negative work attitudes, taking products home, expanding private plots, theft, private production and distribution, and so on. I refer to these behaviours as "counter-action" (*fanxingwei*).[2]

I first came up with the concept of counter-action during a study group meeting in 1992. At the time, I thought counter-action was an academic proper noun (in the sociological sense). What I did not realize was that I had actually constructed this concept myself. Its original meaning carries notions of oppositional or antagonistic behaviour: one cannot understand something as constructed from only a single aspect. For example, the positive does not exist without the negative; for there to be "Yin" there must be "Yang"; and when there is an action there has to be a reaction.[3]

Counter-action thus carries a sense of opposition to a system of rules imposed by the government. This opposition is not necessarily rebellious or violent. Relatively speaking, I would rather say it is a kind of "soft" behaviour (one could also call it "passive"). Thus, it can be considered an unassuming behaviour that forms part of daily life, so subtle that it is dif-ficult to detect. At the same time, it carries a strong sense of deceit.

While counter-action may be related to similar behaviours around the world, I would argue that it entails a high degree of particularity and, in fact, possesses a number of unique characteristics. First, it is a form of resistance. For example, when the upper levels of government assigned production plans, large teams and production teams adopted measures such as "suppressing" and "limiting" production (*yachan, xianchan*) or they "resisted" planned organization (e.g., counter-action resulted in the inability of cotton production to develop properly for many years), as though saying, "whatever it is you need, we will not produce it." Some of the resistance, on the other hand, was much more blatant: for example, when peasants "engaged in grand capitalism," or "took command of the economy," and "grabbed the so-called capitalistic tail". This form of resistance was not necessarily rigid, but it often involved lying or cheating or, at the very least, fabricating excuses.

Second, counter-action is a kind of evasive behaviour. For example, regarding collective labour in the agricultural communes, peasants often "loafed on the job" or snuck out (a partially legal, partially illegal measure) and employed all kinds of evasive methods, including "fleeing from so-called famine areas" in order to avoid collective labour.

Third, counter-action can also be understood as a kind of adaptive behaviour. For example, when it came to land usage, peasants kept private plots and their own "ration-grain" fields or even fixed their own farm quotas on a household basis – a series of rural policies that were reactions to their official counterparts. Indeed, the peasantry often took advantage of the situation in order to achieve its own purpose.

Finally, it was also a sort of corrosive behaviour. For example, with respect to the gains made through collective labour, peasants often privately and illegally distributed that which they produced, or they stole or "borrowed" grain and so on. Quietly, they kept some of what they produced for themselves.

Counter-Action and Collectivization

Before discussing resistance further, I would like to consider the activism and independence peasants exhibited in the face of various unfavourable situations. When the state aggressively initiated the collectivization movement, much of the peasantry believed in the advantages of mutual help and cooperation and so followed the call of the Chinese Communist Party. These peasants consisted mostly of a generation of ambitious young activists who grew up after the land reforms. Under the leadership of the CCP, they formed new militant groups (like the Poor Peasant Society), which were mainly small collectives that went into production with the later village communes. They were different from administrative organizations but still enjoyed special privileges. Some members of these small collectives later went on to become village cadres.

At the same time, it cannot be denied there were also some peasants who joined the collectives in order to avoid government grain quotas (as a collective member, one was well looked after, while labouring outside the collective was much more burdensome). Before the "collectivization storm" of 1955, these "volunteer" collective members made up 14 percent of the total rural population.

Facing the high tide of agricultural collectivization in 1955, peasants felt the "trend of the times": it was impossible not to participate. Large numbers of peasants were swept up by the state, and, within a few months, the number who had joined collectives reached 60 percent of the rural population (by the end of 1955, these collectives were mostly elementary agricultural cooperatives).[4] The remaining 40 percent of the rural population were swept up in the later wave of "advanced" collectivization. Having lost everything they had gained during the land reform movement as well as their original means of production (unlike what one sees in the policy known as "dividends to the shareholders," which is found in lower-stage agricultural producer cooperatives, advanced cooperatives owned the land), they considered themselves "farm hands" who had "joined society" just so they could receive a salary from the government.[5]

By this time, the principles of "free will" and "mutual benefit" that the government had once stressed were, in fact, no longer spoken of. But, as a result of undergoing long periods of Party propaganda regarding "mutual help" and "cooperation," peasants were still under the impression that the new collective organizations were self-determining "collective economies." Consequently, the first round of concealing production and private distribution began nationwide in 1956. From then on, peasants did not dare speak publicly about production needs or actual production. Each person had "individual" rights, but she or he insisted that these were, in fact, "collective" and considered them one of her or his weapons.

Naturally, rushed collectivization led to a reaction. By 1956-57, peasants in some regions had stirred up movements to leave the communes. They used phrases such as "joining a commune is voluntary, so there must be freedom to leave," which evinced convictions that had not been voiced previously. But "leaving the commune" was not an option, and the peasants had no choice but to remain in them. Thus, in 1956, began the practice of contracting output quotas to each farm household.[5]

My research demonstrates that, in the face of an imposed collective economic system, peasants engaged in the following coping behaviours: withdrawing (i.e., leaving the commune, especially in 1956-57), establishing fixed quotas (i.e., contracting output quotas to each farm household [mainly after 1956]), and implementing the so-called "two-sided policy" (after 1962). When peasants realized that withdrawal was not an option, they developed new ideas within the commune. After the Great Leap Forward, the government decided to implement the "three-level ownership" policy, which essentially returned the rural economic system to the times of the agricultural collectives. It was, however, forbidden either to leave the communes or to contract quotas on a household basis. This is what Mao Zedong called the "bottom line," something the peasants had no choice but to accept.

But peasant "acceptance" was not unconditional, and, indeed, peasants eventually adopted a two-sided policy – that is, while they had to adapt to and maintain the collective, they intentionally did not overproduce for it. The two-sided policy reflects the general strategy of the peasants – a strategy that may be referred to as "idling" or "foot dragging." More specifically, it involved suppressing production, loafing on the job, and expanding private plots and other autonomous (or individually managed) lands. On the other hand, peasants also employed a number of means through which to "make good" or "hold together" their own lives (first and foremost by sustaining their existence). These included concealing production and private distribution, theft, "borrowing grain," and so on, and they were already being practised during the early stages of collectivization. Some of these strategies can, in fact, be considered traditional peasant behaviour (e.g., engaging in industry and trade), while only a few seem to be new inventions (e.g., borrowing grain). By this time, however, all such strategies had become normal peasant behaviour and the very core of "resistance." This is particular to peasant behaviour during this period. In the past, such behaviours were considered "negative phenomena" and were harshly criticized by the officials of the CCP. In my opinion, however, these behaviours were, in fact, the peasantry's positive contribution to history, and their significance should not be underestimated. Among such behaviours, "suppressing production" and "limiting production" were the main features of what I earlier refer to as "idling," the importance of which cannot be overstated.

"Suppressing production," as the term suggests, means suppressing the amount one produces. Even today, almost everyone can admit to having loafed on the job. To some, the act of suppressing or limiting production is not seen as being related to loafing; however, the two are actually interconnected. From a certain perspective, they are two sides of the same coin: is the result of loafing on the job not a reduction in (hence a suppression of) production? Although many people have engaged in loafing, they have not looked at it in this way. From another angle, if loafing on the job expresses the peasantry's basic attitude towards the collective economy, then suppressed production reveals the fundamental nature of the collective economic system.

I am concerned that the term "suppressing production" may generate misunderstanding. Commune members worked extremely hard in an effort to increase production. How, therefore, could they have suppressed it? Herein lies the problem. Was it that the collectives could not increase production? Or was it that the peasants did not want to do so? During the course of my research, I realized that, during the collective economic period, it was not that peasants were unable to thresh more grain, it was that they were unwilling to do so. This statement may be said to reveal a truth, and it deserves further research.

The practices of "concealing production and private distribution" and "theft" were also highly influential. They were widely executed via a number of various strategies and remained well hidden. They could not be guarded against, controlled, or truly forbidden. In the words of one rural cadre, "those products were made by us, and they were there with us. If [anyone wanted them] they had to go through our hands first."[7] The practice of "borrowing grain" was even more secretive and technical. Borrowing without returning meant recording grain in the accounting books without actually returning it (or returning it as money instead of as grain). In fact, this can also be considered concealing production or as a form of private distribution. Was there any reason not to let the peasants borrow grain? Their lives were very difficult, and they were often on the verge of starvation. How could this practice be forbidden?

Peasants also "worked outside of the commune." "Working" (i.e., engaging in activities outside of agriculture) or "doing business" consisted mainly of selling small commodities. This was traditional Chinese peasant behaviour. But communes confined peasants to the countryside, allowing them only to engage in agriculture and nothing else. Therefore, whether in poor or developed regions, some peasants attempted to break through these restrictions. Naturally, this had a huge impact on the system.

Last but not least, although contracting quotas on a household basis was not officially allowed, it never ceased to be practised, and many regions engaged in contracting on the sly. Some similar innovations were also practised, such as borrowing land, expanding private plots, subdividing production teams, contracting team output quotas, contracting seasonal household production quotas for certain crops (or land), establishing "ration-grain" fields, the "nine squares" system, and so on. These were much more secretive and destructive than were the practices discussed earlier. Combined, these practices had a significant impact and set the stage for later rural reforms. Through persistent "bullying,"[8] including staging an uprising,[9] peasants managed to reform the system of contracting quotas on a household basis.

Peasant action had a certain comprehensive, or collective, character. In particular, concealing production and private distribution had to be organized by the production team, and each person was accorded a share. One could say that these practices were relatively fair. Borrowing grain was a similar practice, but it was not sufficiently equitable. Theft was the least fair. Moreover, it was not collective behaviour but, rather, behaviour carried out in accordance with a particular individual's agenda. In some locations, however, team leaders purposely allowed commune members to steal a certain amount.[10] This demonstrates that peasant action still exhibited a certain degree of comprehensiveness, even though, as some people would not engage in theft, it was not entirely fair. Thus, it is clear that peasants were not necessarily in search of equality as much as they were in search of some sort of fairness or moral justice. Furthermore, this sort of behaviour was rational. After all, what they took was never in excess: they took only what they needed. This demonstrates that, compared to the high degree of separation of the previous stage of collectivization, there was now a high degree of mutual understanding between village cadres and peasants. In the face of external forces, peasants became much more unified.

Under these conditions, was it still necessary to maintain a "false" collective economy? Was it necessary for the government to force peasants to conceal, steal, borrow, or expand private plots? This was a choice that, at the time, faced everyone. As a result (and under circumstances corresponding to a change in external conditions), the rural agricultural reforms finally took place, at which point the relationship between the peasants and the government entered a new phase.

Although some "democratic" systems did exist in the countryside during the collective era, such as democratic elections and reports made by the masses, none of these prompted the reforms. Similarly, peasants did not engage in stiff resistance to official regulations or rely on any form of public opposition. On the contrary, it was actually peasant "resistance" – the unassuming daily behaviour of dialogue or negotiation – that was effective. Indeed, I would argue that it was the adoption of certain soft behaviours,[11] which were employed to hollow, or void, the rules, that made the difference. Such behaviours included using subtle methods that were not easy to detect and taking advantage of seldom noticed places (e.g., the low end of marginal production outputs) and the limits of government power (e.g., verification of production quantities was extremely challenging). The result was not only a reduction in the effectiveness of the original system – to the point where several modifications were made – but also the creation of a driving force that led to the transformation of the rural system.

Concealed Production and Private Distribution (*manchan sifen*)

Both concealed production and private distribution existed for some time before the creation of the commune system. According to some reports, they appeared around the time that the mutual aid teams were created and very possibly originated from the concealment of collective production quantities by cadres at the township and village levels. However, reports on concealed production and private distribution during the 1950s were rare. In the summer of 1957, for example, it was reported that, when production teams in Zhejiang made production reports to the state, concealment, corruption, and theft on each level were quite common.[12] Hebei's Qingyuan County reported the concealment and private distribution of 1.36 million *jin* of grain. In one area, it was reported that fourteen self-organized communes concealed 270,000 *jin* of grain. These communes became known as "surplus grain communes."[13] When calculating cooperative production in Zhejiang, 25 percent had to be factored in for corruption and grain theft.[14]

While reports on concealed grain production were quite rare in the newspapers published for the general public during the 1950s, they were quite evident in the more restricted internal periodical, *Neibu cankao*. For example, during the summer and fall harvests of 1956 – the first harvests after total collectivization – a focused report appeared in *Neibu cankao*.

The situation regarding the collective concealment of reported production quantities in Jiangsu was quite serious. In Tai County, 80 percent of the agricultural communes were under-reporting. In certain areas of Xinghua County, it was discovered that 1.17 million *jin* of grain had been under-reported and privately concealed. In other areas, commune members would first thrash the rice before reporting the production volume. In this way, they were able to gain more than 1.8 million *jin* of grain for private use. Other practices included collective secrecy towards the higher levels, keeping double accounts, private distribution without reporting, and so on.[15]

In the agricultural communes of Baoying, Xinghua, and other counties, severe concealment of production quantities and storage of grain for private distribution were very common occurrences. The means by which the communes stole included letting grain fall onto the thrashing ground to be swept up later, employing sporadic accounting omissions, cheating during the weighing process in the warehouse, distributing rice right after threshing, exaggerated rounding off, and so on. In the ten agricultural communes in one township in Jiangdu County, the severity of concealing production and private distribution varied. One commune in Baoxing County privately distributed more than 60,000 *jin* of grain, while one production team concealed more than 30,000.[16]

An inspection at Yancheng discovered that 360 people in ninety-four communes were stealing. In one commune, twelve people, including the commune head, collectively stole 3,285 *jin* of rice, and two teams illegally distributed 30,974 *jin*.[17] In Suzhou Prefecture, there were agricultural communes that collectively engaged in corruption (e.g., when storing vegetable seeds in the granary, every one hundred *jin* they weighed was actually reported as eighty).[18]

In Jiangsu, stress was placed on the necessities of the individual commune. Ignoring their obligation to the state, the peasants sought to "distribute first, distribute much, and distribute well." When production was down due to natural disaster, the divergent interests of the state, the collective, and the individual came into even sharper relief. In certain places, grain quantities were under-reported, and some of the surplus and public grain was distributed.[19] In other places, they stopped production, grain stores were watched by guards, and surplus grain was not sold and public grain not exchanged.[20]

In Zhejiang Province, there were many agricultural communes that collectively concealed production quantities. Some of the tactics employed included using an old scale when harvesting grain and the town's scale when recording it, recording less than was distributed, distributing moist grain and applying false discounts, distributing crops other than rice or wheat, not recording the animal feed, and so on – all methods for concealing the true quantity of production. When grain was distributed, the good-quality grain was assigned to the head of the commune, the medium-grade grain was sold to the state, and the lesser-quality grain was paid as agricultural tax.[21]

In Ningbo Prefecture, many agricultural communes experienced corruption and theft. According to incomplete statistics, during the pre-distribution of early harvest grain in Linhai County, theft occurred in 119 communes – 10 percent of all the communes in the county. Production teams falsified production quantity reports and stole collectively through reporting less than what they harvested and distributing more than what they recorded. Some production teams would first hide a portion of the millet and then do the weighing and reporting. Some even used an old scale as the official scale in order to carry out pre-distribution. Some even took advantage of their official authority to falsify accounts.[22]

Many communes in Zhejiang were unwilling to sell their grain or pay the grain tax, so they could privately distribute it as they harvested. While I was gathering information on the "three fixed quotas" (for production, purchase, and marketing of grain), I found that it was not that the cadres were unwilling to admit what they had done, it was that the information was not reliable. Concealing grain production quantities in the agricultural collectives was a very common and frequent occurrence. When it came time to report production numbers, some would practise the "four omissions" (i.e., omitting private plots, omitting roadside or hillside crops, omitting spring crops that increase production, and omitting the few other crops scattered around). As a result of concealing production reports in one township, yield estimates were lowered by as much as 260,000 *jin*.[23]

In Jiangxi Province, many communes, production teams, and groups formed units to collectively conceal grain, form partnerships with commune members, and individually steal crops. According to an investigation of forty-three agricultural communes in eleven counties in Gannan administrative region in October 1956, there were more than forty-three cases in which over one hundred *jin* of grain were concealed or stolen. In the busy chaos between harvest and distribution, it was not uncommon for peasants to steal eight to ten *jin* of grain. However, this was not considered "wrong" as it was for "the common good." At other times, it was feared that the state would over-regulate, buy too much grain, and cause everyone to go hungry. Before joining a commune, no one knew how much others were harvesting, so people were able to hide some of their grain. After entering the commune, however, grain was distributed according to commune rules: certainly they received less than before collectivization.[24]

In Hubei Province, it was discovered that many villages and communes concealed production. One commune in Huangmei concealed the production of seventy thousand *jin* of grain. Of the thirty-four communes in one village, fifteen were found to have concealed production using the methods described above. These communes all concealed their numbers from officials but not from the peasants. They were afraid the government would demand too much of their grain if they reported actual quantities. In Gucheng County, there were occurrences of quantity concealment and grain theft, which some Party members were actually orchestrating.[25]

In the area along the Huai River in Anhui Province, instances of concealed production, corruption, and theft on the part of production teams were very serious. Among the 328 production teams on thirty-three communes in one region of Woyang County, 277 production teams from thirty communes were concealing production; 11 production teams from three communes engaged in corruption; and 118 production teams in twelve communes were stealing.[26]

In Henan Province, some commune cadres took the lead in organizing the collective concealment and private distribution of grain. In Nanyang County, one production team leader even distributed 33,169 *jin* of *yuandou* beans to commune members during the summer harvest. Communes from twenty-two villages in eight districts of Fuyang County stole and distributed more than 210,000 *jin* of wheat.[27]

In Shanxi Province, grain theft and concealment of production numbers were rampant. According to statistics from Danfeng and two other counties, during the fall harvest there were more than four hundred cases of theft. In thirty-eight instances of theft in Hu County, more than twenty thousand *jin* of grain were stolen. The main reason so much grain was stolen was that the peasants were afraid that the official grain allotments would be insufficient.[28]

In Qinghai Province, many communes collectively concealed production numbers from the state and exaggerated natural disasters. Many even distributed grain to commune members before paying the agricultural tax or selling it to the state. Using large rice baskets and "heavy scales" to distribute grain to commune members was a common practice.[29]

In Shanxi Province, many communes lowered production quantities, increased the amount of grain reported for animal feed, reduced harvest numbers for coarse grains, collectively concealed production, and engaged in private distribution in order to reduce the grain quotas demanded by the government. To keep more grain for themselves, production teams in Jinnan Prefecture collectively concealed production quantities by excessively deducting the percentage of moisture when distributing grain, manipulating the scales, and carelessly threshing grain at harvest time so that family members could follow behind and collect what fell. One commune cadre from Yi County concealed 12,967 *jin* of grain and was reported to the government by other commune members.[30]

In Changzhi Prefecture, many communes consciously concealed production numbers. According to an investigation in Gaoping County, some communes stole distribution grain during harvest time, reported less than was harvested, manipulated amounts for storage, exaggerated water percentage, reported a higher population, raised the amount of grain to be kept by commune members, and were careless when harvesting and threshing: more than 324,000 *jin* of grain were concealed. One commune secretly distributed more than 17,000 *jin* of grain to commune members (30 *jin* per person) without factoring it into the total production quantity. Many communes engaged in eight "selective accounting" practices (i.e., accounting for autumn grain but not wheat, accounting for a large fall harvest but not coarse grains, accounting for grains but not tubers, accounting for large corn but not small corn, accounting for harvests from cultivated land but not from uncultivated land, accounting for grain allotted to commune members but not for stored grain, and accounting for unprocessed grain but not for grain already milled).[31]

The year 1956 saw the highest total grain production in Shanxi Province since liberation. The grain quota demanded by the state had never been higher, and the percentage remaining for the peasants was also high. However, even at that point, the collection of state grain quotas was difficult because many communes were exaggerating natural disasters, lowering production figures, over-reporting animal feed, under-recording the harvest of coarse grains, and collectively concealing production quantities for the purpose of private distribution. All of which enabled them to reduce the grain quota meant to be paid to the state.[32]

Production teams in the Liancun communes of Hebei Province seriously concealed production quantities. Some communes calculated one and a half *jin* of grain for every actual *jin* when allotting grain to commune members. Others advised commune members to dig for yams only once and to report the harvest, after which they would dig out the remaining yams in order to distribute them among themselves. According to statistics, the Liancun communes of several counties concealed as much as 520,000 *jin* of grain. Due to bureaucracy, production concealment, and theft, one commune "lost" 1.7 million *jin* of grain.[33]

According to my research, the following seventeen provinces engaged in concealing production quantities and private distribution: Hebei, Jiangsu, Anhui, Shanxi, Shandong, Zhejiang, Sichuan, Hubei, Guizhou, Jiangxi, Liaoning, Heilongjiang, Shaanxi, Henan, Fujian, Guangdong, and Qinghai. Given that the practice was so common and widespread, it is no wonder that some places added 25 percent extra to production numbers to compensate for corruption and misappropriation of grain.[34]

Considering this, it is possible that concealing production and private distribution in the agricultural communes had been a relatively common practice for some time. Besides the provinces mentioned above, similar records were found in Sichuan, Shandong, Heilongjiang, Shanxi, Anhui, Henan, and so on from before the establishment of the communes. How could this situation have arisen? One possible reason is that, while peasants believed communes were truly "collective organizations," they still put their own interests above those of the government. Perhaps they wanted to "have their cake and eat it too."[35]

Because production concealment and private distribution were easier to detect early on, these practices became increasingly secretive. Indeed, peasants gradually came to realize that concealing production and private distribution were, in fact, serious crimes in the eyes of the state. I personally learned of the difficulties in engaging in production concealment and private distribution in the 1970s, when I was an "educated youth" sent to the countryside. At that time, many young people participated in production concealment and private distribution when they were sent to the countryside (especially when they worked as production team accountants). Indeed, these practices were very widespread. If one considers techniques such as reducing water percentage and scale manipulation, then no doubt instances of production concealment and private distribution were even more common.

Can the development of these phenomena be traced? It is clear that, although production concealment and private distribution were brought under control in the early stages of collectivization, they frequently reappeared later on. This development can be attributed largely to the "difficult years," after which these practices spread. A production team cadre whom I know very well (he was an active participant in land reform and communization) told me that "from that time on I had lost faith." That is why, in the first autumn of the Great Leap Forward, when another round of production concealment and private distribution broke out nationwide, Mao Zedong told peasants to "hide in the mountain caves, post guards to sound the alarm, and protect their own products." It was here that he used the term "resistance" (*fankang*) and said that it was "basically rational."[36]

The extensive nature of concealed production and private distribution demonstrates that, when studying China's collective economic system, it is not enough to consider only the "official accounts" and to ignore the so-called "unofficial" ones, to consider only "collective labour" in the communes and to disregard "private behaviour."

From here, we can move one step further and answer this oft-asked question: why did Chinese peasants not revolt? One significant reason can be attributed to the "resistance" they displayed. By employing various techniques, peasants ensured themselves a sustainable existence. To a certain extent, the state even tacitly permitted these techniques; therefore, there was no reason for peasants to rebel or fight for their lives (after all, that could have proven very costly).[37] Furthermore, revolt would have meant struggling with a power that could not be matched. So peasants wisely chose their own battlefields – in the fields and on the ground.

There are many scholars who emphasize this question: Were peasants able to equally distribute privately appropriated grain? In fact, they greatly misunderstand the implications of peasant behaviour. Such behaviour was the result of the relationship between the peasants and the government, an example of "snatching food from the tiger's mouth." Whoever had the means was able to extract more; individually, it was not important who secured a little more or a little less. In effect, it was more like "distribution according to need": not necessarily equitable but certainly demonstrating a degree of fairness.

Theft in the People's Communes

Theft is a phenomenon that has existed from very early on. However, I found in the course of my research that it appeared as though stealing did not exist anywhere. Coming to terms with theft is challenging because it involves individual privacy as well as moral judgment. Relatively speaking, concealed production and private distribution were collective activities. Therefore, at the beginning of my investigation – in a village to which I had earlier been "sent down" as part of a labour team and in which I was confident my connections were reliable (Shanxi Province, TG County) – I encountered a number of difficulties. The peasants did not seem willing to discuss past events, and I often received many different versions of one event.[38]

The former brigade leader of my village said that grain theft began early on in collectivization. Later, thieves were constantly stealing. For example, although some people might notice when someone put some corn into his *luotou* (a small bamboo basket), they did not care. They would say, "it's not ours, it belongs to the brigade," and the thief would take it anyway. A few hundred people could pull the wool over the eyes of just a few cadres. Some peasants, for example, especially the elderley women of the village, collected grain when they went to cut grass. Some said they were going out to dig up field mice. They would mix in some tubers, cover them with two handfuls of earth to mess things up, and openly carry the grain back home.

How much could one steal in one year? At a hundred *jin* per person, thirty-five tons of grain could be stolen (at the time, there were about seven hundred people in a village). Theoretically, one person could steal two hundred *jin*, resulting in seventy tons; but it was probably never that much, more like thirty to thirty-five tons. Before the "four clean-ups" movement (1963-66), the village branch secretary felt that these numbers were more or less accurate. In his opinion, because so much suffering had been endured on account of what happened in the past, nobody dared bother with it, and no one considered it a situation that could be controlled, even if one wanted to.

The aforementioned branch secretary also said that theft was a common occurrence. On many occasions, he came upon someone pulling a cart covered with grass or someone carrying a cloth bag. There were just so many ways to steal. At the time, because the masses were stealing, the cadres, for their part, privately ate and drank their share. But the branch secretary and others stressed that the number of thefts was low and that they were perpetrated only by individuals.

These conflicting reports created a number of problems for me. After only a short period of investigation, it seemed difficult to make any progress. Then one day I heard the talkative companion of a former co-worker say that, for example, if today a guest were to arrive and there were no beans to eat, then she would simply go out and gather some up and put them into a rice jar. Whenever she went to work in the fields, she would always take her *luotou*, cover the top with grass, and carry it back home. It is possible that even the most honest people collected grain this way. Only when she said that the people "did not consider this scandalous" did I realize that this activity had become a part of peasant life. Therefore, it should be differentiated from theft.

But is this view in fact correct? On another day, I met an old peasant who said: "Theft was rare. But grabbing something and taking it home, this was not called theft."[39] From this I learned to use the phrase "grab a handful" (*zhuawo*),[40] which is not considered stealing. The elderly peasant also told me that, if I asked about "grabbing something," well, that happened quite often. Out in the fields, if one person took something, then everyone else would do the same. They would conceal it only from the cadres. Those who were a bit more courageous would take a little more, those less brave would take a little less. If you didn't grab a handful, it would be autumn before you had anything to eat. Taking food home enabled you to eat. The state tried to restrict this behaviour but to no avail. The elderly peasant reckoned that those performing labour were taking one hundred *jin* for themselves; but, in terms of the overall population, it was at most thirty to fifty *jin*. In fact, they were not taking much. Those who took a lot were considered thieves and robbers as they intended mainly to sell it. A former team leader told me that "petty theft couldn't be stopped; many people were just like that. The more daring ones took a little more, and the less daring took a little less. On average it never amounted to one hundred *jin*. People were hungry. If you didn't steal, how could you live? If it was right beside me, I'd help myself too. There's nothing to be afraid of speaking about this now. But if you hadn't come, I wouldn't speak of this."

One friend with whom I had worked in the past asked: "When did this kind of thing actually start? In the 1960s, it was really serious. When you think about it, the country was under tight control, otherwise how could we have been that hungry?" As for the total amount of grain stolen, as far as he was concerned, it could not be calculated: "Some things cannot be clearly explained; everyone has something different to say on the subject."

My village was certainly not the most notorious village in TG as far as stealing was concerned. At the time, Shangcun had the worst reputation for stealing in the area. Shangcun is situated a few miles east of my village, in the middle of which lies a ridge that forms the boundary between Pingchuan and Qiuling. The distribution of surplus in Shangcun was very low. In any given year, one could earn only three cents for a day's labour: people relied primarily on stealing to survive. This was quite well known throughout the county. According to the villagers, the people of Shangcun formed gangs and rode out in carts to steal; some even stole right from the farm. They stole 70 percent of the wheat, whether or not it belonged to the collective, and, as a result, only fifteen *jin* of grain were able to be distributed within the team. In the fields, they would bind together the wheat and shake it to look disorderly; then they would carry it home and say that they had collected it themselves. Sometimes this amounted to more than three hundred *jin*. If your share of the surplus was not enough, you had to steal. Each year the relief grain had to be eaten (according to county sources, the amount of grain borrowed by Shangcun rose to 650,000 *yuan*, about 300 *yuan* per person). In the village, nobody cared. Because stealing was so rampant, no one took responsibility for it. During the corn harvest, when a pile of corn was seen off in the distance, Shangcun villagers would not want it and would say to the people in my village, "you take it away!" Driving carts into the village, they would pass their own homes and throw corn through the front gates.

This situation existed in Shangcun for a number of reasons. For example, in my village we were all living in small village homes; there were no large buildings. In Shangcun, however, there had been many traders in the past (people in my village often said that the landlords in our village were not as wealthy as the middle-level peasants of Shangcun), the land was rich, and the previous generations did not need to rely on farming. Also, many people worked outside of the village and sent money home. Therefore, many people were not dependent on agricultural cooperatives and cared little about collective production.

Were there any other villages like Shangcun in the area? Indeed there were. Except for two, Shangcun's neighbouring villages were all poorly governed. It should be clear that theft was very severe in these villages, although probably not as severe as in Shangcun.

Theft occurred in many ways, and different things were stolen using different methods. Wheat, for instance, was purposely cut crudely and left on the ground so one could return later to pick it up. Some members of the cooperative would ask for time off in order to go and collect wheat. If this was done well, one could gather about ten *jin* in a day. Gathering fallen grain was a traditional custom that had been allowed by landlords. It was part of the commune members' mindset and was quite possibly the one act for which moral condemnation was most unwarranted. For this reason, those who would normally never "grab" anything might gather wheat. In some villages, it was even possible to gather one hundred *jin* (in 1972, for example, this occurred in eight of the villages neighbouring mine).

Most theft occurred during harvest season. People went after millet rather than unhusked rice, while corn and sorghum were stolen most often. These grains could be stolen while people were out working in the fields: one could grab several *liang* on a daily basis. These could either be concealed on one's person or put in a *luotou* and covered with grass. Or they could be dropped to the ground in broad daylight to be picked up later at night. Sometimes they were cooked and eaten right in the fields or on the farm in a "night operation." Beans were often put into jars meant for keeping one's meal and carried home. A certain kind of potato was purposely not dug up when the earth was tilled: people would go back to get them at night. Fumbling through the soil, they would often grab somebody else's hand and not utter a sound.

Generally speaking, cadres could not steal, for, if they did, they would lose the public trust granted to those in a position of power. On the other hand, cadre family members did steal, and because they could rely on the backing of their cadre kin, they often did so rather brazenly. The compensation cadres received allowed them to eat more than others. Adults, elderly women, and children all had different and unique techniques for stealing (children were often beaten back because, even if they were caught, there was no way to deal with them). Those working on the farms or rearing animals also had their own techniques for stealing. People who sowed the fields could steal the seeds, which, generally, were plentiful. Wheat seeds, for example, could afford a loss of approximately 25 percent. Even people living near the villages could steal a lot as they could come and go at their own convenience.

Some people stole at night, some during the day. Stealing at night was considered "grand theft" (*da tou*) as it was committed either by carrying a load on the shoulders or by using a cloth bag that could hold more than one hundred *jin*. Some stole while on the job in the fields during the day. At one time, they could take upwards of ten *jin*. Some would even "grab a handful" at noon when cutting the grass. But these occurrences were all improvised and, therefore, were considered "petty theft" (*xiaotou xiaomo*).

Each village had field patrols, but their usefulness was questionable. Apparently, on any given night, "so and so" would patrol the fields while someone else would go out and steal, and the next night they would reverse roles. On occasion, people from other villages were caught. Sometimes those patrolling the fields would warn the thieves, and then they themselves would steal something. Indeed, a catchy rhyme says it best: "If you don't steal during field patrol, you won't receive grain at all!"

Some people think that, in these villages, theft was a disguised form of private distribution: I can see you, and you can see me, but nobody is telling on anyone. People would stop work early, skip a meal, throw a bag over their back, and go out to gather grain. It happened every day and became very serious. It is said that each household stole at least one hundred *jin* of grain. When there were more mouths to feed, they would take more. Of course, those who moved slower took less. Good people, bad people, all had to steal; otherwise, they would go hungry. People were even encouraged by other villagers: "Why don't you go steal?"

During my research, the former head of TG County told me that theft was most rampant during the "three years of hardship." At that time, everyone was stealing in order to avoid starvation – a point that Thaxton also makes in Chapter 10 of this volume. From that time and into the 1970s, most people were stealing grain in order survive. Theft was everywhere: it was not a phenomenon that occurred in just one or two villages. From another perspective, theft, the county head told me, was not arbitrary: one was not supposed to steal too much. For example, if the field patrol caught someone but could not hold him, it did not matter, as long as there was some measure of control. In general, people stole approximately three hundred *jin* of grain. It was not all stolen at once; people stole on a daily basis so that stealing was tacitly understood. What is worth noting is that these things were all well known by all of us (meaning mainly the county cadres).

Interpretation and Discussion

When I was conducting my research in the early 1990s, the academic world, including both Chinese scholars (those who were interested and those who actually experienced collectivization)[41] as well as academics from overseas (economists, political scientists, and sociologists), became very interested in studying the Chinese collective economy. Apart from conducting research for "revisionist" purposes, the following reasons for doing so were also expressed.

A collective economy was a mainstream agricultural economic system that was implemented in many countries. Though it now appears to be defunct in the former socialist camps, it still constitutes a major event of great historical importance. Because it affected the lives and productivity of millions of peasants, the Chinese collective economy holds a definite position in the history of humankind's existential struggles, especially during times of famine. These were very significant experiences – there are many aspects that, to this day, still have not been clearly explained – and knowledge of them will have a profound effect on the futures of many countries.

Previously, however, the majority of research focused on the "upper level" (i.e., on the process of drawing up and carrying out state policies); at most, it included questions concerning the lower-middle cadres. Such a focus is indeed reasonable; after all, the collective economy was, from the beginning, a planned system devised and implemented at the top. The central leadership did not care about the "free will" or "consent" of the peasants. In the end, however, the planned system had to pass through the peasants (including the base-level cadres) in order to manifest itself. If, during research on the relationship between state and society, one only considers the state and ignores the peasantry, then one overlooks a fundamental level of research.

Why do so many scholars in the PRC neglect or show little interest in peasant behaviour? One reason is that many are bound by conventional thinking. People have the impression that peasants were passive, ignorant, inactive, and submissive. Facing the strength of the state, it would seem, the peasantry did nothing but cower and quietly bear the policies thrust upon them. Therefore, in the past, very few people knew about peasant "oppositional" behaviour. Even if there is a partial understanding of this, it has yet to be summarized concisely. Nor has peasant behaviour been seen as an important element in the composition of the collective economic system. It is my contention that the peasantry should be viewed as one party in a dynamic binary opposition (in game theory, it should be seen as a "player").

Another reason why so many scholars cannot break free from the bounds of conventional thought is that too little research has been conducted on peasant behaviour during this period. The behaviour exhibited by the peasantry was itself a secret and has already become "a thing of the past." Peasants still harbour a secretive attitude towards scholars coming from the outside into their rural communities, and they are not always willing to speak their minds. For many peasants, there is no need to elevate these matters to the level of consciousness. Furthermore, research on peasant behaviour is still considered taboo in China. It has thus been difficult for me to establish this research topic, to secure funding for it (I had to conduct my research without financial help), and to debate it in public.

During the course of my research, I discovered that peasants did not in fact passively accept the system, as many people thought. They had their own expectations, ideas, and demands. It is possible that all along they engaged in consciously "active" behaviour (including the "resistance" described in this chapter); had their own "explanations" for, and made their own "choices" in response to, unfavourable conditions; and changed according to shifts in their environment. During the implementation of rural collectivization, they maintained a form of "oppositional" behaviour and were able to subtly dispel, change, and modify official policies. The result was that the collective economy did not fully correspond either to government intentions or to the hopes of the peasantry; rather, the system was the collective result of mutual struggles between the state and the peasantry, of mutual restraints, of testing each other out, of drawing nearer to one another, and of mutual concessions. This mutual interaction between the government and the peasantry permeated the entire collec- tivization process and continues even to this day. Simply put, peasants are continuously making efforts to re-establish their status: contracting grain quotas on a household basis was just the first step.

In the process of opposing the state, Chinese peasants did not have equal negotiation rights or formal channels through which to negotiate. However, in the end, they still managed to interact with the state – a miracle, con- sidering their predicament. Peasant resistance may be viewed as a kind of "initiative for interaction." Such a view corrects to a large extent the long- held prejudice regarding peasant "passivity" and/or "inactivity." What peasant resistance reveals is exactly what political scientists and sociologists consider to be "society's hidden transcripts," important for understanding daily life.[42] Resistance is, therefore, of great significance.

Thus, in terms of present-day peasant resistance, not only are we able to fill in the blanks of history by rediscovering and rewriting the history of peasants during the collective economic period and carve out a complete image of the history of the Chinese collective economy, but we are also able to study from different angles the role resistance plays in system transformation. This will prove beneficial to both the development of related theories as well as in-depth studies of the relationship between the state and society. However, this research is not merely a theoretical view of history; it also has important practical significance. It can help us analyze the historical background of the relationship between the current government and the peasantry, identify elements influencing the transformation of government policy, reassess questions relating to the "reform and open" policy and its accomplishments, and provide information for future rural development.

From a global perspective, Chinese peasant resistance is unique and difficult to categorize through the use of related analyses of different cultures (for more on this, refer to my research on the history of peasant/tenant-farmer behaviour).[43] Peasant resistance in China did not involve large-scale or violent rebellion. It relied solely on subtle and unassuming daily behaviours to revise and, ultimately, change the system. This was something that was seldom accomplished in other countries. Therefore, the results of this investigation may potentially complement and enrich related areas of sociological theory. Of course, theories and methods from various other disciplines must be employed to more fully analyze these results.

We have only just begun studying peasant resistance, and there are still numerous gaps in our research. It is my hope that many more of my colleagues will pay greater attention to this question and engage in even more in-depth studies. Only then can we gain greater insight into the efforts of the Chinese peasantry. When we listen to their words, we must realize that they have had a significant influence on the making of contemporary Chinese history.

Notes

1 Editor's note: Jean Oi's *State and Peasant in Early China* (Berkeley: University of California Press, 1989) is an important early exception in this regard. See also Ralph Thaxton's chapter in this volume.
2 In *Weapons of the Weak* and *The Moral Economy of the Peasant*, James C. Scott illustrates "everyday forms of (peasant) resistance" in Southeast Asia, such as stealing, "slowing" work production, or faking compliance with authorities. The goal of this strategy is to gain some reasonable material benefits. See James C. Scott, *Weapons of the Weak: Everyday Forms of Peasant Resistance* (New Haven, CT: Yale University Press, 2005); and James C. Scott, *The Moral Economy of the Peasant: Rebellion and Subsistence in Southeast Asia* (New Haven, CT: Yale University Press, 1976).
3 Du Runsheng, who describes this behaviour as "counter-movement" (*fandao erxing*), encouraged me to undertake research on this topic.
4 Vivienne Shue, "Peasant China in Transition" (Los Angeles: University of California Press, 1980), 286.

5   See Gao Wangling, "Jitihua guocheng chongshen" [A Review of the Collectivization Process], unpublished manuscript.

6   According to Du Ruizhi (former head of the Guangdong agricultural committee), by late 1956-57 (at the earliest) peasants (especially wealthy, middle-level peasants) attempted to leave collectives en masse. Only after facing opposition did they begin contracting quotas on a household basis inside the communes. It was because working outside of the commune was prohibited, and one had to farm for oneself, that they began this practice. The historical period of contracting quotas began at this point. See Gao Wangling, "Yige laicuole de difang" [Wrong Place, Wrong Time], unpublished manuscript.

7   Interview, Shanxi, 1994.

8   Du Runsheng claims that, in 1981, the communes of Hebei explained to base-level cadres everywhere that "the masses must be responsible for the system, we do not want to bully them, we are the calves, they are the bulls, we cannot bully them." See Yang Zejiang, former Party secretary of Hebei Province, "Tantan Hebei nongcun de dabaogan" [On the "All-Round" Contracts of Rural Hebei], in *Zhongguo nongcun gaige juece jishi* [A Record of Reform Policies in Rural China] (Beijing: Zhongyang wenxian chubanshe, 1999), 413.

9   Du Ruizhi claims that, in some places, peasants waited for the commune cadres to fall asleep before posting guards and dividing up the fields to work for themselves (conversation with the author, 1980). See Gao, "Yige laicuole de difang."

10 Du Runsheng, conversation with the author, 1995.

11 In the nineteenth chapter of *Xiyouji* [Journey to the West], Sun Wukong says, "do not be deceptive or 'soft' with me." The commentary says that an attitude that manifests a soft and gentle exterior but an evil and unpredictable heart is called "soft." See Wu Cheng'en, *Xiyou ji* [Journey to the West] (Beijing: Renmin wenxue chubanshe, 1981), 244.

12 Zhonggong zhongyang dangxiao chubanshe, ed., "Zhejiang shengwei zhuanfa Yang Xinpei tongzhi guanyu Xianju xian qunzhong naoshi wenti de baogao (1957 nian 6 yue)" [Report of Comrade Yang Xinpei on the Problem of Mass Disturbances in Xianju County, Forwarded by the Provincial Government of Zhejiang (June 1957)], in *Nongye jitihua zhongyao wenjian huibian* [A Compilation of Important Agricultural Collectivization Documents] (Beijing: Zhonggong zhongyang dangxiao chubanshe, 1981), 694.

13 Zhonggong zhongyang dangxiao chubanshe, ed., "Baoding diwei guanyu Xushui, Qingyuan liang xian zai shehuizhuyi xuanchuan yundong zhong fasheng de wenti xiang shengwei de baoago (1957 nian 8 yue)" [Report to the Provincial Government on Problems During the Socialist Propaganda Movement in Xushui and Qingyuan Counties by the Baoding Prefecture Party Committee (August 1957)], in *Nongye jitihua zhongyao wenjian huibian* [A Compilation of Important Agricultural Collectivization Documents] (Beijing: Zhonggong zhongyang dangxiao chubanshe, 1981), 711.

14 For more, see Gao Wangling, "Nongmin fanxingwei yanjiu" [A Study of Peasant Resistance], unpublished manuscript, chap. 3, sec. 3.

15 *Neibu cankao* (hereafter *NBCK*) 2052 (15 November 1956).

16 Ibid. 2060, (24 November 1956).

17 Ibid. 2025 (19 October 1956).

18 Ibid. 1924 (24 November 1956).

19 Ibid. (4 July 1956).

20 Ibid. 2049 (12 November 1956).

21 Ibid. 2031 (24 October 1956).

22 Ibid. 1984 (8 September 1956).

23 Ibid. 2060 (24 November 1956).

24 Ibid. 2030 (23 October 1956).

25 Ibid. 2041 (2 February 1956).

26 Ibid. 1930 (19 July 1956).

27 Ibid. 2066 (30 November 1956).

28 Ibid. 2053 (17 November 1956).

29 Ibid. 2078 (14 December 1956).

30 Ibid. 1961 (17 August 1956).

31 Ibid. 2046 (8 November 1956).

32 Ibid. 2112 (23 January 1957).

33 Ibid. 2072 (7 December 1956).

34 Before this there were serious cases of suppressing consumption quotas for the masses in Hebei Province. In Hejian County, for example, there were villages that were allotting 288 *jin* of grain per person annually or twenty-four *jin* per month for those in their prime. In one village in Huanghua County, each person received at most nineteen *jin* per month. In Gaocheng County, some villages were replacing grain with sweet potatoes and greens, and some were unable to keep feed (other than dried sweet potatoes) for their livestock. In Anping, Shenzhe, Puxian, and other counties, cadres were begging for some grain to be left for the masses but to no avail. They had a theory: "Rural economics make little sense, leave them nothing, and it's as if they have something." See Gao, "Nongmin fanxingwei yanjiu," chap. 2, 48-76.

35 There are, of course, several other possible reasons, for example a number of particular occurrences in 1956. On this, see Gao Wangling, "1956 nian de xiaoyuejin" [The Minor Leap Forward of 1956], unpublished manuscript; and Gao Wangling, "1956 nian de dajianchan" [The Great Reduction in Production of 1956], unpublished manuscript.

36 Zonggong zongyang wenxian yanjiushi, ed., "Zai Zhengzhou huiyishang de jianghua" [Speech Given at the Zhengzhou Conference (February 1959)], in *Jianguo yilai Mao Zedong wengao* [Writings of Mao Zedong since the Establishment of the People's Republic of China] (Beijing: Zhongyang wenxian chubanshe, 1993).

37 Du Runsheng, conversation with the author, 1997.

38 For more, see Gao Wangling, "Huixiang jiwen" [Records of Returning Home], in *Renmin gongshe shiqi Zhongguo nongmin fanxingwei* [Chinese Peasant Resistance at the Time of the People's Communes] (Beijing: Zhonggong dangshi chubanshe, 2006).

39 Interview in Shanxi, 1994.

40 Correspondingly, Liu Shaoqi once used the word *na* ("take"). In 1961, he gave a speech in his hometown of Tanzichong, in which he said: "At present commune members are casually 'taking' things, crops, vegetables, they just 'take' them whenever they feel like it. After the sweet potatoes have been sown, they're just 'taken' away." See *Liu Shaoqi xuanji* [Selected Writings of Liu Shaoqi] (Beijing: Beijing renmin chubanshe, 1981-85), 2:331. This came up in a discussion with Liu Xiaojing in March 2001.

41 Gao Huamin, *Nongye hezuohua yundong shimo* [The Whole Story of the Collectivization of Agriculture] (Beijing: Qingnian chubanshe, 1999); Luo Pinghan, *Nongye hezuoshe yundong shi* [The History of the Agricultural Cooperative Movement] (Fuzhou: Fujian renmin chubanshe, 2004); Luo Pinghan, *Gongshe! Gongshe! Nongcun renmingongshe shi* [Commune! Commune! The History of the Rural People's Commune] (Fuzhou: Fujian renmin chubanshe, 2003).

42 James C. Scott, *Domination and the Arts of Resistance: Hidden Transcripts* (New Haven, CT: Yale University Press, 1990).

43 Gao Wangling, *Zudian guanxi: Dizhu, nongmin he dizu* [A New Perspective on Tenant-Landlord Relationships: Landlords, Peasants, and Land Rent] (Shanghai: Shanghai shudian chubanshe, 2005). Without doubt, many of the techniques employed by the peasantry have historical origins. However, peasant "opposition" to rent and peasant "resistance" under the collective economy differ greatly: the latter incorporates the relationship between state and society, while the former only identifies problems between individuals within rural society.

Bibliography

Adorno, Theodor W. *Soziologische Schriften: Band I* [Sociological Writings: Volume 1]. Frankfurt: Suhrkamp Verlag, 2003.

Andors, Phyllis. *The Unfinished Liberation of Chinese Women, 1949-1980*. Bloomington: Indiana University Press, 1983.

Anhui difangzhi bianzhuan weiyuanhui, ed. *Anhui shengzhi: Liangshizhi* [Anhui Provincial Gazetteer: Food Volume]. Hefei: Anhui renmin chubanshe, 1991.

–, ed. *Anhui shengzhi: Nongyezhi* [Anhui Provincial Gazetteer: Agriculture Volume]. Hefei: Anhui renmin chubanshe, 1996.

–, ed. *Anhui shengzhi: Renkouzhi* [Anhui Provincial Gazetteer: Population Volume]. Hefei: Anhui renmin chubanshe, 1995.

Anhui xinsijun lishi yanjiuhui, ed. *Jinian Zeng Xisheng wenji* [Collected Writings Commemorating Zeng Xisheng]. Beijing: Dangdai Zhongguo chubanshe, 2005.

Apter, David Ernest, and Tony Saich. *Revolutionary Discourse in Mao's Republic*. Cambridge, MA: Harvard University Press, 1994.

Ash, Robert. "Squeezing the Peasants: Grain Extraction, Food Consumption, and Rural Living Standards in Mao's China." *China Quarterly* 188 (2006): 959-98.

Ashton, Basil, and Kenneth Hill. "Famine in China, 1958-1961." *Population and Development Review* 10, 4 (1984): 613-45.

Austen, Jane. *Sense and Sensibility*. Ware, UK: Wordsworth Classics, 1979.

Bachman, David M. *Bureaucracy, Economy, and Leadership in China: The Institutional Origins of the Great Leap Forward*. New York: Cambridge University Press, 1991.

Ban Wang. "Revolutionary Realism and Revolutionary Romanticism: The Song of Youth." In *The Columbia Companion to Modern East Asian Literature*, ed. Joshua Mostov, 471-75. New York: Columbia Univerity Press, 2003.

Basu, Amrita. *Two Faces of Protest*. Berkeley: University of California Press, 1992.

Becker, Jasper. *Hungry Ghosts: Mao's Secret Famine*. London: John Murray, 1996.

Bernstein, Thomas B. "Mao Zedong and the Famine of 1959-1960: A Study in Wilfulness." *China Quarterly* 186 (2006): 421-45.

–. "Stalinism, Famine, and Chinese Peasants." *Theory and Society* 13 (1984): 339-77.

Bernstein, Thomas P. "Cadre and Peasant Behavior under Conditions of Insecurity and Deprivation: The Grain Supply Crisis of the Spring of 1955." In *Chinese Communist Politics in Action*, ed. A. Doak Barnett, 365-99. Seattle: University of Washington Press, 1969.

Bianco, Lucien. *Peasants without the Party*. New York: M.E. Sharpe, 2001.

Bo Yibo. *Ruogan zhongda juece yu shijian de huigu (xiudingben)* [Reflections on Certain Major Decisions and Events]. Vol. 2. Beijing: Renmin chubanshe, 1997.

Brady, Anne-Marie. *Making the Foreign Serve China: Managing Foreigners in the People's Republic*. Lanham, MD: Rowman and Littlefield, 2003.

Brown, Jeremy. "Crossing the Rural-Urban Divide in Twentieth-Century China." PhD diss., University of California, San Diego, 2008.

Brown, Jeremy, and Paul Pickowicz, eds. *Dilemmas of Victory: The Early Years of the People's Republic of China.* Cambridge, MA: Harvard University Press, 2007.

–. "The Early Years of the People's Republic of China: An Introduction." In *Dilemmas of Victory: The Early Years of the People's Republic of China,* ed. Jeremy Brown and Paul Pickowicz, 1-18. Cambridge, MA: Harvard University Press, 2007.

Cai Chang. "Guanxin funü jiankang baochi wangsheng ganjin" [Take Care of Women's Health in Order to Protect Their Exuberant Spirit]. *Zhongguo funü* [Chinese Women] 3 (1959): 1-2.

–. "Quanguo fulian Cai Chang zhuxi zai shoudu gejie funü jinian 'sanba' jie dahui shang de jianghua" [The All China Women's Federation Chair Cai Chang's Speech at the Capital's Women's Meeting Commemorating the "March Eighth" Holiday]. *Zhongguo funü* [Chinese Women] 6 (1959): 1-4.

–. "Quanguo fulian dangzu dui xian fulian zuzhi cunzai wenti de yijian" [The All China Women's Federation Party Committee's Recommendations on the Problems Existing in County Women's Federation Organizations]. In *Zhongguo funü wushi nian* [Fifty Years of the Chinese Women's Movement], ed. Quanguo fulian funü yanjiusuo. CD ROM. Beijing: Zhongguo funü chubanshe, 1999 [1958].

–. "Tigao juewu xue hao benling wei jianshe shehuizhuyi fenyong qianjin" [Raise Consciousness and Study Skills Well in Order to Forge Ahead Courageously in the Construction of Socialism]. *Zhongguo funü* [Chinese Women] 18 (1958): 6-11.

Calhoun, Craig Jackson. "The Radicalism of Tradition: Community Strength or Venerable Disguise and Borrowed Language?" *American Journal of Sociology* 88, 5 (1983): 886-914.

Cao Guanqun. "Guanyu heli zuzhi yu shiyong funü laodongli wenti" [The Problems Regarding Reasonably Organizing and Using Women's Labour]. In *Zhongguo funü yundong wenxian ziliao huibian* [A Compilation of Historical Documents of the Chinese Women's Movement], 272-75. Beijing: Zhongguo funü chubanshe, 1988 [1957].

Cao Shuji. "1959-61 nian Zhongguo de renkou siwang jiqi chengyin" [The Death Rate of China's Population and Its Contributing Factors from 1959 to 1961]. *Zhongguo renkou kexue* [Chinese Population Science] 1 (2005): 14-28.

–. *Dajihuang* [The Great Famine]. Hong Kong: Shidai guoji chuban youxian gongsi, 2005.

Cao Xingsui, et al. *Minguo shiqi de nongye* [Agriculture during the Republican Era]. Nanjing: Jiangsu wenshi ziliao bianjibu, 1993.

Chan, Alfred. "The Campaign for Agricultural Development in the Great Leap Forward: A Study of Policy-Making and Implementation in Liaoning." *China Quarterly* 129 (1992): 52-71.

–. *Mao's Crusade: Politics and Policy Implementation in China's Great Leap Forward.* Oxford: Oxford University Press, 2001.

Chan, Anita, Richard Madsen, and Jonathan Unger. *Chen Village under Mao and Deng: The Recent History of a Peasant Community in Mao's China.* Berkeley: University of California Press, 1992.

Chan, Ching-kiu Stephen. "Split China or the Historical/Imaginary: Toward a Theory of the Displacement of Subjectivity in Modern China." In *Politics, Ideology, and Literary Discourse in Modern China*, ed. Kang Liu and Tang Xiaobing, 70-101. Durham: Duke University Press, 1993.

Chan, Kam Wing. "The Chinese Hukou System at 50." *Eurasian Geography and Economics* 50, 2 (2009): 197-221.

Chang, Gene Hsin, and Guanzhong James Wen. "Food Availability versus Consumption Efficiency: Causes of the Chinese Famine." *China Economic Review* 9, 2 (1998): 157-65.

Chen Boda. "Quanxin de shehui, quanxin de ren" [All New Society, All New Men]. *Hongqi* [Red Flag] 4 (1958): 7-8.

Chen, Jian. *Mao's China and the Cold War.* Chapel Hill, NC: University of North Carolina Press, 2001.

Chen Minzhi, and Ding Dong, eds. *Gu Zhun riji* [The Diary of Gu Zhun]. Beijing: Jingji ribaoshe, 1997.

Chen, Tina Mai. "Female Icons, Feminist Iconography? Social Rhetoric and Women's Agency in 1950s China." *Gender and History* 15, 2 (2003): 268-95.

Chen, Yixin. "Cold War Competition and Food Production in China, 1957-1962." *Agricultural History* 83, 1 (2009): 51-78.

– "When Food Became Scarce: Life and Death in Chinese Villages during the Great Leap Forward Famine." *Journal of the Historical Society* 2, (June 2010): 117-65.

Chen Yung-fa. *Zhongguo gongchan geming qishinian* [Seventy Years of the Chinese Communist Revolution]. Vol. 2. Taipei: Lianjing chubanshe, 2001.

Cheng, Tiejun, and Mark Selden. "The Construction of Spatial Hierarchies: China's Hukou and Danwei Systems." In *New Perspectives on State Socialism in China*, ed. Timothy Cheek and Tony Saich, 23-50. New York: M.E. Sharpe, 1997.

Ching Kwan Lee, and Guobin Yang, eds. *Re-Envisioning the Chinese Revolution: The Politics and Poetics of Collective Memories in Reform China*. Washington, DC: Woodrow Wilson Center Press, 2007.

Choy, Howard Y.F. *Remapping the Past: Fictions of History in Deng's China, 1979-1997*. Boston: Brill, 2008.

Commission of the Central Committee of the C.P.S.U.(B.), ed. *History of the Communist Party of the Soviet Union (Bolsheviks) Short Course*. Moscow: Foreign Languages Publishing House, 1939.

Cooper, Ellie McCallie, and William Liu. *Grace: An American Woman in China, 1934-1974*. New York: Soho Press, 2002.

Dangdai Zhongguo congshu bianjibu, ed. *Dangdai Zhongguo de Tianjin* [Contemporary China's Tianjin]. Vol. 1. Beijing: Zhongguo caizheng jingji chubanshe, 1999.

Dangdai Zhongguo nongye hezuohua bianjishi, ed. *Zhongguo hezuohua lishi ziliao* [Materials Regarding the History of Collectivization]. Beijing: Dangdai Zhongguo nongye hezuohua bianjishi, 1987.

–. "Guangdong shengwei guanyu muqian nongcun gongzuo qingkuang he bushu de baogao" [Guangdong Provincial Committee Report on Present Labour Conditions in Rural Areas]. In *Jianguo yilai nongye hezuohua shiliao huibian* [Compilation of Documents on Agricultural Cooperativization since the Founding of the People's Republic of China]. Beijing: Zhonggongdangshi chubanshe, 1992.

–. "Niandi quanguo nongcun gonggong shitang fazhan qingkuang (1959)" [The Development of Public Dining Halls in Rural Areas throughout the Country at the End of 1959]. In *Jianguo yilai nongye hezuohua shiliao huibian* [Compilation of Documents on Agricultural Cooperativization since the Founding of the People's Republic of China]. Beijing: Zhonggongdangshi chubanshe, 1992.

–. "Qiliying renmin gongshe zhangcheng cao'an" [The Draft Constitution of Qiliying People's Commune]. In *Jianguo yilai nongye hezuohua shiliao huibian* [Compilation of Documents on Agricultural Cooperativization since the Founding of the People's Republic of China]. Beijing: Zhonggongdangshi chubanshe, 1992.

–. "Zhonggong Hebei shengwei guanyu guanche bajie qizhong quanhui jingshen de baogao" [Hebei Provincial Committee Report on Carrying on the Spirit of the Seventh Plenary Session of the Eighth Central Committee]. In *Jianguo yilai nongye hezuohua shiliao huibian* [Compilation of Documents on Agricultural Cooperativization since the Founding of the People's Republic of China]. Beijing: Zhonggongdangshi chubanshe, 1992.

–. "Zhonggong Zhongyang guanyu renmin gongshe xiashou fenpei de zhishi" [Central Committee Instructions for Commune Summer Harvest Distribution]. In *Jianguo yilai nongye hezuohua shiliao huibian* [Compilation of Documents on Agricultural Cooperativization since the Founding of the People's Republic of China]. Beijing: Zhonggongdangshi chubanshe, 1992.

–. "Zhonggong Zhongyang pizhuan nongyebu dangzu guanyu Lushan huiyi yilai nong-cun xingshi de baogao" [Ministry of Agriculture's Report on Rural Developments since the Lushan Conference, Circulated by the Central Committee]. In *Jianguo yilai nongye hezuohua shiliao huibian* [Compilation of Documents on Agricultural Cooperativization since the Founding of the People's Republic of China]. Beijing: Zhonggongdangshi chubanshe, 1992.

Davin, Delia. *Woman-Work: Women and the Party in Revolutionary China.* Oxford: Oxford University Press, 1976.

Davis, Mike. *Late Victorian Holocausts: El Nino Famines and the Making of the Third World.* New York: Verso, 2001.

Davis, R.W., and Stephen Wheatcroft. *The Years of Hunger: Soviet Agriculture, 1931-1933.* New York: Palgrave Macmillan, 2004.

De Waal, Alex. *Famine Crimes: Politics and the Disaster Relief Industry in Africa.* Blooming-ton, IN: Indiana University Press, 1997.

Deng Zhiwang. "Jianlun renmin gongshe chuqi de fenpei zhidu" [A Short Analysis of the Initial Phase of the People's Commune Supply System]. *Ershiyi shiji* [Twenty-First Century] 11 (2004): http://www.usc.cuhk.edu.hk/wk.asp.

Deng Zili. *Kanke rensheng* [Rough Human Life]. Chengdu: Sichuan wenyi chubanshe, 2000.

Devereux, Stephen. *Theories of Famine.* New York: Havester/Wheatsheaf, 1993.

Diamant, Neil. *Revolutionizing the Family: Politics, Love, and Divorce in Urban and Rural China, 1949-1958.* Berkeley: University of California Press, 2000.

Diamond, Norma. "Collectivization, Kinship, and the Status of Women in Rural China." *Bulletin of Concerned Asian Scholars* 7 (1975): 25-32.

–. "Household, Kinship, and the Status of Women in Taitou Village, Shandong Province." In *Agricultural and Rural Development in China Today*, ed. Randolph Barker and Beth Rose, 78-96. Ithaca: International Agricultural Program, New York State College of Agricultural Life Sciences, Cornell University, 1983.

Ding Xueliang. "Geming huiyilu zhiwu: Wo zuizao yudao de 'chi butong zhengjian zhe'" [Five Recollections from the Revolution: My Earliest Encounter with a "Dissident"]. *Xinbao caijing xinwen* [Hong Kong Economic Journal], 13 February 2001, 24.

Dittmer, Lowell. "Chinese Informal Politics." *China Journal* 34 (1995): 1-34.

Domenach, Jean-Luc. *The Origins of the Great Leap Forward.* Boulder, CO: Westview Press, 1995.

Domes, Jürgen. *Socialism in the Chinese Countryside: Rural Societal Policies in the People's Republic of China.* Montreal: McGill-Queen's University Press, 1980.

Dong Bian, Cai Asong, and Tan Deshan, eds. *Women de hao dajie Cai Chang* [Our Good Elder Sister Cai Chang]. Beijing: Zhongyang wenxian chubanshe, 1992.

Dong Fu. *Maimiao qing, caihua huang* [Wheat Sprouts Green, Rape Flowers Yellow]. Hong Kong: Tianyuan shuwu, 2008.

Downs, Jennifer Eileen. "Famine Policy and Discourses on Famine in Ming China, 1368-1644." PhD diss., University of Minnesota, 1995.

Dreze, Jean, and Amartya K. Sen. *Hunger and Public Action.* New York: Oxford University Press, 1989.

Du Hong. *20 shiji Zhongguo nongcun wenti* [Issues in 20th-Century China's Countryside]. Beijing: Zhongguo shehui chubanshe, 1998.

Du Runsheng. *Dangdai Zhongguo de nongye hezuozhi* [The Agricultural Cooperative System of Contemporary China]. Beijing: Dangdai Zhongguo chubanshe, 2001.

Duke, Michael S. "Past, Present, and Future in Mo Yan's Fiction of the 1980s." In *From May Fourth to June Fourth: Fiction and Film in 20th-Century China*, ed. David Der-wei Wang and Ellen Widmer, 43-70. Cambridge, MA: Harvard University Press, 1993.

Ellman, Michael. "The 1947 Soviet Famine and the Entitlement Approach to Famine." *Cambridge Journal of Economics* 24, 5 (2000): 603-30.

Endrey, Andrew. "Zhiliang: Hungry Mountain Village – Excerpts." *Renditions* 68 (2007): 112-42.

Evans, Harriet. *Women and Sexuality in China: Female Sexuality and Gender since 1949.* New York: Continuum, 1997.

Farquhar, Judith. *Appetites: Food and Sex in Post-Socialist China.* London: Duke University Press, 2002.

Feuerwerker, Yi'tsi. *Ideology, Power, Text: Self-Representation and the Peasant "Other" in Modern Chinese Literature.* Stanford: Stanford University Press, 1998.

Foucault, Michel. *Die Ordnung des Diskurses* [The Order of the Discourse]. Frankfurt: Fischer, 2003.

Friedman, Edward, Paul Pickowicz, and Mark Selden. *Chinese Village, Socialist State.* New Haven, CT: Yale University Press, 1991.

–. *Revolution, Resistance, and Reform.* New Haven, CT: Yale University Press, 2005.

Fu Shenglun. *Gaobie ji'e* [Farewell to Hunger]. Beijing: Renmin chubanshe, 1999.

Fu Xiutao. "Quanmin jie bing" [People in Arms]. *Hongqi* [Red Flag] 10, (1958).

Fu Yutian et al., comps. *Dangdai Zhongguo de Jiangxi* [Jiangxi in Contemporary China]. Vol. 1. Beijing: Dangdai Zhongguo chubanshe, 1991.

Gang Yue. *The Mouth that Begs: Hunger, Cannibalism, and the Politics of Eating in Modern China.* London: Duke University Press, 1999.

Gao Huamin. *Nongye hezuohua yundong shimo* [The Whole Story of the Collectivization of Agriculture]. Beijing: Qingnian chubanshe, 1999.

Gao, Mobo C.F. *Gao Village: Rural Life in Modern China.* London: Hurst and Company, 1999.

Gao Wangling. "1956 nian de dajianchan" [The Great Reduction in Production of 1956]. Unpublished manuscript.

–. "1956 nian de xiaoyuejin" [The Minor Leap Forward of 1956]. Unpublished manuscript.

–. "Guanyu Du Runsheng huiyi de huiyi" [On the Recollection of the Memory of Du Runsheng]. Unpublished manuscript.

–. "Huixiang jiwen" [Records of Returning Home]. In *Renmin gonshe shiqi Zhongguo nongmin fanxingwei* [Chinese Peasant Resistance at the Time of the People's Communes]. Beijing: Zhonggong dangshi chubanshe, 2006.

–. "Jitihua guocheng chongshen" [A Review of the Collectivization Process]. Unpublished manuscript.

–. "Nongmin fanxingwei yanjiu" [A Study of Peasant Resistance]. Unpublished manuscript.

–. *Renmin gongshe shiqi Zhongguo nongmin "fanxingwei" diaocha* [Investigations of Counter-Action: The Chinese Peasants in the Era of the People's Commune]. Beijing: Zhonggongdangshi chubanshe, 2006.

–. "Wo yan zhong de dayuejin" [The Great Leap Forward in My Eyes]. Unpublished manuscript.

–. "Yige laicuole de difang" [Wong Place, Wrong Time]. Unpublished manuscript.

–. *Zhengfu zuoyong he juese wenti de lishi kaocha* [A Historical Examination of the Function and Role of Government]. Beijing: Haiyang chubanshe, 2003.

–. *Zudian guanxi: Dizhu, nongmin he dizu* [A New Perspective on Tenant-Landlord Relationships: Landlords, Peasants, and Land Rent]. Shanghai: Shanghai shudian chubanshe, 2005.

Gao, Xiaoxian. "'The Silver Flower Contest': Rural Women in 1950s China and the Gendered Division of Labour." *Gender and History* 18, 3 (2006): 594-612.

Gaoshan xianzhi [Gaoshan County Annal]. Shanghai: Shanghai shehui kexueyuan chubanshe, 1994.

Geng Chen. "Liushi niandai chuqi Tianjin shi kaifang tanfan shichang de qianqian houhou" [The Whole Story of Opening Peddlers' Markets in Tianjin in the Early 1960s]. *Tianjin wenshi ziliao xuanji* [Collected Historical and Cultural Records of Tianjin] 79 (October 1998).

Gilmartin, Christina K. *Engendering the Chinese Revolution: Radical Women, Communist Politics, and Mass Movements in the 1920s.* Berkeley: University of California Press, 1995.

Goldstein, Joshua S. "Scissors, Surveys, and Psycho-Prophylactics." *Journal of Historical Sociology* 1, 2 (1998): 153-84.

Goldstone, Jack A. "Toward a Fourth Generation of Revolutionary Theory." *Annual Review of Political Science* 4 (2001): 139-87.

Greene, Felix. *A Curtain of Ignorance.* London: Jonathan Cape, 1965.

Gries, Peter Hays, and Stanley Rosen. "Introduction: Popular Protest and State Legitimation in 21st-Century China." In *State and Society in 21st-Century China*, ed. Peter Hays Gries and Stanley Rosen, 1-23. New York: RoutledgeCurzon, 2004.

"Guanyu jianguo yilai dang de ruogan lishi wenti de jueyi" [Resolution on Some Questions Regarding the History of the Party since the Founding of the People's Republic of China]. Beijing: Renmin chubanshe, 1985.

"Guanyu jianguo yilai dang de ruogan lishi wenti de jueyi mingci jieshi" [Resolution on Some Questions Regarding the History of the Party since the Founding of the People's Republic of China]. *Renmin ribao* [People's Daily], 1981.

"Guanyu kaizhan nongcun funü zigong tuochui de fangzhi gongzuo de tongzhi" [A Notice Regarding the Commencement of Prevention Work on Prolapsed Uteruses (among) Rural Women]. *Funü gongzuo* [Woman-Work], 7 August 1959, 12.

Gui Yingchao, ed. *Cong fangniuwa dao shengzhang: Huang Yan zhuanlüe* [From a Child Cowherd to Provincial Governor: A Short Biography of Huang Yan]. Hefei: Anhui renmin chubanshe, 1994.

Guo Fengqi, ed. *Tianjin tongzhi: Gong'anzhi* [Tianjin Gazetteer: Public Security Gazetteer]. Tianjin: Tianjin renmin chubanshe, 2001.

Guo Moruo, and Zhou Yang, eds. *Hongqi geyao* [Red Flag Ballads]. Beijing: Renmin wenxue chubanshe, 1979 [1959].

Guo Shutian. *Shiheng de Zhongguo: Nongcun chengshihua de guoqu, xianzai yu weilai* [Unbalanced China: The Past, Present, and Future of the Urbanization of the Countryside]. Shijiazhuang: Hebei renmin chubanshe, 1990.

Guo Weilian. "Pi-Shi-Hang gongcheng xingjian shi de Liu'an diwei shuji Du Weiyou" [The Liu'an Prefectural Party Secretary Du Weiyou during the Construction of the Pi-Shi-Hang engineering project]. *Jianghuai wenshi* [Anhui Cultural and Historical Records] 4 (1999): 77-82.

Guojia tongjiju zonghesi, ed. *Quanguo gesheng, zizhiqu, zhixiashi lishi tongji ziliao huibian, 1949-1989* [A Compilation of Historical Statistical Data on Provinces, Autonomous Regions, and Municipalities, 1949-1989]. Beijing: Zhongguo tongji chubanshe, 1990.

Han Fudong and Lei Min. "Xiaogang cun dabaogan daitouren: Yan Junchang jiangshu gaige kaifang 30 nian" [Xiaogang Village's Pioneering of the Household Responsibility System: Yan Junchang Talks about the Thirty Years of Reform and Opening]. http://news.xinhuanet.com/.

Hao Jan [Ran]. *Bright Clouds.* Beijing: Foreign Language Press, 1974.

Hao Ran. "Dawn Clouds Red as Flame." Hadyn Shook and Richard King, trans. *Renditions* 68 (2007): 18-49.

–. *Hao Ran zuopin yanjiu ziliao* [Research Materials on Hao Ran's Works]. Nanjing: Nanjing daxue Zhongwenxi, 1974.

–. "Song caizi" [Sending in Vegetable Seed]. In *Bright Clouds*, 40-50. Beijing: Foreign Language Press, 1974.

–. *Wode rensheng: Hao Ran koushu zizhuan* [My Life: Hao Ran's Oral Autobiography]. Beijing: Huayi chubanshe, 2000.

– *Xin chun qu* [Songs of a New Dawn]. Beijing: Zhongguo qingnian chubanshe, 1960.

–. "Zhaoxia hong si huo" [Dawn Clouds Red as Flame]. *Wenyi hongqi* [Red Flag in the Arts] May 1959.

He Qifang. *Wenxue yishu de chuntian* [Spring in Literature and Art]. Beijing: Zuojia chubanshe, 1964.

He Youliang. "Dangdai Jiangxi nongye shilüe" [A Brief Agricultural History of Contemporary Jiangxi]. *Nongye kaogu* [Agricultural Archaeology] 3 (2003): http://www.guoxue. com.

Hebei sheng minzhengting, ed. *Hebei sheng xingzheng quhua biangeng ziliao, 1949-1984*. [Changes in the Administrative Divisions of Hebei Province, 1949-1984]. Shijiazhuang: 1985.

Heilongjiang sheng difangzhi bianzhuan weiyuanhui, ed. *Helongjiang shengzhi: Guoying nongchang zhi* [Heilongjiang Chronicle: The State Farm Volume]. Harbin: Heilongjiang renmin chubanshe, 1992.

Hershatter, Gail. "Birthing Stories: Rural Midwives in 1950s China." In *Dilemmas of Victory: The Early Years of the People's Republic of China*, ed. Jeremy Brown and Paul G. Pickowicz, 337-58. Cambridge, MA: Harvard University Press, 2007.

–. "The Gender of Memory: Rural Chinese Women and the 1950s." *Signs* 28, 1 (2002): 43-70.

–. "Local Meanings of Gender and Work in Rural Shaanxi in the 1950s." In *Redrawing Boundaries*, ed. Barbara Entwistle and Gail E. Henderson, 79-96. Berkeley: University of California Press, 2000.

–. *The Workers of Tianjin, 1900-1949*. Stanford: Stanford University Press, 1986.

–. "Virtue at Work: Rural Shaanxi Women Remember the 1950s." In *Gender in Motion: Divisions of Labor and Cultural Change in Late Imperial and Modern China*, ed. Bryna Goodman and Wendy Larson, 309-28. Lanham, MD: Rowman and Littlefield, 2005.

Hinton, William. *Shenfan: The Continuing Revolution in a Chinese Village*. New York: Random House, 1983.

Hood, Johanna, and Robert Mackie. "A Brief Biography of Li Shuangshuang." *Renditions* 68 (2007): 52-76.

Hou Yong, et al., eds. *Dangdai Anhui jianshi* [A Brief History of Contemporary Anhui]. Beijing: Dangdai Zhongguo chubanshe, 2001.

Hu Sheng, ed. *Zhongguo gongchandang de qishi nian* [Seventy Years of the Chinese Communist Party]. Beijing: Zhonggong dangshi chubanshe, 1991.

Huang Jun. "60 niandai chu liangshi kuifa kunjing xia de chengzhen jingjian renkou: Yi Jiangsu sheng wei ge'an." [The Reduction of the Urban Population against the Background of the Lack of Grain in the Early Sixties: Jiangsu Province as an Example]. Paper from the Second Annual Graduate Seminar on China, Hong Kong, 2006.

Huang Zhiquan, et al., eds. *Zhongguo ziran ziyuan congshu: Jiangxi juan* [A Series on China's Natural Resources: Jiangxi]. Beijing: Zhongguo huanjing kexue chubanshe, 1995.

Huoyue xianzhi [Huoyue County Annal]. Zhengzhou: Zhongzhou guji chubanshe, 1993.

Jia Yanmin. *Dayuejin shiqi xiangcun zhengzhi de dianxing: Henan Chayashan weixing renmin gongshe yanjiu* [A Typical Example of Rural Politics during the Great Leap Forward: A Study of Henan's Chayashan Satellite Commune]. Beijing: Zhishi chanquan chubanshe, 2006.

Jiang Yihua. "Zongxu" [General Introduction]. In *Geming yu xiangcun, guojia, sheng, xian yu liangshi tonggou tongxiao zhidu, 1953-1957* [The Revolution and the Countryside: The Central State, the Province, the County, and the System of Controlled Grain Allocation, 1953-1957], Tian Xiquan, ed., 2-3. Shanghai: Shanghai shehui kexue chubanshe, 2006.

Jin Chongji, and Chen Qun, eds. *Chen Yun zhuan* [Biography of Chen Yun]. Beijing: Zhongyang wenxian chubanshe, 2005.

Jin Feng. *Lishi de shunjian: Yige xinwen jizhe de huiyi* [A Glimpse of History: Memoirs of a Journalist]. Beijing: Zhongguo wenlian chubanshe, 1986.

Jin, Qiu. *The Culture of Power: The Lin Biao Incident in the Cultural Revolution*. Stanford, CA: Stanford University Press, 1999.

Johnson, Kay Ann. *Women, the Family, and Peasant Revolution in China.* Chicago: University of Chicago Press, 1983.

Judd, Ellen R. "Feminism from Afar." In *Ethnographic Feminisms*, ed. Sally Cole and Lynne Phillips, 37-51. Ottawa: Carleton University Press, 1995.

–. *Gender and Power in Rural North China.* Stanford, CA: Stanford University Press, 1994.

–. "Niangjia: Chinese Women and Their Natal Families." *Journal of Asian Studies* 48, 3 (1989): 525-44.

Kai'en, Pengyi. *Zhongguo de dajihuang* [The Great Famine in China]. Beijing: Zhongguo shehui kexue chubanshe, 1993.

Kampwirth, Karen. *Women and Guerrilla Movements: Nicaragua, El Salvador, Chiapas, Cuba.* University Park: Pennsylvania State University Press, 2002.

Kane, Penny. *Famine in China, 1959-61: Demographic and Social Implications.* New York: St. Martin's Press, 1988.

Kang Jian. *Huihuang de huanmie: Renmin gongshe jingshilu* [The Death of Glory: An Alarming Account of a People's Commune]. Beijing: Zhongguo shehui chubanshe, 1998.

Ke Jiadong. "Cheng-xiang eryuan shehui shi zenyang xingcheng de?" [How Did the Dual Society Take Shape?]. *Shuwu* [Book Room] 5 (2003): http://www.360doc.com/.

Kelliher, Daniel. *Peasant Power in China: The Era of Rural Reform, 1979-1989.* New Haven, CT: Yale University Press, 1993.

King, Richard. "The Hundred Flowers." In *The Columbia Companion to Modern East Asian Literature*, ed. Joshua Mostow, 476-80. New York: Columbia University Press, 2003.

–, ed. *Heroes of China's Great Leap Forward: Two Stories.* Honolulu: University of Hawai'i Press, 2010.

Krog, Antjie. *Country of My Skull: Guilt, Sorrow, and the Limits of Forgiveness in the New South Africa.* New York: Random House, 1998.

Kueh, Y.Y. *Agricultural Instability in China, 1931-1991: Weather, Technology, and Institutions.* Oxford: Clarendon Press, 1995.

Kung, James K., and Justin Y. Lin. "The Causes of China's Great Leap Famine, 1959-1961." *Economic Development and Cultural Change* 52 (2003): 51-73.

LaCapra, Dominick. *Representing the Holocaust: History, Theory, Trauma.* Ithaca: Cornell University Press, 1994.

Landwehr, Achim. *Geschichte des Sagbaren: Eine Einfürung in die Historische Diskursanalyse* [The History of What Can Be Said: An Introduction to Historical Discourse Analysis]. Tübingen: Edition Discord, 2001.

Leys, Simon. *The Chairman's New Clothes: Mao and the Cultural Revolution.* New York: St. Martin's Press, 1977.

Li Chengrui. "'Dayuejin' yinqi de renkou biandong" [Changes in Demography as Induced by the "Great Leap Forward"]. *Zhonggong dangshi yanjiu* [Research on CCP History] 2 (1997): 1-13.

Li Chunfeng. "Jinnian lai 'dayuejin' shiqi gonggong shitang yanjiu zongshu" [The State of the Art Research of the Last Years Regarding Public Dining Halls during the Period of the "Great Leap Forward"]. *Gaoxiao sheke dongtai* [Trends of Social Science in Higher Education] 2 (2007): 17-22.

Li Dequan. "Guanxin funü jiankang baochi wangsheng ganjin" [Take Care of Women's Health in Order to Protect Their Exuberant Spirit]. *Zhongguo funü* [Chinese Women] 3 (1959): 1-2.

Li Huaiyin. "The Great Leap Forward and Its Aftermath." Unpublished paper.

Li Jingneng, ed. *Zhongguo renkou, Tianjin fence* [China's Population, Tianjin Volume]. Beijing: Zhongguo caizheng jingji chubanshe, 1987.

Li, Lillian. *Fighting Famine in North China.* Stanford: Stanford University Press, 2007.

Li Lin, and Ma Guangyao, eds. *Henan nongcun jingji tizhi biangeshi* [A History of the Economic Transformation of Rural Henan]. Beijing: Zhonggongdanshi chubanshe, 2000.

Li Rui. *Dayuejin qinliji* [Personal Account of the Great Leap Forward]. Vols. 1-2. Haikou: Nanfang chubanshe, 1999.

–. *Lushan huiyi shilu, zengdingben* [Memorandum on the Lushan Conference]. Zhengzhou: Henan renmin chubanshe, 1995.

–. "Xinyang shijian" [The Xinyang Incident]. *Yanhuang chunqiu* [China Chronicle] 4 (2002): 19-22.

Li Ruojian. "Dayuejin yu kunnan shiji de shehui dongdang yu kongzhi" [Social Turbulence and Social Control during the Great Leap Forward and the Period of Difficulty]. *Ershiyi shijie* [Twenty-First Century] 4, 62 (2002): http://www.xschina.org/.

Li Wenhai, et al. *Zhongguo jindai shida zaihuang* [Ten Great Famines in Modern China]. Shanghai: Shanghai renmin chubanshe, 1994.

Li Xiangjun. *Qingdai huangzheng yanjiu* [A Study of the Failed Government of the Qing Dynasty]. Beijing: Zhongguo nongye chubanshe, 1995.

Li Xiwen, and Wei Rengzheng. *Liu Junxiu zhuan* [Biography of Liu Junxiu]. Beijing: Zhongyang wenxian chubanshe, 1996.

Li Youjiu. "Henan Xinyang laixin" [A Letter from Xinyang, Henan]. *Hongqi* [Red Flag] 7 (1958).

Li Zhisui. *The Private Life of Chairman Mao.* New York: Random House, 1994.

Li Zhun. "Bu neng zou neitiao lu" [Not That Road]. In *Not That Road and Other Stories*, 1-23, Beijing: Foreign Language Press, 1962.

–. *Li Shuangshuang.* Shanghai: Shanghai Film Studio, 1962.

–. *Li Shuangshuang.* Text by Lu Zhongjian. Illustrations by He Youzhi. Shanghai: Shanghai renmin chubanshe, 1977.

–. *Li Shuangshuang xiaozhuan* [The Story of Li Shuangshuang]. Beijing: Renmin wenxue chubanshe, 1977.

–. "The Story of Li Shuang-shuang." Translated and abbreviated by Tang Sheng. *Chinese Literature* (June 1960): 3-25.

Liang Shoufu. "Chaoqi chaoluo" [The Tide Came In, the Tide Went Out]. *Huaxia wenzhai zengkan* [China News Digest Supplementary Issues] 682 (29 December 2008). http://www.cnd.org.

Lieberthal, Kenneth. "The Great Leap Forward and the Split in the Yan'an Leadership, 1958-1965." In *Politics of China, 1949-1989*, ed. Roderick MacFarquhar, 87-147. Cambridge: Cambridge University Press, 1993.

–. "The Great Leap Forward and the Split in the Yan'an Leadership, 1958-1965." In *Cambridge History of China*, Vol. 14, ed. John K. Fairbank and Roderick MacFarquhar, 293-359. Cambridge: Cambridge University Press, 1987.

–. *Revolution and Tradition in Tientsin, 1949-1952.* Stanford: Stanford University Press, 1980.

Lin, Justin Yifu, and Dennis Tao Yang. "Food Availability, Entitlements, and the Chinese Famine of 1959-61." *Economic Journal* 110 (2000): 136-58.

–. "On the Causes of China's Agricultural Crisis and the Great Leap Famine." *China Economic Review* 9, 2 (1998): 125-40.

Liu Mianyu, and Hu Shaochun. *Fang Zhichun zhuan* [Biography of Fang Zhichun]. Nanchang: Jiangxi renmin chubanshe, 2005.

Liu Pichang. "Chentong de huiyi" [Painful Memories]. *Tianjin wenshi ziliao xuanji* [Collected Historical and Cultural Records of Tianjin] 79 (1998): 114.

Liu Shaoqi. *Liu Shaoqi xuanji* [Selected Writings of Liu Shaoqi]. Beijing: Beijing renmin chubanshe, 1981-85.

Liu Yanpei. "Li Shinong fandang jituan shijian de zhenxiang jiqi lishi jingyan" [The Truth and the Historical Lessons of the Incident of the Li Shinong Anti-Party Clique]. *Jianghuai wenshi* [Anhui Cultural and Historical Records] 1 (2006): 68-176.

Lu Fangshang. "Kangzhan qian Jiangxi de nongye gailiang yu nongcun gaijin shiye, 1933-37" [Agricultural Reforms and Rural Improvements in Jiangxi Prior to the War against Japan, 1933-37]. In *Jindai Zhongguo nongye jingjishi lunwenji* [Symposium of Rural Economic History of Modern China], ed. Zhongyang yanjiuyuan jindaishisuo, 517-56. Taipei: Zhongyang yanjiuyuan jindaishisuo, 1989.

Lü Hongbin. "Wo dui aiguo nongye shengchan hezuoshe de huiyi, xia" [My Memory of the Aiguo Agricultural Cooperative]. *Zhongguo nongye hezuohuashi ziliao* [Documentation on the Agricultural Cooperativization of China] 3 (1986).

Lü, Xiaobo. *Cadres and Corruption: The Organizational Involution of the Chinese Communist Party.* Stanford, CA: Stanford University Press, 2000.

Luo Pinghan. *Daguofan: Gonggong shitang shimo* [Eating out of the Big Pot: The History of the Public Dining Halls]. Nanning: Guangxi renmin chubanshe, 2001.

–. *Gongshe! Gongshe! Nongcun renmingongshe shi* [Commune! Commune! The History of the Rural People's Commune]. Fuzhou: Fujian renmin chubanshe, 2003.

–. *Nongye hezuohua yundong shi* [The History of the Agricultural Cooperative Movement]. Fuzhou: Fujian renmin chubanshe, 2004.

–. "Renmin gongshe gongjizhi tanxi" [Analysis of the People's Commune Supply System]. *Dangdai Zhongguoshi yanjiu* [Research on Modern Chinese History] 3 (2000): 38-46.

Luthi, Lorenz. *The Sino-Soviet Split: Cold War in the Communist World.* Princeton, NJ: Princeton University Press, 2008.

Ma Juxian, Shi Yuan, and Yi Yiqu, ed. *Zhongguo renkou: Jiangxi fence* [Chinese Population: Jiangxi Volume]. Beijing: Zhongguo caizheng jingji chubanshe, 1989.

MacFarquhar, Roderick. *The Origins of the Cultural Revolution.* 3 vols. New York: Columbia University Press, 1974-97.

MacFarquhar, Roderick. *The Coming of the Cataclysm, 1961-1966.* Oxford: Oxford University Press; New York: Columbia University Press, 1997.

Mallory, Walter Hampton. *China: Land of Famine.* New York: American Geographical Society, 1926.

Manning, Kimberley Ens. "Communes, Canteens, and Crèches: The Gendered Politics of Remembering the Great Leap Forward." In *Re-Envisioning the Chinese Revolution*, ed. Ching Kwan Lee and Guobin Yang, 93-118. Stanford: Woodrow Wilson and Stanford University Press, 2007.

–. "Making a Great Leap Forward? The Politics of Women's Liberation in Maoist China." *Gender and History* 18, 3 (2006): 574-93.

–. "The Sino-Japanese War and the Second Maternalist Front." Paper presented at Historical Society for Twentieth Century China, Honolulu, Hawaii, 2008.

Mao Zedong. *Ausgewählte Werke: Band V* [Selected Works: Volume 5]. Beijing: Verlag für Fremdsprachige Literatur, 1977.

–. Investigation of the Peasant Movement in Hunan. In *Selected Works of Mao Zedong.* Beijing: Renmin chubanshe, 1968, 23-62.

–. "Reply to Li Shu-yi." In *Mao Tse-Tung: Poems.* Beijing: Foreign Language Press, 1976.

–. "Zai Zhengzhou huiyishang de jianghua" [Speech Given at Zhengzhou Conference]. In *Mao Zedong wenji* [Collected Works of Mao Zedong]. Vol. 8. Beijing: Renmin chubanshe, 1999.

Mao Zedong tongzhi de qingshaonian shidai [The Childhood and Youth of Comrade Mao Zedong]. Beijing: Renmin chubanshe, 1951.

Mao Zhuxi shi-ci jangjie [Explanations of Chairman Mao's Poetry]. Shenyang: Liaoning daxue Zhongwenxi xiandai wenxue jiao-yan shi, 1973.

Meisner, Maurice J. "Marx, Mao, and Deng on the Division of Labour in History." In *Marxism and the Chinese Experience*, ed. Arif Dirlik and Maurice Meisner, 79-116. London: M.E. Sharpe, 1989.

Middell, Matthias, and Felix Wemheuer, eds. *Hunger and Scarcity under Socialist Rule.* Leipzig: University of Leipzig Press, forthcoming 2010.

Migdal, Joel S. *State in Society: Studying How States and Societies Transform and Constitute One Another.* New York: Cambridge University Press, 2001.

Migdal, Joel, Atul Kohli, and Vivienne Shue. "Introduction: Developing a State-in-Society Perspective." In *State Power and Social Forces*, ed. Joel Migdal, Atul Kohli, and Vivienne Shue, 293-326. Cambridge: Cambridge University Press, 1994.

Mo Yan. *Big Breasts and Wide Hips.* London: Methuen, 2006.

–. "Chishi san pian" [Three Pieces about Eating]. In *Qingxing de shuo meng zhe* [A Clear-Headed Dreamer]. Jinan: Shandong wenyi chubanshe, 2002.

–. *Fengru feitun* [Big Breasts, Wide Hips]. Beijing: Dangdai shijie chubanshe, 2004.

–. "Liangshi" [Grain]. In *Zuiguo: Duanpian xiaoshuoji* [Guilty: Collection of Short Stories]. Jinan: Shandong wenyi chubanshe, 2002.

–. "Muzhikao" [Thumbscrew]. In *Muzhikao: Duanpian xiaoshuoji* [Thumbscrew: Collection of Short Stories]. Jinan: Shandong wenyi chubanshe, 2002.

Mo Yan, and Howard Goldblatt, trans. *Big Breasts, Wide Hips.* New York: Arcade Publishing, 2004.

Mo Yan, and Janice Wickeri, trans. *Explosions and Other Stories.* Hong Kong: Renditions Paperback, 1991.

Moore, Barrington. *Social Origins of Dictatorship and Democracy: Lord and Peasant in the Making of the Modern World.* Boston: Beacon Press, 1966.

Mueggler, Erik. *The Age of Wild Ghosts: Memory, Violence, and Place in Southwest China.* Berkeley: University of California Press, 2001.

"Nankai daxue Zhonggong dangshi jiangyi bianxiezu: Zhongguo gongchandang lishi jiangyi" [Lecture on the History of the Chinese Communist Party]. Tianjin, 1976.

Nolan, Peter. "The Causation and Prevention of Famines: A Critique of A.K. Sen." *Journal of Peasant Studies* 21, 1 (1993): 4-5.

O'Grada, Cormac. *Famine: A Short History.* Princeton: Princeton University Press, 2008.

Oi, Jean Chun. "Communism and Clientelism: Rural Politics in China." *World Politics* 37, 2 (1985): 238-66.

–. *State and Peasant in Contemporary China: The Political Economy of Village Government.* Berkeley: University of California Press, 1989.

Oksenberg, Michael. "Local Leaders in Rural China, 1962-65: Individual Attributes, Bureaucratic Positions, and Political Recruitment." In *Chinese Communist Politics in Action*, ed. A. Doak Barnett, 155-215. Seattle: University of Washington Press, 1969.

Paige, Jeffrey M. *Agrarian Revolution.* New York: Free Press, 1975.

Pang Xianzhi, and Jin Chongji. *Mao Zedong zhuan (1949-1976)* [Biography of Mao Zedong (1949-1976)]. Beijing: Zhongyang wenxian chubanshe, 2003.

Parish, William L., and Martin King Whyte. *Village and Family in Contemporary China.* Chicago: University of Chicago Press, 1978.

Peng, Xizhe. "Demographic Consequences of the Great Leap Forward in China's Provinces." *Population and Development Review* 13, 4 (1987): 639-70.

Perry, Elizabeth. *Challenging the Mandate of Heaven: Social Protest and State Power in China.* New York: M.E. Sharpe, 2002.

–. *Patrolling the Revolution: Worker Militias, Citizenship, and the Modern Chinese State.* Lanham: Rowman and Littlefield, 2006.

–. "Trends in the Study of Chinese Politics." *China Quarterly* 139 (1994): 704-13.

Plum, M. Colette. "Unlikely Heirs: War Orphans during the Second Sino-Japanese War, 1937-1945." Phd diss., Stanford University, 2006.

Potter, Jack, and Sulamith H. Potter. *China's Peasants: The Anthropology of a Revolution.* Cambridge: Cambridge University Press, 1990.

Potter, Sulamith H., and Jack Potter. "The Position of Peasants in Modern China's Social Order." *Modern China* 9, 4 (1983): 465-99.

Qiang Xiaochu, Li Li'an, and Ji Yeli. *Ma Mingfang zhuanlüe* [The Brief Biography of Ma Mingfang]. Xi'an: Shaanxi renmin chubanshe, 1990.

Qiao Peihua. *Xinyang shijian* [The Xinyang Disaster]. Hong Kong: Kaifang chubanshe, 2009.

Quanguo fulian funü yanjiusuo, ed. "Zhuanfa Ningxia Huizu zizhiqu fulian: Guanyu funü laodongli baohu qingkuang'de diaocha baogao" [Distribution of the Investigative Report from the Ningxia Minority Autonomous Region Women's Federation: The Situation of Women's Labour Protection]. In *Zhongguo funü wushi nian* [Fifty Years of Chinese Women]. Beijing: Zhongguo funü chubanshe, 1999 [1959].

Ragvald, Lars. "The Emergence of Worker-Writers in Shanghai." In *Shanghai: Revolution and Development in an Asian Metropolis*, ed. Christopher Howe, 302-25. Cambridge: Cambridge University Press, 1981.

Renmin chubanshe, ed. "Guanyu jianguo yilai dang de ruogan lishi wenti de jueyi" [Resolution on Some Questions Regarding the History of the Party since the Founding of the People's Republic of China], in *Guanyu jianguo yilai dang de ruogan lishi wenti de jueyi zhushiben*. Beijing: Renmin chubanshe, 1985.

Renmin chubanshe ziliaoshi, ed. *Pipan ziliao: Zhongguo Heluxiaofu Liu Shaoqi fangeming xiuzhengzhuyi yanlun ji 1958.6-1967.7* [Materials for Criticism: Collection of Counter-Revolutionary Revisionist Utterances by China's Khruschev, June 1958-July 1967]. Beijing: Renmin chubanshe ziliaoshi, 1967.

Riemenschnitter, Andrea. "Nationale Mythen und Konfigurationen kulturellen Wandels in der chinesischen Literatur des 20.Jahrhunderts" [National Myths and Configurations of Cultural Change in the Chinese Literature of the 20th Century]. Unveröffentlichte Habilitationsschrift [Habilitation Thesis], University of Heidelberg, 2001.

Riskin, Carl. "Seven Questions about the Chinese Famine of 1959-61." *China Economic Review* 9, 2 (1998): 111-24.

Rittenberg, Sidney, and Amanda Bennett. *The Man Who Stayed Behind.* Durham: Duke University Press, 2001.

Rogaski, Ruth. *Hygenic Modernity: Meanings of Health and Disease in Treaty-Port China.* Berkeley: University of California Press, 2004.

Schneider, Helen. "On the Homefront: Women's Work Corps and Social Welfare in the Sino-Japanese War." Paper presented at the Southeast Conference of the Association for Asian Studies, Lexington, Kentucky, 2005.

Schneider, Leander. "High on Modernity? Explaining the Failings of Tanzanian Villagization." *African Studies* 66, 1 (2007): 9-38.

Schnönegger-Men, Angelika. "Beherrscht von Hunger und Leid: Übersetzung und gesellschaftspolitischer Kommentar zu vier autobiographischen Geschichten und zwei kurzen Erzählungen von Mo Yan" [Ruled by Hunger and Misery: Commentary on Four Autobiographical Stories and Two Short Stories by Mo Yan]. Diploma thesis, University of Vienna, 2004.

Schoenhals, Michael. *Doing Things with Words in Chinese Politics.* Berkeley: University of California Press, 1992.

–. *Saltationist Socialism: Mao Zedong and the Great Leap Forward.* Stockholm: University of Stockholm Department of Oriental Languages, 1987.

Schurmann, Franz. *Ideology and Organization in Communist China.* Berkeley: University of California Press, 1968.

Scott, James C. "Everyday Forms of Resistance." In *Everyday Forms of Peasant Resistance*, ed. Forrest D. Colburn, 3-33. New York: M.E. Sharpe, 1989.

–. "Hegemony and the Peasantry." *Politics and Society* 7 (1977): 267-96.

–. *The Moral Economy of the Peasant: Rebellion and Subsistence in Southeast Asia.* New Haven, CT: Yale University Press, 1976.

–. *Seeing Like a State: How Certain Schemes to Improve the Human Condition Have Failed.* New Haven, CT: Yale University Press, 1998.

–. *Weapons of the Weak: Everyday Forms of Peasant Resistance.* New Haven, CT: Yale University Press, 2005.

Scott, Joan. "Experience." In *Feminists Theorize the Political,* ed. Judith Butler and Joan Scott, 22-40. New York: Routledge, 1992.

Sen, Amartya K. "The Causation and Prevention of Famines: A Reply." *Journal of Peasant Studies* 21, 1 (1993): 29-40.

–. *Poverty and Famine: An Essay on Entitlement and Deprivation.* Oxford: Clarendon Press, 1997.

"Shandong Madian gongshe xunsu zhizhi chiqing touqing xianxiang" [The Madian Peoples' Commune in Shandong Province Swift Stoppage of the Phenomena of Eating and Stealing the Green Crops]. *Xinhuashe Jinan 20 ri xun* [New China News Agency, Jinan, Day 20 Report], 1960.

Shandong tonggoutongxiao shouce [Shandong's Handbook for the State Monopoly for Purchase and Marketing]. Jinan: Shandong sheng liangshiting, 1957.

Shangyebu dangdai Zhongguo liangshi gongzuo bianjibu, ed. *Dangdai Zhongguo de shiliao* [Historical Data on Food Work in Contemporary China]. Baoding: Hebei sheng gongxiaoshe yinshuachang, 1989.

Shao Hua. *Shuo jiahua niandai* [A Generation of Liars]. Changchun: Changchun wenyi chubanshe, 1999.

Shao Shiping. *Shao Shiping riji* [The Diary of Shao Shiping]. Nanchang: Jiangxi renmin chubanshe, 1983.

Shapiro, Judith. *Mao's War against Nature: Politics and the Environment in Revolutionary China.* Cambridge: Cambridge University Press, 2001.

She Dehong. "Guanyu 'Xinyang shijian' de yishu" [Memories of the "Xinyang Incident"]. In *Zhongguo nongcun yanjiu 2002 juan* [Research on the Chinese Countryside 2002], ed. Zhongguo nongcunyanjiu bianji weiyuanhui. Beijing: Zhongguo shehui kexue chubanshe, 2003.

Sheehan, Brett. *Trust in Troubled Times: Money, Banks, and State-Society Relations in Republican Tianjin.* Cambridge, MA: Harvard University Press, 2003.

Shue, Vivienne. *Peasant China in Transition.* Los Angeles: University of California Press, 1980.

–. *The Reach of the State: Sketches of the Chinese Body Politic.* Stanford: Stanford University Press, 1988.

Shui Jing. *Teshu de jiaowang: Shengwei diyishuji furen de huiyilu* [Unique Interactions: The Reminiscences of the Wife of a Provincial First Party Secretary]. Nanjing: Jiangsu wenyi chubanshe, 1992.

Siu, Helen F. *Agents and Victims in South China: Accomplices in Rural Revolution.* New Haven, CT: Yale University Press, 1989.

Skocpol, Theda. *States and Social Revolutions: A Comparative Analysis of France, Russia, and China.* New York: Cambridge University Press, 1979.

Song Liansheng. *Zongluxian, dayuejin, renmingongshehua yundong shimo* [The General Line, the Great Leap Forward, and the People's Commune Movement]. Kunming: Yunnan renmin chubanshe, 2002.

Song Renqiong. *Song Renqiong huiyilu* [Song Renqiong's Memoirs]. Beijing: Jiefangjun chubanshe, 1994.

Song Yongyi, and Ding Shu. *Dayuejin – dajihuang: Lishi he bijiao shiye xia de shishi he sibian* [Great Leap Forward – Great Leap Famine: The Truth and Analysis under Historical and Comparative Perspectives]. Hong Kong: Tianyuan shuwu, 2009.

Stacey, Judith. *Patriarchy and Socialist Revolution in China.* Berkeley: University of California Press, 1983.

Strauss, Julia. "Editor's Introduction: In Search of PRC History." *China Quarterly* 188 (2006): 855-69.

Su Hua, et al., comps. *Dangdai Zhongguo de Anhui* [Anhui in Contemporary China]. Vol. 1. Beijing: Dangdai Zhongguo chubanshe, 1992.

Sun Dongfang. "Dui 1957 nongcun shehuizhuyi jiaoyu yundong de lishi kaocha" [Historical Investigation of the Rural Socialist Education Campaign in 1957]. *Beijing dangshi* [Beijing Party History] 1 (2006): 8-11.

Sun Jian. *Zhonghua renmin gongheguo jingjishi* [An Economic History of the People's Republic of China]. Beijing: Zhongguo renmin daxue chubanshe, 1992.

Szonyi, Michael. *Cold War Island*. Cambridge: Cambridge University Press, 2008.

Tao Lujia. *Mao zhuxi jiaodao women dang shengwei shuji* [Chairman Mao Taught Us to Be Provincial Party Secretaries]. Beijing: Zhongyang wenxian chubanshe, 2003.

Teiwes, Frederick. "Provincial Politics in China: Themes and Variations." In *China: Management of a Revolutionary Society*, ed. John Lindbeck, 116-92. Seattle: University of Washington Press, 1971.

Teiwes, Frederick, and Warren Sun. *China's Road to Disaster: Mao, Central Politicians, and Provincial Leaders in the Unfolding of the Great Leap Forward, 1955-1959*. London: M.E. Sharpe, 1999.

Tenshin chīki shi kenkyū kai, ed. *Tenshin shi: Saisei suru toshi no toporojī* [Tianjin History: Topology of a Reborn City]. Tokyo: Tōhō shoten, 1999.

Thaxton, Ralph A. *Catastrophe and Contention in Rural China: Mao's Great Leap Forward Famine and the Origins of Righteous Resistance in Da Fo Village*. New York: Cambridge University Press, 2008.

Thorborg, Marina. "Chinese Employment Policy in 1949-78 with Special Emphasis on Women in Rural Production." In *Chinese Economy Post Mao: A Compendium of Papers*, 535-604. Washington, DC: US Government Printing Office, 1978.

Tian Xiquan. "Liangshi gouxiao zhidu de xingcheng ji qi zai Tanghe xian de yunzuo" [How the System of Unified Purchase and Sale of Grain Was Set up and How It Was Run in Tanghe County]. PhD diss., Fudan University, 2004.

Tianjin shi dang'anguan, ed. *Jindai yilai Tianjin chengshihua jincheng shilu* [Record of the Process of Urbanization in Modern Tianjin]. Tianjin: Tianjin renmin chubanshe, 2005.

"Tibet: Proving Truth from the Facts." http://www.tibet.net/.

Unger, Jonathan. "State and Peasant in Post-Revolution China." *Journal of Peasant Studies* 17, 1 (1989): 114-36.

–. *The Transformation of Rural China*. Armonk: M.E. Sharpe, 2002.

Vernon, James. *Hunger: A Modern History*. Cambridge, MA: Belknap Press of Harvard University Press, 2007.

Viterna, Jocelyn S. "Pulled, Pushed, and Persuaded: Explaining Women's Mobilization into the Salvadoran Guerrilla Army." *American Journal of Sociology* 112, 1 (2006): 1-45.

Walker, Kenneth R. *Food Grain Procurement and Consumption in China*. Cambridge: Cambridge University Press, 1984.

Wan Xiaotang jinian wenji bianjizu, ed. *Wan Xiaotang jinian wenji* [Collected Writings Commemorating Wan Xiaotang]. Tianjin: Tianjin renmin chubanshe, 2001.

Wang Feng. "Poets Old and Young." In *Chinese Women in the Great Leap Forward*. Beijing: Foreign Language Press, 1960.

Wang Gengjin, et al. *Xiangcun sanshi nian: Fengyang nongcun shehui jingji fazhan shilu (1949-1983)* [Thirty Years in the Countryside: A Record of the Social and Economic Development of Fengyang Village, 1949-1983]. Beijing: Nongcun duwu chubanshe, 1989.

Wang Jialiang, and Jin Han. *Zhongguo xian-dangdai wenxue* [Modern and Contemporary Chinese Literature]. Hangzhou: Zhejiang daxue chubanshe, 2001.

Wang Juefei. *Shizhe rusi* [Time Passes Like the Flow of Water]. Beijing: Zhongguo qingnian chubanshe, 2001.

Wang Junyi, and Ding Dong, eds. *Koushu lishi* [Oral History]. Vol. 1. Beijing: Zhongguo shehui kexue chubanshe, 2003.

Wang Man. "Liushiliu nian de huigu" [Recollections of Sixty-Six Years]. Unpublished memoir.

Wang Yanni. "Cong Macheng xian kan gongshehua de ABC" [Introduction to the People's Communes in Macheng County]. MA thesis, Renmin University of China, 2004.

Wang, Zheng. "Dilemmas of Inside Agitators: Chinese State Feminists in 1957." *China Quarterly* 188 (2006): 913-32.

Wang Zhiliang. *Ji'e de shancun* [A Starving Mountain Village]. Guilin: Lijiang chubanshe, 1994.

Wei Junyi. *Sitonglu* [Recollections of a Bitter Past]. Beijing: Beijing shiyue wenyi chubanshe, 1998.

Wei Li, and Dennis Tao Yang. "The Great Leap Forward: Anatomy of a Central Planning Disaster." *Journal of Political Economy* 113 (2005): 840-77.

Weigelin-Schweidrzik, Susanne. "The Distance between State and Rural Society in the PRC." *Journal of Environmental Management* 87, 2 (2008): 216-25.

–. "Party Historiography in the People's Republic of China." *Australian Journal of Chinese Affairs* 17 (1987): 77-94.

–. "Trauma and Memory: The Case of the Great Famine in the People's Republic of China (1959-1961)." *Historiography East and West* 1, 1 (2003): 39-67.

Wemheuer, Felix. *China's "Großer Sprung nach vorne" (1958-1961) Von der kommunistischen Offensive in die Hungersnot: Intellektuelle erinnern sich* [China's "Great Leap Forward" (1958-1961): From the Communist Offensive to Famine: Intellectuals Remember]. Münster: Lit-Verlag, 2004.

–. "Dealing with the Great Leap Famine in China: The Question of Responsibilty." *China Quarterly* 201 (2010): 176-94.

–. "Regime Changes of Memories: Creating Official History of the Ukrainian and Chinese Famine under State Socialism after the Cold War." *Kritika: Explorations in Russian and Eurasian History* 10, 1 (2009): 31-59.

–. *Steinnudeln: Ländliche Erinnerungen und staatliche Vergangenheitsbewältigung der "Großen Sprung" – Hungersnot in der chinesischen Provinz Henan* [Stone Noodles: Rural and Official Memory of the Great Leap Famine in the Chinese Province of Henan]. Frankfurt: Peter Lang, 2007.

Wen, Guanzhong James, and Gene Chang. "Communal Dining and the Chinese Famine of 1958-1961." *Economic and Cultural Change* 46 (1997): 2-34.

Wenhe xianzhi [Wenhe County Annal]. Zhengzhou: Zhongzhou guji chubanshe, 1992.

Wheatcroft, Stephen. "Soviet and Chinese Famines in Historical Perspective." In *Hunger and Scarcity under Socialist Rule*, ed. Matthias Middell and Felix Wemheuer. Leipzig: University of Leipzig Press, forthcoming 2010.

White, Tyrene. "The Origins of China's Birth Planning Policy." In *Engendering China: Women, Culture, and the State*, ed. Christina K. Gilmartin, Gail Hershatter, Lisa Rofel, and Tyrene White, 250-78. Cambridge, MA: Harvard University Press, 1994.

Will, Pierre-Etienne, and R. Bin Wong. *Nourish the People: The State Civilian Granary System in China, 1650-1850.* Ann Arbor: Center for Chinese Studies, University of Michigan, 1991.

Wolf, Eric. *Peasant Wars of the Twentieth Century.* New York: Harper and Row, 1969.

Wong, R. Bin. *China Transformed: Historical Change and the Limits of the European Experience.* Ithaca, NY: Cornell University Press, 1997.

Wordsworth, William. "French Revolution as It Appeared to Enthusiasts at Its Commencement." 1805. http://www.poetryfoundation.org/.

Wu Cheng'en. *Xiyouji* [Journey to the West]. Beijing: Renmin wenxue chubanshe, 1981.

Wu Deyong. "Dayudao cunyuye hezuohuashi" [A History of the Cooperativization of Dayudao Village Fishery]. *Zhongguo nongye hezuohuashi ziliao* [Documentation on the Agricultural Cooperativization of China] 6 (1989).

Wu Lengxi. *Yi Mao zhuxi: Wo qinshen jingli de ruogan zhongda lishi shijian pianduan* [Remembering Mao Zedong: Several Important Historical Events that I Personally Experienced]. Beijing: Xinhua chubanshe, 1995.

Wu Ren, ed. *Renmin gongshe he gongchanzhuyi* [People's Communes and Communism]. Beijing: Gongren chubanshe, 1958.

Wu Zhipu. "Lun renmin gongshe" [On the People's Communes]. *Xuanchuan jianbao* [Propaganda Bulletin], 25 August 1958.

–. "Yuejin de zhexue yu zhexue de yuejin" [The Philosophy of the Great Leap and a Great Leap in Philosophy]. *Zhexue yanjiu* [Philosophical Research] 6 (1958).

Xiao Donglian. "Zhongguo eryuan shehuijiegou xingcheng de lishikaocha" [A Historical Investigation of the Dual System of the Chinese Society]. *Dangshi yanjiu* [Research on Party History] 1 (2005): 8-11.

Xie Chuntao. *Dayuejin kuanglan* [The Raging Tide of the Great Leap Forward]. Beijing: Zhongguo shehui chubanshe, 1990.

Xin, Liu. "Remember to Forget: Critique of a Critical Case Study." *Historiography East and West* 2, 1 (2004): 45-85.

Xin Yi. "Guanyu nongcun renmin gongshe de fenqi" [A Timeline for the People's Commune]. *Shandong shifan daxue xuebao* [Journal of Shangong Normal University] 1 (2000): 23-27.

Xiong Mengjue. "Yi feng gongkai de xin-tan Dongbei funü gongzuo" [An Open Letter to Discuss Women-Work in the Northeast]. In *Zhongguo funü yundong lishi ziliao* [Historical Materials of the Chinese Women's Movement, 1945-49], ed. Hu Lipei, 128-31. Beijing: Zhongguo funü chubanshe, 1991 [1947].

Xiong Yuezhi, ed. *Shanghai tongshi* [A Comprehensive History of Shanghai]. Vol. 11. Shanghai: Shanghai renmin chubanshe, 1999.

Xu Quanxing. *Mao Zedong wannian de lilun yu shijian (1956-1976)* [Mao Zedong's Theory and Practice in His Later Years (1956-1976)]. Beijing: Zhongguo dabaike chubanshe, 1995.

Yan, Sun. *Corruption and Market in Contemporary China*. Ithaca, NY: Cornell University Press, 2004.

Yang, Dali L. *Calamity and Reform in China: State, Rural Society, and Institutional Change since the Great Leap Famine*. Stanford: Stanford University Press, 1996.

Yang, Dennis Tao. "China's Agricultural Crisis and Famine of 1959-1961: A Survey and Comparison to Soviet Famines." *Comparative Economic Studies* 50 (2008): 1-29.

Yang Jisheng. *Mubei: Zhongguo liushi niandai dajihuang jishi* [Tombstone: A Report on the Great Famine of the 1960s in China]. Hong Kong: Tiandi tushu, 2008.

Yang Nanying, ed. *Zhonghua quanguo funü lianhehui sishi nian* [Forty Years of Chinese Women: Forty Years of the All China Women's Federation]. Beijing: Zhongguo funü chubanshe, 1991.

Yang Peijin. *Yang Shaokui zhuan* [Biography of Yang Shaokui]. Beijing: Zhongyang wenxian chubanshe, 2000.

Yang Zejiang. "Tantan Hebei nongcun de dabaogan" [On the "All-Round" Contracts of Rural Hebei]. In *Zhongguo nongcun gaige juece jishi* [A Record of Reform Policies in Rural China]. Beijing: Zhongyang wenxian chubanshe, 1999.

Yao Wenyuan. "Shengqi-bobo de nongcun tuhua" [Vibrant Images of Rural Life]. In *Zai qianjin de daolu shang* [On the Road Going Forward], 226-39. Beijing: Renmin wenxue chubanshe, 1965.

Ye Shengtao. "Xin nongcun de xin mianmao: Du *xique deng zhi*" [The New Face of the New Countryside: On Reading *The Magpie Climbs the Branch*]. *Dushu* [Reading] 14 (1958): 109-20.

Ye Yongjie. *Fanyoupai shimo* [The Whole History of the Anti-Rightist Campaign]. Vol. 2. Wulumuqi: Xinjiang renmin chubanshe, 2000.

Yi Shabei, and Mai Gang. "Fenqi yu xieyi: Fenxi shehui guifan bianqian de yizhong yanjiu lujing" [Divergence and Agreement: A Research Avenue for Model Changes in Social Analysis]. In *Qinghua shehuixue pinglun, teji* [Qinghua Discussion on Sociology, Special Issue] (2000).

"Yige dangzong zhi shuiji jing xiang fuyu zhongnong 'qingzui'" [A Party Secretary of the Party General Branch Surprisingly Pleads Guilty to Rich Middle-Level Peasants in Xinhuashe Guiyang] Guiyang: New China News Agency, 1959.

Young, Helen Praeger. *Choosing Revolution: Chinese Women Soldiers on the Long March.* Urbana: University of Illinois Press, 2001.

Yu Hua. *Chronicle of a Blood Merchant.* New York: Pantheon Books, 2003.

–. "Huozhe" [To Live]. In *Yu Hua zuopinji* [Collected Works of Yu Hua]. Shanghai: Shanghai wenyi chubanshe, 2004 [1993].

–. *To Live.* New York: Anchor Books, 2000.

–. *Xu Sanguan mai xue ji* [An Account of Xu Sanguan Selling His Blood]. Shanghai: Shanghai wenyi chubanshe, 2004.

Yu, Lin. "Why Did It Go So High? Political Mobilization and Agricultural Collectivization in China." *China Quarterly* 187 (2006): 732-43.

Yu Xiguang. *Dayuejin: Kurizi* [The Great Leap Forward: A Bitter Life]. Hong Kong: Shidai chaoliu chubanshe, 2005.

Yuan Lin. *Xibei zaihuang shi* [A History of Famine in Xibei]. Lanzhou: Gansu renmin chubanshe, 1994.

Zhang Huaisan jinian wenji bianjizu, ed. *Zhang Huaisan jinian wenji* [Collected Writings Commemorating Zhang Huaisan]. Tianjin: Tianjin renmin chubanshe, 1999.

Zhang Kaifan. *Zhang Kaifan huiyilu* [Memoir of Zhang Kaifan]. Hefei: Anhui renmin chubanshe, 2004.

Zhang Letian. *Gaobie lixiang: Renmin gongshe zhidu yanjiu* [Farewell to Idealism: A Study of the People's Commune System]. Shanghai: Dongfang chuban zhongxin, 1998.

Zhang Lihua, Ru Haitao, and Dong Naiqiang. "Jianguo sishi nian funü tushu gaikuang." [A Survey of Forty Years of Books on Women, 1981-1990]. In *Zhongguo funü lilun yanjiu shinian, 1981-1990* [Ten Years of research on Chinese Women's Theory, 1981-1990], ed. Xiong Yumei, Liu Xiaocong, and Qu Wen, 592-605. Beijing: Zhongguo funü chubanshe, 1992.

Zhang, Naihua. "The All-China Women's Federation, Chinese Women, and the Women's Movement, 1949-1993." PhD diss., Michigan State University, 1996.

Zhang Shufan. "Xinyang shijian: Yige chentong de lishi jiaoxun" [The Xinyang Incident: Bitter Lessons from History]. *Bainian chao* [Current Century] 12 (1998): 39-44.

Zhang Suhua. *Bianju: Qiqianren dahui shimo* [The Change: From the Beginning to the End of the Seven Thousand People's Conference]. Beijing: Zhongguo qingnian chubanshe, 2006.

Zhang Wenhe, and Li Yan. *Kouhao yu Zhongguo* [Slogans and China]. Beijing: Zhonggong dangshi chubanshe, 1998.

Zhang, Xiaojun. "Land Reform in Yang Village: Symbolic Capital and Determination of Class Status." *Modern China* 30, 1 (2004): 3-45.

Zhang Yigong. "Fanren Li Tongzhong de gushi" [The Story of the Criminal Li Tongzhong]. Haydn Shook, Richard King, Carmen So, and Aaron Ward, eds. In *Heroes of China's Great Leap Forward*, ed. Richard King, 63-128. Honolulu: University of Hawaii Press, 2010.

Zhang Zhanbin, Liu Jiehui, and Zhang Guohua, eds. *"Dayuejiin" he sannian kunnan shiqi de Zhongguo* [China during the "Great Leap Forward" and the Three Difficult Years]. Beijing: Zhongguo shangye chubanshe, 2001.

Zhao Yunshan, and Zhao Bensong. "Xushui xian gongchanzhuyi shidian shimo" [A History of Xushui County's Communist Pilot Project]. *Dangshi tongxun* [Communiqué of Party] 6 (1987).

Zheng Rui. *Zhengcheng huimou* [My Journey in Retrospect]. Beijing: Renmin chubanshe, 2005.

Zheng Zhiying, ed. *Tianjin shi 45 nian dashiji* [Forty-Five-Year Chronology of Tianjin]. Tianjin: Tianjin renmin chubanshe, 1995.

Zhonggong Anhui shengwei bangongting, ed. *Zhonggong Anhui shengwei wenjian xuanbian, 1958-1962* [Selected Documents of the Anhui Provincial Committee of the Chinese Communist Party, 1958-1962]. Hefei: Anhui shiyou kantan gongsi yinshuachang, 2004.

Zhonggong Beijing shiwei bianxiezu, ed. *Liu Ren zhuan* [The Biography of Liu Ren]. Beijing: Beijing chubanshe, 2000.

Zhonggong Hebei shengwei, Hebei si qing tongxun bianji bu. *Hebei nongcun jieji douzheng dianxing cailiao* [Representative Materials on Class Struggle in Hebei Villages]. Shijiazhuang: 1966.

Zhonggong Jiangsu shengwei dangshi gongzuo bangongshi, ed., *Zhonggong Jiangsu difangshi, di er juan* [History of the CCP in Jiangsu]. Nanjing: Jiangsu renmin chubanshi, 2001.

Zhonggong zhonyang dangxiao chubanse, ed., "Baoding diwei guanyu Xushui, Qingyuan liang xian zai shehuizhuyi xuanchuan yundong zhong fasheng de wenti xiang shengwei de baoago (1957 nian 8 yue)" [Report to the Provincial Government on Problems during the Socialist Propaganda Movement in Xushui and Qingyuan Counties by the Baoding Prefecture Party Committee (August 1957)]. In *Nongye jitihua zhongyao wenjian huibian* [A Compilation of Important Agricultural Collectivization Documents]. Beijing: Zhonggong zhongyang dangxiao chubanshe, 1981.

–, ed. "Zhejiang shengwei zhuanfa Yang Xinpei tongzhi guanyu Xianjuxian qunzhong naoshi wenti de baogao (5 nian 6 yue)" [Report of Comrade Yang Xinpei on the Problem of Mass Disturbances in Xianju County, Forwarded by the Provincial Government of Zhejiang (June 1957)]. Beijing: Zhonggong zhongyang dangxiao chubanshe, 1981.

"Zhonggong zhongyang guowuyuan guanyu cujin nongmin zengjia shouru ruogan zhengce yijian" [Chinese Communist Party Central Committee and State Council Resolution on Some Political Suggestions for Boosting Peasant Incomes]. http://www.zjkjt.gov.cn/.

Zhonggong zhongyang wenxian yanjiushi, ed. "Chayashan weixing renmin gongshe shixing jianzhang (caogao)" [Trial Constitution of Chayashan People's Satellite Commune (Draft)]. In *Jianguo yilai zhongyao wenxian xuanbian* [Selected Important Documents since the Founding of the People's Republic of China]. Beijing: Zhongyang wenxian chubanshe, 1995.

–, ed. "Guanyu renmin gongshe ruogan wenti de jueyi" [Resolution on Several Issues Concerning People's Communes]. In *Jianguo yilai zhongyao wenxian xuanbian* [Selected Important Documents since the Founding of the People's Republic of China]. Beijing: Zhongyang wenxian chubanshe, 1995.

–, ed. "Guanyu renmin gongshe shiba ge wenti" [Eighteen Questions on People's Communes]. In *Jianguo yilai zhongyao wenxian xuanbian* [Selected Important Documents since the Founding of the People's Republic of China]. Beijing: Zhongyang wenxian chubanshe, 1996.

–, ed. "Hubei shengwei guanyu shengwei kuoda huiyi de qingkuang baogao" [Hubei Provincial Committee Report on the Proceedings of the Provincial Committee's Expanded Conference]. In *Jianguo yilai zhongyao wenxian xuanbian* [Selected Important Documents since the Founding of the People's Republic of China]. Beijing: Zhongguo wenxian chubanshe, 1996.

–, ed. *Jianguo yilai Mao Zedong wengao* [Writings of Mao Zedong since the Establishment of the People's Republic of China]. Vol. 7. Beijing: Zhongyang wenxian chubanshe, 1992.

–, ed. *Jianguo yilai Mao Zedong wengao* [Writings of Mao Zedong since the Establishment of the People's Republic of China]. Vol. 8. Beijing: Zhongguo wenxian chubanshe, 1993.

–, ed. *Jianguo yilai Mao Zedong wengao* [Writings of Mao Zedong since the Establishment of the People's Republic of China]. Vol. 11. Beijing: Zhongguo wenxian chubanshe, 1995.

–, ed. "Mao Zedong tongzhi de jianghua" [The Speech of Comrade Mao Zedong]. In *Jianguo yilai zhongyao wenxian xuanbian* [Selected Important Documents since the Founding of the People's Republic of China] Beijing: Zhonggong zhongyang wenxian chubanshe, 1996.

–, ed. "Nongcun renmin gongshe gongzuo tiaoli (xiuzheng cao'an)" [Work Regulations in People's Communes (Revised Draft)]. In *Jianguo yilai zhongyao wenxian xuanbian* [Selected Important Documents since the Founding of the People's Republic of China]. Beijing: Zhongyang wenxian chubanshe, 1997.

–, ed. "Zai Zhengzhou huiyishang de jianghua" [Speech Given at the Zhengzhou Conference (February 1959)]. In *Jianguo yilai Mao Zedong wengao* [Writings of Mao Zedong since the Establishment of the People's Republic of China]. Beijing: Zhongyang wenxian chubanshe, 1993.

–, ed. "Zhonggong Hubei shengwei kuoda huiyi 'Guanyu renmin gongshe de shiba ge wenti' de taolun jiyao" [Hubei Provincial Committee's Summary of the Expanded Conference on the "Eighteen Questions on People's Communes"]. In *Jianguo yilai zhongyao wenxian xuanbian* [Selected Important Documents since the Founding of the People's Republic of China]. Beijing: Zhongyang wenxian chubanshe, 1996.

–, ed. "Zhonggong zhongyang guanyu ba xiaoxing de nongye hezuoshe shidang de hebing wei dashe de yijian" [View of the Central Committee on the Merger of the Small Collectives into Big Collectives]. In *Jianguo yilai zhongyao wenxian xuanbian* [Selected Important Documents since the Founding of the People's Republic of China]. Beijing: Zhonggong zhongyang wenxian chubanshe, 1995.

–, ed. "Zhonggong zhongyang guanyu fazhan difang gongye wenti de yijian" [View of the Central Committee regarding the Development of Local Industry]. In *Jianguo yilai zhongyao wenxian xuanbian* [Selected Important Documents since the Founding of the People's Republic of China]. Beijing: Zhonggong zhongyang wenxian chubanshe, 1995.

–, ed. "Zhonggong zhongyang guanyu minbing wenti de jueding" [The Decision of the Central Committee regarding the Problem of the People's Militia]. In *Jianguo yilai zhongyao wenxian xuanbian* [Selected Important Documents since the Founding of the People's Republic of China]. Beijing: Zhonggong zhongyang wenxian chubanshe, 1995.

–, ed. "Zhonggong zhongyang guanyu nongcun jianshe renmin gongshe wenti de jueyi" [Resolution of the Central Committee of the CCP Regarding Problems with the Establishment of the People's Communes in the Countryside]. In *Jianguo yilai zhongyao wenxian xuanbian* [Selected Important Documents since the Founding of the People's Republic of China]. Beijing: Zhonggong zhongyang wenxian chubanshe, 1995.

–, ed. "Zhonggong zhongyang guanyu nongcun renmin gongshe dangqian zhengce wenti de jinji zhishixin" [Central Committee Emergency Instructions on Present Problems with Commune Policies]. In *Jianguo yilai zhongyao wenxian xuanbian* [Important documents since the founding of the People's Republic of China]. Beijing: Zhongyang wenxian chubanshe, 1996.

–, ed. "Zhonggong zhongyang guanyu nongye de wutiao jinji zhishi" [Central Committee's Five Emergency Measures for Agriculture]. In *Jianguo yilai zhongyao wenxian xuanbian* [Selected Important Documents since the Founding of the People's Republic of China]. Beijing: Zhongyang wenxian chubanshe, 1996.

–, ed. "Zhonggong zhongyang guanyu sheyuan siyang jiaqin, jiachu he ziliudi deng sige wenti de zhishi" [Central Committee Instructions on Raising Poultry, Keeping Livestock, and Cultivating Private Plots]. In *Jianguo yilai zhongyao wenxian xuanbian*

[Selected Important Documents since the Founding of the People's Republic of China]. Beijing: Zhongyang wenxian chubanshe, 1996.

–, ed. "Zhonggong zhongyang guanyu zai nongcun jianli renmin gongshe wenti de jueyi" [Central Committee Resolution on the Establishment of People's Communes in the Countryside]. In *Jianguo yilai zhongyao wenxian xuanbian* [Selected Important Documents since the Founding of the People's Republic of China]. Beijing: Zhongyang wenxian chubanshe, 1995.

–, ed. "Zhonggong zhongyang pizhuan Shanxi shengwei 'Guanyu liuji ganbu huiyi qingkuang de baogao'" [Central Committee Commentary on the Shanxi Provincial Committee's "Report on the Six Levels Cadres Council"]. In *Jianguo yilai zhongyao wenxian xuanbian* [Selected Important Documents since the Founding of the People's Republic of China]. Beijing: Zhongyang wenxian chubanshe, 1996.

–, ed. *Zhou Enlai nianpu* [Chronicle of Zhou Enlai]. Vol. 2. Beijing: Zhongyang wenxian chubanshe, 1997.

–, ed. *Zhou Enlai zhuan*. [Biography of Zhou Enlai]. Vol. 4. Beijing: Zhongyang wenxian chubanshe, 1998.

"Zhongguo gongchandang shici luxian douzheng jiangyi (chugao)" [Lecture on the Ten Inner Party Line Struggles of the Chinese Communist Party (First Draft)]. N.d.

Zhonghua renmin gongheguo guojia nongye weiyuanhui bangongting, ed. *Nongye jitihua zhongyao wenjian huibian* [Important Documents Regarding the Collectivization of Agriculture]. Beijing: Zhongyangdangxiao chubanshe, 1981.

Zhonghua renmin gongheguo nongyebu jihuasi, ed. *Zhongguo nongcun jingji tongji daquan, 1949-1980* [Comprehensive Statistics of China's Rural Economy, 1949-1980]. Vol. 1989. Beijing: Nongye chubanshe, 1989.

Zhonghua renmin gongheguo nongyebu zhengce faguisi, and Zhonghua renmin gongheguo guojia tongjiju nongyesi, eds. *Zhongguo nongcun 40 nian* [Forty Years in Rural China]. Beijing: Zhongyuan nongmin chubanshe, 1989.

–, ed. "Zhonghua renmin gongheguo nongyeshui tiaoli" [The Agricultural Tax Regulations of the People's Republic of China]. In *Jianguo yilai zhongyao wenxian xuanbian* [Selected Important Documents since the Founding of the People's Republic of China]. Beijing: Zhongyang wenxian chubanshe, 1995.

Zhou Benli, et al., ed. *Zhongguo ziran ziyuan congshu: Anhui juan* [A Series on China's Natural Resources: Anhui Volume]. Beijing: Zhongguo huanjing kexue chubanshe, 1995.

Zhou Enlai. "Lun 'xianqi liangmu' yu muzhi" [On Good Wives, Loving Mothers and the Duties of Motherhood]. In *Zhongguo funü yundong lishi ziliao, 1937-1945* [Historical Materials of the Chinese Women's Movement, 1937-1945], ed. Wang Menglan, 608-11. Beijing: Zhongguo funü chubanshe, 1991 [1942].

Zhou Jun. "Caifang Pi-Shi-Hang guangai gongcheng zhuiyi" [Recollection of My Reporting the Pi-Shi-Hang Irrigation Engineering Project]. *Jianghuai wenshi* [Anhui Cultural and Historical Records] 3 (1999): 121-34.

Zhou, Kate Xiao. *How the Farmers Changed China: Power of the People.* Boulder, CO: Westview Press, 1996.

Zhou Weiren. *Jia Tuofu zhuan* [The Biography of Jia Tuofu]. Beijing: Zhonggong dangshi chubanshe, 1993.

Zhou Yang. "Xin minge kaituole shige xin daolu" [New Folk Songs Have Opened a New Road for Poetry]. *Hongqi* [Red Flag] 1 (1958): 33-38.

Zhu Chengxia. "Dabieshan yi nian lai de funü gongzuo" [A Year of Woman-Work in Dabieshan]. In *Zhongguo funü yundong lishi ziliao* [Historical Materials of the Chinese Women's Movement, 1937-1945], ed. Wang Menglan, 214-27. Beijing: Zhongguo funü chubanshe, 1991 [1939].

Zhu De. "Zai jiefangqu funü gongzuo huiyi shang de jianghua" [A Speech Given at the Woman-Work Meeting in the Liberated Areas]. In *Zhongguo funü yundong lishi ziliao*

[Historical Materials of the Chinese Women's Movement, 1937-1945], ed. Hu Lipei, 276-80. Beijing: Zhongguo funü chubanshe, 1991 [1948].

Zhu Di. *1957: Da zhuanwan zhi mi – zhengfeng fanyou shilu* [1957: The Puzzle of the Great Turn: A True Record of the Rectification and Anti-Rightist Movement]. Taiyuan: Shanxi renmin chubanshe, 1995.

Zhu Zheng. *Xiaoshu sheng dashidai* [The Little Book that Gave Birth to a Great Generation]. Beijing: Beijing daxue, 1999.

Zhuan Xiezu. *Dong Biwu zhuan* [The Biography of Dong Biwu]. Beijing: Zhongyang wenxian chubanshe, 2006.

Zhuo Wen. "Guanyu nongcun renmin gongshe de fenqi" [A Timeline for the People's Commune]. *Shandong shifan daxue xuebao* [Academic Journal of Shandong Normal University] 1 (2000).

Zubkova, Elena. *Russia after the War: Hopes, Illusions, and Disappointment, 1945-1957.* London: M.E. Sharpe, 1998.

Zweig, David. *Agrarian Radicalism in China, 1968-1981.* Cambridge, MA: Harvard University Press, 1989.

Contributors

Jeremy Brown is an assistant professor in the Department of History at Simon Fraser University, Canada.

Chen Yixin is an associate professor in the Department of History at the University of North Carolina, United States.

Gao Hua is a professor in the Department of History at Nanjing University, People's Republic of China.

Gao Wangling is a professor in the Department of Qing History at the People's University, People's Republic of China.

Richard King is the director of the Centre for Asia Pacific Initiatives and an associate professor of Chinese in the Department of Pacific and Asian Studies, University of Victoria, Canada.

Kimberley Ens Manning is an assistant professor in the Department of Political Science at Concordia University, Canada.

Ralph Thaxton is a professor in the Department of Politics at Brandeis University, United States.

Wang Yanni is a graduate of the People's University, People's Republic of China.

Susanne Weigelin-Schwiedrzik is the chair and a professor of Sinology at the Institute for East Asian Studies/Sinology for the University of Vienna, Austria.

Felix Wemheuer is an assistant professor at the Institute for East Asian Studies/Sinology at the University of Vienna, Austria.

Xin Yi is an associate professor at the Institute for the History of the Chinese Communist Party at the People's University, People's Republic of China.

Index

Printed and bound in Canada by Friesens

Set in Arrus and Futura by Artegraphica Design Co. Ltd.

Copy editor: Joanne Richardson

Proofreader: Dallas Harrison